TABLE OF CONTENTS

Title Page

Copyright

Dedication

Contents

Preface

Understanding the Bible as a Revelation of Christ

How to Use This Book

Chapter 1: The True House of God: A Living Bride

Chapter 2: Adam and Eve: Type of Christ and the Church

Chapter 3: The Passover Lamb: A Type of Christ's Sacrifice

Chapter 4: The Exodus and Red Sea Crossing: A Type of Baptism and Deliverance

Chapter 5: Manna from Heaven: A Type of Christ as the Bread of Life

Chapter 6: The Bronze Serpent: A Type of Christ's Crucifixion

Chapter 7: The Ark of Noah: A Type of Salvation in Christ

Chapter 8: The Levitical Priesthood and Sacrifices: A Type of Christ's High Priesthood

Chapter 9: The Tabernacle: A Type of Christ's Ministry

Chapter 10: The Feasts of Israel: Types of Christ and Future Events

Chapter 11: Jonah: A Type of Christ's Death, Burial, and Resurrection

Chapter 12: Joseph: A Type of Christ

Chapter 13: The Sacrifice of Isaac: A Type of Christ's Sacrifice

Chapter 14: The Sabbath: A Type of the Eternal Rest in Christ

Chapter 15: Melchizedek: A Type of Christ's Eternal Priesthood

Chapter 16: The Exodus Plagues: A Type of Judgment and Deliverance

Chapter 17: Boaz and Ruth: A Type of Christ as the Kinsman-Redeemer

Chapter 18: The Tabernacle's Veil: A Type of Christ's Flesh

Chapter 19: Joshua: A Type of Jesus Leading God's People into Rest

Chapter 20: The Cities of Refuge: A Type of Christ as Our Refuge

Chapter 21: The Rock in the Wilderness: A Type of Christ the Living Water

Chapter 22: The Scapegoat: A Type of Christ Bearing Our Sins

Chapter 23: The Feasts of Israel: Types of Christ's Ministry and the Church

Chapter 24: Samson: A Type of Christ's Sacrificial Strength

Chapter 25: The Manna and Quail: A Type of God's Provision in Christ

Chapter 26: The Deliverance from Babylon: A Type of Spiritual Redemption

Chapter 27: David as a Type of Christ the King

Chapter 28: Moses as a Mediator: A Type of Christ the Mediator

Chapter 29: Elijah as a Type of John the Baptist

Chapter 30: The High Priest's Garments: A Type of Christ's Role as High Priest

Chapter 31: The Golden Lampstand: A Type of Christ as the Light of the World

Chapter 32: Jonah in the Belly of the Fish: A Type of Christ's Resurrection

Chapter 33: The Judges: Types of Christ as Deliverer

Chapter 34: The Alpha and the Omega: Christ as the Fulfillment of All Typology

Chapter 35: Christ, the Fulfillment of All Typology

Bible Verse Index for All Chapters

Glossary of Theological Terms

Author's Note

3 Temples

Types and Shadows

Eric C Alger

Eternal Roots Ltd

Copyright © 2024 Eternal Roots LTD

All rights reserved. No part of this book may be reproduced, stored in a retrieval system, or transmitted in any form or by any means, electronic, mechanical, photocopying, recording, or otherwise, without the prior written permission of the publisher.
3 Temples: Types and Shadows
Registered with the U.S. Copyright Office: TXu002450572

To my Heavenly Father,
Who authored the ultimate temple and plan of redemption.
To my Lord and Savior, Jesus Christ,
The true cornerstone, whose sacrifice opened the way for us to become His living temple.
And to the Holy Spirit,
Who dwells in the hearts of all believers, guiding us into all truth.

May this book bring glory to You and draw others closer to Your eternal purpose.

To my mother and father, who brought me up to know Christ in the way that I do, thank you for grounding me in faith and teaching me the value of God's Word. Your guidance has shaped the person I am today, and I am forever grateful for the spiritual foundation you built in me.

To my "Sold Out Brothers in Christ," Bobby and Scott—Proverbs 18:24 says, "there is a friend who sticks closer than a brother." God's timing in our talks, these books, and the ideas we share is no coincidence. His divine providence is all over it, and I thank Him for placing you in my life during these seasons.

To my son, Benjamin—I pray that as you continue to grow, you hold fast to the faith that has already taken root in your heart. You are strong, and my hope is that one day you will fully realize the depth of God's love for you. May this book serve as a reminder of the rich spiritual heritage you have, and may you always seek to walk in God's truth.

Finally, to every reader who embarks on this journey, may this book deepen your understanding of God's Word and help you see the beauty of His redemptive plan through the types and shadows revealed in Scripture.

PREFACE

The Bible offers a rich tapestry of types and shadows, especially in the forms of two monumental physical structures: Solomon's Temple and the Second Temple. These buildings, built with human hands, brick, mortar, and adorned with animal skins, timber, and precious metals, were far more than just places of worship. They held the very presence of God, housed over the Ark of the Covenant, which was placed in the Holy of Holies. Surrounding this sacred space were the courts—the outer court representing the Gentiles and the inner court representing Israel (Ephesians 2:14). The law, written by God's own hand on two stone tablets, rested inside the Ark, serving as a reminder of His covenant with Israel.

But these physical temples were only temporary, earthly representations of something far greater to come. The prophets of old spoke of a time when God would establish a "New Covenant" (Jeremiah 31; Zechariah 4), a New Testament, wherein He would no longer dwell in structures built by human hands. Instead, God declared that His ultimate temple would be the hearts of men and women, where He would dwell through the Holy Spirit, establishing His bride—the Church—as the final temple (Hebrews 10:5).

This prophetic transition is marked by compound layers of meaning. When Jesus said, "Destroy this temple, and in three days I will raise it up" (John 2:19), He was not only speaking of His physical resurrection but also prophesying about His body, the Church. Christ is the cornerstone, and His people form the living stones of the third and final temple. The destruction of the previous temples foreshadowed the end of the old sacrificial system, while Christ's resurrection signaled the establishment of the New Covenant.

Even in the Old Testament, God laid the foundation for this transformation. Moses led the Israelites out of Egypt, not just to build a temporary tabernacle, but as a type of Christ, pointing to a future deliverer who would lead His people out of the bondage of sin. Abraham left his home in search of a city with foundations not made by human hands, but designed and built by God (Hebrews 11:8-10). Through each step in Israel's history, from the tabernacle to the physical temples, God was preparing humanity for the spiritual temple to come.

The Old Testament temples, while magnificent in their splendor and craftsmanship, were shadows of a greater reality. They pointed forward to Christ, who would fulfill every prophecy and serve as the true temple. The progression from physical structures to spiritual dwelling places reveals God's redemptive plan: to inhabit not a building, but His people.

INVITATION TO THE READER

Isaiah 1:18 beckons us with these words: "Come now, and let us reason together, saith the Lord: though your sins be as scarlet, they shall be as white as snow; though they be red like crimson, they shall be as wool." God invites us to the table, to delve deep into the rich treasures of Scripture, to feast upon the truths that reveal the mystery of His plan. From the Old Testament to the New, God has been unveiling His purposes, showing us how the past foreshadowed the present and the future.

In the following pages, we will explore the profound symbolism of the three temples—the earthly temples built by men and the spiritual temple God is building through Christ. This journey will reveal that one cannot fully understand the New Testament without grasping the types and shadows of the Old. As Jesus said in Matthew 13:52, "Every scribe who has been instructed in the kingdom of heaven is like a householder who brings out of his treasure things new and old." By understanding the old, we can fully embrace the new.

THE IMPORTANCE OF OLD TESTAMENT TYPES AND SHADOWS

The Scriptures are filled with examples that point to a greater fulfillment in Christ. The Apostle Paul, in 1 Corinthians 10:11, reminds us that "these things happened to them as examples and were written down as warnings for us, on whom the culmination of the ages has come." The types and shadows of the Old Testament—whether in the sacrifices, the feasts, or the temples—were not just historical events, but prophetic revelations of what Christ would accomplish. Hebrews 10:1 says, "For the law, having a shadow of the good things to come, and not the very image of the things..." This chapter will explore how the Old Testament types reveal the nature of God's plan for redemption, fulfilled through Christ.

Every type and shadow are an actual prophecy.

Matthew 13:52

Then said He unto them, "Therefore every scribe which is instructed unto the kingdom of heaven is like unto a man that is an householder, which bringeth forth out of his treasure things new and old."

A wise man studies both, for one cannot understand the New Testament without understanding the Old Testament.

Hebrews 10:6

Now these things occurred as examples to keep us from setting our hearts on evil things as they did.

Colossians 2:16-17

Therefore let no one pass judgment on you in questions of food and drink, or with regard to a festival or a new moon or a Sabbath. These are a shadow of the things to come, but the substance belongs to Christ.

UNDERSTANDING THE BIBLE AS A REVELATION OF CHRIST

The Bible is not simply a history of the Jewish people, nor is it merely a collection of rules, moral lessons, or grand stories. From Genesis to Revelation, the Bible is a complete Revelation of Jesus Christ. Every event, person, and action points directly to Him. When we look at Scripture through the lens of types and shadows, we see that God's purpose in revealing Himself wasn't just historical; it was prophetic. God used types and shadows purposefully to display the fullness of His plan, which is centered entirely on Christ (Revelation 22:13).

Each story, each character—from King David to the prophets and even figures like Samson—wasn't just a hero of their own time, but a vessel through which God was displaying His redemptive plan. These were not merely human actions; they were the workings of God Himself within them (2 Peter 1:21). The Spirit of God moved in them to show a deeper reality, often hidden but now revealed in Christ (1 Peter 1:9-11).

WHY TYPES AND SHADOWS ARE IMPORTANT TODAY

God didn't just randomly weave types and shadows into Scripture; it was His intentional method to reveal Christ through prophetic imagery. Every type and shadow served a purpose. When Paul spoke in 1 Corinthians 15:3-4 about how the Scriptures foretold Christ's death and resurrection, he wasn't referencing a single direct quote from the Old Testament, but rather the prophetic shadow of Jonah in the belly of the fish for three days and nights. This is an example of how God's plan was hidden within the Old Testament narratives, waiting to be revealed to those who seek His truth (Matthew 11:25).

God purposely hid His redemptive plan within the types and shadows of the Old Testament to reveal it to the humble and teachable, like babes (Job 23:12). Every type and shadow is a prophecy in itself. As Christ Himself said in Matthew 13:52, a wise man draws from both the old and the new. Understanding the Old Testament is crucial to fully grasping the truth revealed in the New Testament.

Paul also emphasizes this in 1 Corinthians 10:11, explaining that everything in the Old Testament happened as examples for us, upon whom the ends of the world have come. The law, as Hebrews 10:1 tells us, is a shadow of the good things to come. Colossians 2:16-17 reiterates that these festivals, new moons, and Sabbaths were shadows of the things to come, but the substance is found in Christ.

To truly appreciate the New Testament, we must understand the types and shadows that prepared the way for Christ. The Old Testament is not a separate or lesser part of Scripture—it is the treasure chest from which both old and new treasures are brought forth, revealing the fullness of God's plan (Matthew 13:52).

UNDERSTANDING TYPOLOGY: A KEY TO BIBLICAL INTERPRETATION

Opening Analogy

Imagine you're reading the first chapter of a mystery novel. The author scatters small, seemingly unrelated clues throughout the story. At first, these hints don't make sense, but as the plot progresses, each clue begins to fit into a larger, more meaningful picture. Then, at the climactic moment, everything comes together in a stunning revelation.

Typology works in a similar way. Throughout the **Old Testament**, God places **types** and **shadows**—small, powerful hints that point toward a greater reality fulfilled in **Jesus Christ**. Much like a mystery unfolding, these types initially seem isolated, but as we journey through **Scripture**, we see how they all lead us to the final revelation of **God's redemptive plan**.

For example, consider the **Passover Lamb** in **Exodus 12**. What seems like a singular event in history—a lamb sacrificed to protect the Israelites—turns out to be a **blueprint** for the ultimate sacrifice of **Christ**, the **Lamb of God**, who takes away the sins of the world (**John 1:29**). The **Old Testament** is more than a collection of stories—it is a beautifully orchestrated narrative in which each **type** and **shadow** finds its fulfillment in **Christ**.

THE ROLE OF THE HOLY SPIRIT IN TYPOLOGY

The Holy Spirit plays a critical role in guiding believers to understand the profound depths of **typology** within **Scripture**. Just as the Spirit inspired the authors of the Bible, He now illuminates the hearts of believers, revealing how these **types** and **shadows** foreshadow **Christ**.

In **1 Corinthians 2:14**, Paul explains that "the natural person does not accept the things of the Spirit of God, for they are folly to him, and he is not able to understand them because they are spiritually discerned." Without the **Holy Spirit**, the rich layers of **types** and **shadows** remain hidden or misunderstood.

Through the **Holy Spirit**, we are able to recognize the deeper connections between the **Old** and **New Testaments**, as He reveals the significance of **Old Testament** events and figures that point toward **Christ's work of redemption**. For example, when we read about the **Passover Lamb**, it is the **Holy Spirit** who helps us understand that this event foreshadows the sacrificial death of **Christ**.

When approaching typology, invite the **Holy Spirit** to guide your study, and trust Him to lead you into a deeper understanding of **God's redemptive plan**.

TYPOLOGY IN CHURCH HISTORY: A RICH TRADITION

Typology has deep roots in **Christian theology**, with contributions from theologians such as **Irenaeus, Augustine,** and **John Calvin**. Each helped shape our modern understanding of how the **Old Testament** and **New Testament** are linked.

WHAT IS TYPOLOGY?

At its core, **typology** is a method of interpreting **Scripture** where certain **events, persons,** or **institutions** in the **Old Testament** serve as **types**—**blueprints**—for greater realities called **antitypes**, revealed in the **New Testament**. Unlike allegory, which is symbolic, **typology** is rooted in **historical events** that prefigure **Christ**.

For example, **Adam** is a type of **Christ. Adam's disobedience** brought death to humanity, while **Christ's obedience** brings life and redemption (**Romans 5:14**). This **blueprint** helps us understand the overarching narrative of **Scripture**—moving from **creation** to **fall**, and ultimately to **redemption** in **Christ**.

TYPES AND SHADOWS: A BLUEPRINT FOR FULFILLMENT

Much like an **architectural blueprint, types** and **shadows** in the **Old Testament** outline a **divine design** that is completed in the **New Testament**.

1. **Types**: These are **specific blueprints**—historical figures or events that prefigure **Christ**. For example, **Moses** delivering **Israel** from physical slavery is a **type of Christ**, who delivers us from spiritual slavery.

2. **Shadows**: These are **broader outlines**—systems or practices such as the **sacrificial system** or the **temple**—that point toward a greater fulfillment in **Christ**. Just as the **blueprint** is incomplete without the finished building, these **shadows** were meant to point forward to **Christ's perfect sacrifice**.

VISUALIZING TYPOLOGY: TYPES AS FADED PAINTINGS

Think of **types** and **shadows** as faded paintings in the **Old Testament**. When we look at these paintings, we can make out the basic shapes and outlines, but the details remain hidden. Only in the **New Testament**, when **Christ** comes, is the painting fully restored, revealing all its rich colors and depth.

For example, the **tabernacle**—God's dwelling place among His people—was a shadow of the true, eternal dwelling that would be realized in **Christ**. In **John 1:14**, we learn that **Jesus** "dwelt among us," which literally means He "tabernacled" with humanity. The **tabernacle** was just a **blueprint**; **Jesus** is the finished structure.

WHY TYPOLOGY MATTERS TODAY

Typology isn't just a theological exercise; it holds practical significance for believers today. Understanding **types** and **shadows** deepens our relationship with **God** and enhances our understanding of **Scripture**. When we see how **Christ** is prefigured throughout the **Old Testament**, it helps us appreciate the consistency of **God's plan** for redemption.

Seeing **Christ** as the fulfillment of types like the **Passover Lamb** enriches our understanding of His sacrifice and draws us closer to Him. Each **type** and **shadow** reveals a part of the **blueprint**, helping us see that **God** has been orchestrating our salvation from the very beginning.

MISUNDERSTANDING OR MISUSING TYPOLOGY

While **typology** is a powerful interpretative tool, it is crucial to approach it with care. Misunderstanding or misusing **typology** can lead to forced connections or over-spiritualizing texts.

TYPOLOGY—A BLUEPRINT FOR GOD'S REDEMPTIVE PLAN

From the Tabernacle to Solomon's Temple to the Second Temple, the progression of God's dwelling among His people points toward a final and eternal fulfillment in Christ. The tearing of the temple veil at Jesus' crucifixion signifies the end of separation between God and humanity, and the beginning of the Church as the living temple, indwelt by the Spirit.

Solomon's Temple was the physical dwelling place of God among His people, where the Ark of the Covenant resided. As magnificent as it was, it served as a shadow of a greater reality. The destruction of this temple symbolized the passing of the old covenant system, pointing forward to the time when God's presence would dwell fully in Christ, the true Temple. The physical structure of the temple was temporary, but it laid the foundation for the spiritual temple found in Christ.

The Second Temple, rebuilt after the exile, held great significance for the Jewish people. It was the site of Jesus' ministry, and although it lacked the glory of Solomon's Temple, it still foreshadowed a greater fulfillment in Christ. The destruction of the Second Temple, as prophesied by Jesus, marks the end of the old sacrificial system and the transition to a new covenant where God's presence is no longer confined to a building but resides in Christ and His Church. Jesus, the ultimate Temple, fulfills what the Second Temple could only symbolize.

As we study **typology**, we begin to see that the **Old Testament** is not merely a historical account of **Israel** but a **blueprint** for the work of **Christ**. **Types**—specific foreshadowing's—give us a clearer picture of how key figures and events point to **Christ**. **Shadows**—broader practices and systems—serve as outlines, helping us see how **Christ** fulfills all things.

Through both **types** and **shadows**, we uncover the intricate **blueprint** of **God's redemptive plan**, which finds its final fulfillment in **Jesus Christ**.

INSPIRATIONAL PRAYER

As you embark on this journey of exploring **types** and **shadows** in **Scripture**, I invite you to pray:

Heavenly Father, we thank You for the richness of Your Word, and how You have woven Your redemptive plan through every story, event, and person. As we study the types and shadows that point to Christ, open our hearts and minds through the power of the Holy Spirit. Help us to see the beauty of Your plan and deepen our awe and love for Jesus, who fulfills all things. Guide us to understand Your Word more deeply and to draw nearer to You in faith and worship. In Jesus' name, Amen.

HOW TO USE THIS BOOK

3 Temples: Types and Shadows delves into rich theological themes and concepts that are woven throughout the Bible. For some readers, this may include terminology or ideas that are less familiar. To assist you in gaining a deeper understanding of these topics, we've included a comprehensive **Glossary** at the end of the book.

As you read, if you encounter a term or concept that you'd like to learn more about, feel free to flip to the Glossary for a simplified explanation. This will help clarify key theological points and provide context for the ideas discussed in each chapter.

Whether you are well-versed in Christian theology or exploring these topics for the first time, this book is designed to guide you through the profound symbolism and biblical truths surrounding the temples, covenants, and the redemptive plan of God. Don't hesitate to reference the Glossary as often as needed throughout your journey.

CHAPTER 1: THE TRUE HOUSE OF GOD: A LIVING BRIDE

Solomon's Temple, while magnificent, was ultimately a temporary dwelling for God's presence—a shadow of the greater reality to come. Just as the physical temple housed the glory of God, Christ's body becomes the true temple, and we, the Church, are joined to Him as living stones, creating a spiritual temple (1 Peter 2:5).

The house of God is not a physical building made of stone and mortar; it is a living body, a collective of vessels called the Bride. She is called out of the world's systems, separated from the religious constructs men have built—systems that will ultimately come to nothing. Just as the Pharisees and Sadducees prided themselves on their Hebrew lineage while rejecting and persecuting the prophets, so too will the institutions built by men fail if they are not aligned with God's divine purpose. This transition from a physical temple to a spiritual body is one of the most profound themes in Scripture, and understanding it allows us to see the full scope of God's redemptive plan.

The Bride, as described throughout Scripture, represents the Church—those who have been called out of the world to be united with Christ. This calling is not only a rejection of worldly systems but an invitation to enter into a divine relationship with God through Christ. The symbolic nature of the Bride reflects the intimacy, purity, and sanctification that God desires for His people. Understanding the development of this metaphor throughout the Bible helps us grasp the deeper spiritual truths concerning the Church's role in God's eternal plan.

1. THE OLD TESTAMENT TEMPLES: SOLOMON'S TEMPLE AND THE SECOND TEMPLE

The Second Temple, rebuilt after the exile, held great significance for the Jewish people. It was the site of Jesus' ministry, and although it lacked the glory of Solomon's Temple, it still foreshadowed a greater fulfillment in Christ. The destruction of the Second Temple, as prophesied by Jesus, marks the end of the old sacrificial system and the transition to a new covenant where God's presence is no longer confined to a building but resides in Christ and His Church. Jesus, the ultimate Temple, fulfills what the Second Temple could only symbolize.

Historical Context and Significance

Solomon's Temple, built around 957 BC, represented the pinnacle of Israel's religious and political power. It was a place where heaven and earth met—a physical space where God's presence was believed to dwell among His people. The temple's construction was an important moment in Israel's history, marking the fulfillment of God's promises to David, as outlined in 1 Chronicles 22:10, that his son would build a house for the Lord.

Solomon's Temple was constructed with the utmost care and reverence. The detailed craftsmanship, the gold that covered the interior, the cherubim that adorned the inner sanctum, and the Holy of Holies—all pointed to the grandeur and holiness of God. This temple was not just a building; it was a visual representation of the covenant relationship between God and His people. Yet, despite its physical beauty, the temple was ultimately a shadow of a greater reality to come.

The **Holy of Holies**, the innermost part of the temple, was where God's presence dwelled in a visible form through the **Shekinah**

glory. Only the high priest could enter this sacred space once a year on the Day of Atonement (Leviticus 16:34), highlighting the separation between God and humanity due to sin. This division pointed to the need for a greater mediator, one who could permanently remove the barrier between God and His people. Solomon's Temple, as grand as it was, could only hint at the ultimate plan of redemption that God would accomplish through Christ.

The Destruction of Solomon's Temple and the Loss of the Ark

When Solomon's Temple was destroyed by the Babylonians in 586 BC, it marked the end of an era for Israel. The destruction of the temple was not just a physical loss; it was a profound theological event. The loss of the Ark of the Covenant, which had been housed in the Holy of Holies, symbolized the departure of God's presence from among His people. **1 Samuel 4:21** echoes the sentiment of this loss: "Ichabod, the glory has departed from Israel."

This loss foreshadowed the spiritual reality that God would no longer dwell in temples made with human hands. It signaled that something greater was coming—a new temple, not built by men, but established by God Himself. This idea finds its fulfillment in Christ, who referred to His own body as the true temple that would be destroyed and raised up in three days (John 2:19).

The Second Temple and its Symbolism

The Second Temple, rebuilt after the exile, held great significance for the Jewish people. It was the site of Jesus' ministry, and although it lacked the glory of Solomon's Temple, it still foreshadowed a greater fulfillment in Christ. The destruction of the Second Temple, as prophesied by Jesus, marks the end of the old sacrificial system and the transition to a new covenant where God's presence is no longer confined to a building but resides in Christ and His Church. Jesus, the ultimate Temple, fulfills what the Second Temple could only symbolize.

The Second Temple, rebuilt under the leadership of Zerubbabel, Ezra, and Nehemiah after the return from Babylonian exile, stood as a symbol of restoration and hope. It was completed around 516 BC, and though it lacked the grandeur of Solomon's Temple, it represented a new chapter in Israel's history. However, the **Second Temple** also lacked something critical: the **Shekinah glory** of God never returned to this temple as it had to Solomon's. The Ark of the Covenant was lost, and with it, the tangible manifestation of God's presence.

The Second Temple, rebuilt after the exile, held great significance for the Jewish people. It was the site of Jesus' ministry, and although it lacked the glory of Solomon's Temple, it still foreshadowed a greater fulfillment in Christ. The destruction of the Second Temple, as prophesied by Jesus, marks the end of the old sacrificial system and the transition to a new covenant where God's presence is no longer confined to a building but resides in Christ and His Church. Jesus, the ultimate Temple, fulfills what the Second Temple could only symbolize.

The Second Temple stood as a reminder of the promises that were yet to be fulfilled. The glory that filled Solomon's Temple pointed to a future reality—the coming of the Messiah, who would inaugurate a new era of divine presence and blessing. The **Prophet Haggai** spoke of this future glory, declaring that the glory of the latter house would be greater than the former (Haggai 2:9). This promise finds its ultimate fulfillment not in a physical building, but in the coming of Christ, who embodies the true temple and brings the fullness of God's presence to His people.

The Second Temple, rebuilt after the exile, held great significance for the Jewish people. It was the site of Jesus' ministry, and although it lacked the glory of Solomon's Temple, it still foreshadowed a greater fulfillment in Christ. The destruction of the Second Temple, as prophesied by Jesus, marks the end of the old sacrificial system and the transition to a new covenant where God's presence is no longer confined to a building but resides in Christ and His Church. Jesus, the ultimate Temple, fulfills what the Second Temple could only symbolize.

By the time Jesus arrived on the scene, the Second Temple had been renovated by King Herod and had become a symbol of the religious elite's control over Israel's worship. While the temple remained vital to Jewish life, it had also become a place of corruption and hypocrisy, as seen in Jesus' cleansing of the temple (Matthew 21:12-13). This act of driving out the moneychangers was not just about restoring order but about signaling the impending end of the temple's role in God's redemptive plan.

The Second Temple, rebuilt after the exile, held great significance for the Jewish people. It was the site of Jesus' ministry, and although it lacked the glory of Solomon's Temple, it still foreshadowed a greater fulfillment in Christ. The destruction of the Second Temple, as prophesied by Jesus, marks the end of the old sacrificial system and the transition to a new covenant where God's presence is no longer confined to a building but resides in Christ and His Church. Jesus, the ultimate Temple, fulfills what the Second Temple could only symbolize.

>Jesus predicted the destruction of the Second Temple (Matthew 24:1-2), which occurred in AD 70 when the Romans sacked Jerusalem. This event marked the definitive end of the physical temple's significance and foreshadowed the age of the spiritual temple—the Church, the Body of Christ.

The Second Temple, rebuilt after the exile, held great significance for the Jewish people. It was the site of Jesus' ministry, and although it lacked the glory of Solomon's Temple, it still foreshadowed a greater fulfillment in Christ. The destruction of the Second Temple, as prophesied by Jesus, marks the end of the old sacrificial system and the transition to a new covenant where God's presence is no longer confined to a building but resides in Christ and His Church. Jesus, the ultimate Temple, fulfills what the Second Temple could only symbolize.

---

2. THE TRANSITION FROM THE PHYSICAL TEMPLE TO THE SPIRITUAL TEMPLE

The Sacrificial System as a Foreshadowing of Christ

The sacrificial system of the Old Testament served as a shadow of the ultimate sacrifice to come. The constant offering of sacrifices in the temple, whether for sin, peace, or thanksgiving, pointed to the inadequacy of animal blood to permanently remove sin (Hebrews 10:4). While the sacrifices allowed Israel to maintain a temporary relationship with God, they were a signpost pointing to the perfect Lamb who would take away the sin of the world.

Hebrews 9 provides an extensive comparison between the Old Testament sacrificial system and the sacrifice of Christ. It emphasizes that Christ entered the heavenly Holy of Holies—not with the blood of goats and calves, but with His own blood—once for all, securing eternal redemption (Hebrews 9:12). This event was the culmination of everything the physical temple and its rituals had foreshadowed.

Jesus as the True Temple

In **John 2:19**, Jesus made the revolutionary statement: *"Destroy this temple, and in three days I will raise it up."* This confused His listeners, who thought He was referring to the physical temple in Jerusalem. But Jesus was speaking of His body, the true dwelling place of God. In Christ, the fullness of God's presence was made manifest (Colossians 2:9). His death and resurrection marked the end of the physical temple's role in mediating the relationship between God and humanity.

The tearing of the temple veil at the moment of Jesus' death (Matthew 27:51) symbolized the removal of the barrier between God and His people. No longer would access to God be restricted to a specific place or a specific person (the high priest). Through Christ, every believer now has direct access to the Father (Hebrews 10:19-22). This radical shift from a physical building to a spiritual reality is one of the defining features of the New Covenant.

The Ark of the Covenant and the Indwelling of God's Presence

The Ark of the Covenant, which was lost during the Babylonian exile, represented God's presence among His people. It contained the tablets of the Law, Aaron's rod, and a jar of manna—symbols of God's covenant with Israel. Its loss was a devastating blow to the people, symbolizing the departure of God's glory from Israel.

However, the **Ark of the Covenant** was merely a symbol of something greater to come. The New Covenant, established through Christ, promised the indwelling of the Holy Spirit within every believer. No longer would God's presence be confined to a physical object or a specific location. In **Jeremiah 31:33**, God promised to write His law on the hearts of His people, and this promise was fulfilled through the Holy Spirit's work in the New Covenant.

In the Old Testament, God's presence was often distant and mediated through specific individuals like priests and prophets. But in the New Covenant, the Holy Spirit indwells every believer, making their body the temple of God (1 Corinthians 6:19). This is the ultimate fulfillment of the symbolism of the Ark and the temple. God is no longer dwelling in a specific place; He is dwelling within His people.

---

3. THE FRAGILITY OF HUMAN EFFORTS

Psalm 127:1 declares, *"Except the LORD build the house, they labour in vain that build it: except the LORD keep the city, the watchman waketh but in vain."* This verse is a stark reminder of the futility of human efforts when they are disconnected from God's will. Human ambition, even in religious pursuits, is doomed to failure if it is not aligned with God's purpose.

The Tower of Babel: A Cautionary Tale

The story of the Tower of Babel in Genesis 11:1-9 serves as an archetype of human pride and ambition. The people of Babel sought to build a tower that reached the heavens, believing that they could make a name for themselves and establish their own legacy. Their project was a symbol of human autonomy and self-sufficiency—a rejection of dependence on God.

However, their efforts were frustrated when God confused their language, causing them to scatter across the earth. This story illustrates the principle that human endeavors, no matter how impressive, will ultimately fail if they are undertaken in rebellion against God's will.

Religious Systems: The Danger of Legalism

In a similar way, religious systems throughout history have often fallen into the trap of legalism and self-reliance. The Pharisees and Sadducees, two of the leading religious groups during Jesus' time, are prime examples of this. They prided themselves on their strict observance of the Law and their lineage as descendants of Abraham, yet their hearts were far from God.

Jesus frequently rebuked them for their hypocrisy, calling them "whitewashed tombs" (Matthew 23:27). Outwardly, they appeared righteous, but inwardly they were full of dead men's bones. Their obsession with maintaining religious traditions had blinded them to the deeper truths of God's kingdom. This serves as a warning to modern religious institutions that can become so focused on external forms of worship that they neglect the inward transformation that God desires.

Legalism, the belief that righteousness can be attained through strict adherence to rules and rituals, is a trap that has ensnared many throughout history. It leads to a false sense of security and self-righteousness, causing people to rely on their own efforts rather than on God's grace. The Pharisees, despite their knowledge of Scripture and their religious zeal, missed the heart of the Law, which was love for God and love for neighbor (Matthew 22:37-40).

In contrast, Jesus' teachings emphasized the importance of a heart transformed by God's grace. In **Matthew 5:8**, He declared, *"Blessed are the pure in heart, for they shall see God."* True righteousness, according to Jesus, is not about outward conformity to rules but about the inward purity that comes from a heart surrendered to God.

4. THE CALL TO SEPARATE FROM CORRUPTION

In **Revelation 18:4**, God issues a clear command to His people: *"Come out of her, my people, that ye be not partakers of her sins, and that ye receive not of her plagues."* This call to separate from the world's corrupt systems is as relevant today as it was in the time of the early Church. Babylon, in this context, represents the idolatrous and corrupt systems of the world that stand in opposition to God's kingdom.

Babylon as a Symbol of Worldly Corruption

Throughout Scripture, **Babylon** serves as a symbol of human rebellion and idolatry. The historical Babylon was a city of great wealth and power, known for its pagan practices and its oppression of God's people. It was Babylon that destroyed Solomon's Temple and took the Israelites into exile. In the Book of Revelation, Babylon is portrayed as the ultimate symbol of human pride, idolatry, and rebellion against God.

The call to "come out of her" is not just a call to physical separation but to spiritual and moral separation. As believers, we are called to live in the world but not be of the world (John 17:14-16). This means that while we engage with the world and seek to bring the light of the Gospel to those around us, we must guard against being conformed to the values, practices, and systems that oppose God.

Holiness as Separation

Holiness, in its most basic sense, means to be set apart. God's people are called to be holy because He is holy (1 Peter 1:16). This call to holiness is not about isolation but about distinction. We are called to live lives that reflect the character of God, marked by love, purity, and righteousness.

The pursuit of holiness involves a continual process of sanctification, in which the Holy Spirit works in us to conform us to the image of Christ (Romans 8:29). It is a daily decision to reject the values of the world and to embrace the values of God's kingdom. Holiness is not an abstract concept; it is lived out in the choices we make, the way we treat others, and the way we conduct ourselves in the world.

In **2 Corinthians 6:17-18**, Paul echoes the call to separation, writing, *"Wherefore come out from among them, and be ye separate, saith the Lord, and touch not the unclean thing; and I will receive you, and will be a Father unto you, and ye shall be my sons and daughters, saith the Lord Almighty."* This passage reinforces the idea that separation from the world is not just about avoiding sin but about maintaining a close and intimate relationship with God.

The Church, as the Bride of Christ, is called to be pure and unblemished, ready for her union with the Bridegroom. This purity is not something we achieve on our own; it is the result of Christ's work in us. He is the one who sanctifies and cleanses His Church, preparing her for the day when she will be presented to Him in glory (Ephesians 5:25-27).

---

5. THE PROPHETS AND THE REJECTION OF GOD'S MESSENGERS

Acts 7:52 reminds us of Israel's tragic history of rejecting God's prophets. From Moses to Jeremiah to John the Baptist, God sent messengers to call His people back to Himself, but they were often met with rejection, persecution, and even death. This pattern of rejection reached its climax in the crucifixion of Jesus, the ultimate Prophet, who came to bring salvation but was rejected by His own people (John 1:11).

The Ministry of the Prophets: Calling People Back to God

The Old Testament prophets had a dual role: they were both **forthtellers** and **foretellers**. As forthtellers, they delivered God's message to the people, calling them to repentance and faithfulness to the covenant. As foretellers, they predicted future events, often pointing to the coming of the Messiah and the establishment of God's kingdom.

The prophets were often a voice crying in the wilderness, confronting the idolatry, injustice, and immorality of their time. **Isaiah**, for example, warned of impending judgment if Israel did not turn back to God, but he also spoke of a future hope—the coming of a suffering servant who would bear the sins of many (Isaiah 53).

Jeremiah is another example of a prophet who faced intense opposition. Known as the "weeping prophet," Jeremiah's ministry was marked by rejection and persecution. He was imprisoned, thrown into a cistern, and continually opposed by the religious and political leaders of his time. Yet, Jeremiah remained faithful to his calling, delivering God's message of judgment and hope. His perseverance in the face of rejection is a model for believers today, reminding us that faithfulness to God's calling often comes with opposition.

Prophets as a Foreshadowing of Christ

The rejection of the Old Testament prophets foreshadowed the ultimate rejection of Christ. Just as the people of Israel rejected God's messengers, they also rejected His Son. In **Matthew 21:33-46**, Jesus tells the parable of the wicked tenants, in which a landowner sends multiple servants (representing the prophets) to collect the fruit of the vineyard, but they are beaten and killed by the tenants. Finally, the landowner sends his son (representing Jesus), but the tenants kill him as well. This parable illustrates the hard-heartedness of those who reject God's message and highlights the tragic culmination of this pattern in the rejection of Christ.

Jesus' crucifixion was not just the rejection of a prophet; it was the rejection of God's ultimate offer of salvation. Yet, through His death and resurrection, Jesus fulfilled the very promises that the prophets had foretold. He became the suffering servant of **Isaiah 53**, bearing the sins of the world, and through His sacrifice, He made a way for humanity to be reconciled to God.

6. THE TEMPLE OF THE HOLY SPIRIT: A NEW DWELLING PLACE

In **1 Corinthians 6:19**, Paul makes a profound statement: *"What? know ye not that your body is the temple of the Holy Ghost which is in you, which ye have of God, and ye are not your own?"* This declaration represents one of the most significant shifts in redemptive history. No longer is God's presence confined to a physical building or location; instead, He dwells within every believer through the Holy Spirit. This transition from the physical temple to the spiritual temple of the believer's body signifies the fulfillment of the Old Covenant and the inauguration of the New Covenant.

The Indwelling of the Holy Spirit as the Fulfillment of God's Promises

The indwelling of the Holy Spirit in the hearts of believers is the ultimate fulfillment of the promises made in the Old Testament. In **Ezekiel 36:26-27**, God promises, *"A new heart also will I give you, and a new spirit will I put within you: and I will take away the stony heart out of your flesh, and I will give you a heart of flesh. And I will put my spirit within you, and cause you to walk in my statutes, and ye shall keep my judgments, and do them."* This promise finds its fulfillment in the New Testament when the Holy Spirit comes to dwell within believers, enabling them to live lives that are pleasing to God.

The indwelling of the Holy Spirit marks the transition from the external observance of the Law to the internal transformation of the heart. In the Old Covenant, the Law was written on tablets of stone and imposed from the outside. In the New Covenant, the Law is written on the hearts of believers through the work of the Holy Spirit (Jeremiah 31:33). This internal transformation is what enables believers to live in obedience to God's commands, not out of obligation, but out of love and gratitude for His grace.

The Holy Spirit as the Seal of Our Inheritance

In **Ephesians 1:13-14**, Paul describes the Holy Spirit as the seal of our inheritance, guaranteeing what is to come. This sealing signifies that we belong to God and that He will fulfill His promises to us. Just as a king's seal on a document represented his authority and guarantee, the Holy Spirit's presence in our lives is God's guarantee that we are His and that He will bring us to completion in Christ (Philippians 1:6).

The presence of the Holy Spirit also serves as a foretaste of the glory to come. In **Romans 8:23**, Paul writes that we have "the firstfruits of the Spirit," meaning that the Holy Spirit's presence in our lives is a down payment on the full inheritance we will receive in eternity. The Holy Spirit not only empowers us to live for God in the present but also gives us the assurance of our future hope—the redemption of our bodies and the restoration of all things.

---

7. THE REVELATION OF THE BRIDE

In **Revelation 21:2-3**, the apostle John receives a vision of the ultimate fulfillment of God's plan. The holy city, New Jerusalem, comes down from heaven, prepared as a bride adorned for her husband. This moment represents the culmination of redemptive history, where God's people are finally united with Christ, their Bridegroom, in eternal fellowship.

The New Jerusalem as a Symbol of the Bride

The **New Jerusalem** is not just a physical city; it is a symbol of the glorified and perfected Church. In the Old Testament, Jerusalem was the center of Israel's worship and identity. It was the place where the temple stood, where sacrifices were offered, and where God's presence was believed to dwell. However, in the New Covenant, the New Jerusalem represents something far greater. It is the dwelling place of God with His people for all eternity.

The description of the New Jerusalem as a **bride adorned for her husband** emphasizes the intimate relationship between Christ and His Church. Just as a bride prepares herself for her wedding day, so too is the Church being prepared for her eternal union with Christ.

This preparation is ongoing, as believers are sanctified through the work of the Holy Spirit, being made ready for that glorious day.

The Marriage Supper of the Lamb

The image of the Bride is also tied to the **Marriage Supper of the Lamb** in **Revelation 19:7-9**. This great celebration marks the final union between Christ and His Church. Throughout Scripture, marriage is used as a metaphor for the covenant relationship between God and His people. In the Old Testament, God is often portrayed as the **husband** of Israel, while Israel is described as His **bride**. However, Israel's repeated unfaithfulness led to her separation from God, symbolized by the exile and the destruction of the temple.

In the New Testament, Christ is portrayed as the Bridegroom who comes to redeem His bride—the Church. The **Marriage Supper of the Lamb** is the culmination of this redemption, where the Bride is presented to Christ in all her glory, having been purified and made holy through His sacrificial love.

The **Marriage Supper** also reflects the **eschatological** hope of believers. Just as a wedding feast is a time of joy, celebration, and fellowship, the **Marriage Supper of the Lamb** will be a time of eternal joy, as the redeemed from every nation, tribe, and tongue come together to worship and glorify Christ. This is the ultimate fulfillment of the **Feast of Tabernacles**, which celebrated God's provision and presence with His people.

---

8. THE ETERNAL TEMPLE: PILLARS OF FAITH

In **Revelation 3:12**, Jesus promises that those who overcome will be made pillars in the temple of God. This promise speaks to the eternal nature of the believer's union with Christ. Pillars are symbols of strength, permanence, and stability. In the eternal temple, those who remain faithful to Christ will have a permanent place of honor.

Pillars in Ancient Architecture

In ancient architecture, pillars were not only functional but also symbolic. They provided support and stability, bearing the weight of the structure. They also served as symbols of strength, endurance, and beauty. In the same way, believers who remain faithful to Christ are described as pillars in the eternal temple of God. They are foundational to God's kingdom, standing firm in the face of opposition and reflecting the beauty of Christ's glory.

This imagery is also used in **Galatians 2:9**, where Paul refers to **James, Peter, and John** as pillars of the Church. These men were foundational leaders in the early Church, providing strength and stability to the growing body of believers. In the same way, every believer who overcomes through faith in Christ is promised a place of honor and permanence in the eternal temple of God.

The Overcomer's Reward

The promise of being made a pillar in the temple of God is tied to the idea of overcoming. Throughout the letters to the seven churches in **Revelation**, the overcomer is promised various rewards, all of which point to eternal life and fellowship with God. In **Revelation 3:12**, the overcomer is promised not only a place in the eternal temple but also the name of God and the name of the New Jerusalem written upon them. This signifies ownership, identity, and intimate relationship with God.

The overcomer's reward is not just about surviving trials or enduring hardship; it's about remaining faithful to Christ in the face of temptation, persecution, and worldly pressures. Those who overcome will be marked by God's name, signifying their eternal security and their place in His kingdom.

---

9. THE CONSUMMATION OF GOD'S PLAN: THE BRIDE AND THE BRIDEGROOM

The union between Christ and the Church is the culmination of God's redemptive plan. Just as Eve was taken from Adam's side and brought to him as his bride, so too is the Church being prepared as the Bride of Christ. In **Ephesians 1:10**, Paul writes that God's plan is to *"gather together in one all things in Christ, both which are in heaven, and which are on earth; even in him."* This gathering together of all things in Christ is the ultimate goal of history—the moment when the Bride and the Bridegroom are united for all eternity.

The Marriage of Adam and Eve as a Type of Christ and the Church

The marriage of **Adam and Eve** serves as a **type** of the relationship between Christ and the Church. In **Genesis 2:21-24**, God creates Eve from Adam's side and presents her to him as his bride. This act of creation foreshadows the creation of the Church, which is taken from the side of Christ, the second Adam, through His death and resurrection.

In the same way that Adam and Eve were united in marriage, Christ and the Church will be united in the **Marriage Supper of the Lamb**. This union is not just a legal or contractual relationship; it is a relationship of love, intimacy, and fellowship. Just as a husband and wife become one flesh in marriage, so too will Christ and the Church be united in perfect oneness for all eternity.

The Millennial Reign of Christ: The Honeymoon of the Bride and the Bridegroom

The **Millennial Reign** of Christ, described in **Revelation 20:1-6**, can be seen as the "honeymoon" of the Bride and the Bridegroom. During this thousand-year reign, Christ will rule the earth with justice, peace, and righteousness, and the Church will reign with Him. This period of time will be a foretaste of the eternal kingdom, where the Bride will enjoy intimate fellowship with the Bridegroom.

The **Millennium** is also a fulfillment of the **Feast of Tabernacles**, which celebrated God's provision and presence with His people. Just as the Israelites lived in booths during the Feast of Tabernacles to commemorate their journey through the wilderness, so too will believers' dwell with Christ during the **Millennial Reign**, celebrating His victory over sin and death.

10. ETERNAL REST AND REWARD: THE BRIDE'S ETERNAL HOME

Finally, in **Revelation 21:2-3**, we see the fulfillment of God's plan: the Bride, the New Jerusalem, descends from heaven, and God dwells with His people forever. This eternal rest, described in **Hebrews 4:9-11**, is the final reward for the faithful. No longer will there be separation between God and His people. The Bride will dwell with the Bridegroom in perfect unity, love, and fellowship for all eternity.

The New Heavens and New Earth

The **New Heavens and New Earth**, described in **Revelation 21:1**, represent the ultimate renewal of all creation. In the beginning, God created the heavens and the earth, and He declared them to be "very good" (Genesis 1:31). However, sin entered the world through Adam and Eve's disobedience, and creation was subjected to futility and decay (Romans 8:20-22). The new creation, however, will be free from the effects of sin and death, and it will become the eternal home of the Bride and the Bridegroom.

In the **New Heavens and New Earth**, there will be no more pain, no more sorrow, and no more death (Revelation 21:4). God Himself will dwell with His people, and they will experience the fullness of His love and glory for all eternity. The relationship between

Christ and the Church, which began in the Garden of Eden and was redeemed at the cross, will be consummated in the new creation, where the Bride and the Bridegroom will dwell together in perfect harmony.

CHAPTER 2: ADAM AND EVE: TYPE OF CHRIST AND THE CHURCH

The narrative of Adam and Eve in the opening chapters of Genesis is foundational to the Christian faith. Not only does it explain the origins of humanity, sin, and death, but it also provides a rich typological framework for understanding Christ and the Church. Paul explicitly identifies Adam as a "type" of Christ in **Romans 5:14**, highlighting the theological parallels between Adam's role in the fall and Christ's role in redemption. Similarly, Eve's creation from Adam's side and their union as "one flesh" prefigures the Church's intimate relationship with Christ, as outlined in **Ephesians 5:31-32**. This expanded chapter will explore these themes in greater depth, providing additional theological insights, historical perspectives, and practical applications for believers today.

I. ADAM AS A TYPE OF CHRIST (ROMANS 5:14)

Romans 5:14 states, "Adam, who is a type of the one who was to come," revealing that the first man, Adam, serves as a foreshadowing of Christ. Adam's actions in the Garden of Eden introduced sin and death into the world, but Christ, the second Adam, would bring redemption and life. The typological relationship between Adam and Christ is both instructive and profound, illustrating the grand scope of God's redemptive plan throughout human history.

A. Adam, the First Man, Brings Sin into the World

The story of Adam begins in **Genesis 1-2**, where he is created by God and placed in the Garden of Eden. Adam is the first human, made in the image of God (Genesis 1:27), and tasked with ruling over creation. However, despite his privileged position, Adam's disobedience in eating from the tree of the knowledge of good and evil introduces sin and death into the world. **Genesis 3** recounts the tragic fall, in which Adam and Eve succumb to the serpent's temptation, violating God's command and bringing about catastrophic consequences for themselves and for all of humanity.

1. Theological Implications of Adam's Fall: Sin, Death, and Separation from God

Adam's sin has far-reaching theological implications. His disobedience leads to **original sin**, the doctrine that all of humanity inherits a sinful nature from Adam. **Romans 5:12** states, "Therefore, just as sin came into the world through one man, and death through sin, and so death spread to all men because all sinned." Adam's sin brought both spiritual and physical death into the world. Theologically, death is understood as **separation from God**, and Adam's act of disobedience resulted in a rupture between humanity and its Creator.

The curse that follows Adam's fall is extensive. Not only does it affect Adam and Eve personally—causing pain in childbirth and toil in labor—but it also curses the entire created order. **Genesis 3:17-19** states that the ground is cursed because of Adam's sin, resulting in thorns and thistles, making Adam's labor difficult and unproductive. The harmony that once existed between humanity and creation is shattered. Adam's disobedience affects not only himself but all of creation.

This act of rebellion represents a **reversal of the divine order**. In creation, God established a hierarchy: God over humanity, humanity over creation. By listening to the serpent (a creature) instead of God, Adam inverted this order. The consequences of this inversion are felt throughout human history, with humanity struggling to maintain its role as steward of creation while being subjected to the curse of sin and death.

2. Adam's Headship: The Federal Headship of Humanity

Adam's fall also introduces the theological concept of **federal headship**. As the first human, Adam represents all of humanity. His actions in the Garden of Eden are not merely personal but corporate. Adam's disobedience brought sin and death to all who would come after him, and as a result, all humans are born in a state of sin. Paul makes this point explicitly in **Romans 5:19**, saying, "For as by the one man's disobedience the many were made sinners."

Federal headship refers to the idea that Adam acted as the representative of all humanity. His decision to disobey God resulted in a fallen condition for all his descendants. This is why every person is born into a state of sin, with an inherent bent toward rebellion against God. This corporate identity in Adam sets the stage for the need for another representative, a second Adam, to bring redemption.

B. Jesus, the Second Adam, Brings Redemption and New Life

Where Adam brought sin and death, Christ brings righteousness and life. **1 Corinthians 15:22** says, "For as in Adam all die, so also in Christ shall all be made alive." This establishes the contrast between Adam and Christ: the first man's failure brought ruin, but the second Adam's obedience brings restoration. Christ is the head of a new humanity, and His obedience reverses the curse brought by Adam's disobedience.

1. The Obedience of Christ: Reversing Adam's Failure

The key difference between Adam and Christ lies in their responses to temptation. Adam, though created in a perfect environment, failed when faced with a relatively simple command—do not eat from one tree. In contrast, Christ, who was born into a fallen world and faced far greater trials and temptations, remained perfectly obedient to the Father's will. **Philippians 2:8** emphasizes Christ's submission: "And being found in human form, he humbled himself by becoming obedient to the point of death, even death on a cross."

Christ's obedience undoes the damage caused by Adam's disobedience. Where Adam brought condemnation, Christ brings justification. **Romans 5:18-19** declares, "Therefore, as one trespass led to condemnation for all men, so one act of righteousness leads to justification and life for all men. For as by the one man's disobedience the many were made sinners, so by the one man's obedience the many will be made righteous." Through His life, death, and resurrection, Christ restores what Adam lost—righteousness, life, and fellowship with God.

2. The Second Adam and the New Humanity

As the second Adam, Christ becomes the head of a **new humanity**. Just as all who are in Adam inherit sin and death, all who are in Christ inherit righteousness and eternal life. This idea is central to Paul's theology, particularly in **Romans 6**, where he describes the believer's union with Christ in His death and resurrection. Through faith, believers are united with Christ, sharing in His victory over sin and death.

The new humanity that Christ inaugurates is characterized by **grace**, in contrast to the condemnation that marks those who remain in Adam. **1 Corinthians 15:45** describes Christ as the "last Adam," who is a "life-giving spirit." While Adam brought death, Christ brings life through the Spirit, offering a new kind of existence for those who belong to Him.

This new humanity is no longer under the curse of sin and death. **Romans 8:1** triumphantly declares, "There is therefore now no condemnation for those who are in Christ Jesus." Those who are in Christ have been transferred from the realm of Adam's fall into the realm of Christ's grace. They are justified, sanctified, and will one day be glorified in the presence of God.

II. EVE AS A TYPE OF THE CHURCH (GENESIS 2-3; EPHESIANS 5:31-32)

Eve, the first woman, serves as a type of the Church, the bride of Christ. Just as Eve was created from Adam's side, the Church is born from the side of Christ, and their union as "one flesh" points to the spiritual union between Christ and His Church. The parallels between Eve and the Church provide a rich understanding of the intimate relationship God desires with His people.

A. Eve Was Taken from Adam's Side, Signifying the Church Coming from Christ

The creation of Eve from Adam's side in **Genesis 2:21-22** is one of the most beautiful and symbolic moments in Scripture. God causes Adam to fall into a deep sleep, takes a rib from his side, and fashions Eve from it. Eve is not created from the dust, like Adam, but from his own flesh. This act signifies the deep connection between Adam and Eve and prefigures the relationship between Christ and the Church.

1. The Creation of Eve as a Prefiguration of the Church's Birth

Early Christian theologians often interpreted Eve's creation from Adam's side as a prefiguration of the Church's birth from Christ's side. Just as Eve was brought forth from Adam during his sleep, the Church is brought forth from Christ's sacrificial death. When Jesus died on the cross, a soldier pierced His side, and blood and water flowed out (John 19:34). This event symbolizes the birth of the Church, which is washed in the blood of Christ and given new life through the water of baptism.

The imagery of Eve being taken from Adam's side highlights the idea of **union**. Eve is not a separate entity from Adam but is intimately connected to him—"bone of his bones and flesh of his flesh" (Genesis 2:23). Similarly, the Church is not a separate entity from Christ but is united with Him in a profound spiritual bond. The Church is born from Christ's side, and believers share in His life, His death, and His resurrection.

2. Eve as Adam's Helper and the Church's Role as Christ's Partner

Eve's role as Adam's **helper** (Genesis 2:18) is another key aspect of the typology. The Hebrew word for "helper" (ezer) is often used in Scripture to describe God Himself as the helper of Israel (e.g., **Psalm 33:20**), indicating that Eve's role is one of dignity and importance. Eve was created to be Adam's companion and partner in fulfilling God's command to multiply and have dominion over the earth (Genesis 1:28). This partnership is a reflection of the Church's role in relation to Christ.

The Church is often described as the **bride of Christ**, and her role is to partner with Christ in His mission of redemption. Just as Eve was Adam's helper in the work of tending the garden and ruling over creation, the Church is Christ's helper in spreading the Gospel and building His kingdom. **Ephesians 3:10** speaks of the Church displaying the manifold wisdom of God to the world. This is a high calling, as the Church is entrusted with the mission of making disciples, proclaiming the good news, and being a light in the world.

B. The Two Becoming One Flesh Prefigures the Union Between Christ and the Church

The union of Adam and Eve in marriage, described in **Genesis 2:24** as the two becoming "one flesh," is a profound foreshadowing of the spiritual union between Christ and His Church. In **Ephesians 5:31-32**, Paul quotes this verse from Genesis and reveals that it refers to Christ and the Church, describing this union as a "profound mystery."

1. The Profound Mystery of Marriage and the Gospel

The biblical concept of marriage is not merely a social contract or a legal arrangement; it is a **covenant relationship** that reflects the relationship between Christ and His Church. This is why Paul emphasizes the sacrificial nature of Christ's love for the Church in **Ephesians 5:25-27**: "Husbands, love your wives, as Christ loved the church and gave himself up for her, that he might sanctify her, having cleansed her by the washing of water with the word."

In marriage, the husband and wife become "one flesh," symbolizing the deep and intimate union that exists between Christ and His Church. Just as Adam and Eve were united in a bond of love, Christ and His Church are united in an unbreakable covenant. Christ gave Himself up for His bride, the Church, sanctifying her and preparing her to be holy and blameless. This sacrificial love forms the foundation of the Church's identity and mission.

2. The Church as the Bride of Christ: Covenant and Faithfulness

The relationship between Christ and the Church is often described as a **covenant**, similar to the covenant of marriage. Just as a husband and wife pledge their faithfulness to one another, Christ pledges His faithfulness to the Church, and the Church responds in kind. **Ephesians 5:32** makes clear that this "one flesh" union is ultimately a picture of the Gospel, where Christ and the Church are joined together in a relationship of mutual love and commitment.

This covenant relationship is marked by the **faithfulness** of Christ. The Church can trust in Christ's unwavering love and care. He is the "bridegroom" who will return for His bride, and the Church eagerly awaits the day when she will be united with Him in glory. The **Marriage Supper of the Lamb** in **Revelation 19:7-9** is the culmination of this covenant, where the bride, the Church, is presented to Christ in splendor.

The covenant between Christ and the Church is eternal and unbreakable. While human marriages may falter or fail, the union between Christ and His Church is secure. This covenant is sealed by Christ's blood and will be fully consummated at His return, when the Church will dwell with Him in perfect fellowship for all eternity.

III. COVENANT THEOLOGY: THE CONTRAST BETWEEN THE COVENANT OF WORKS AND THE COVENANT OF GRACE

The story of Adam and Eve is deeply connected to the broader biblical theme of **covenants**. Theologically, Adam's life in the Garden of Eden is understood as being governed by the **Covenant of Works**—an agreement that promised life for obedience and death for disobedience. After Adam's fall, however, God instituted the **Covenant of Grace**, through which salvation is offered through faith in Christ, the second Adam.

A. The Covenant of Works: Life for Obedience, Death for Disobedience

In the Garden of Eden, Adam was placed under a covenant with God, sometimes called the **Covenant of Works**. While the term itself is not explicitly found in Scripture, the concept is drawn from the structure of the narrative in Genesis 2-3. Adam was commanded not to eat from the tree of the knowledge of good and evil, with the promise of life if he obeyed and the threat of death if he disobeyed (Genesis 2:16-17). This covenant was based on Adam's works—his ability to obey or disobey God's command.

Adam's failure under this covenant resulted in death and the curse of sin. However, even in the midst of judgment, God gave a promise of redemption. In **Genesis 3:15**, often called the **protoevangelium** (the first Gospel), God declares that the seed of the woman would crush the serpent's head, pointing to the coming of Christ, who would defeat sin and death.

B. The Covenant of Grace: Redemption through Christ

After Adam's failure under the Covenant of Works, God instituted the **Covenant of Grace**—a covenant that offers salvation not based on human works but on the work of Christ. The Covenant of Grace is first hinted at in Genesis 3:15 and unfolds throughout the rest of Scripture, culminating in the person and work of Jesus Christ. While Adam's covenant required perfect obedience for life, the Covenant of Grace offers life through faith in the perfect obedience of Christ.

Romans 5:17 explains this transition: "For if, because of one man's trespass, death reigned through that one man, much more will those who receive the abundance of grace and the free gift of righteousness reign in life through the one man Jesus Christ." The contrast between these two covenants highlights the depth of God's grace. While Adam's disobedience brought condemnation, Christ's obedience brings justification and eternal life.

IV. PATRISTIC AND HISTORICAL PERSPECTIVES ON ADAM AND EVE'S TYPOLOGY

The typological relationship between Adam, Eve, Christ, and the Church has been a central theme in Christian theology throughout the ages. Early Church fathers, medieval theologians, and Reformers all reflected on the significance of Adam and Eve as types of Christ and the Church, providing rich insights that have shaped Christian doctrine and spirituality.

A. The Early Church Fathers on Adam and Eve

The early Church fathers often emphasized the typology of Adam and Christ as part of their reflections on redemption. **Irenaeus of Lyons**, writing in the 2nd century, developed the concept of **recapitulation**, arguing that Christ "recapitulated" or summed up all of humanity in Himself, succeeding where Adam had failed. Irenaeus viewed Christ's work as a reversal of Adam's disobedience, restoring humanity to its intended state.

Tertullian and **Augustine** also reflected on the typology of Adam and Christ, emphasizing the contrast between Adam's sin and Christ's righteousness. Augustine's doctrine of original sin was deeply influenced by the idea that all humanity is born in Adam and must be reborn in Christ.

B. Medieval and Reformation Theologians on the Bride of Christ

In the medieval period, theologians such as **Bernard of Clairvaux** and **Thomas Aquinas** explored the idea of the Church as the bride of Christ. Bernard's sermons on the **Song of Songs** are particularly noteworthy for their exploration of the mystical union between Christ and His Church. Bernard viewed the relationship between Christ and the Church as one of profound intimacy, likening it to the love between a bridegroom and his bride.

During the Reformation, theologians such as **John Calvin** and **Martin Luther** further developed the idea of the Church as the bride of Christ. Luther, in particular, emphasized the covenantal nature of this relationship, viewing the union between Christ and the Church as a reflection of God's grace and faithfulness. Calvin's doctrine of **union with Christ** was central to his theology, stressing that believers are united with Christ in both His death and resurrection.

V. THE SYMBOLIC AND ESOTERIC DIMENSIONS: THE GARDEN OF EDEN AND THE NEW CREATION

The Garden of Eden is often viewed not only as a historical place but also as a symbol of the ideal relationship between God and humanity. The Garden represents the state of **shalom**—wholeness, peace, and perfect fellowship with God—that was lost through Adam's sin but will be restored in the new creation. This symbolic understanding of Eden is woven throughout Scripture, from Genesis to Revelation.

A. The Tree of Life and the Tree of Knowledge

The **Tree of Life** in the Garden of Eden represents eternal life and fellowship with God. After Adam and Eve's sin, they were barred from accessing the Tree of Life, symbolizing their separation from God's presence. However, in the book of Revelation, the Tree of Life reappears in the **New Jerusalem**, signifying the restoration of eternal life for the redeemed (Revelation 22:2). This progression from Eden to the New Jerusalem highlights the **eschatological hope** of believers—that what was lost in the fall will be fully restored in Christ.

B. The New Creation: A Return to Eden

The **new creation** described in Revelation is often seen as a return to the ideal state of Eden but on a grander scale. In the new heavens and new earth, God will dwell with His people in perfect fellowship, and there will be no more death, pain, or suffering (Revelation 21:1-4). The **Marriage Supper of the Lamb** in Revelation 19 marks the ultimate consummation of the relationship between Christ and His Church, and the new creation is the eternal home of this united people.

VI. PRACTICAL APPLICATIONS FOR BELIEVERS TODAY

The typology of Adam and Eve as it relates to Christ and the Church has profound implications for how we live as believers. It shapes our understanding of our identity, our relationships, and our mission as the people of God.

A. Understanding Our Identity as the Bride of Christ

As believers, we are part of the **bride of Christ**, united with Him in an intimate, covenantal relationship. This identity gives us a profound sense of purpose and security. We are loved, cherished, and pursued by Christ, and our ultimate destiny is to be united with Him forever. This understanding of our identity shapes how we live, motivating us to pursue holiness and faithfulness in response to Christ's sacrificial love.

B. The Call to Holiness and Purity

Just as Eve was created to be a pure and holy companion for Adam, the Church is called to be **holy and blameless** in her relationship with Christ. **Ephesians 5:25-27** emphasizes that Christ's love for the Church is sanctifying, cleansing her by the washing of water with the word. As the bride of Christ, we are called to live in a way that reflects His holiness, forsaking the ways of the world and walking in purity.

C. The Mission of the Church: Partnering with Christ in Redemption

Eve's role as Adam's helper prefigures the Church's role as Christ's partner in His mission of redemption. The Church is entrusted with the task of proclaiming the Gospel and making disciples of all nations (Matthew 28:18-20). As Christ's bride, we are called to be His hands and feet in the world, working alongside Him to bring about the redemption of creation.

D. The Hope of the Consummation: The Marriage Supper of the Lamb

Finally, the typology of Adam and Eve points us to the **future hope** of the consummation of the relationship between Christ and His Church. Just as Adam and Eve were united as one flesh, we too will be united with Christ in perfect fellowship at the end of the age. The **Marriage Supper of the Lamb** in Revelation 19 is the ultimate celebration of this union, and it gives us hope and assurance as we live in anticipation of Christ's return.

The Gospel in Adam and Eve

From the Tabernacle to Solomon's Temple to the Second Temple, the progression of God's dwelling among His people points toward a final and eternal fulfillment in Christ. The tearing of the temple veil at Jesus' crucifixion signifies the end of separation between God and humanity, and the beginning of the Church as the living temple, indwelt by the Spirit.

Solomon's Temple was the physical dwelling place of God among His people, where the Ark of the Covenant resided. As magnificent as it was, it served as a shadow of a greater reality. The destruction of this temple symbolized the passing of the old covenant system, pointing forward to the time when God's presence would dwell fully in Christ, the true Temple. The physical structure of the temple was temporary, but it laid the foundation for the spiritual temple found in Christ.

The Second Temple, rebuilt after the exile, held great significance for the Jewish people. It was the site of Jesus' ministry, and although it lacked the glory of Solomon's Temple, it still foreshadowed a greater fulfillment in Christ. The destruction of the Second Temple, as prophesied by Jesus, marks the end of the old sacrificial system and the transition to a new covenant where God's presence is no longer confined to a building but resides in Christ and His Church. Jesus, the ultimate Temple, fulfills what the Second Temple could only symbolize.

The story of Adam and Eve is much more than an account of humanity's origins; it is a profound revelation of the **Gospel**. Adam, the first man, serves as a type of Christ, whose obedience brings life where Adam's disobedience brought death. Eve, the first bride, points to the Church, the bride of Christ, who is united with Him in a bond of sacrificial love and covenant faithfulness.

Through Adam and Eve, we see the grand narrative of salvation unfold. Where Adam's fall plunged humanity into sin, Christ's work as the second Adam brought redemption and new life. Where Eve was taken from Adam's side to be his companion, the Church is born from Christ's side and becomes His bride. Together,

Adam and Eve provide a picture of the Gospel—a picture of sin, redemption, and ultimate union with God.

CHAPTER 3: THE PASSOVER LAMB: A TYPE OF CHRIST'S SACRIFICE

Just as the blood of the lamb saved Israel from judgment, Christ's blood delivers us from eternal death (Exodus 12, 1 Corinthians 5:7). This wasn't just a historical event but a prophecy pointing to Christ, the perfect and final Passover Lamb whose sacrifice provides ultimate deliverance from sin. As Paul declares in 1 Corinthians 5:7, "For Christ, our Passover lamb, has been sacrificed." The Passover lamb in Exodus 12, one of the most significant types of Christ in the Old Testament, played a key role in the deliverance of the Israelites from Egypt. It foreshadows Christ's ultimate sacrifice on the cross. Just as the blood of the Passover lamb spared the Israelites from physical death and ensured their deliverance from slavery, the blood of Christ spares believers from spiritual death and delivers them from the bondage of sin. This chapter explores the profound connection between the Passover lamb in Egypt and Christ's redemptive work, illustrating how this Old Testament event points to its New Testament fulfillment in Jesus.

I. THE PASSOVER LAMB IN EGYPT (EXODUS 12)

The story of the Passover is a central event in the narrative of the Exodus, when God delivered the Israelites from slavery in Egypt. On the night before their deliverance, God instituted the Passover as a lasting ordinance for the people of Israel. The instructions for the Passover lamb, described in **Exodus 12**, are filled with symbolic meaning that points forward to Christ's sacrificial death.

A. The Blood of the Lamb Spared the Israelites from Death

In **Exodus 12**, God commanded the Israelites to select a lamb without blemish, slaughter it, and apply its blood to the doorposts and lintel of their houses. This act of faith would protect them from the final plague—the death of the firstborn. God promised that when He saw the blood on the doorposts, He would "pass over" those houses, sparing the firstborn from death (Exodus 12:13).

This act of applying the lamb's blood marked a significant turning point in the Exodus story. The lamb's blood was the means by which the Israelites were spared from judgment and death. Without the blood, the firstborn of the household would die. The Passover lamb, therefore, served as a substitute, standing in the place of the firstborn and bearing the penalty of death.

1. The Significance of the Lamb Without Blemish

God's requirement that the Passover lamb be "without blemish" (Exodus 12:5) is crucial to understanding its typological significance. A lamb with any defect would not suffice; it had to be perfect. This points forward to Christ, who was without sin and perfect in every way. **1 Peter 1:19** describes Christ as the Lamb "without blemish or spot," emphasizing His sinlessness and perfection. Just as the Passover lamb had to be without defect to serve as an acceptable sacrifice, Christ's sinless life made Him the perfect sacrifice for humanity's sins.

The lamb's unblemished nature also underscores the idea of holiness and purity. In the same way that the Israelites were commanded to offer a lamb without defect, God's ultimate plan for salvation involved sending His Son, who was pure and holy, to offer Himself as the spotless Lamb who would take away the sins of the world.

2. The Substitutionary Nature of the Sacrifice

The Passover lamb was not merely a ritualistic offering; it was a **substitute** for the firstborn in every household. The lamb's life was taken so that the firstborn could live. This substitutionary aspect is a key theme throughout the sacrificial system in the Old Testament and reaches its fulfillment in the death of Christ. The lamb's blood, applied to the doorposts, marked the household as being under God's protection and judgment passed over it.

This substitutionary element foreshadows Christ's sacrifice, where He serves as the substitute for humanity. Just as the lamb's blood was applied to the Israelites' houses, Christ's blood is applied to the believer's life through faith. **Isaiah 53:5** points to this substitution, saying, "He was wounded for our transgressions, He was bruised for our iniquities; the chastisement for our peace was upon Him, and by His stripes we are healed."

B. Deliverance Through the Blood of the Lamb

The Passover marked the moment when God began to deliver His people from Egyptian slavery. The death of the lamb and the application of its blood were the means by which the Israelites were spared from death and ultimately set free. Following the Passover, God led the Israelites out of Egypt, demonstrating His power over Pharaoh and His faithfulness to His promises.

1. Liberation from Slavery

The blood of the Passover lamb not only spared the Israelites from death but also marked the beginning of their **liberation from slavery**. After the final plague, Pharaoh finally agreed to let the Israelites go, and they began their journey toward the Promised Land. This act of deliverance from physical slavery serves as a powerful symbol of the spiritual deliverance that Christ would later bring to His people.

In the same way that the Israelites were delivered from bondage in Egypt, believers are delivered from the bondage of sin through the blood of Christ. **Romans 6:17-18** speaks of this transformation, saying, "But thanks be to God, that you who were once slaves of sin have become obedient from the heart to the standard of teaching to which you were committed, and, having been set free from sin, have become slaves of righteousness." The Passover lamb's blood points to the greater deliverance that would come through Christ, the Lamb of God.

2. A Perpetual Memorial

God commanded the Israelites to observe the Passover as a **perpetual memorial** (Exodus 12:14), reminding them of their deliverance from Egypt. This annual celebration was meant to keep the memory of God's saving work alive in the hearts of His people. In the same way, the Church observes the Lord's Supper (or Communion) as a memorial of Christ's sacrifice. **1 Corinthians 11:24-26** reminds believers to "do this in remembrance of Me," pointing to the continuity between the Passover and the new covenant in Christ's blood.

II. JESUS AS THE TRUE PASSOVER LAMB

The New Testament explicitly connects the Passover lamb in Exodus with Christ's sacrifice on the cross. **John 1:29** records John the Baptist's declaration upon seeing Jesus: "Behold, the Lamb of God, who takes away the sin of the world!" This title directly identifies Jesus as the true and greater Passover Lamb, whose death brings spiritual deliverance to all who believe in Him.

A. Jesus Fulfills the Passover Sacrifice

In the New Testament, the writers often link Jesus' death with the Passover lamb. Paul makes this connection clear in **1 Corinthians 5:7**, where he writes, "For Christ, our Passover lamb, has been sacrificed." Jesus' crucifixion occurred during the Passover festival, further underscoring the connection between His death and the Passover lamb.

1. The Lamb of God Takes Away the Sin of the World

John the Baptist's proclamation of Jesus as the "Lamb of God" in **John 1:29** is a powerful declaration of Jesus' role as the ultimate sacrifice. While the Passover lamb in Egypt protected the Israelites from physical death, Jesus, the Lamb of God, takes away the sins of the world, delivering humanity from spiritual death. His sacrifice is once and for all, unlike the annual Passover lamb sacrifices that merely pointed forward to the true Lamb.

In this way, Jesus fulfills the typology of the Passover lamb, taking upon Himself the punishment for sin and offering His blood as the means of atonement. **Hebrews 9:12** emphasizes that Christ "entered once for all into the holy places, not by means of the blood of goats and calves but by means of His own blood, thus securing an eternal redemption."

2. Jesus, the Perfect and Sinless Sacrifice

Just as the Passover lamb had to be without blemish, Jesus lived a sinless life, making Him the only acceptable sacrifice for the sins of humanity. **1 Peter 1:18-19** describes Jesus as the "Lamb without blemish or defect," drawing a direct parallel between the Passover lamb and Christ. His sinlessness qualified Him to bear the sins of the world and to offer His life as a ransom for many (Mark 10:45).

Christ's perfection was essential to His role as the Lamb of God. Only a sinless sacrifice could atone for the sins of the world. Throughout His ministry, Jesus remained fully obedient to the Father, fulfilling all righteousness (Matthew 3:15) and living in perfect accordance with God's will. This obedience culminated in His death on the cross, where He willingly gave His life as the ultimate Passover Lamb.

B. The Blood of Christ Saves Us from Spiritual Death

Just as the blood of the Passover lamb spared the Israelites from physical death, the blood of Christ spares believers from **spiritual death**. This theme is central to the New Testament's understanding of salvation. **Ephesians 1:7** declares, "In Him we have redemption through His blood, the forgiveness of our trespasses, according to the riches of His grace." The blood of Christ is the means by which believers are forgiven and set free from the penalty of sin.

1. Redemption and Forgiveness Through the Blood of Christ

The New Testament frequently emphasizes the importance of Christ's blood in the work of salvation. **Hebrews 9:22** states, "Without the shedding of blood, there is no forgiveness of sins," underscoring the necessity of a blood sacrifice for the remission of sin. Christ's blood, like the Passover lamb's blood, serves as the means of redemption, delivering believers from the consequences of sin and offering them eternal life.

Through His death, Jesus establishes a new covenant in His blood. **Luke 22:20** records Jesus' words at the Last Supper: "This cup that is poured out for you is the new covenant in my blood." This new covenant replaces the old system of sacrifices and offers a permanent solution to the problem of sin. Christ's blood secures eternal redemption, and those who are covered by His blood are spared from the judgment that sin brings.

2. Deliverance from the Bondage of Sin

In the same way that the blood of the Passover lamb led to the Israelites' deliverance from slavery, the blood of Christ delivers believers from the **bondage of sin**. Paul writes in **Romans 6:6-7**, "We know that our old self was crucified with Him in order that the body of sin might be brought to nothing, so that we would no longer be enslaved to sin. For one who has died has been set free from sin." The blood of Christ breaks the chains of sin and frees believers to live a new life in Him.

Christ's sacrifice not only removes the penalty of sin but also breaks its power. Believers are no longer slaves to sin but are empowered by the Holy Spirit to live in righteousness. This deliverance from sin's bondage is a direct parallel to the Israelites' deliverance from Egypt. Just as the Israelites were freed from physical slavery, believers are freed from spiritual slavery through the blood of Christ.

III. PRACTICAL IMPLICATIONS FOR BELIEVERS

The typology of the Passover lamb and its fulfillment in Christ has profound implications for believers today. Understanding Christ as the Passover Lamb deepens our appreciation for His sacrifice and shapes the way we live as His followers.

A. The Importance of the Blood of Christ

The blood of Christ is central to the Christian faith. It is through His blood that we are forgiven, redeemed, and set free from sin. As believers, we are called to trust in the sufficiency of Christ's sacrifice and to live in the light of His redemptive work. **Hebrews 10:19** encourages believers to "have confidence to enter the holy places by the blood of Jesus." The blood of Christ gives us access to God and secures our eternal salvation.

B. Living in Freedom from Sin

Just as the Israelites were called to leave Egypt and live as God's chosen people, believers are called to live in **freedom from sin**. Christ's sacrifice delivers us from the bondage of sin and enables us to live in righteousness. **Romans 6:11** instructs believers to "consider yourselves dead to sin and alive to God in Christ Jesus." As those who have been redeemed by the blood of the Lamb, we are called to walk in newness of life, no longer enslaved to sin but living in obedience to God.

C. A Perpetual Remembrance of Christ's Sacrifice

Just as the Israelites observed the Passover as a perpetual memorial of their deliverance, the Church observes the Lord's Supper as a continual reminder of Christ's sacrifice. **1 Corinthians 11:24-26** calls believers to "do this in remembrance of Me" as we partake of the bread and the cup. The Lord's Supper is a powerful reminder of the blood that was shed for our salvation and the body that was broken for our deliverance. It points us back to the cross and reminds us of the great cost of our redemption.

D. The Hope of Eternal Deliverance

Finally, the Passover lamb points us to the **ultimate deliverance** that Christ will bring at His second coming. Just as the Israelites looked forward to the Promised Land, believers look forward to the new heavens and the new earth, where Christ will reign in glory and righteousness. **Revelation 7:9-10** describes a great multitude standing before the throne, clothed in white robes and holding palm branches, crying out, "Salvation belongs to our God who sits on the throne, and to the Lamb!" The Passover lamb not only delivers us from sin in this life but also guarantees our eternal salvation.

The Passover Lamb as a Foreshadowing of Christ's Sacrifice

From the Tabernacle to Solomon's Temple to the Second Temple, the progression of God's dwelling among His people points toward a final and eternal fulfillment in Christ. The tearing of the temple veil at Jesus' crucifixion signifies the end of separation between God and humanity, and the beginning of the Church as the living temple, indwelt by the Spirit.

Solomon's Temple was the physical dwelling place of God among His people, where the Ark of the Covenant resided. As magnificent as it was, it served as a shadow of a greater reality. The destruction of this temple symbolized the passing of the old covenant system, pointing forward to the time when God's presence would dwell fully in Christ, the true Temple. The physical structure of the temple was temporary, but it laid the foundation for the spiritual temple found in Christ.

The Second Temple, rebuilt after the exile, held great significance for the Jewish people. It was the site of Jesus' ministry, and although it lacked the glory of Solomon's Temple, it still foreshadowed a greater fulfillment in Christ. The destruction of the Second Temple, as prophesied by Jesus, marks the end of the old sacrificial system and the transition to a new covenant where God's presence is no longer confined to a building but resides in Christ and His Church. Jesus, the ultimate Temple, fulfills what the Second Temple could only symbolize.

The Passover lamb in **Exodus 12** is a powerful type of Christ's sacrifice on the cross. Just as the blood of the lamb spared the Israelites from death and delivered them from slavery, the blood of Christ, the true Passover Lamb, spares believers from spiritual death and delivers them from the bondage of sin. The typology of the Passover lamb points forward to the ultimate sacrifice of Jesus, whose perfect and sinless life made Him the only acceptable substitute for the sins of humanity.

As believers, we are called to remember Christ's sacrifice, live in the freedom He has provided, and look forward to the day when we will be fully and finally delivered from the presence of sin. Christ, our Passover Lamb, has been sacrificed, and through His blood, we are redeemed.

CHAPTER 4: THE EXODUS AND RED SEA CROSSING: A TYPE OF BAPTISM AND DELIVERANCE

The story of the Exodus is one of the most profound and significant events in the Bible, marking the moment when God delivered the Israelites from slavery in Egypt and led them into freedom. Beyond its historical importance, the Exodus also serves as a powerful type—a symbolic foreshadowing of greater spiritual truths, particularly baptism and deliverance. The Red Sea crossing, in particular, represents the believer's passage from death to life, from bondage to freedom, as it prefigures the spiritual deliverance brought through Christ. In this chapter, we will explore how the Exodus narrative functions as a type of baptism and spiritual liberation, showing how the Israelites' journey out of Egypt foreshadows the believer's journey out of sin and into new life in Christ.

I. THE EXODUS: ISRAEL'S DELIVERANCE FROM EGYPT (EXODUS 14)

The Exodus was a defining moment in the history of Israel and in the unfolding of God's redemptive plan. After enduring centuries of slavery in Egypt, the Israelites cried out to God, and He answered by raising up Moses to lead them to freedom. The plagues that God sent upon Egypt culminated in the Passover, in which the blood of a lamb saved the Israelites from the final plague—the death of the firstborn. After this devastating blow, Pharaoh finally agreed to let the Israelites go, and they began their journey out of Egypt, heading toward the Promised Land.

However, Pharaoh soon changed his mind and pursued the Israelites with his army, trapping them at the shores of the Red Sea. In this moment of crisis, God performed one of the most dramatic miracles in the Bible: He parted the waters of the Red Sea, allowing the Israelites to cross on dry ground. When the Egyptians followed, the waters returned, drowning Pharaoh's army and securing the Israelites' deliverance once and for all.

The parting of the Red Sea is more than just a historical event; it is a powerful symbol of salvation and deliverance. In the New Testament, Paul explicitly links the Exodus and the Red Sea crossing with baptism, highlighting the spiritual significance of this event for believers today.

A. The Red Sea Crossing as a Type of Baptism

In 1 Corinthians 10:1-2, Paul draws a clear parallel between the Exodus and baptism, stating, "For I do not want you to be unaware, brothers, that our fathers were all under the cloud, and all passed through the sea, and all were baptized into Moses in the cloud and in the sea." Here, Paul is identifying the crossing of the Red Sea as a type of baptism, in which the Israelites passed through the waters and were, in a sense, baptized into Moses, their leader and deliverer. This prefigures the Christian sacrament of baptism, in which believers pass through the waters and are baptized into Christ, their ultimate Deliverer.

1. The Waters of Baptism: From Death to Life

The parting of the Red Sea represents a powerful metaphor for baptism, where believers pass through the waters and are brought from death to life. Just as the Israelites passed through the waters of the Red Sea and were delivered from death at the hands of Pharaoh's army, believers pass through the waters of baptism and are delivered from spiritual death. Romans 6:3-4 speaks of baptism as a participation in Christ's death and resurrection: "Do you not know that all of us who have been baptized into Christ Jesus were baptized into his death? We were buried therefore with him by baptism into death, in order that, just as Christ was raised from the dead by the glory of the Father, we too might walk in newness of life."

In this way, the Red Sea crossing symbolizes the transformative power of baptism. The Israelites, standing on the shores of the Red Sea, were facing certain death—trapped between the sea and Pharaoh's advancing army. But through the waters, they passed from death to life, emerging on the other side as free people, no longer slaves. In the same way, believers pass through the waters of baptism, leaving behind their old life of sin and death and emerging as new creations in Christ, free from the bondage of sin.

2. Baptized into Christ: The New Moses

Paul's reference to the Israelites being baptized into Moses in 1 Corinthians 10:2 underscores another important typological connection: just as the Israelites were baptized into their leader, Moses, believers are baptized into Christ, the true and greater Deliverer. Moses, as the leader of the Exodus, serves as a type of Christ, who leads His people out of the slavery of sin and into the freedom of new life.

In baptism, believers are not merely undergoing a symbolic washing but are being united with Christ, their Deliverer. Galatians 3:27 emphasizes this union: "For as many of you as were baptized into Christ have put on Christ." Just as Moses led the Israelites through the waters of the Red Sea, Christ leads His people through the waters of baptism, delivering them from sin and death and bringing them into new life.

B. Egypt as a Type of Sin and Bondage

The story of the Exodus is not just about the Israelites escaping from physical slavery; it is also a profound spiritual allegory for the believer's deliverance from the bondage of sin. In typology, Egypt represents the state of sin and bondage, while the Red Sea crossing signifies the believer's escape from that bondage through the saving work of Christ.

1. Slavery in Egypt as a Type of Sin's Bondage

In the Exodus narrative, the Israelites were enslaved in Egypt, forced to labor under the harsh rule of Pharaoh. This slavery to Pharaoh is a powerful picture of humanity's slavery to sin. Romans 6:16-18 describes how, before coming to Christ, all people are enslaved to sin: "Do you not know that if you present yourselves to anyone as obedient slaves, you are slaves of the one whom you obey, either of sin, which leads to death, or of obedience, which leads to righteousness?"

Just as the Israelites could not free themselves from Pharaoh's grip, so too humanity is unable to free itself from the power of sin. Deliverance from sin requires a divine intervention, just as the Israelites' deliverance from Egypt required God's mighty hand.

2. Crossing the Sea: Freedom Through Christ

The crossing of the Red Sea symbolizes the moment of deliverance when the Israelites were finally set free from Egypt. After passing through the waters, they were no longer slaves but free people, destined for the Promised Land. This crossing prefigures the believer's experience of salvation, in which Christ delivers them from the bondage of sin and brings them into the freedom of new life.

Paul writes in Romans 6:6-7, "We know that our old self was crucified with him in order that the body of sin might be brought to nothing, so that we would no longer be enslaved to sin. For one who has died has been set free from sin." Just as the waters of the Red Sea drowned Pharaoh's army, symbolizing the complete defeat of Egypt's power over the Israelites, the waters of baptism symbolize the believer's liberation from sin's power through Christ's death and resurrection.

In the same way that Pharaoh's army was destroyed, leaving the Israelites free from their former oppressors, sin's dominion over the believer is broken through the work of Christ. The believer is no longer a slave to sin but is free to walk in newness of life, just as the Israelites walked freely into the wilderness, no longer bound by Egypt's chains.

Fun Fact: The Red Sea Crossing and the Significance of the Sea

Did you know that the name "Red Sea" might be more accurately translated as the Sea of Reeds? The original Hebrew name, *Yam Suph*, means "Sea of Reeds," suggesting that the body of water the Israelites crossed was a large marshy area, not necessarily the deep sea as we often imagine. However, regardless of the exact location, the miracle of parting the waters remains a powerful demonstration of God's control over nature and His ability to make a way where there seems to be no way.

II. TYPOLOGY OF THE EXODUS AND RED SEA CROSSING: A SPIRITUAL JOURNEY OF DELIVERANCE

The Exodus and the Red Sea crossing are not just historical events; they are also spiritual paradigms for the believer's journey from sin to salvation. The Old Testament narrative of God leading His people out of Egypt is a type that prefigures the spiritual deliverance God accomplishes through Christ. Each element of the story—from the plagues to the Passover, from the Red Sea to the Promised Land—carries deep spiritual meaning that foreshadows the believer's journey of salvation.

The Exodus as a Picture of Salvation

The Exodus narrative is much more than a historical account; it is a profound typology of salvation through Christ. The Red Sea crossing, like baptism, represents the believer's passage from death to life, from bondage to freedom. Just as God delivered the Israelites from Egypt through the waters of the Red Sea, He delivers believers from sin through the waters of baptism. The journey of sanctification and freedom, prefigured by the Exodus, continues as believers walk in newness of life in Christ, with the promise of eternal rest in the true Promised Land.

CHAPTER 5: MANNA FROM HEAVEN: A TYPE OF CHRIST AS THE BREAD OF LIFE

In the Old Testament, the story of **manna from heaven** stands as one of the most compelling demonstrations of God's provision. After the Israelites were freed from slavery in Egypt, they found themselves in the wilderness with no food, and God miraculously provided them with manna—a mysterious bread-like substance that appeared each morning on the ground, sustaining them throughout their 40 years in the desert. The manna was a direct and tangible expression of God's care for His people.

However, the significance of manna extends far beyond its historical and literal meaning. In the New Testament, Jesus refers to Himself as the **bread of life**, identifying Himself as the true and greater fulfillment of the manna in the wilderness. While the manna sustained the Israelites physically, Jesus, as the bread of life, sustains believers spiritually, offering eternal life. This chapter explores how the story of manna in the wilderness serves as a **type** that prefigures Christ as the bread of life, showing how God provides for both the physical and spiritual needs of His people.

I. MANNA IN THE WILDERNESS (EXODUS 16)

The story of manna begins in **Exodus 16**, shortly after the Israelites had crossed the Red Sea and begun their journey through the wilderness. Having been delivered from slavery, the Israelites now faced the harsh realities of life in the desert, where food and water were scarce. In their desperation, they began to **grumble** against

Moses and Aaron, accusing them of leading them into the wilderness to die of hunger. Despite their lack of faith, God responded with grace and provided for their needs by sending manna from heaven.

The manna appeared each morning like dew on the ground, described in **Exodus 16:14** as "a small round substance, as fine as frost." The Israelites were instructed to gather just enough for each day, trusting that God would provide more the following day. The manna was to be collected six days a week, with a double portion provided on the sixth day so that the people could rest on the Sabbath.

A. Manna: God's Provision for Physical Sustenance

Manna was God's supernatural provision for the physical sustenance of the Israelites during their time in the wilderness. It served as their daily bread, sustaining them throughout their long journey to the Promised Land. In this way, the manna was both a **gift of grace** and a **test of faith**—a reminder that God is the provider of all things, and that His people must trust in His daily provision.

1. Daily Dependence on God's Provision

One of the key lessons that the manna taught the Israelites was the importance of daily dependence on God. Each day, they were to gather just enough manna for their needs, trusting that God would provide again the next day. This was a **test of faith**, as they were not allowed to hoard or store up manna beyond what they needed for that day (except on the Sabbath). Any excess manna would rot and spoil, as described in **Exodus 16:20**: "But they did not listen to Moses; some left part of it till the morning, and it bred worms and stank."

This daily dependence on God's provision is a theme that runs throughout Scripture. In the Lord's Prayer, Jesus teaches His disciples to pray, "Give us this day our daily bread" (**Matthew 6:11**), emphasizing the need to rely on God for daily sustenance, both physically and spiritually. The manna in the wilderness was a physical demonstration of this principle, reminding the Israelites (and by extension, believers today) that God is faithful to meet their needs, one day at a time.

2. The Sabbath Rest and Trust in God

The instructions regarding the collection of manna also emphasized the importance of the **Sabbath** as a day of rest and trust in God's provision. On the sixth day, the Israelites were to gather a double portion of manna so that they would not need to work on the Sabbath. Unlike the other days, the extra manna gathered on the sixth day did not spoil, allowing the Israelites to rest in confidence that God had provided enough.

This aspect of the manna narrative teaches the principle of **trusting in God's provision even in times of rest**. The Sabbath rest, which was established at creation, is a reminder that God is the ultimate provider and sustainer. Just as the Israelites were called to rest on the Sabbath and trust that God would meet their needs, believers today are called to rest in Christ, the true Sabbath rest, knowing that He has already accomplished the work of salvation on their behalf.

B. Manna as a Type of Christ: The Bread of Life

While the manna provided physical sustenance for the Israelites in the wilderness, its deeper significance is revealed in the New Testament, where Jesus identifies Himself as the **true bread from heaven**. In **John 6**, after feeding the five thousand with just five loaves of bread and two fish, Jesus engages in a conversation with the crowd about the meaning of this miracle. The people recall the story of manna in the wilderness and ask Jesus to perform a similar sign. In response, Jesus declares that He is the true **bread of life**, who gives eternal life to all who believe in Him.

1. The Bread from Heaven: Jesus as the True Manna

In **John 6:31-35**, the crowd says to Jesus, "Our fathers ate the manna in the wilderness; as it is written, 'He gave them bread from heaven to eat.'" In their minds, they are comparing Jesus to Moses, who they believed provided the manna for their ancestors. However,

Jesus corrects their misunderstanding, saying, "Truly, truly, I say to you, it was not Moses who gave you the bread from heaven, but my Father gives you the true bread from heaven. For the bread of God is he who comes down from heaven and gives life to the world."

Here, Jesus shifts the focus from the **physical manna** that sustained the Israelites to the **spiritual bread** that sustains eternal life. He declares in **John 6:35**, "I am the bread of life; whoever comes to me shall not hunger, and whoever believes in me shall never thirst." In this statement, Jesus identifies Himself as the fulfillment of the manna in the wilderness. While the manna sustained physical life, Jesus offers the **bread of life** that sustains spiritual life and leads to eternal salvation.

2. The Superiority of Christ's Provision

The manna in the wilderness was a temporary provision, meeting the Israelites' physical needs for a time, but it did not grant them eternal life. In fact, **John 6:49** states, "Your fathers ate the manna in the wilderness, and they died." The physical manna could not save them from death, nor could it sustain them beyond their earthly lives. In contrast, Jesus offers something far greater—eternal life. He says in **John 6:50-51**, "This is the bread that comes down from heaven, so that one may eat of it and not die. I am the living bread that came down from heaven. If anyone eats of this bread, he will live forever."

Jesus, as the **true bread of life**, offers something that the manna in the wilderness could not. While the manna temporarily satisfied physical hunger, Jesus satisfies the deepest spiritual hunger of the human soul. Those who come to Him in faith are promised eternal life, never to hunger or thirst spiritually again. This is the ultimate fulfillment of the typology of manna.

II. THE DEEPER SPIRITUAL MEANING OF MANNA: LIFE IN CHRIST

The manna in the wilderness was more than just physical sustenance for the Israelites; it was a **signpost** pointing to a deeper spiritual truth about God's provision for His people. In the same way that the Israelites had to **trust** God for their daily bread, believers are called to trust in **Christ** as their ultimate source of spiritual nourishment. Just as the manna appeared each morning to sustain the Israelites, Jesus offers Himself as the daily bread that sustains the believer's spiritual life.

A. Spiritual Nourishment: Feeding on Christ

In **John 6:53-56**, Jesus makes a radical statement about what it means to receive the bread of life: "Truly, truly, I say to you, unless you eat the flesh of the Son of Man and drink his blood, you have no life in you. Whoever feeds on my flesh and drinks my blood has eternal life, and I will raise him up on the last day. For my flesh is true food, and my blood is true drink."

While this passage can be difficult to understand, it is clear that Jesus is speaking in spiritual terms. To "eat" His flesh and "drink" His blood is to **participate in His life** and **death** through faith. It is a metaphor for **union with Christ**—just as physical food sustains the body, so too does Christ sustain the soul. Feeding on Christ means coming to Him in faith, receiving His grace, and relying on His Spirit for spiritual life and strength.

1. Abiding in Christ

The idea of "feeding" on Christ is closely connected to the concept of **abiding** in Christ, which Jesus later teaches in **John 15:4**: "Abide in me, and I in you. As the branch cannot bear fruit by itself, unless it abides in the vine, neither can you, unless you abide in me." Just as the Israelites were sustained by the manna in the wilderness, believers are sustained by their abiding relationship with Christ. He is the source of all spiritual nourishment, and without Him, we can do nothing.

The manna that appeared each morning in the wilderness was a reminder to the Israelites of their dependence on God's daily provision. In the same way, believers are called to **daily abide in**

Christ, drawing their spiritual sustenance from Him. He is the true bread of life, and apart from Him, there is no spiritual life.

2. Communion: Remembering Christ's Sacrifice

The language of **eating** Christ's flesh and **drinking** His blood also points forward to the **Lord's Supper**, or **Communion**, which Jesus instituted at the Last Supper. In Communion, believers participate in a symbolic meal that reminds them of Christ's sacrifice on the cross. The bread represents Christ's body, broken for them, and the wine represents His blood, shed for the forgiveness of sins.

While the bread and wine in Communion are physical symbols, they point to the deeper spiritual reality of Christ's sacrifice. Just as the Israelites ate the manna in the wilderness to sustain their physical lives, believers partake of Communion to remember the spiritual life they have received through Christ's death and resurrection. **1 Corinthians 11:26** says, "For as often as you eat this bread and drink the cup, you proclaim the Lord's death until he comes."

Communion serves as a regular reminder that Jesus is the bread of life, the one who sustains believers through His grace. By participating in this meal, believers are reminded of their **ongoing need** for Christ's sustaining presence and are spiritually nourished as they remember His sacrifice.

Fun Fact: The Taste of Manna

Have you ever wondered what manna tasted like? According to **Exodus 16:31**, manna was described as "like coriander seed, white, and the taste of it was like wafers made with honey." Later, in **Numbers 11:8**, it is described as tasting like "cakes baked with oil." This description suggests that manna was not only nourishing but also sweet and pleasant to eat, a gift that was both sustaining and enjoyable.

Some scholars have speculated that manna was a naturally occurring substance, such as resin from tamarisk trees, which could appear in desert regions. However, the biblical narrative clearly presents manna as a **supernatural provision** from God, not something that could be explained by natural phenomena. Regardless of its exact composition, manna was a miraculous gift that pointed to God's care for His people and foreshadowed the spiritual nourishment that Christ would one day provide as the true bread of life.

III. LESSONS FROM MANNA: FAITH, OBEDIENCE, AND GRATITUDE

The story of manna in the wilderness offers several important lessons for believers today, particularly in the areas of **faith**, **obedience**, and **gratitude**. Just as the Israelites were called to trust God for their daily provision, believers are called to trust Christ for their spiritual sustenance. The manna also teaches the importance of **obedience** to God's commands and the need for **gratitude** in recognizing His ongoing provision.

A. Faith: Trusting in God's Daily Provision

One of the primary lessons of the manna narrative is the importance of trusting in **God's daily provision**. The Israelites had to gather just enough manna for each day, trusting that God would provide again the next day. In the same way, believers are called to trust in **Christ's sufficiency** for their daily spiritual needs.

Matthew 6:34 reminds us not to worry about tomorrow: "Therefore do not be anxious about tomorrow, for tomorrow will be anxious for itself. Sufficient for the day is its own trouble." Just as the Israelites were instructed to gather manna daily, we are called to come to Christ daily for our spiritual nourishment, trusting that He will provide what we need each day.

1. The Temptation to Hoard

One of the temptations the Israelites faced was the desire to **hoard** manna, trying to gather more than they needed for the day. However, when they did this, the manna spoiled and became worthless. This temptation to hoard reflects a lack of trust in God's provision and a desire for self-sufficiency. In the same way, believers today may be tempted to rely on their own efforts or resources rather than trusting in God's provision.

The lesson here is clear: God provides what we need, and we must trust Him daily. Just as the Israelites had to learn to rely on God for their physical sustenance, we must learn to rely on Christ for our spiritual sustenance. Hoarding spiritual "manna" by relying on our own efforts or worrying about the future only leads to frustration and emptiness.

2. Learning to Be Content

The Israelites' experience with manna also teaches the importance of **contentment**. Throughout their time in the wilderness, the Israelites often grumbled and complained about the manna, longing for the food they had in Egypt (Numbers 11:4-6). Despite the miraculous nature of God's provision, they were not satisfied and desired more.

This attitude of discontentment can easily creep into the life of a believer. Instead of being satisfied with the spiritual nourishment that Christ provides, we may find ourselves longing for the pleasures or distractions of the world. However, true contentment comes from recognizing that **Christ is enough**—He is the bread of life who satisfies the deepest longings of our souls.

Philippians 4:11-13 teaches the secret of contentment: "I have learned in whatever situation I am to be content. I know how to be brought low, and I know how to abound. In any and every circumstance, I have learned the secret of facing plenty and hunger, abundance and need. I can do all things through him who strengthens me." When we trust in Christ as our source of strength and sustenance, we find contentment in Him, no matter the circumstances.

B. Obedience: Following God's Instructions

Another key lesson from the manna narrative is the importance of **obedience** to God's instructions. God gave the

Israelites specific commands regarding how to gather and use the manna, and their willingness (or unwillingness) to follow these commands revealed the condition of their hearts. Similarly, our obedience to God's Word is a reflection of our trust in His provision and care.

1. Gathering Just Enough

The Israelites were instructed to gather just enough manna for each day, with a double portion on the sixth day to cover the Sabbath. This required **obedience** to God's instructions and a willingness to trust His provision. Some Israelites, however, disobeyed by attempting to gather more than they needed, and the extra manna spoiled.

This act of disobedience illustrates the danger of **self-reliance** and the importance of trusting in God's provision. When we try to take matters into our own hands, rather than obeying God's commands, we often find ourselves in trouble. Obedience to God's Word is essential for experiencing the fullness of His provision in our lives.

2. Observing the Sabbath

The manna narrative also emphasizes the importance of **rest** and **observing the Sabbath**. God instructed the Israelites to gather a double portion of manna on the sixth day so that they could rest on the seventh day, the Sabbath. This required trust in God's provision and a willingness to follow His command to rest.

For believers today, the Sabbath rest points to the spiritual rest we have in **Christ**. Just as the Israelites rested from their labor on the Sabbath, we are called to rest in the finished work of Christ, trusting that He has provided everything we need for our salvation. **Hebrews 4:9-10** speaks of this spiritual rest: "So then, there remains a Sabbath rest for the people of God, for whoever has entered God's rest has also rested from his works as God did from his."

In a world that often values **busyness** and **self-sufficiency**, the call to rest in Christ can be challenging. However, just as the Israelites were called to observe the Sabbath and trust in God's provision, we are called to rest in Christ, knowing that He is our ultimate provider.

C. Gratitude: Recognizing God's Ongoing Provision

The manna in the wilderness was a daily reminder of God's **faithfulness** and **provision**. However, instead of responding with gratitude, the Israelites often complained and grumbled about the manna. Their ingratitude serves as a warning for believers today, reminding us of the importance of **gratitude** in recognizing God's ongoing provision in our lives.

1. Avoiding Grumbling and Complaining

Despite the miraculous nature of the manna, the Israelites often grumbled and complained, longing for the food they had in Egypt. **Numbers 11:4-6** describes their dissatisfaction: "Now the rabble that was among them had a strong craving. And the people of Israel also wept again and said, 'Oh that we had meat to eat! We remember the fish we ate in Egypt that cost nothing, the cucumbers, the melons, the leeks, the onions, and the garlic. But now our strength is dried up, and there is nothing at all but this manna to look at.'"

This grumbling reflects a **lack of gratitude** for God's provision and a distorted memory of the past. The Israelites forgot the harshness of their slavery in Egypt and instead longed for the temporary pleasures they had left behind. In the same way, believers today can fall into the trap of complaining about their circumstances, forgetting the blessings and provisions that God has provided.

Philippians 2:14-15 urges believers to "Do all things without grumbling or disputing, that you may be blameless and innocent, children of God without blemish in the midst of a crooked and twisted generation, among whom you shine as lights in the world." Gratitude is an essential aspect of the Christian life, and it reflects our trust in God's goodness and faithfulness.

2. Cultivating an Attitude of Thanksgiving

Instead of grumbling, the Israelites should have responded to the manna with **gratitude**, recognizing that God was providing for their needs each day. In the same way, believers are called to cultivate an attitude of **thanksgiving**, acknowledging that every good and perfect gift comes from God (James 1:17).

1 Thessalonians 5:16-18 encourages believers to "Rejoice always, pray without ceasing, give thanks in all circumstances; for this is the will of God in Christ Jesus for you." Gratitude is not dependent on our circumstances but is a reflection of our trust in God's ongoing provision and care. When we recognize that Christ is the **bread of life**, who provides for our deepest spiritual needs, we can respond with gratitude, no matter what challenges we may face.

IV. THE PROMISE OF ETERNAL SATISFACTION IN CHRIST

The manna in the wilderness was a temporary provision, meeting the Israelites' physical needs for a time, but it pointed forward to the greater and eternal provision found in **Christ**. Jesus, as the true bread of life, offers something far greater than the manna—**eternal satisfaction** and life in Him.

A. Eternal Life Through Christ

While the manna sustained the Israelites physically, it could not grant them eternal life. In contrast, Jesus offers **eternal life** to all who come to Him in faith. He declares in **John 6:40**, "For this is the will of my Father, that everyone who looks on the Son and believes in him should have eternal life, and I will raise him up on the last day."

The promise of eternal life is central to the message of the **gospel**. Through His sacrificial death and resurrection, Jesus has made a way for believers to experience **eternal satisfaction** in Him. Just as the Israelites were sustained by the manna during their journey to the Promised Land, believers are sustained by Christ during their journey toward **eternal life**.

B. Never Hunger or Thirst Again

In **John 6:35**, Jesus promises that those who come to Him will "never hunger" and "never thirst" again. This statement reflects the **complete satisfaction** that is found in Christ. While the things of this world may leave us empty and unfulfilled, Christ offers true and lasting satisfaction.

The **hunger** and **thirst** that Jesus speaks of are not physical but spiritual. They reflect the deep longings of the human soul for **meaning**, **purpose**, and **fulfillment**—longings that can only be satisfied in a relationship with Christ. Those who come to Him in faith will find that He is more than enough to meet their deepest needs.

Psalm 107:9 echoes this truth: "For he satisfies the longing soul, and the hungry soul he fills with good things." In Christ, we find the **true bread of life**, the one who satisfies our deepest longings and sustains us for eternity.

Manna as a Type of Christ, the Bread of Life

From the Tabernacle to Solomon's Temple to the Second Temple, the progression of God's dwelling among His people points toward a final and eternal fulfillment in Christ. The tearing of the temple veil at Jesus' crucifixion signifies the end of separation between God and humanity, and the beginning of the Church as the living temple, indwelt by the Spirit.

Solomon's Temple was the physical dwelling place of God among His people, where the Ark of the Covenant resided. As magnificent as it was, it served as a shadow of a greater reality. The destruction of this temple symbolized the passing of the old covenant system, pointing forward to the time when God's presence would dwell fully in Christ, the true Temple. The physical structure of the temple was temporary, but it laid the foundation for the spiritual temple found in Christ.

The Second Temple, rebuilt after the exile, held great significance for the Jewish people. It was the site of Jesus' ministry, and although it lacked the glory of Solomon's Temple, it still foreshadowed a greater fulfillment in Christ. The destruction of the Second Temple, as prophesied by Jesus, marks the end of the old sacrificial system and the transition to a new covenant where God's presence is no longer confined to a building but resides in Christ and His Church. Jesus, the ultimate Temple, fulfills what the Second Temple could only symbolize.

The story of manna in the wilderness is a powerful reminder of God's faithfulness and provision for His people. It teaches important lessons about **faith**, **obedience**, and **gratitude**, while also pointing forward to the greater spiritual provision found in **Christ**, the true **bread of life**. Just as the manna sustained the Israelites during their journey through the wilderness, Christ sustains believers on their journey of faith, offering eternal life and satisfaction to all who come to Him.

As we reflect on the manna, we are reminded that Christ is the source of all **spiritual nourishment**. He is the bread of life, the one who satisfies the deepest longings of the human soul. By coming to Him in faith, we receive the **gift of eternal life** and are sustained by His grace each day. Just as the Israelites had to gather manna daily, we are called to abide in Christ daily, trusting Him to meet our every need.

In Christ, we find **true satisfaction**—a satisfaction that the world cannot offer. As we partake of the bread of life, we are reminded that He is more than enough to sustain us, both now and for eternity.

CHAPTER 6: THE BRONZE SERPENT: A TYPE OF CHRIST'S CRUCIFIXION

In the Old Testament, one of the most striking and unusual symbols of deliverance occurs in **Numbers 21:4-9** with the account of the **bronze serpent**. During their wilderness journey, the Israelites faced a deadly plague of venomous snakes, and in their desperation, they turned to God for help. God instructed Moses to craft a bronze serpent and raise it on a pole, promising that anyone who looked at the serpent would be healed.

Though peculiar in its details, this event serves as a powerful **type** that points forward to the **crucifixion of Jesus Christ**. Just as the Israelites were healed by looking at the bronze serpent lifted up in the wilderness, Jesus draws on this imagery to explain His own death. In **John 3:14-15**, Jesus says, "And as Moses lifted up the serpent in the wilderness, so must the Son of Man be lifted up, that whoever believes in Him may have eternal life." This chapter explores how the bronze serpent prefigures the crucifixion of Christ, demonstrating how God's plan of salvation unfolds in both the Old and New Testaments.

I. THE BRONZE SERPENT IN THE WILDERNESS (NUMBERS 21:4-9)

The story of the bronze serpent takes place during the **Israelites' journey through the wilderness**, a time marked by trials, rebellion, and divine intervention. After being freed from slavery in Egypt, the Israelites often complained about their hardships, despite God's ongoing provision for them. On one such occasion, their rebellion against God and Moses led to a severe judgment in the form of **venomous serpents**.

In **Numbers 21:5-6**, we read, "The people spoke against God and against Moses, 'Why have you brought us up out of Egypt to die in the wilderness? For there is no food and no water, and we loathe this worthless food.' Then the Lord sent fiery serpents among the people, and they bit the people, so that many of the people of Israel died."

The venomous snakes were a direct result of the people's rebellion. Yet, in their distress, they repented and cried out to God for deliverance. **Numbers 21:7** continues, "And the people came to Moses and said, 'We have sinned, for we have spoken against the Lord and against you. Pray to the Lord, that He take away the serpents from us.' So Moses prayed for the people."

A. The Bronze Serpent: God's Unusual Means of Healing

God's response to the Israelites' plea for deliverance was not to remove the serpents but to provide a **means of healing**. In **Numbers 21:8-9**, the Lord instructs Moses, "Make a fiery serpent and set it on a pole, and everyone who is bitten, when he sees it, shall live. So Moses made a bronze serpent and set it on a pole. And if a serpent bit anyone, he would look at the bronze serpent and live."

This solution seems strange at first glance—why would looking at a **bronze serpent** bring healing from a deadly snake bite? Yet, this was the method God chose to teach the Israelites about faith and obedience. The people were not healed through medical intervention or by removing the snakes; they were healed by **looking at the bronze serpent**, trusting in God's promise that they would be saved.

1. The Serpent as a Symbol of Judgment

The serpent itself is significant. Throughout the Bible, the serpent is often a symbol of **sin** and **judgment**. In the Garden of Eden, it was the serpent that tempted Eve and led humanity into sin (Genesis 3). By instructing Moses to create a serpent, God was using a symbol of the very thing that was afflicting the Israelites. The **bronze**

serpent lifted on a pole was a visual representation of the **judgment** they were under because of their rebellion.

Bronze, in biblical symbolism, is often associated with **judgment** and **atonement**. For instance, the **bronze altar** in the tabernacle was where sacrifices were made for the sins of the people (Exodus 27:1-2). Therefore, the bronze serpent on the pole was a visible reminder of the **judgment** the Israelites deserved, yet it also pointed to God's provision of a way of escape.

2. Healing Through Faith and Obedience

The healing came not from the bronze serpent itself but from the **act of looking** at it in faith. God provided the means of healing, but the Israelites had to trust Him and obey His command to look at the serpent in order to be healed. This required an acknowledgment of their sin, a turning away from their rebellion, and an act of faith in God's provision.

This act of **faith** foreshadows the way salvation works in the New Testament. Just as the Israelites were called to look at the serpent and live, so too are believers called to **look to Christ** in faith to receive salvation and eternal life. The simplicity of the solution—just looking at the serpent—emphasizes that salvation is a gift of grace and not something earned through human effort.

B. The Typology of the Bronze Serpent: Pointing to Christ's Crucifixion

In **John 3:14-15**, Jesus makes a direct connection between the bronze serpent and His own crucifixion. He says, "And as Moses lifted up the serpent in the wilderness, so must the Son of Man be lifted up, that whoever believes in Him may have eternal life." This typological connection reveals that the bronze serpent was a **foreshadowing** of Christ's work on the cross.

1. The Serpent Lifted Up: Christ Lifted Up on the Cross

The act of **lifting up** the bronze serpent on a pole is a clear type of Christ being **lifted up** on the cross. In both cases, the lifting up is a public display, and in both cases, the lifting up provides a means of salvation for those who look in faith. The Israelites were physically healed by looking at the bronze serpent, while believers are spiritually healed—saved from sin and death—by looking to Christ's sacrifice on the cross.

Isaiah 45:22 says, "Turn to me and be saved, all the ends of the earth! For I am God, and there is no other." This call to "turn" or "look" reflects the simplicity and yet profound significance of faith. Just as the Israelites had to look to the serpent to be saved, so too must people today look to Christ, lifted up on the cross, to receive eternal life.

2. The Serpent as a Representation of Sin and Judgment

The bronze serpent represented the **sin** and **judgment** of the Israelites. In the same way, Jesus, who knew no sin, became **sin for us** when He was lifted up on the cross. **2 Corinthians 5:21** says, "For our sake, He made Him to be sin who knew no sin, so that in Him we might become the righteousness of God." Just as the serpent represented the consequences of the Israelites' rebellion, Jesus bore the punishment for humanity's sin on the cross.

The bronze serpent, which symbolized the very thing that was killing the Israelites, was the object they had to look at for healing. In a similar way, Jesus, though He was sinless, took on the form of sinful humanity and became the object of God's wrath so that those who look to Him might be healed of the deadly effects of sin.

II. THE DEEPER SPIRITUAL MEANING: FAITH, SALVATION, AND CHRIST'S SACRIFICE

The story of the bronze serpent teaches profound truths about **faith**, **salvation**, and the **nature of Christ's sacrifice**. In both the Old Testament and the New Testament, healing and salvation come not through human effort or merit but through an act of **faith**—looking to God's provision for deliverance. The bronze serpent foreshadows the cross, showing that salvation is a gift of grace received through faith in Christ's atoning work.

A. Faith and Healing: The Simplicity of Looking to Christ

One of the most significant aspects of the bronze serpent story is the **simplicity** of the Israelites' healing. They did not have to perform elaborate rituals or offer sacrifices; they simply had to **look** at the serpent on the pole and believe that God would heal them. This simplicity is mirrored in the gospel message—salvation is not achieved by works or human effort but by **faith** in Christ's finished work on the cross.

1. The Act of Looking: A Picture of Faith

The act of **looking** at the bronze serpent is symbolic of the act of **faith**. The Israelites had to believe that by looking at the serpent, they would be healed. This required them to acknowledge their sin, trust in God's provision, and obey His command. Similarly, salvation in Christ requires an acknowledgment of our **sin**, faith in His sacrifice, and a response of obedience to His call.

Hebrews 12:2 encourages believers to "fix our eyes on Jesus, the author and perfecter of our faith." Just as the Israelites had to fix their eyes on the bronze serpent, believers are called to fix their eyes on Christ, trusting that He is the source of their salvation and healing.

2. The Necessity of Faith for Salvation

The story of the bronze serpent underscores the necessity of **faith** for salvation. The Israelites who looked at the serpent were healed, but those who refused to look remained under judgment. In the same way, salvation through Christ is available to all, but it must be received by **faith**. **John 3:16** follows Jesus' reference to the bronze serpent, emphasizing that "whoever believes in Him shall not perish but have eternal life."

Faith is the means by which we appropriate the gift of salvation. It is not enough to acknowledge Christ's sacrifice intellectually; we must **personally trust** in His work on the cross for our salvation. **Romans 10:9** says, "If you declare with your mouth, 'Jesus is Lord,' and believe in your heart that God raised Him from the dead, you will be saved."

Fun Fact: The Symbol of the Serpent in Medicine

Did you know that the symbol of the **serpent on a pole** is often associated with the medical field today? The **Rod of Asclepius**, a staff with a single snake wrapped around it, is commonly used as a symbol for healing and medicine. While its origins are rooted in Greek mythology, some scholars believe the symbol may have been influenced by the biblical story of the bronze serpent in Numbers 21. Both symbols represent healing, and the connection between serpents and healing is a theme that spans cultures and history. However, in the biblical narrative, the healing power comes not from the serpent itself but from God's grace and the act of faith in His provision.

III. CHRIST AS THE FULFILLMENT OF THE BRONZE SERPENT: THE CROSS AS THE ULTIMATE MEANS OF SALVATION

The typology of the bronze serpent finds its ultimate fulfillment in **Christ's crucifixion**. Just as the serpent was lifted up on a pole to bring healing to the Israelites, Christ was lifted up on the cross to bring salvation to all who believe. The parallel between the two events is a powerful reminder that God's plan of salvation was foreshadowed long before Jesus' death, and the cross is the culmination of that plan.

A. The Necessity of Christ's Crucifixion

The **lifting up** of the bronze serpent in the wilderness was a temporary solution to a specific problem, but the lifting up of Christ on the cross was a **permanent solution** to the problem of sin. In **John 12:32**, Jesus says, "And I, when I am lifted up from the earth, will draw all people to myself." The crucifixion was not an afterthought or a tragic accident; it was the **necessary means** by which salvation would be made available to the world.

1. Christ as the Substitute for Sin

The bronze serpent, which symbolized the **judgment** the Israelites deserved, pointed forward to Christ, who became our **substitute** on the cross. Just as the serpent was lifted up to represent the sin and judgment of the people, Christ was lifted up on the cross to bear the punishment for our sins. **Isaiah 53:5** prophesies this substitutionary act: "But He was pierced for our transgressions; He was crushed for our iniquities; the punishment that brought us peace was on Him, and by His wounds we are healed."

Through His death, Christ bore the **wrath of God** on behalf of humanity, taking the place of sinners and offering His life as a ransom. Just as the bronze serpent provided a way of escape from physical death, Christ's crucifixion provides a way of escape from **spiritual death** and eternal separation from God.

2. The Cross as the Pinnacle of God's Redemptive Plan

The lifting up of Christ on the cross was the **pinnacle** of God's redemptive plan, foreseen in the bronze serpent and prophesied throughout the Old Testament. The cross is the **means by which God reconciled the world to Himself**, offering forgiveness and eternal life to all who look to Christ in faith. **Colossians 2:14** describes how Christ's crucifixion dealt with the problem of sin: "He canceled the record of the charges against us and took it away by nailing it to the cross."

Just as the bronze serpent was lifted up to provide healing, Christ's crucifixion is the ultimate expression of God's love and grace, offering healing for the soul and eternal life for all who believe.

B. The Universal Call to Look to Christ

The story of the bronze serpent demonstrates that God's provision of healing was available to all Israelites who chose to look at the serpent in faith. In the same way, **salvation through Christ** is available to all who look to Him in faith, regardless of background, nationality, or past sins. Jesus' statement in **John 3:14-15** makes it clear that "whoever believes in Him may have eternal life."

1. Salvation Available to All

The **universality** of Christ's invitation is a central theme in the gospel. **John 3:16** declares, "For God so loved the world, that He gave His only Son, that whoever believes in Him should not perish but have eternal life." Just as anyone who looked at the bronze serpent could be healed, anyone who looks to Christ and places their trust in Him can be saved.

This is the heart of the gospel message: salvation is not limited to a select few; it is available to all who will turn to Christ in faith. The bronze serpent foreshadowed this inclusivity by offering healing to any Israelite who would look at the serpent, regardless of their status, past actions, or level of understanding. In the same way, Jesus offers eternal life to anyone who will believe in Him.

2. The Simplicity of Salvation Through Faith

The act of **looking** at the bronze serpent required no great effort, skill, or qualification. It was a simple act of faith, trusting that God's provision was sufficient for their healing. This simplicity mirrors the gospel message: salvation is not something we can earn or achieve through our own efforts. It is a **gift of grace**, received through **faith** in Christ's atoning work on the cross.

Ephesians 2:8-9 emphasizes this truth: "For by grace you have been saved through faith. And this is not your own doing; it is the gift of God, not a result of works, so that no one may boast." Just as the Israelites were healed by looking at the serpent, we are saved by **looking to Christ**—acknowledging our sin, trusting in His sacrifice, and receiving the gift of eternal life.

IV. THE CROSS AS THE CURE FOR SIN: HEALING FOR THE NATIONS

The bronze serpent brought physical healing to the Israelites, but Christ's crucifixion brings **spiritual healing** for the nations. Just as the venomous snakes represented the **consequences of sin**, so too does sin act like a poison, infecting every aspect of human life and leading to death. The cross is the **cure** for this poison, offering a way of escape from the deadly consequences of sin.

A. Sin as a Deadly Poison

In the story of the bronze serpent, the venomous snakes were a **consequence of the Israelites' rebellion** against God. The snakes bit the people, and the venom led to death unless they looked at the bronze serpent for healing. This imagery of a **deadly poison** is a powerful metaphor for **sin**, which similarly leads to spiritual death.

Romans 6:23 states, "For the wages of sin is death, but the free gift of God is eternal life in Christ Jesus our Lord." Sin, like the venom of the snakes, spreads throughout humanity, infecting every person and leading to separation from God. Without intervention, the result is spiritual death and eternal separation from God.

1. The Global Nature of Sin's Poison

The effects of sin are not limited to a single group of people; sin's **poison** has spread throughout the entire world. From the fall of Adam and Eve in the Garden of Eden, sin has infected all of humanity, leading to broken relationships, suffering, and death. **Romans 5:12** explains, "Therefore, just as sin came into the world through one man, and death through sin, and so death spread to all men because all sinned."

The bronze serpent, lifted up in the wilderness, provided healing for the Israelites who were bitten by the snakes. Similarly, Christ's crucifixion provides healing for all who have been "bitten" by sin. His sacrifice on the cross offers a way of escape from the deadly consequences of sin for all who look to Him in faith.

2. The Cross as the Cure for Sin

The **cross** is the ultimate **cure** for sin's poison. Just as the Israelites were healed by looking at the bronze serpent, we are healed—spiritually, emotionally, and physically—by looking to Christ's sacrifice on the cross. The cross is where sin's power is broken, where the poison is neutralized, and where new life is offered to all who believe.

Isaiah 53:4-5 prophesies about the healing power of Christ's sacrifice: "Surely He has borne our griefs and carried our sorrows; yet we esteemed Him stricken, smitten by God, and afflicted. But He was pierced for our transgressions; He was crushed for our iniquities; upon Him was the chastisement that brought us peace, and with His wounds we are healed."

Through Christ's wounds—His suffering and death on the cross—healing is made available to the nations. Just as the bronze serpent brought physical healing to the Israelites, Christ's crucifixion brings spiritual healing to all who trust in Him.

B. The Global Call to Look to Christ for Healing

The story of the bronze serpent is a picture of **God's mercy** and **grace**, not only for the Israelites but for the entire world. Just as the serpent was lifted up for all to see, Christ was lifted up on the cross for the sake of the nations. His death provides healing and salvation for all who look to Him in faith.

1. Christ's Sacrifice for the Nations

The scope of Christ's sacrifice is **universal**. **John 12:32** emphasizes this global call: "And I, when I am lifted up from the earth, will draw all people to myself." Jesus' crucifixion was not just for the benefit of a select group of people; it was for the salvation of the world. **Revelation 5:9** proclaims the global impact of Christ's sacrifice: "Worthy are You to take the scroll and to open its seals, for You were slain, and by Your blood You ransomed people for God from every tribe and language and people and nation."

The bronze serpent provided healing for the Israelites, but Christ's crucifixion provides healing for the nations. Through His death, people from every corner of the earth are invited to come to the cross and receive the gift of salvation.

2. The Church's Mission to Proclaim Christ's Healing

As recipients of this **healing**, the Church is called to proclaim the message of Christ's salvation to the nations. Just as the bronze serpent was lifted up for all to see, so too must the message of the cross be lifted up in every corner of the world. **Matthew 28:19** gives the Great Commission: "Go therefore and make disciples of all nations, baptizing them in the name of the Father and of the Son and of the Holy Spirit."

The healing power of Christ's crucifixion is available to all, but it must be proclaimed and shared. As the Church, we are called to lift up Christ in our words and actions, pointing others to the **healing** and **salvation** found in Him alone.

The Bronze Serpent as a Picture of Christ's Crucifixion

From the Tabernacle to Solomon's Temple to the Second Temple, the progression of God's dwelling among His people points toward a final and eternal fulfillment in Christ. The tearing of the temple veil at

Jesus' crucifixion signifies the end of separation between God and humanity, and the beginning of the Church as the living temple, indwelt by the Spirit.

Solomon's Temple was the physical dwelling place of God among His people, where the Ark of the Covenant resided. As magnificent as it was, it served as a shadow of a greater reality. The destruction of this temple symbolized the passing of the old covenant system, pointing forward to the time when God's presence would dwell fully in Christ, the true Temple. The physical structure of the temple was temporary, but it laid the foundation for the spiritual temple found in Christ.

The Second Temple, rebuilt after the exile, held great significance for the Jewish people. It was the site of Jesus' ministry, and although it lacked the glory of Solomon's Temple, it still foreshadowed a greater fulfillment in Christ. The destruction of the Second Temple, as prophesied by Jesus, marks the end of the old sacrificial system and the transition to a new covenant where God's presence is no longer confined to a building but resides in Christ and His Church. Jesus, the ultimate Temple, fulfills what the Second Temple could only symbolize.

The story of the **bronze serpent** in the wilderness is one of the most powerful **types** of Christ's crucifixion in the Old Testament. Just as the serpent was lifted up on a pole to provide physical healing for the Israelites, Christ was lifted up on the cross to provide **spiritual healing** and **eternal life** for all who believe in Him. The bronze serpent pointed forward to the ultimate act of salvation—Christ's death on the cross, where He bore the punishment for our sins and made a way for us to be reconciled to God.

The simplicity of the Israelites' healing—just looking at the serpent—reflects the simplicity of the gospel. Salvation is not earned through human effort but is received through **faith** in Christ's finished work on the cross. As we look to Him, we find healing, forgiveness, and eternal life.

The call to "look and live" is as relevant today as it was in the wilderness. Just as the Israelites were healed by looking at the bronze serpent, so too are we saved by looking to **Christ**, the one who was lifted up on the cross for our sins. In Him, we find the **cure** for sin's poison, the **healing** for our souls, and the **hope** of eternal life.

CHAPTER 7: THE ARK OF NOAH: A TYPE OF SALVATION IN CHRIST

The story of **Noah's Ark** is one of the most well-known and beloved narratives in the Bible, found in **Genesis 6-9**. This account of God's judgment on a corrupt world through a devastating flood, and the deliverance of Noah and his family through the ark, contains deep symbolic meaning beyond the literal events. In Christian theology, Noah's ark serves as a **type** of **Christ**, pointing forward to the salvation that Jesus provides from the ultimate judgment of sin. Just as Noah and his family were saved from the floodwaters by entering the ark, believers are saved from the consequences of sin by being "in Christ," who shelters them from God's righteous judgment.

In this chapter, we will explore the typological significance of **Noah's Ark**, examining how it prefigures the salvation offered in Christ. We will also explore the parallels between the flood and baptism, as highlighted in **1 Peter 3:20-21**, and how the story of Noah and the flood teaches us about faith, judgment, and God's mercy. Through the lens of typology, we see how the ark is not only a vessel of physical salvation but also a powerful symbol of **spiritual deliverance** in Christ.

I. THE STORY OF NOAH'S ARK (GENESIS 6-9)

The story of **Noah's Ark** takes place during a time when humanity had fallen into deep sin and corruption. In the opening chapters of **Genesis**, we learn that the world had become so filled with wickedness that God, in His holiness, could no longer tolerate the evil that permeated His creation. **Genesis 6:5** tells us, "The Lord saw that the wickedness of man was great in the earth, and that every intention of the thoughts of his heart was only evil continually."

In response to this rampant sinfulness, God declared His intention to bring judgment upon the earth through a **great flood** that would wipe out all living creatures. However, in the midst of this announcement of judgment, we also see a display of God's grace and mercy. **Genesis 6:8** says, "But Noah found favor in the eyes of the Lord." God chose to spare Noah, a righteous man, and his family by instructing him to build an ark that would preserve them from the coming destruction.

A. The Ark: God's Provision for Salvation

The **ark** that Noah built, under God's direction, was a massive vessel designed to save Noah, his family, and representatives of the animal kingdom from the floodwaters. **Genesis 6:14-16** describes the specifications for the ark, including its size, materials, and construction. The ark was to be made of **gopher wood** and coated with **pitch** inside and out to make it watertight. It was to have three decks and a single door on its side, and it was large enough to accommodate all the people and animals God intended to save.

The ark represents God's **provision** of salvation. While the rest of humanity would be swept away by the floodwaters, Noah and his family were spared because they took refuge in the ark. The ark itself became a place of **refuge** and **protection** from the judgment that God was about to pour out on the world. In this way, the ark serves as a type or foreshadowing of Christ, who is the ultimate provision for salvation.

1. The Significance of the Ark's Construction

The detailed instructions for the ark's construction in **Genesis 6:14-16** carry symbolic meaning. The fact that the ark was made of **wood** and covered with **pitch** points to the necessity of atonement and protection from God's judgment. The **pitch**, in particular, is significant because the Hebrew word for pitch (**kopher**) is related to the word for **atonement**. Just as the pitch made the ark watertight and kept the floodwaters of judgment out, the atoning work of Christ covers and protects believers from the judgment they deserve.

Moreover, the ark had only **one door**, which Noah and his family had to enter to be saved. This singular door points to Christ, who in **John 10:9** declares, "I am the door. If anyone enters by me, he will be saved." Just as there was only one way into the ark, there is only one way to salvation—through Jesus Christ. **Acts 4:12** affirms this truth: "And there is salvation in no one else, for there is no other name under heaven given among men by which we must be saved."

2. Noah's Obedience and Faith

Noah's obedience in building the ark is a model of **faith** and **trust** in God's word. **Hebrews 11:7** highlights Noah's faith: "By faith Noah, being warned by God concerning events as yet unseen, in reverent fear constructed an ark for the saving of his household. By this he condemned the world and became an heir of the righteousness that comes by faith."

Noah had no tangible evidence that a flood was coming—he had only God's word. Yet, he trusted God and obeyed His command to build the ark. This act of faith not only saved Noah and his family but also condemned the unbelieving world. Similarly, believers are called to trust in God's promise of salvation through Christ, even though we may not yet see the full extent of that salvation.

B. The Flood: A Picture of God's Judgment

The **flood** itself represents the **judgment** of God upon a sinful and rebellious world. In **Genesis 6:17**, God declares, "For behold, I will bring a flood of waters upon the earth to destroy all flesh in which is the breath of life under heaven. Everything that is on the earth shall die." The floodwaters were God's means of cleansing the earth of its wickedness, wiping out all life except for those who were safely inside the ark.

1. The Severity of God's Judgment

The flood serves as a sobering reminder of the **severity** of God's judgment against sin. God is holy and cannot tolerate evil, and the flood was a demonstration of His righteous anger against a world that had become utterly corrupt. Yet, even in the midst of this judgment, God's mercy is evident in the way He provided a means of escape for Noah and his family.

The flood also points forward to the **final judgment** that is to come. In **2 Peter 3:6-7**, the apostle Peter draws a connection between the flood and the future judgment of the world: "By these waters also the world of that time was deluged and destroyed. By the same word, the present heavens and earth are reserved for fire, being kept for the day of judgment and destruction of the ungodly." Just as the flood brought judgment on the ancient world, so too will there be a future day when God will judge the world in righteousness.

2. The Cleansing Nature of Water

In addition to symbolizing judgment, the floodwaters also represent **cleansing** and **renewal**. The flood was not merely an act of destruction; it was a means of purifying the earth from the wickedness that had taken root. In the same way, the waters of **baptism**, which Peter connects to the flood in **1 Peter 3:20-21**, symbolize the washing away of sin and the beginning of new life in Christ.

Water is often used in Scripture as a symbol of both judgment and renewal. Just as the floodwaters washed away the old, sinful world and made way for a new beginning, the waters of baptism represent the washing away of sin and the believer's entrance into a new life in Christ. **Titus 3:5** speaks of the "washing of regeneration and renewal of the Holy Spirit," which occurs in the life of a believer.

II. THE ARK AS A TYPE OF CHRIST

The **ark** that saved Noah and his family from the flood is a clear **type of Christ**. In typology, a type is a person, event, or object in the Old Testament that prefigures a greater fulfillment in the New Testament. In the case of Noah's ark, it serves as a symbol of the **salvation** that Christ provides for believers, sheltering them from the judgment of sin and delivering them into new life.

A. The Ark as a Place of Refuge

One of the primary parallels between the ark and Christ is that both provide a **place of refuge** from God's judgment. Just as the ark shielded Noah and his family from the floodwaters, Christ shields believers from the wrath of God that is poured out on sin. **Romans 5:9** declares, "Since, therefore, we have now been justified by His blood, much more shall we be saved by Him from the wrath of God."

In both cases, those who take refuge in the ark or in Christ are spared from destruction. The ark was the only means of salvation for Noah and his family, just as Christ is the only means of salvation for humanity. **John 14:6** emphasizes this exclusivity: "Jesus said to him, 'I am the way, and the truth, and the life. No one comes to the Father except through me.'"

1. The Door of the Ark: Christ as the Only Way

The fact that the ark had only **one door** is a significant typological detail. There was only one way into the ark, and once Noah and his family entered, God Himself shut the door (**Genesis 7:16**), sealing them safely inside. This points to the **exclusive nature of salvation** in Christ. Just as there was only one way into the ark, there is only one way to be saved from the judgment of sin—through Jesus Christ.

Jesus refers to Himself as the **door** in **John 10:9**, saying, "I am the door. If anyone enters by me, he will be saved and will go in and out and find pasture." In the same way that Noah and his family had to enter the ark to be saved, we must enter into a relationship with Christ to receive salvation.

2. The Ark as a Place of Safety

Once inside the ark, Noah and his family were safe from the storm that raged outside. The ark was their **shelter** in the midst of the flood, protecting them from the waters of judgment. This is a powerful picture of the **security** believers have in Christ. Just as the ark provided a place of safety for Noah, Christ provides a place of spiritual safety for those who trust in Him.

Romans 8:1 assures believers of this safety: "There is therefore now no condemnation for those who are in Christ Jesus."

When we are "in Christ," we are safe from the condemnation that sin brings, just as Noah was safe from the floodwaters inside the ark. The **security of salvation** in Christ is one of the central themes of the gospel.

B. Salvation in Christ: The Ultimate Ark

While Noah's ark provided physical salvation for Noah and his family, **Christ** provides **spiritual salvation** for all who believe in Him. The ark was a temporary solution to a specific act of judgment, but Christ's salvation is **eternal** and extends to all who place their faith in Him.

1. The Universality of Salvation in Christ

The story of Noah's ark highlights the fact that only those who were inside the ark were saved from the flood. In a similar way, **only those who are in Christ** will be saved from the judgment of sin. **Acts 4:12** makes this clear: "And there is salvation in no one else, for there is no other name under heaven given among men by which we must be saved."

Christ's offer of salvation is **universal** in its invitation but **exclusive** in its means. Just as there was only one ark, there is only one way to be saved—through faith in Jesus Christ. **John 3:16** declares, "For God so loved the world, that He gave His only Son, that whoever believes in Him should not perish but have eternal life."

2. The Symbolism of Water and Baptism

In **1 Peter 3:20-21**, the apostle Peter draws a direct connection between the **flood** and **baptism**, explaining how both are symbols of salvation. He writes, "God's patience waited in the days of Noah, while the ark was being prepared, in which a few, that is, eight persons, were brought safely through water. Baptism, which corresponds to this, now saves you, not as a removal of dirt from the body but as an appeal to God for a good conscience, through the resurrection of Jesus Christ."

Just as Noah and his family were saved through the waters of the flood by being in the ark, believers are saved through the waters of **baptism** by being "in Christ." Baptism is a **symbol** of the believer's identification with Christ in His death, burial, and resurrection. The waters of baptism represent the **washing away of sin** and the entrance into new life, just as the floodwaters symbolized the cleansing of the earth and the beginning of a new creation.

It is important to note that Peter emphasizes that baptism itself does not save; rather, it is an outward sign of an **inward reality**—a demonstration of the believer's faith in Christ and their appeal to God for a clean conscience. Just as the ark provided salvation from the physical waters of the flood, Christ provides salvation from the spiritual consequences of sin.

Fun Fact: The Ark's Dimensions and Modern Ships

Did you know that the **dimensions of Noah's Ark**, as described in **Genesis 6:15**, have been studied by naval architects for their remarkable stability and seaworthiness? The ark was about 450 feet long, 75 feet wide, and 45 feet high, giving it a **6-to-1 length-to-width ratio**, which is nearly ideal for a vessel designed to withstand rough seas. Modern cargo ships and ocean liners often use similar dimensions to maximize stability in stormy waters.

This fact underscores the **practical wisdom** embedded in the Bible's account of the ark, showing that God's instructions to Noah were not only spiritually significant but also practically sound. The ark was designed to protect its occupants from the chaos of the floodwaters, just as Christ is the perfect "ark" who protects believers from the storms of life and the judgment to come.

III. LESSONS FROM THE FLOOD: JUDGMENT, MERCY, AND NEW BEGINNINGS

The story of Noah's ark is not only about **judgment** but also about **mercy** and **new beginnings**. While the flood was a severe act of judgment on a sinful world, it was also an opportunity for a fresh start—a new beginning for humanity and creation. In the same way, the salvation offered in Christ is both a rescue from judgment and the beginning of a new life in Him.

A. The Flood as a Foreshadowing of Final Judgment

The flood was an act of **divine judgment** against the wickedness of the world, but it also serves as a foreshadowing of the **final judgment** that is to come. In **Matthew 24:37-39**, Jesus compares the days of Noah to the time of His second coming: "For as were the days of Noah, so will be the coming of the Son of Man. For as in those days before the flood they were eating and drinking, marrying and giving in marriage, until the day when Noah entered the ark, and they were unaware until the flood came and swept them all away, so will be the coming of the Son of Man."

Just as the flood came suddenly and unexpectedly, so too will the final judgment come at a time when the world is unprepared. The floodwaters of Noah's day were a **warning** of the greater judgment to come, and the ark is a symbol of the **safety** found in Christ for those who place their trust in Him.

1. The Call to Repentance

The story of Noah's ark is a call to **repentance**. Just as the people in Noah's day were given a chance to repent and turn to God, so too is the world today given the opportunity to turn to Christ before the final judgment. **2 Peter 3:9** reminds us that God is patient, "not wishing that any should perish, but that all should reach repentance."

Noah was described as a **preacher of righteousness (2 Peter 2:5)**, warning the people of his generation about the coming judgment. In the same way, believers today are called to share the message of salvation through Christ and to warn others of the judgment that is to come. The story of the flood is a reminder that God's judgment is real, but so too is His offer of mercy and salvation.

2. The Promise of Deliverance for the Righteous

While the flood was a judgment on the wicked, it was also a **deliverance** for Noah and his family, who were described as **righteous** in God's sight. The ark was their means of escape, and through it, they were brought safely through the waters to a new life. In the same way, believers are promised **deliverance** from the final judgment through faith in Christ.

1 Thessalonians 5:9 assures us of this deliverance: "For God has not destined us for wrath, but to obtain salvation through our Lord Jesus Christ." Just as Noah and his family were not destined for the floodwaters of judgment, so too are believers not destined for the wrath of God. Through Christ, we are **saved** and delivered into the safety of eternal life.

B. New Beginnings: The Covenant with Noah and Creation

After the floodwaters receded, God established a **covenant** with Noah and his descendants, as well as with all living creatures. This covenant marked the beginning of a **new creation**—a fresh start for humanity and the world. **Genesis 9:12-13** records the words of God to Noah: "This is the sign of the covenant that I make between me and you and every living creature that is with you, for all future generations: I have set my bow in the cloud, and it shall be a sign of the covenant between me and the earth."

1. The Rainbow as a Sign of God's Mercy

The **rainbow** became the **sign of God's covenant**, symbolizing His promise never again to destroy the earth with a flood. This sign was a reminder of God's **mercy** and **faithfulness** to His creation. Even though humanity would continue to sin, God promised to show restraint in His judgment, offering opportunities for repentance and reconciliation.

The rainbow also points forward to the **new covenant** that God would establish through Christ. Just as the rainbow signified God's promise to preserve life on earth, the new covenant in Christ promises **eternal life** for those who believe in Him. **Hebrews 9:15** speaks of Christ as the mediator of the new covenant, through whom we receive "the promised eternal inheritance."

2. The New Creation in Christ

The story of Noah's ark ends with a **new beginning** for humanity. After the flood, Noah and his family stepped out of the ark into a cleansed world, where they were called to **be fruitful and multiply** and to fill the earth once again. This new beginning is a picture of the **new creation** that believers experience in Christ.

2 Corinthians 5:17 declares, "Therefore, if anyone is in Christ, he is a new creation. The old has passed away; behold, the new has come." Just as the flood washed away the old, sinful world, so too does the work of Christ wash away the old life of sin and bring about a new creation in the believer. Through Christ, we are given a fresh start, free from the power of sin and death.

The Ark of Noah as a Type of Salvation in Christ

From the Tabernacle to Solomon's Temple to the Second Temple, the progression of God's dwelling among His people points toward a final and eternal fulfillment in Christ. The tearing of the temple veil at Jesus' crucifixion signifies the end of separation between God and humanity, and the beginning of the Church as the living temple, indwelt by the Spirit.

Solomon's Temple was the physical dwelling place of God among His people, where the Ark of the Covenant resided. As magnificent as it was, it served as a shadow of a greater reality. The destruction of this temple symbolized the passing of the old covenant system, pointing forward to the time when God's presence would dwell fully in Christ, the true Temple. The physical structure of the temple was temporary, but it laid the foundation for the spiritual temple found in Christ.

The Second Temple, rebuilt after the exile, held great significance for the Jewish people. It was the site of Jesus' ministry, and although it lacked the glory of Solomon's Temple, it still foreshadowed a greater fulfillment in Christ. The destruction of the Second Temple, as prophesied by Jesus, marks the end of the old sacrificial system and the transition to a new covenant where God's presence is no longer confined to a building but resides in Christ and His Church. Jesus, the ultimate Temple, fulfills what the Second Temple could only symbolize.

The story of **Noah's Ark** is much more than an account of a great flood and a man's survival. It is a profound **foreshadowing** of the salvation that is offered in **Jesus Christ**. The ark that saved Noah and his family from the floodwaters is a picture of the **spiritual salvation** that Christ provides for all who believe in Him. Just as the ark sheltered Noah from the judgment of the flood, Christ shelters believers from the judgment of sin, offering them refuge and eternal life.

The flood serves as a warning of the coming **final judgment**, but it also highlights God's mercy in providing a way of escape. The story of Noah's ark calls us to **repentance**, to faith in God's provision, and to trust in Christ as the ultimate **ark of salvation**. As we look to the story of the ark, we are reminded of the security we have in Christ, the safety we find in His saving work, and the new beginning He offers to all who place their faith in Him.

Through the lens of typology, the ark becomes a powerful symbol of God's plan of redemption, pointing us to the cross of Christ and the salvation that is found in Him alone. Just as Noah and his family were saved by entering the ark, we are saved by entering into a relationship with Christ, who is our refuge, our shelter, and our salvation.

CHAPTER 8: THE LEVITICAL PRIESTHOOD AND SACRIFICES: A TYPE OF CHRIST'S HIGH PRIESTHOOD

In the Old Testament, the **Levitical priesthood** and the sacrificial system were central to Israel's relationship with God. The priests, particularly the high priest, served as mediators between God and the people, offering sacrifices to atone for their sins. This system was instituted by God as a way to maintain holiness among the people and to provide a temporary solution to the problem of sin. However, the Levitical priesthood and the sacrifices they offered were never meant to be permanent. They were **types**—foreshadowings of a greater reality to come. The priesthood and the sacrifices pointed forward to **Jesus Christ**, who would fulfill the role of the **true High Priest** and offer the **ultimate sacrifice** for sin.

In this chapter, we will explore how the **Levitical priesthood** and the **sacrifices** outlined in the book of **Leviticus** serve as types that prefigure Christ's work as our High Priest. We will delve into the role of the Levitical priests, the significance of the **Day of Atonement**, and how Jesus' sacrifice on the cross fulfills and surpasses the sacrificial system of the Old Covenant. Through this exploration, we will gain a deeper understanding of how Christ's priesthood brings about a better covenant, one based not on repeated animal sacrifices but on His once-for-all sacrifice.

I. THE LEVITICAL PRIESTHOOD (LEVITICUS 8-10)

The **Levitical priesthood** was established by God through Moses as part of the covenant He made with Israel at Mount Sinai. The priests, all descendants of **Levi**, were set apart to serve in the tabernacle (and later the temple), where they performed the daily rituals, sacrifices, and ceremonies that were essential for maintaining Israel's relationship with God. The priests acted as **mediators** between God and the people, ensuring that the covenant relationship was upheld and that the people's sins were atoned for through the prescribed sacrifices.

A. The Role of the Priests as Mediators

The primary function of the Levitical priests was to **mediate** between God and Israel. Sin had created a barrier between humanity and God, and the priests were tasked with bridging that gap through the offering of sacrifices. These sacrifices were necessary because God is holy, and sin cannot dwell in His presence. The priests, therefore, played a vital role in ensuring that the people could approach God in a state of **ritual purity**.

1. The Consecration of the Priests

In **Leviticus 8**, we read about the **consecration** of the priests, specifically **Aaron** and his sons, who were the first to serve in this role. Moses was instructed by God to consecrate Aaron and his sons by washing them, clothing them in the priestly garments, anointing them with oil, and offering sacrifices on their behalf. This consecration ceremony symbolized the **purification** and **dedication** of the priests to their holy duties.

The priestly garments, including the **ephod**, **breastplate**, and **turban**, were designed to reflect the holiness of the office and to signify that the priests were set apart for God's service. The high priest, in particular, wore garments that were intricately detailed, symbolizing his unique role in representing the people before God.

The **consecration** of the priests foreshadows the **consecration of Christ** as our High Priest. While the Levitical priests needed to be purified before they could serve, Christ was already perfect and sinless. **Hebrews 7:26** describes Christ as "holy, innocent, unstained, separated from sinners, and exalted above the heavens."

Christ's priesthood is superior because He did not need to be consecrated through sacrifices; instead, He offered Himself as the perfect, sinless sacrifice.

2. The Priests' Daily Duties

The daily duties of the Levitical priests included offering **burnt offerings**, **grain offerings**, **sin offerings**, and **peace offerings** on behalf of the people. These sacrifices were performed according to specific instructions given by God, and they served to atone for both the intentional and unintentional sins of the people. In addition to offering sacrifices, the priests also maintained the **lampstand**, the **table of showbread**, and the **altar of incense** in the tabernacle.

The priest's role as a **mediator** between God and the people is a direct type of Christ's role as the ultimate mediator. **1 Timothy 2:5** declares, "For there is one God, and there is one mediator between God and men, the man Christ Jesus." While the Levitical priests offered sacrifices daily, Christ's **once-for-all sacrifice** on the cross mediates the new covenant between God and humanity. The priests were limited by their humanity and their sinfulness, but Christ, as the sinless Son of God, is the perfect and eternal mediator.

B. The Limitations of the Levitical Priesthood

Despite the important role that the Levitical priests played, their priesthood had significant **limitations**. The sacrifices they offered were **temporary** and had to be repeated daily and yearly. Moreover, the priests themselves were sinners and had to offer sacrifices for their own sins before they could offer sacrifices for the people. These limitations point to the **need for a better priesthood**—one that could offer a permanent solution to the problem of sin.

1. The Temporary Nature of the Sacrifices

The sacrifices offered by the Levitical priests were **inadequate** to provide a permanent solution to sin. **Hebrews 10:1** explains, "For since the law has but a shadow of the good things to come instead of the true form of these realities, it can never, by the same sacrifices that are continually offered every year, make perfect those who draw near." The repeated nature of the sacrifices indicated that they were not sufficient to **fully cleanse** the people from sin. Each time a person sinned, another sacrifice was required.

These sacrifices were a **shadow** of the ultimate sacrifice to come. They pointed forward to Christ, who would offer Himself as the **final sacrifice** for sin. Once Christ's sacrifice was made, there would no longer be a need for repeated sacrifices because His offering was **perfect** and **complete**. **Hebrews 9:12** states, "He entered once for all into the holy places, not by means of the blood of goats and calves but by means of His own blood, thus securing an eternal redemption."

2. The Sinfulness of the Priests

Another limitation of the Levitical priesthood was the **sinfulness** of the priests themselves. Because the priests were human, they were subject to the same weaknesses and temptations as the people they served. Before offering sacrifices for the people, the priests had to offer sacrifices for their own sins. This is highlighted in **Leviticus 9**, where Aaron is commanded to offer a **sin offering** and a **burnt offering** for himself before offering sacrifices for the people.

This stands in stark contrast to Christ, who is the **sinless** High Priest. Unlike the Levitical priests, Christ did not need to offer a sacrifice for Himself. He was "tempted in every way, just as we are—yet He did not sin" (**Hebrews 4:15**). Because of His sinlessness, Christ was able to offer Himself as the perfect sacrifice for the sins of others. His priesthood is superior to the Levitical priesthood because He is not hindered by sin.

II. THE SACRIFICIAL SYSTEM: POINTING TO CHRIST'S PERFECT SACRIFICE

The **sacrificial system** in Leviticus was the primary means by which the people of Israel maintained their covenant relationship with God. Through various offerings, the priests atoned for the sins of the people, ensuring that they could continue to live in the presence of a holy God. However, like the priesthood, the sacrificial system was **imperfect** and **temporary**. The sacrifices were a **shadow** of the greater sacrifice to come—the sacrifice of Christ on the cross, which would **fulfill** and **replace** the old system.

A. The Types of Sacrifices in Leviticus

The book of Leviticus outlines several types of sacrifices that the priests were to offer on behalf of the people. Each type of sacrifice served a specific purpose and addressed different aspects of sin, guilt, and the need for **reconciliation** with God. These sacrifices were an essential part of the **Old Covenant**, but they ultimately pointed forward to the **New Covenant**, which would be established through the blood of Christ.

1. The Burnt Offering

The **burnt offering** (Leviticus 1) was one of the most common sacrifices in Israel's worship. In this offering, the entire animal was burned on the altar, symbolizing the complete **dedication** of the person making the offering to God. The burnt offering was made to atone for **general sins** and to seek God's favor.

The burnt offering is a type of Christ's **total dedication** to the will of the Father. Just as the entire animal was consumed by fire, Christ offered His entire life as a sacrifice for sin. **Hebrews 10:5-7** quotes Psalm 40, applying it to Christ: "Sacrifices and offerings you have not desired, but a body have you prepared for me; in burnt offerings and sin offerings you have taken no pleasure. Then I said, 'Behold, I have come to do your will, O God.'" Christ's willingness to lay down His life was the ultimate fulfillment of the burnt offering, as He gave Himself completely to the Father's will for the redemption of humanity.

2. The Grain Offering

The **grain offering** (Leviticus 2) was a gift of grain, flour, or bread presented to God as an expression of **thanksgiving** for His provision. While the grain offering did not involve the shedding of blood, it was often offered alongside other sacrifices that atoned for sin. The grain offering symbolized the worshiper's gratitude for God's sustenance and blessings.

In the New Testament, Christ refers to Himself as the **bread of life (John 6:35)**, indicating that He is the one who sustains and nourishes the spiritual life of believers. The grain offering, in this sense, points to Christ as the one who provides **spiritual sustenance** through His life and sacrifice. Just as the grain offering was a way for the Israelites to express their gratitude for God's provision, Christ's sacrificial death is the means by which believers give thanks for the gift of eternal life.

3. The Peace Offering

The **peace offering** (Leviticus 3) was a sacrifice offered to express **thankfulness** and to celebrate the **peace** and **fellowship** that existed between the worshiper and God. Unlike the burnt offering, in which the entire animal was consumed, the peace offering allowed the worshiper to eat part of the sacrificial animal as a **communal meal** with God.

The peace offering prefigures the **reconciliation** and **peace** that Christ's sacrifice brings between God and humanity. **Ephesians 2:14** declares, "For He Himself is our peace, who has made us both one and has broken down in His flesh the dividing wall of hostility." Through His death on the cross, Christ made peace between God and sinners, reconciling us to God and establishing a new relationship of fellowship and communion. This peace is celebrated in the **Lord's Supper**, where believers partake of the bread and the cup as a **symbol** of their unity with Christ.

4. The Sin Offering

The **sin offering** (Leviticus 4) was a sacrifice made to atone for **unintentional sins** and to cleanse the worshiper from **impurity**. This offering emphasized the seriousness of sin and the need for **forgiveness** in order to maintain a right relationship with God. The blood of the sacrificed animal was sprinkled on the **altar** and on the

veil of the tabernacle, symbolizing the cleansing of sin and the restoration of the sinner to fellowship with God.

The sin offering is perhaps the clearest type of **Christ's sacrifice** on the cross. **Hebrews 9:22** states, "Without the shedding of blood, there is no forgiveness of sins." Just as the sin offering in the Old Testament involved the shedding of blood to atone for sin, Christ's death on the cross involved the **shedding of His blood** to atone for the sins of the world. **1 John 2:2** declares, "He is the atoning sacrifice for our sins, and not only for ours but also for the sins of the whole world." Christ's sacrifice fulfilled the sin offering once and for all, providing a permanent solution to the problem of sin.

5. The Guilt Offering

The **guilt offering** (Leviticus 5) was made to atone for specific sins, particularly those that involved **desecration** of holy things or **damage** to another person's property. In addition to offering an animal sacrifice, the guilty person was required to make **restitution** for the wrong they had committed, often adding an additional **fifth** of the value of the restitution.

The guilt offering points to the fact that sin often involves **consequences** that must be addressed, both in terms of our relationship with God and with others. Christ, through His sacrifice, made **full restitution** for our sins, satisfying the demands of God's justice and restoring our relationship with Him. **Colossians 2:14** describes how Christ "canceled the record of debt that stood against us with its legal demands. This He set aside, nailing it to the cross." Through His death, Christ paid the debt we owed for our sins, making restitution on our behalf and freeing us from the burden of guilt.

B. The Temporary Nature of the Sacrifices

While the sacrifices in Leviticus were necessary for maintaining Israel's relationship with God, they were **incomplete** and **temporary**. The sacrifices had to be repeated regularly, indicating that they were not sufficient to provide a permanent solution to the problem of sin. The sacrificial system was a **shadow** of the greater sacrifice to come—the sacrifice of Christ, which would provide a once-for-all solution to sin.

1. The Repetition of Sacrifices

One of the most significant limitations of the Levitical sacrifices was their **repetitive nature**. The daily, weekly, and yearly sacrifices had to be offered again and again because they could not fully cleanse the people from sin. **Hebrews 10:1-4** explains, "For since the law has but a shadow of the good things to come instead of the true form of these realities, it can never, by the same sacrifices that are continually offered every year, make perfect those who draw near. Otherwise, would they not have ceased to be offered, since the worshipers, having once been cleansed, would no longer have any consciousness of sins? But in these sacrifices there is a reminder of sins every year. For it is impossible for the blood of bulls and goats to take away sins."

The repeated sacrifices served as a constant **reminder of sin**, but they could not remove sin completely. They pointed forward to the day when a perfect sacrifice would be offered—one that would **remove sin** entirely and provide eternal redemption. This perfect sacrifice was fulfilled in Christ, whose death on the cross was sufficient to atone for all sin, once and for all.

2. The Imperfection of Animal Sacrifices

Another limitation of the Levitical sacrifices was the fact that they involved **animals**, not humans. While the blood of bulls and goats could serve as a temporary substitute, it could not fully address the problem of human sin. Only a **perfect human** could atone for the sins of humanity.

Christ, as both fully **God** and fully **man**, was the perfect sacrifice for sin. His sacrifice was sufficient because He was without sin and because He willingly offered Himself as a substitute for sinners. **Hebrews 9:14** explains, "How much more will the blood of Christ, who through the eternal Spirit offered Himself without blemish to God, purify our conscience from dead works to serve the living God." Christ's sacrifice was superior to the animal sacrifices because He was the perfect, sinless Son of God, and His sacrifice had the power to **purify** not only the external actions of the worshiper but also the **conscience**.

III. THE DAY OF ATONEMENT: A SHADOW OF CHRIST'S SACRIFICE

The **Day of Atonement**, described in **Leviticus 16**, was the most important day in Israel's religious calendar. On this day, the high priest would enter the **Holy of Holies** in the tabernacle (and later the temple) to offer sacrifices for the sins of the entire nation. This annual ritual was a solemn reminder of the people's sinfulness and their need for atonement. However, like the other sacrifices, the Day of Atonement was a **shadow** of the greater atonement to come—the atonement that Christ would accomplish through His death on the cross.

A. The Role of the High Priest on the Day of Atonement

On the Day of Atonement, the **high priest** played a central role in mediating between God and the people. He was the only person who could enter the **Holy of Holies**, the innermost part of the tabernacle where the **Ark of the Covenant** was kept. Before entering the Holy of Holies, the high priest had to offer a **bull** as a sin offering for himself and his household, ensuring that he was purified before offering sacrifices for the nation.

1. The Scapegoat

One of the most striking elements of the Day of Atonement was the ritual involving two **goats**. One goat was sacrificed as a sin offering, and its blood was sprinkled on the **mercy seat** in the Holy of Holies, symbolizing the atonement for the sins of the people. The other goat, known as the **scapegoat**, was brought before the high priest, who laid his hands on its head and confessed the sins of the people over it. The scapegoat was then sent out into the wilderness, symbolically carrying the sins of the people away from the camp.

The scapegoat ritual points to the **removal of sin** that Christ accomplished through His death. **Isaiah 53:6** prophesies about Christ's role as the scapegoat: "The Lord has laid on Him the iniquity of us all." Just as the scapegoat carried away the sins of Israel, Christ bore the sins of humanity on the cross and removed them as far as the east is from the west (**Psalm 103:12**).

2. Entering the Holy of Holies

The high priest's entry into the **Holy of Holies** was a dangerous and awe-inspiring event. Only the high priest could enter this sacred space, and only once a year on the Day of Atonement. He entered with the blood of the sin offering, which he sprinkled on the **mercy seat** (the cover of the Ark of the Covenant) to atone for the sins of the people.

This act prefigures Christ's **ascension** into the true Holy of Holies—**heaven itself**—after His resurrection. **Hebrews 9:24** explains, "For Christ has entered, not into holy places made with hands, which are copies of the true things, but into heaven itself, now to appear in the presence of God on our behalf." Just as the high priest entered the Holy of Holies to offer atonement, Christ entered heaven to present His own blood as the atoning sacrifice for sin.

B. Christ as the Fulfillment of the Day of Atonement

While the Day of Atonement provided **temporary** atonement for the sins of Israel, Christ's sacrifice on the cross provided **permanent** atonement for the sins of the world. His death fulfilled and replaced the Day of Atonement, rendering the annual sacrifices of the high priest unnecessary. **Hebrews 9:11-12** declares, "But when Christ appeared as a high priest of the good things that have come, then through the greater and more perfect tent (not made with hands, that is, not of this creation) He entered once for all into the holy places, not by means of the blood of goats and calves but by means of His own blood, thus securing an eternal redemption."

1. The Once-for-All Sacrifice

One of the key differences between the sacrifices of the Old Testament and the sacrifice of Christ is that Christ's sacrifice was made **once for all**. While the high priest had to offer sacrifices every year on the Day of Atonement, Christ's sacrifice was **final** and **complete**. **Hebrews 10:12** states, "But when Christ had offered for all time a single sacrifice for sins, He sat down at the right hand of God."

This once-for-all sacrifice means that there is no longer any need for repeated sacrifices. Christ's death on the cross fully satisfied the demands of God's justice and provided a way for sinners to be reconciled to God permanently. Through His sacrifice, Christ accomplished what the Levitical priests and sacrifices could not—**eternal redemption**.

2. The Perfect High Priest

Not only is Christ's sacrifice superior, but He is also the **perfect High Priest** who offers it. Unlike the Levitical high priests, who were sinful and had to offer sacrifices for themselves, Christ was **sinless** and offered Himself as the perfect sacrifice for the sins of others. **Hebrews 7:26-27** says, "For it was indeed fitting that we should have such a high priest, holy, innocent, unstained, separated from sinners, and exalted above the heavens. He has no need, like those high priests, to offer sacrifices daily, first for His own sins and then for those of the people, since He did this once for all when He offered up Himself."

Christ's priesthood is superior because He is both the priest and the sacrifice. As the sinless Son of God, He was able to offer Himself as the **perfect sacrifice**, fulfilling the requirements of the law and securing salvation for all who believe in Him.

Fun Fact: The Scapegoat in Modern Language

Did you know that the term **"scapegoat"** comes directly from the **Day of Atonement** ritual described in **Leviticus 16**? In modern language, a scapegoat refers to someone who is unfairly blamed for the wrongdoings of others. This concept is rooted in the biblical practice of the high priest confessing the sins of the people over the head of the scapegoat and sending it into the wilderness, symbolically carrying away their sins. While the modern usage of the term often has a negative connotation, the biblical scapegoat represents the **removal of sin** and the **forgiveness** that comes through the atoning work of Christ.

IV. THE NEW COVENANT: CHRIST'S HIGH PRIESTHOOD AND SACRIFICE

The **Levitical priesthood** and the **sacrificial system** were part of the **Old Covenant**, a covenant that was based on the law and the repeated offering of sacrifices to atone for sin. However, through His death and resurrection, Christ established the **New Covenant**, a covenant that is based on His **once-for-all sacrifice** and the forgiveness of sins. Christ's role as the **High Priest** of the New Covenant is central to this new relationship between God and humanity.

A. The New Covenant in Christ's Blood

In the Upper Room, on the night before His crucifixion, Jesus instituted the **Lord's Supper** and spoke of the **New Covenant** that would be established through His death. In **Luke 22:20**, He says, "This cup that is poured out for you is the new covenant in My blood." This New Covenant is radically different from the Old Covenant because it is based on the **finished work of Christ**, not on the repeated sacrifices of animals.

1. The Forgiveness of Sins

The central promise of the New Covenant is the **forgiveness of sins**. While the Old Covenant provided a temporary covering for sin through the sacrificial system, the New Covenant provides **complete forgiveness** through the sacrifice of Christ. **Hebrews 8:12** quotes God's promise regarding the New Covenant: "For I will be merciful toward their iniquities, and I will remember their sins no more."

This forgiveness is made possible because Christ's sacrifice was perfect and sufficient to atone for all sin. As the true High Priest, Christ entered the Holy of Holies in heaven and presented His own blood as the atoning sacrifice. Because of His sacrifice, believers can approach God with **confidence**, knowing that their sins have been forgiven and that they are reconciled to God.

2. Access to God

Under the Old Covenant, only the high priest could enter the **Holy of Holies**, and even then, only once a year on the Day of Atonement. However, under the New Covenant, all believers have **direct access** to God through Christ. **Hebrews 10:19-20** declares, "Therefore, brothers, since we have confidence to enter the holy places by the blood of Jesus, by the new and living way that He opened for us through the curtain, that is, through His flesh."

Christ's sacrifice tore down the **barrier** between God and humanity, allowing believers to come into God's presence with confidence and boldness. This access to God is one of the greatest blessings of the New Covenant, as believers no longer need a human mediator to approach God. Instead, Christ, as the true High Priest, provides us with **continuous access** to the Father.

B. The Eternal Priesthood of Christ

Unlike the Levitical priests, who were mortal and had to be replaced when they died, Christ's priesthood is **eternal**. **Hebrews 7:23-24** explains, "The former priests were many in number, because they were prevented by death from continuing in office, but He holds His priesthood permanently, because He continues forever." Christ's priesthood is superior because it is not limited by death, and His ministry as High Priest is ongoing.

1. Christ's Intercession for Believers

One of the most important aspects of Christ's eternal priesthood is His role as an **intercessor** for believers. **Hebrews 7:25** declares, "Consequently, He is able to save to the uttermost those who draw near to God through Him, since He always lives to make intercession for them." Christ's intercession means that He continually represents believers before the Father, pleading on their behalf and ensuring that they remain in God's grace.

This intercessory role is a great source of comfort for believers, as it means that Christ is always **advocating** for them, even in their weakness and sin. His priesthood is not limited to the past; it is ongoing, and His work of intercession continues to this day.

2. The Hope of Eternal Life

Because Christ's priesthood is eternal, believers can have **confidence** in the **hope of eternal life**. The sacrifices of the Old Covenant could not provide eternal life because they were temporary and insufficient. However, Christ's sacrifice guarantees eternal life for all who trust in Him. **Hebrews 9:15** explains, "Therefore He is the mediator of a new covenant, so that those who are called may receive the promised eternal inheritance, since a death has occurred that redeems them from the transgressions committed under the first covenant."

The **eternal inheritance** that Christ provides is the hope of eternal life in the presence of God. Just as Christ's priesthood is eternal, so too is the salvation that He offers. Believers can be assured that they are **secure** in Christ and that His priesthood guarantees their eternal future.

The Levitical Priesthood and Sacrifices as Types of Christ's High Priesthood

From the Tabernacle to Solomon's Temple to the Second Temple, the progression of God's dwelling among His people points toward a final and eternal fulfillment in Christ. The tearing of the temple veil at Jesus' crucifixion signifies the end of separation between God and humanity, and the beginning of the Church as the living temple, indwelt by the Spirit.

Solomon's Temple was the physical dwelling place of God among His people, where the Ark of the Covenant resided. As magnificent as it was, it served as a shadow of a greater reality. The destruction of this temple symbolized the passing of the old covenant system, pointing forward to the time when God's presence would dwell fully in Christ, the true Temple. The physical structure of the temple was temporary, but it laid the foundation for the spiritual temple found in Christ.

The Second Temple, rebuilt after the exile, held great significance for the Jewish people. It was the site of Jesus' ministry, and although it lacked the glory of Solomon's Temple, it still foreshadowed a greater fulfillment in Christ. The destruction of the Second Temple, as prophesied by Jesus, marks the end of the old sacrificial system and the transition to a new covenant where God's presence is no longer confined to a building but resides in Christ and His Church. Jesus, the ultimate Temple, fulfills what the Second Temple could only symbolize.

The **Levitical priesthood** and the **sacrificial system** were central to Israel's worship under the Old Covenant, but they were always intended to be **temporary** and **incomplete**. The priests and sacrifices served as **types**—foreshadowings of the greater High Priest and the greater sacrifice that were to come in **Jesus Christ**. Through His death and resurrection, Christ fulfilled and replaced the old system, offering a **once-for-all sacrifice** that provides **eternal redemption** and **complete forgiveness** for sins.

As the **true High Priest**, Christ is both the mediator of the New Covenant and the perfect sacrifice that brings about reconciliation between God and humanity. His priesthood is eternal, and His work of intercession on behalf of believers continues to this day. Through His sacrifice, believers have **direct access** to God, the **forgiveness of sins**, and the **hope of eternal life**.

The story of the Levitical priests and sacrifices is not merely a historical account; it is a **picture** of the salvation that is offered in Christ. Just as the priests offered sacrifices on behalf of the people, Christ offered Himself as the perfect sacrifice on behalf of all who believe in Him. Through His priesthood, we are given the **assurance** of salvation, the **security** of eternal life, and the **privilege** of approaching God with confidence and boldness.

CHAPTER 9: THE TABERNACLE: A TYPE OF CHRIST'S MINISTRY

As with the Tabernacle, Solomon's Temple represented God's dwelling among His people. However, even as the Second Temple was rebuilt, it lacked the Shekinah glory that filled the first. This absence symbolized the anticipation of the true fulfillment in Christ, in whom 'the fullness of deity dwells bodily' (Colossians 2:9). Jesus not only fulfills the typology of the Tabernacle but surpasses it, offering His own body as the ultimate temple.

Solomon's Temple was the physical dwelling place of God among His people, where the Ark of the Covenant resided. As magnificent as it was, it served as a shadow of a greater reality. The destruction of this temple symbolized the passing of the old covenant system, pointing forward to the time when God's presence would dwell fully in Christ, the true Temple. The physical structure of the temple was temporary, but it laid the foundation for the spiritual temple found in Christ.

The Second Temple, rebuilt after the exile, held great significance for the Jewish people. It was the site of Jesus' ministry, and although it lacked the glory of Solomon's Temple, it still foreshadowed a greater fulfillment in Christ. The destruction of the Second Temple, as prophesied by Jesus, marks the end of the old sacrificial system and the transition to a new covenant where God's presence is no longer confined to a building but resides in Christ and His Church. Jesus, the ultimate Temple, fulfills what the Second Temple could only symbolize.

The **Tabernacle**, described in detail in **Exodus 25-31**, was a portable sanctuary constructed by the Israelites under God's command during their time in the wilderness. It served as the dwelling place of God among His people and was the center of their worship. The Tabernacle's significance, however, extends far beyond its immediate historical and religious function. In Christian theology, the Tabernacle serves as a **type** of **Christ's ministry**, prefiguring His work of salvation and His role as the mediator between God and humanity.

Each part of the Tabernacle—its design, furnishings, and rituals—symbolically pointed forward to the work of Christ. From the **altar** where sacrifices were made, to the **Holy of Holies** where the Ark of the Covenant was kept, every detail was imbued with spiritual meaning, illustrating aspects of the gospel and Christ's role in the redemption of humanity. This chapter will explore the **typology** of the Tabernacle, highlighting how it foreshadowed the **ministry of Jesus**, and how the Ark of the Covenant, with its **mercy seat**, represents Christ's role as the true atonement for sin.

I. THE WILDERNESS TABERNACLE: A TEMPORARY DWELLING FOR GOD'S PRESENCE (EXODUS 25-31)

The **Wilderness Tabernacle**, also known as the **Tent of Meeting**, was designed by God and constructed by the Israelites as they journeyed from Egypt to the Promised Land. It was intended to be a **temporary dwelling place** for God's presence among His people until the construction of the permanent Temple in Jerusalem. Despite its temporary nature, the Tabernacle was carefully designed to reflect God's holiness and to illustrate the process by which sinful humans could approach a holy God.

A. The Purpose of the Tabernacle: God Dwelling Among His People

The primary purpose of the Tabernacle was to provide a **dwelling place** for God's presence in the midst of the Israelites. In **Exodus 25:8**, God says, "And let them make Me a sanctuary, that I may dwell in their midst." The Tabernacle was the place where God's glory rested and where He met with His people. It was also the location where the priests offered **sacrifices** on behalf of the people to atone for their sins.

The concept of God dwelling among His people in the Tabernacle is a powerful foreshadowing of the **incarnation** of Christ. Just as God dwelt in the Tabernacle in the wilderness, **Jesus**—God in human flesh—came to dwell among us. **John 1:14** declares, "And the Word became flesh and dwelt among us, and we have seen His glory, glory as of the only Son from the Father, full of grace and truth." The word "dwelt" in this verse is the Greek word for "tabernacled," indicating that Jesus' incarnation was the fulfillment of the symbolism of the Tabernacle.

1. The Tabernacle as a Picture of Christ's Humanity

The **Tabernacle** was a **temporary** structure, made of earthly materials, that housed the glory of God. This is a picture of Christ's **humanity**. While Jesus is fully divine, He also took on a **temporary human body**, dwelling in the midst of sinful humanity. Just as the Tabernacle was made from humble materials but contained the glory of God, Christ's human body veiled His divine glory. **Philippians 2:6-7** describes this mystery: "Who, though He was in the form of God, did not count equality with God a thing to be grasped, but emptied Himself, by taking the form of a servant, being born in the likeness of men."

The Tabernacle was also a **temporary solution** for housing God's presence until the more permanent Temple was built. In the same way, Christ's earthly ministry was temporary, but it pointed to the **eternal** work of redemption that would be completed through His death, resurrection, and exaltation.

2. The Tabernacle as a Place of Worship and Atonement

The Tabernacle was the center of **worship** for the Israelites, and it was where **atonement** for sin was made. The priests offered sacrifices at the Tabernacle's **altar**, and the high priest entered the **Holy of Holies** once a year to offer blood on the **mercy seat** of the Ark of the Covenant to atone for the sins of the people. This ritual foreshadows Christ's role as both the **sacrifice** and the **High Priest**, who offers Himself as the perfect atonement for sin.

In the Tabernacle, sinful people could only approach God through the **mediation** of the priests and through the offering of blood sacrifices. In the same way, humanity can only approach God through the mediation of **Jesus Christ**, who offered His own blood as a once-for-all sacrifice for sin. **Hebrews 9:12** states, "He entered once for all into the holy places, not by means of the blood of goats and calves but by means of His own blood, thus securing an eternal redemption."

B. The Parts of the Tabernacle: Symbolizing Christ's Work in Salvation

Each part of the Tabernacle—the **altar**, the **bronze basin**, the **lampstand**, the **table of showbread**, the **altar of incense**, and the **Holy of Holies**—had symbolic meaning and pointed forward to the **work of Christ** in salvation. These parts of the Tabernacle served both a practical function in Israel's worship and a spiritual function in illustrating the process of salvation that would ultimately be fulfilled in Christ.

1. The Bronze Altar: A Symbol of Sacrifice

The **bronze altar**, located in the outer court of the Tabernacle, was where the priests offered **burnt offerings** and **sacrifices** for sin. This altar was the first thing worshipers encountered as they approached the Tabernacle, signifying that **atonement for sin** was necessary before entering into God's presence. The shedding of blood on the altar foreshadowed the **sacrificial death of Christ** on the cross.

Just as the blood of animals was shed on the bronze altar to atone for the sins of the people, **Jesus' blood** was shed on the cross to atone for the sins of the world. **Hebrews 9:22** reminds us that "without the shedding of blood there is no forgiveness of sins." Christ's sacrifice was the **ultimate fulfillment** of the sacrifices made on the altar, providing a **once-for-all** solution to the problem of sin.

2. The Bronze Basin: A Symbol of Cleansing

The **bronze basin**, also located in the outer court, was used by the priests to **wash** themselves before entering the holy place. This washing symbolized the **purification** necessary for those who ministered before God. It points to the need for spiritual cleansing, which Christ provides through His **word** and **Spirit**.

In **Ephesians 5:26**, Paul describes how Christ cleanses His Church "by the washing of water with the word." The bronze basin symbolizes the **cleansing power** of Christ's word, which purifies believers and prepares them for fellowship with God. This cleansing is also reflected in **Titus 3:5**, which speaks of the "washing of regeneration and renewal of the Holy Spirit." Just as the priests needed to be cleansed before entering God's presence, believers are cleansed by the blood of Christ and the work of the Holy Spirit.

3. The Lampstand: A Symbol of Christ's Light

Inside the Tabernacle, in the **holy place**, stood the **golden lampstand**, which provided light for the priests as they ministered before the Lord. The lampstand, with its seven branches, was a symbol of **light** and **life**, and it pointed forward to **Christ**, who is the **light of the world**.

In **John 8:12**, Jesus declares, "I am the light of the world. Whoever follows me will not walk in darkness, but will have the light of life." The lampstand in the Tabernacle was a reminder that God is the source of all light and life, and that His presence brings **illumination** and **truth**. Just as the lampstand provided light in the Tabernacle, Christ provides spiritual light to those who follow Him, leading them out of darkness and into the light of eternal life.

4. The Table of Showbread: A Symbol of Christ's Provision

Opposite the lampstand, in the holy place, was the **table of showbread**, on which twelve loaves of bread were placed each week as an offering to the Lord. These loaves represented the **twelve tribes of Israel** and symbolized God's **provision** for His people. The bread was a reminder that God sustained His people in the wilderness and that He continues to provide for their needs.

The showbread points forward to **Christ**, who is the **bread of life**. In **John 6:35**, Jesus says, "I am the bread of life; whoever comes to me shall not hunger, and whoever believes in me shall never thirst." Just as the showbread symbolized God's physical provision for the Israelites, Christ is the **spiritual provision** for believers, satisfying their deepest needs and offering them **eternal life**.

5. The Altar of Incense: A Symbol of Intercession

The **altar of incense** was located just outside the **Holy of Holies** in the holy place, and the priests burned incense on it every morning and evening. The rising smoke from the incense symbolized the **prayers** of the people ascending to God. The altar of incense points to Christ's role as our **intercessor**, who continually offers prayers on our behalf before the Father.

Hebrews 7:25 says, "He is able to save to the uttermost those who draw near to God through Him, since He always lives to make intercession for them." Just as the incense on the altar represented the prayers of the people, Christ's intercession for believers ensures that they are always in God's favor and that their prayers are heard.

6. The Veil and the Holy of Holies: A Symbol of Separation and Access

The **veil** that separated the **holy place** from the **Holy of Holies** was a symbol of the **separation** between God and humanity due to sin. Only the high priest could enter the Holy of Holies, and only once a year, on the **Day of Atonement**, to offer blood on the **mercy seat** of the Ark of the Covenant. This veil represented the barrier between sinful humanity and a holy God.

When Christ died on the cross, the veil in the Temple was **torn in two** from top to bottom (**Matthew 27:51**), symbolizing that the barrier between God and humanity had been **removed**. Through Christ's sacrifice, believers now have **direct access** to God. **Hebrews 10:19-20** declares, "Therefore, brothers, since we have confidence to enter the holy places by the blood of Jesus, by the new and living way that He opened for us through the curtain, that is, through His flesh."

The tearing of the veil was a powerful symbol of the **new covenant** in Christ, in which believers can approach God with confidence because their sins have been atoned for. The Holy of Holies, once off-limits to all but the high priest, is now open to all who are **in Christ**.

II. THE ARK OF THE COVENANT: A SYMBOL OF GOD'S PRESENCE AND CHRIST'S ATONEMENT

At the heart of the Tabernacle, in the **Holy of Holies**, was the **Ark of the Covenant**, a wooden chest overlaid with gold. The Ark contained the **tablets of the law**, a jar of **manna**, and Aaron's **rod** that budded. The **mercy seat** (or **atonement cover**) rested on top of the Ark, and it was here that the high priest sprinkled the blood of the sin offering on the **Day of Atonement**. The Ark and its contents were the most sacred objects in the Tabernacle, representing God's **presence**, His **covenant** with Israel, and His provision for their spiritual and physical needs.

A. The Ark as a Symbol of God's Presence

The Ark of the Covenant was the visible **symbol of God's presence** among His people. When the Tabernacle was completed, God's **glory** filled the Holy of Holies, and His presence was manifest above the mercy seat between the two **cherubim** that adorned the Ark. In **Exodus 25:22**, God says, "There I will meet with you, and from above the mercy seat, from between the two cherubim that are on the ark of the testimony, I will speak with you about all that I will give you in commandment for the people of Israel."

The Ark served as a reminder that God was **with** His people, guiding them and providing for them. It also symbolized the **covenant**

relationship between God and Israel, in which God promised to be their God, and they were to be His people. However, the Ark's location in the Holy of Holies, separated by the veil, also emphasized the **holiness** of God and the need for atonement before approaching Him.

In the New Testament, **Jesus** is the ultimate fulfillment of the Ark's symbolism. Just as the Ark represented God's presence among the Israelites, **Jesus** is the embodiment of God's presence among humanity. **Colossians 2:9** declares, "For in Him the whole fullness of deity dwells bodily." Jesus is the **"Emmanuel"**, which means **"God with us"** (**Matthew 1:23**), and through Him, we have access to the presence of God.

B. The Mercy Seat: Christ as the True Atonement

The most important feature of the Ark of the Covenant was the **mercy seat** (also called the **atonement cover**), which was the place where the high priest sprinkled the blood of the sin offering on the Day of Atonement. The mercy seat was where God's **wrath** against sin was **propitiated**, or satisfied, through the shedding of blood. It was the place where **atonement** was made for the sins of the people, allowing them to remain in covenant relationship with God.

The mercy seat points forward to **Christ**, who is the true **atonement** for sin. In **Romans 3:25**, Paul writes, "God presented Christ as a sacrifice of atonement, through the shedding of His blood—to be received by faith." The Greek word translated as "atonement" (or "propitiation") in this verse is **hilasterion**, which is the same word used for the **mercy seat** in the Greek translation of the Old Testament (the **Septuagint**). This indicates that Christ is the **fulfillment** of the mercy seat—He is the one who provides atonement for sin through His sacrificial death on the cross.

1. The Blood of the Atonement

Just as the high priest sprinkled **blood** on the mercy seat to atone for the sins of Israel, Christ shed **His blood** on the cross to atone for the sins of the world. The blood of animals offered on the Day of Atonement provided **temporary** forgiveness for the people, but

Christ's blood provides **eternal** forgiveness for all who trust in Him. **Hebrews 9:12** states, "He entered once for all into the holy places, not by means of the blood of goats and calves but by means of His own blood, thus securing an eternal redemption."

The blood of Christ is the ultimate **sacrifice** for sin, and it fulfills the symbolism of the blood sprinkled on the mercy seat. Through His death, Christ **propitiated** (satisfied) the wrath of God, and His blood provides **cleansing** and **forgiveness** for all who believe.

2. The Mercy Seat and Reconciliation

The **mercy seat** was the place where **reconciliation** between God and Israel was made each year on the Day of Atonement. This reconciliation was temporary, and the sacrifices had to be repeated year after year. However, Christ's sacrifice on the cross provides **permanent reconciliation** between God and humanity. **2 Corinthians 5:18** says, "All this is from God, who through Christ reconciled us to Himself and gave us the ministry of reconciliation."

Through Christ's death and resurrection, the **barrier** between God and humanity has been removed, and believers are now **reconciled** to God. This reconciliation is not just for a year or a season but for **eternity**. Christ's role as the true **mercy seat** ensures that all who come to Him in faith are forgiven and brought into right relationship with God.

III. THE TABERNACLE AS A FORESHADOWING OF CHRIST'S MINISTRY

The **Tabernacle** and its rituals were not just temporary measures for Israel's worship; they were a **foreshadowing** of the **ministry of Christ**. Every detail of the Tabernacle, from its structure to its furnishings to its rituals, pointed forward to the **greater reality** that would be fulfilled in Christ. As **Hebrews 8:5** explains, the Tabernacle was "a copy and shadow of the heavenly things." The earthly Tabernacle was a **shadow** of the **heavenly reality** that Christ would bring about through His ministry.

A. The Temporary Nature of the Tabernacle

One of the most significant aspects of the Tabernacle is that it was a **temporary structure**, designed to be set up and taken down as the Israelites moved from place to place in the wilderness. This temporary nature of the Tabernacle points to the **temporary** nature of the **Old Covenant** and the **sacrificial system**. The Tabernacle was always intended to be a **shadow** of the **greater reality** that would come in Christ.

Just as the Tabernacle was replaced by the more permanent **Temple** in Jerusalem, so too the Old Covenant was replaced by the **New Covenant** in Christ. The sacrifices, rituals, and priesthood of the Old Covenant were **shadows** of the ultimate **sacrifice** and **priesthood** of Christ. **Hebrews 10:1** says, "For since the law has but a shadow of the good things to come instead of the true form of these realities, it can never, by the same sacrifices that are continually offered every year, make perfect those who draw near."

1. Christ as the True Tabernacle

While the Tabernacle was a temporary dwelling for God's presence, Christ is the **true Tabernacle**, the **permanent dwelling** of God's presence among humanity. **Colossians 1:19** declares, "For in Him all the fullness of God was pleased to dwell." Christ is the **Emmanuel**, the **God with us**, who came to dwell among humanity not in a temporary structure but in the **flesh**.

The **glory of God**, which dwelt in the Tabernacle in the wilderness, is now revealed in the **person of Jesus Christ**. **John 1:14** proclaims, "And the Word became flesh and dwelt among us, and we have seen His glory, glory as of the only Son from the Father, full of grace and truth." The Greek word for "dwelt" in this verse can also be translated as **"tabernacled."** This emphasizes the idea that Jesus is the fulfillment of the Tabernacle, the place where God's glory dwells and where His people can meet with Him.

2. The Permanent Ministry of Christ

The ministry of the **Levitical priests** was temporary, and their sacrifices had to be repeated year after year. However, the ministry of Christ is **permanent**. **Hebrews 7:23-24** contrasts the two priesthoods: "The former priests were many in number, because they were prevented by death from continuing in office, but He holds His priesthood permanently, because He continues forever."

Because Christ's priesthood is eternal, His ministry of **intercession** and **atonement** is also eternal. He is able to **save to the uttermost** those who draw near to God through Him, as **Hebrews 7:25** declares. Christ's work on the cross is a **once-for-all sacrifice**, and His role as our **High Priest** is ongoing. Just as the Tabernacle was the place where God's presence dwelt, Christ is now the **mediator** of God's presence for all who believe.

Fun Fact: The Symbolism of the Cherubim on the Mercy Seat

The **cherubim** that adorned the **mercy seat** on the Ark of the Covenant are an interesting detail of the Tabernacle. These angelic beings, with their wings outstretched, symbolized the **heavenly hosts** who surround God's throne in worship and adoration. In ancient Near Eastern cultures, cherubim were often depicted as guardians of sacred spaces, emphasizing the **holiness** and **sacredness** of the Ark.

The presence of the cherubim on the mercy seat also recalls the **Garden of Eden**, where cherubim were stationed to guard the entrance to the **Tree of Life** after Adam and Eve were expelled (**Genesis 3:24**). In this way, the cherubim on the mercy seat can be seen as symbols of **God's holiness** and the **separation** between humanity and God due to sin. However, through Christ, the way to **God's presence** has been opened, and the cherubim, once symbols of separation, now point to the **reconciliation** made possible through the **atoning work** of Jesus.

The Tabernacle as a Type of Christ's Ministry

From the Tabernacle to Solomon's Temple to the Second Temple, the progression of God's dwelling among His people points toward a final and eternal fulfillment in Christ. The tearing of the temple veil at Jesus' crucifixion signifies the end of separation between God and humanity, and the beginning of the Church as the living temple, indwelt by the Spirit.

Solomon's Temple was the physical dwelling place of God among His people, where the Ark of the Covenant resided. As magnificent as it was, it served as a shadow of a greater reality. The destruction of this temple symbolized the passing of the old covenant system, pointing forward to the time when God's presence would dwell fully in Christ, the true Temple. The physical structure of the temple was temporary, but it laid the foundation for the spiritual temple found in Christ.

The Second Temple, rebuilt after the exile, held great significance for the Jewish people. It was the site of Jesus' ministry, and although it lacked the glory of Solomon's Temple, it still foreshadowed a greater fulfillment in Christ. The destruction of the Second Temple, as prophesied by Jesus, marks the end of the old sacrificial system and the transition to a new covenant where God's presence is no longer confined to a building but resides in Christ and His Church. Jesus, the ultimate Temple, fulfills what the Second Temple could only symbolize.

      The **Tabernacle** was much more than a temporary dwelling place for God's presence; it was a **foreshadowing** of the **ministry of Christ**. Every part of the Tabernacle—the altar, the bronze basin, the lampstand, the table of showbread, the altar of incense, the veil, the Holy of Holies, and the Ark of the Covenant—symbolically pointed forward to Christ's work of salvation. The Tabernacle illustrated the **process of redemption**, showing how sinful humanity could be reconciled to a holy God through **sacrifice**, **cleansing**, **illumination**, **provision**, **intercession**, and **atonement**.

      In Christ, the **symbolism** of the Tabernacle is **fulfilled**. He is the **true Tabernacle**, the place where God's presence dwells among humanity. He is the **Lamb of God**, the **bread of life**, the **light of the world**, and the **High Priest** who offers His own blood as the atoning sacrifice for sin. Through His death and resurrection, the **veil** of separation has been torn, and believers now have **direct access** to God through Christ.

The Tabernacle, with all its details and rituals, pointed to the **greater reality** of Christ's ministry. It was a **shadow** of the **heavenly reality** that would be fully realized in Christ, the one who **tabernacled** among us, offered Himself as the ultimate sacrifice, and now serves as our **eternal High Priest**. Through Christ, we have been reconciled to God, and we can now **enter His presence** with confidence, knowing that our sins have been atoned for and that we are **forgiven**.

CHAPTER 10: THE FEASTS OF ISRAEL: TYPES OF CHRIST AND FUTURE EVENTS

The Feast of Tabernacles not only recalled Israel's time in temporary shelters but also pointed to the future, where God would dwell permanently among His people. While Solomon's Temple stood as a physical representation of God's presence, it foreshadowed the true and eternal temple—Christ, whose body is the ultimate tabernacle.

In the Old Testament, God instituted a series of **feasts** for the Israelites to observe throughout the year. These feasts, outlined in **Leviticus 23**, were not only times of worship, celebration, and remembrance of God's provision and protection, but they also served as **prophetic types**, pointing forward to the work of **Jesus Christ** and the unfolding of **God's redemptive plan** for humanity. Each feast carries deep symbolic meaning that is fulfilled in the person and ministry of Christ and holds significance for **future prophetic events**.

In this chapter, we will explore the **seven major feasts** of Israel—**Passover, Unleavened Bread, Firstfruits, Pentecost**, the **Feast of Trumpets**, the **Day of Atonement**, and the **Feast of Tabernacles**—and examine how each one prefigures Christ and relates to key events in **God's timeline** for humanity, from the **death of Christ** to His **second coming** and the establishment of His **Millennial Kingdom**.

I. PASSOVER: FORESHADOWING CHRIST'S DEATH AS THE LAMB OF GOD (LEVITICUS 23:5)

The **Feast of Passover** is the first of the seven major feasts and is arguably the most well-known. It commemorates the night when the Israelites were delivered from **slavery in Egypt** by God's mighty hand. On that night, God sent the **tenth and final plague** upon Egypt, striking down the firstborn of every household. However, the Israelites were spared from this plague by sacrificing a lamb and applying its blood to the **doorposts** of their homes. When the angel of death saw the blood, he "passed over" those houses, sparing the firstborn within.

The symbolism of Passover is clear: the **lamb** sacrificed during Passover foreshadows **Jesus Christ**, the **Lamb of God**, who would be sacrificed to deliver humanity from **sin and death**. Just as the blood of the Passover lamb saved the Israelites from physical death, the **blood of Christ** saves believers from **spiritual death**.

A. Christ as the Passover Lamb

The **New Testament** makes a direct connection between the Passover lamb and Jesus Christ. **John 1:29** records John the Baptist's declaration about Jesus: "Behold, the **Lamb of God** who takes away the sin of the world!" Jesus is the ultimate fulfillment of the Passover lamb, and His sacrificial death provides **atonement** for the sins of the world.

1 Corinthians 5:7 also confirms this typology: "For Christ, our **Passover lamb**, has been sacrificed." Jesus was crucified during the time of Passover, further cementing the connection between the feast and His death. The timing of Christ's crucifixion was not accidental but rather part of **God's sovereign plan**, demonstrating that He is the true Passover Lamb whose sacrifice brings **eternal salvation**.

1. The Blood of the Lamb and Protection from Judgment

In the original Passover event, the blood of the lamb applied to the doorposts was the **sign** that protected the Israelites from God's judgment. This is a powerful picture of how the blood of Christ, applied to the lives of believers through faith, protects them from **God's wrath**. **Romans 5:9** states, "Since we have now been justified by His blood, how much more shall we be saved from God's wrath through Him!"

Just as the Israelites were delivered from **slavery in Egypt**, Christians are delivered from the **slavery of sin** through Christ's sacrifice. **Romans 6:6** explains, "For we know that our old self was crucified with Him so that the body ruled by sin might be done away with, that we should no longer be slaves to sin."

2. The Unblemished Lamb and Christ's Perfection

The Passover lamb had to be **without blemish** or defect (Exodus 12:5). This requirement foreshadowed the **sinlessness** of Christ, the perfect Lamb of God. **1 Peter 1:18-19** affirms, "For you know that it was not with perishable things such as silver or gold that you were redeemed...but with the precious blood of Christ, a lamb **without blemish or defect**."

Jesus, as the sinless Lamb, was the only one who could offer Himself as the perfect **sacrifice** for humanity's sins. His death on the cross fulfilled the prophetic significance of Passover, providing salvation for all who place their faith in Him.

II. THE FEAST OF UNLEAVENED BREAD: REPRESENTING CHRIST'S SINLESS LIFE AND THE NEED FOR PURITY (LEVITICUS 23:6)

The **Feast of Unleavened Bread** began the day after Passover and lasted for seven days. During this feast, the Israelites were commanded to remove all **leaven** (yeast) from their homes and to eat only **unleavened bread**. Leaven, in Scripture, is often symbolic of **sin** and **corruption**, and the removal of leaven from the home during this feast represented the need for **purity** and **holiness** before God.

A. Christ's Sinless Life

The Feast of Unleavened Bread points to **Christ's sinless life**. Just as unleavened bread is free from yeast, Christ was free from sin. Throughout His life, Jesus was **perfectly obedient** to the Father, and He fulfilled the law in its entirety. **Hebrews 4:15** declares, "For we do not have a high priest who is unable to sympathize with our weaknesses, but we have one who has been tempted in every way, just as we are—yet He did not sin."

Because Jesus was sinless, He was able to be the perfect **sacrifice** for the sins of the world. His sinlessness is also a model for believers, who are called to live lives of **holiness** and to "put away the old leaven" of sin.

1. The Removal of Leaven as a Picture of Sanctification

The removal of leaven from the Israelites' homes during the Feast of Unleavened Bread is symbolic of the process of **sanctification** in the life of a believer. **Sanctification** is the process by which Christians are made holy, growing in their relationship with God and becoming more like Christ. **1 Corinthians 5:7** urges believers to "Get rid of the old yeast, so that you may be a new unleavened batch—as you really are. For Christ, our Passover lamb, has been sacrificed."

Just as the Israelites had to search their homes to find any trace of leaven, Christians are called to examine their lives and remove anything that might **hinder** their relationship with God. The Feast of Unleavened Bread, therefore, points not only to Christ's sinless life but also to the believer's call to **live in purity** and holiness.

2. The Bread of Life

The unleavened bread used during this feast also symbolizes **Christ as the Bread of Life**. In **John 6:35**, Jesus declares, "I am the bread of life. Whoever comes to me will never go hungry, and whoever believes in me will never be thirsty." Just as the Israelites relied on the unleavened bread for physical sustenance during the

Feast of Unleavened Bread, believers rely on **Christ** for spiritual sustenance. He is the source of **eternal life**, and only through Him can we be truly satisfied.

III. THE FEAST OF FIRSTFRUITS: TYPIFYING CHRIST'S RESURRECTION AS THE FIRSTFRUITS OF THE DEAD (LEVITICUS 23:10)

The **Feast of Firstfruits** was celebrated on the day after the **Sabbath** during the Feast of Unleavened Bread. This feast marked the beginning of the **harvest season**, and the Israelites were commanded to bring the **first and best** of their crops as an offering to the Lord. This act of offering the firstfruits was a way of acknowledging God's **provision** and giving thanks for the harvest that was to come.

The Feast of Firstfruits points to **Christ's resurrection**, which occurred on the day after the Sabbath during the Feast of Unleavened Bread. Jesus is described as the **firstfruits** of the dead, signifying that His resurrection is the **guarantee** of the future resurrection of believers.

A. Christ as the Firstfruits of the Resurrection

The apostle Paul explicitly connects the Feast of Firstfruits to Christ's resurrection in **1 Corinthians 15:20**: "But Christ has indeed been raised from the dead, the **firstfruits** of those who have fallen asleep." Just as the firstfruits offering in the Old Testament was a **pledge** of the full harvest to come, Christ's resurrection is a **pledge** of the future resurrection of all believers. His resurrection is the **first** of many, and those who are in Christ will follow in the **resurrection of the dead**.

1. The Promise of Future Resurrection

Christ's resurrection as the firstfruits assures believers that they, too, will be raised from the dead. **1 Corinthians 15:23** states, "But each in turn: Christ, the firstfruits; then, when He comes, those who belong to Him." The Feast of Firstfruits, therefore, points to the **hope of resurrection** and **eternal life** for all who trust in Christ. Just as the firstfruits offering was a **promise** of the harvest to come, Christ's resurrection is the **promise** of the resurrection of all believers at His second coming.

2. The Significance of the Timing of Christ's Resurrection

It is significant that Christ's resurrection occurred on the exact day of the Feast of Firstfruits. This timing was not coincidental but was part of God's **sovereign plan** to demonstrate that Jesus is the **fulfillment** of the feast. Just as the firstfruits offering signaled the beginning of the harvest, Christ's resurrection signals the beginning of the **new creation**—a new era in which death has been defeated and eternal life is available to all who believe in Him.

IV. PENTECOST: SYMBOLIZING THE COMING OF THE HOLY SPIRIT AND THE BIRTH OF THE CHURCH (LEVITICUS 23:15-22)

The **Feast of Pentecost**, also known as the **Feast of Weeks** or **Shavuot**, occurred **fifty days** after the Feast of Firstfruits. It was a celebration of the **wheat harvest** and marked the conclusion of the grain harvest season. During this feast, the Israelites presented an offering of **two loaves of bread** made from the first wheat of the harvest, symbolizing God's **provision** and **blessing**.

In the New Testament, the Feast of Pentecost is fulfilled by the **coming of the Holy Spirit** and the **birth of the Church**. On the day of Pentecost, fifty days after Christ's resurrection, the Holy Spirit descended upon the disciples, empowering them to proclaim the gospel and marking the beginning of the Church.

A. The Coming of the Holy Spirit

In **Acts 2**, we read about the day of **Pentecost**, when the Holy Spirit was poured out on the disciples who were gathered in Jerusalem. The coming of the Holy Spirit on Pentecost was the fulfillment of Jesus' promise in **John 14:16-17**, where He told His disciples that He would send them the **Helper**, the **Spirit of truth**. The outpouring of the Holy Spirit empowered the disciples to speak in different languages and proclaim the message of the **gospel** to the diverse crowd gathered in Jerusalem for the feast.

The coming of the Holy Spirit on Pentecost marked the **birth of the Church** and the beginning of the Church's mission to spread the gospel to the ends of the earth. **Acts 2:41** records that about **three thousand people** were baptized and added to the Church that day, demonstrating the power of the Holy Spirit to **bring people to faith** in Christ.

1. The Two Loaves of Bread: A Picture of Jews and Gentiles United in Christ

The two loaves of bread offered during the Feast of Pentecost can be seen as a **type** of the **unity** of **Jews and Gentiles** in the Church. Prior to Pentecost, the people of God were primarily the **Jewish nation**, but with the coming of the Holy Spirit, the gospel was proclaimed to **all nations**, and both Jews and Gentiles were united as one body in Christ.

Ephesians 2:14 speaks of this unity: "For He Himself is our peace, who has made the two groups one and has destroyed the barrier, the dividing wall of hostility." The two loaves of bread offered during Pentecost symbolize the **one Church** made up of both Jews and Gentiles, united by the Holy Spirit and by their faith in Christ.

2. The Beginning of the Harvest of Souls

Just as the Feast of Pentecost celebrated the **harvest**, the day of Pentecost in Acts 2 marked the beginning of the **spiritual harvest**—the harvest of **souls** brought into the kingdom of God through the preaching of the gospel. **Matthew 9:37-38** uses the metaphor of a harvest to describe the work of evangelism: "The harvest is plentiful, but the workers are few. Ask the Lord of the harvest, therefore, to send out workers into His harvest field."

The outpouring of the Holy Spirit on Pentecost empowered the disciples to begin this work of evangelism, and it continues to this day as believers are filled with the Holy Spirit and sent out to share the gospel with the world.

V. THE FEAST OF TRUMPETS: POINTING TO THE FUTURE RAPTURE OF THE CHURCH (LEVITICUS 23:23-25)

The **Feast of Trumpets**, or **Rosh Hashanah**, is the next feast on Israel's calendar. This feast marked the **beginning of the civil new year** and was celebrated by the blowing of trumpets (or **shofars**) to announce the arrival of the feast and to call the people to **repentance** in preparation for the **Day of Atonement**, which followed ten days later.

In Christian eschatology, the Feast of Trumpets is seen as a type of the **rapture** of the Church, the future event in which **believers** will be caught up to meet the Lord in the air at the **sound of the trumpet**.

A. The Blowing of Trumpets and the Rapture

The connection between the **blowing of trumpets** and the rapture is made in **1 Thessalonians 4:16-17**, which states, "For the Lord Himself will descend from heaven with a shout, with the voice of the archangel, and with the **trumpet of God**. And the dead in Christ will rise first. Then we who are alive and remain shall be caught up together with them in the clouds to meet the Lord in the air."

The **trumpet blast** that announces the Feast of Trumpets is seen as a type of the **trumpet of God** that will announce the rapture of the Church. Just as the Feast of Trumpets was a call to **gather** the people of Israel, the rapture will be the gathering of **believers** to meet the Lord and to be with Him forever.

1. The Call to Repentance

The Feast of Trumpets also served as a **call to repentance**, as it preceded the **Day of Atonement**, the holiest day of the year for Israel. Similarly, the rapture of the Church will serve as a **wake-up call** for the world, signaling that the time of **God's judgment** is near and that there is a need for repentance before it is too late.

2. The Future Fulfillment of the Feast of Trumpets

While the rapture has not yet occurred, the Feast of Trumpets points forward to this **future event.** Just as the trumpet blast announced the beginning of the new year in Israel's calendar, the **trumpet of God** will announce the **beginning of a new era** in God's redemptive plan—the rapture of the Church and the events that will lead to the **second coming of Christ**.

VI. The Day of Atonement: Prefiguring the Future National Redemption of Israel (Leviticus 23:27-32)

The **Day of Atonement**, or **Yom Kippur**, is the holiest day in the Jewish calendar. On this day, the high priest entered the **Holy of Holies** to offer a sacrifice for the **sins of the nation**. The Day of Atonement was a day of **fasting, prayer**, and **repentance**, and it provided temporary atonement for the sins of Israel for the previous year.

In Christian eschatology, the Day of Atonement prefigures the **future national redemption of Israel,** when the nation will recognize **Jesus Christ** as their Messiah and be reconciled to God.

A. The Future Redemption of Israel

The **apostle Paul** speaks of the future redemption of Israel in **Romans 11:26**, where he writes, "And so all Israel will be saved, as it is written: 'The Deliverer will come from Zion; He will turn godlessness away from Jacob.'" This future event will occur at the **second coming of Christ**, when the **Jewish people** will finally recognize Jesus as their Messiah and experience **national redemption**.

The **Day of Atonement** serves as a **type** of this future event, as it was the day when the sins of the nation were atoned for. In the same way, at Christ's second coming, the nation of Israel will experience a **spiritual atonement** and be brought into a **right relationship** with God through faith in Christ.

1. The High Priest and Christ's Role as Mediator

On the Day of Atonement, the high priest entered the Holy of Holies to offer a **sacrifice** for the sins of the people. This act prefigures Christ's role as our **High Priest**, who entered the **heavenly Holy of Holies** and offered His own blood as the final atonement for sin. **Hebrews 9:12** says, "He entered once for all into the holy places, not by means of the blood of goats and calves but by means of His own blood, thus securing an eternal redemption."

While Christ's atonement is available to all who believe, the Day of Atonement points to the **future reconciliation** of the nation of Israel, when they will recognize Christ as their **Messiah** and **Savior**.

2. The National Repentance of Israel

The Day of Atonement was a time of **national repentance** for Israel, and it points to the **future repentance** of the Jewish nation. **Zechariah 12:10** prophesies about this event: "And I will pour out on the house of David and the inhabitants of Jerusalem a spirit of grace and supplication. They will look on Me, the one they have pierced, and they will mourn for Him as one mourns for an only child, and grieve bitterly for Him as one grieves for a firstborn son."

This prophecy speaks of the **national mourning** that will occur when Israel recognizes Jesus as the **one they have pierced** and repents for rejecting Him. The **Day of Atonement** is a foreshadowing of this future event, when Israel will experience **spiritual restoration** through faith in Christ.

VII. THE FEAST OF TABERNACLES: SYMBOLIZING THE MILLENNIAL KINGDOM AND GOD DWELLING WITH HIS PEOPLE (LEVITICUS 23:33-43)

The final feast in Israel's calendar is the **Feast of Tabernacles**, or **Sukkot**. This feast was a time of **joyful celebration** and **thanksgiving** for the **harvest**, and it also commemorated the time when the Israelites lived in **temporary shelters** (or tabernacles) during their journey through the wilderness. During the feast, the Israelites would build and dwell in these shelters as a reminder of God's **provision** and **faithfulness** during their time in the wilderness.

The Feast of Tabernacles points forward to the **Millennial Kingdom**—the future time when Christ will **reign** on earth and **dwell** among His people in the **New Jerusalem**.

A. The Millennial Kingdom

The **Feast of Tabernacles** symbolizes the time when God will once again **dwell** among His people during the **Millennial Kingdom**. This future period is described in **Revelation 20:4-6**, when Christ will reign on earth for **one thousand years**, bringing peace, justice, and righteousness.

During this time, **Zechariah 14:16-19** prophesies that the nations of the world will come to **Jerusalem** to celebrate the Feast of Tabernacles and worship the **King**, the Lord Almighty. This is a picture of the **universal reign** of Christ, when all nations will acknowledge Him as King and come to worship Him.

1. God Dwelling with His People

One of the most significant aspects of the Feast of Tabernacles is its emphasis on **God dwelling with His people**. In the wilderness, God's presence was with the Israelites in the **Tabernacle**, a temporary dwelling. However, in the Millennial Kingdom, God will dwell with His people in a **permanent** and **glorious** way. **Revelation 21:3** speaks of this future reality: "And I heard a loud voice from the throne saying, 'Look! God's dwelling place is now among the people, and He will dwell with them. They will be His people, and God Himself will be with them and be their God.'"

The **temporary shelters** used during the Feast of Tabernacles serve as a reminder of our **temporary** lives on earth, but they also point forward to the **eternal dwelling** we will have with God in the **new heavens** and **new earth**.

2. The New Creation

The **Feast of Tabernacles** also points forward to the **new creation** described in **Revelation 21-22**, when God will make all things new and dwell with His people forever. In this new creation, there will be no more death, mourning, crying, or pain, for the **old order of things** will have passed away. The **Feast of Tabernacles** is a celebration of **God's faithfulness** and provision, and it ultimately looks forward to the **eternal celebration** that believers will experience in the **presence of God** in the new creation.

Fun Fact: The "Water Libation Ceremony" and Christ as the Living Water

During the Feast of Tabernacles, there was a special ceremony called the **Water Libation Ceremony**, in which water was drawn from the **Pool of Siloam** and poured out at the **Temple** as an offering to God. This ceremony symbolized God's provision of **rain** and water for the crops, but it also had **spiritual significance**, pointing to the **living water** that God provides for His people.

In **John 7:37-38**, during the Feast of Tabernacles, Jesus stood up and proclaimed, "Let anyone who is thirsty come to Me and drink. Whoever believes in Me, as Scripture has said, rivers of living water will flow from within them." Here, Jesus identifies Himself as the **source of living water**, fulfilling the symbolism of the Water Libation Ceremony and offering **spiritual life** and refreshment to all who come to Him.

The Feasts of Israel as Types of Christ and Future Events

The Feast of Tabernacles not only recalled Israel's time in temporary shelters but also pointed to the future, where God would dwell permanently among His people. While Solomon's Temple stood as a physical representation of God's presence, it foreshadowed the true and eternal temple—Christ, whose body is the ultimate tabernacle.
From the Tabernacle to Solomon's Temple to the Second Temple, the progression of God's dwelling among His people points toward a final and eternal fulfillment in Christ. The tearing of the temple veil at Jesus' crucifixion signifies the end of separation between God and humanity, and the beginning of the Church as the living temple, indwelt by the Spirit.

Solomon's Temple was the physical dwelling place of God among His people, where the Ark of the Covenant resided. As magnificent as it was, it served as a shadow of a greater reality. The destruction of this temple symbolized the passing of the old covenant system, pointing forward to the time when God's presence would dwell fully in Christ, the true Temple. The physical structure of the temple was temporary, but it laid the foundation for the spiritual temple found in Christ.

The Second Temple, rebuilt after the exile, held great significance for the Jewish people. It was the site of Jesus' ministry, and although it lacked the glory of Solomon's Temple, it still foreshadowed a greater fulfillment in Christ. The destruction of the Second Temple, as prophesied by Jesus, marks the end of the old sacrificial system and the transition to a new covenant where God's presence is no longer confined to a building but resides in Christ and His Church. Jesus, the ultimate Temple, fulfills what the Second Temple could only symbolize.

The **Feasts of Israel** were not only times of worship and celebration for the Israelites but also **prophetic types** that point to the work of **Christ** and the unfolding of **God's redemptive plan**. From **Passover**, which foreshadows Christ's death as the **Lamb of God**, to the **Feast of Tabernacles**, which points to the **Millennial Kingdom** and **God dwelling with His people**, each feast carries deep **theological significance** and highlights different aspects of Christ's ministry and future events.

The Feast of Tabernacles not only recalled Israel's time in temporary shelters but also pointed to the future, where God would dwell permanently among His people. While Solomon's Temple stood as a physical representation of God's presence, it foreshadowed the true and eternal temple—Christ, whose body is the ultimate tabernacle.

Through the **feasts**, God provided His people with a **pattern** and **timeline** that pointed forward to the coming of the **Messiah** and the **fulfillment** of His promises. Today, as we look back at these feasts through the lens of the **New Testament**, we see how each one finds its ultimate **fulfillment** in Christ and how they point us to the **hope** of **future events** in God's redemptive plan, including the **rapture**, the **Millennial Kingdom**, and the **new creation**.

The Feasts of Israel are a beautiful reminder of God's **faithfulness**, **provision**, and **sovereign plan**, and they continue to speak to us today as we await the **return of Christ** and the **consummation** of all things.

The Feast of Tabernacles not only recalled Israel's time in temporary shelters but also pointed to the future, where God would dwell permanently among His people. While Solomon's Temple stood as a physical representation of God's presence, it foreshadowed the true and eternal temple—Christ, whose body is the ultimate tabernacle.

CHAPTER 11: JONAH: A TYPE OF CHRIST'S DEATH, BURIAL, AND RESURRECTION

Jonah in the Belly of the Fish

Jonah's three days in the belly of the great fish prefigured the three days Christ would spend in the tomb (Jonah 1:17, Matthew 12:40). This event wasn't just an isolated occurrence; it was a prophetic shadow of Christ's death, burial, and resurrection. Jesus Himself referenced this in Matthew 12:40, drawing a direct parallel to His own death and resurrection: "For just as Jonah was three days and three nights in the belly of the great fish, so will the Son of Man be three days and three nights in the heart of the earth."

I. JONAH'S CALL AND FLIGHT: THE BEGINNING OF A FORESHADOWING (JONAH 1:1-3)

The story of Jonah is one of the most fascinating and well-known narratives in the Bible, often remembered for its depiction of Jonah being swallowed by a great fish. However, beneath the surface of this dramatic tale lies profound theological significance. Jonah's experience in the belly of the fish serves as a type of Christ's death, burial, and resurrection. Jesus Himself draws a direct parallel between Jonah's three days in the fish and His own three days in the tomb, affirming Jonah's experience as a foreshadowing of His redemptive work.

The book of Jonah opens with a clear directive from God: Jonah, a prophet of Israel, is commanded to go to Nineveh, the capital of Assyria, and preach against its wickedness. Instead of obeying, Jonah flees in the opposite direction, boarding a ship bound for Tarshish. Jonah's initial flight from God's command sets the stage for the events that will follow, and his disobedience mirrors, in some ways, humanity's tendency to flee from God and our need for redemption.

A. Jonah's Rebellion and Humanity's Disobedience

Jonah's decision to flee can be seen as a type of humanity's disobedience to God's commands. Just as Jonah tried to escape God's will, humanity, through sin, has turned away from God. Romans 3:23 reminds us that "all have sinned and fall short of the glory of God." Jonah's flight to Tarshish represents the broader human experience of rebellion against God and the consequences that follow.

II. JONAH IN THE BELLY OF THE FISH: A TYPE OF CHRIST'S DEATH AND BURIAL (JONAH 1:17)

The turning point in Jonah's story comes when he is thrown overboard during a violent storm, and God sends a great fish to swallow him. Jonah's three days in the belly of the fish is a clear type of Christ's death and burial. As Jonah was buried in the depths of the sea, Christ was laid in the tomb. Jesus' reference to Jonah (Matthew 12:40) affirms that this event foreshadowed His own burial after His crucifixion.

A. Jonah's Descent into the Depths and Christ's Burial

Jonah's descent into the sea symbolizes a type of death, surrounded by chaos and judgment. This descent mirrors Christ's burial in the tomb, where He bore the weight of the sins of the world. Jonah's imagery of being engulfed by the sea (Jonah 2:5-6) is reminiscent of Christ's descent into the realm of death on behalf of humanity.

B. Three Days and Three Nights in the Heart of the Earth

Jonah's three days in the fish correspond to Christ's three days in the tomb. This time symbolizes the fullness of death. Jonah was completely engulfed, just as Christ was fully enclosed in the grave. But just as Jonah was delivered after three days, Christ rose from the dead, victorious over death, securing eternal salvation for all who believe in Him.

III. JONAH'S PRAYER OF DELIVERANCE: A PICTURE OF CHRIST'S TRIUMPH OVER DEATH (JONAH 2:1-9)

While in the belly of the fish, Jonah prays a prayer of repentance and thanksgiving, acknowledging God's power to save him. Jonah's prayer reflects his faith in God's deliverance and mirrors Christ's triumph over death.

A. Deliverance from the Grave

Jonah's deliverance from the belly of the fish prefigures Christ's resurrection. Just as Jonah was brought up from the depths of the sea, Christ was raised from the grave, defeating death and offering eternal life to those who trust in Him.

IV. JONAH'S DELIVERANCE FROM THE FISH: A TYPE OF CHRIST'S RESURRECTION (JONAH 2:10)

After three days, God commands the fish to release Jonah, delivering him onto dry land. This moment of deliverance serves as a type of Christ's resurrection. Jonah's emergence from the belly of the fish mirrors Christ's victory over the grave, signifying the new life that comes through resurrection.

V. JONAH'S PREACHING AND THE REPENTANCE OF NINEVEH: A FORESHADOWING OF SALVATION FOR THE GENTILES (JONAH 3)

After being delivered, Jonah goes to Nineveh and preaches a message of repentance. The people of Nineveh respond by turning from their sins, and God shows them mercy. This act foreshadows the extension of salvation to the Gentiles through Christ. Jonah's mission to Nineveh serves as a type of Christ's offer of salvation to all nations.

JONAH AS A TYPE OF CHRIST'S DEATH, BURIAL, AND RESURRECTION

Jonah's story is much more than a dramatic tale of survival. It is a powerful type of Christ's death, burial, and resurrection, as Jesus Himself pointed out in Matthew 12:40. Jonah's three days and nights in the fish prefigured Christ's burial, and his deliverance foreshadowed Christ's resurrection. Through Jonah's story, we are reminded of the depths of God's mercy and the power of salvation. Just as Jonah was delivered from the belly of the fish, so are we delivered from sin and death through Christ's resurrection.

CHAPTER 12: JOSEPH: A TYPE OF CHRIST

The story of **Joseph** is one of the most detailed and dramatic narratives in the book of **Genesis**, spanning **chapters 37-50**. Joseph's life is marked by hardship, betrayal, and suffering, but it is ultimately a story of triumph, forgiveness, and divine purpose. Through all of Joseph's trials, God's hand was at work, orchestrating events that would lead to the **salvation of many lives**. This narrative has long been recognized as a **type** of **Christ**—a prefiguration of Jesus' own life, suffering, betrayal, exaltation, and ultimate mission to save humanity.

In this chapter, we will explore how **Joseph's life** serves as a powerful type of Christ, examining the parallels between the events of Joseph's life and the key elements of Jesus' mission. From being betrayed by his brothers and sold into slavery, to his rise to power in Egypt and his role in saving his family and the nations from famine, Joseph's story provides a **prophetic picture** of the **life and work of Jesus Christ**.

I. JOSEPH'S EARLY LIFE AND FAVOR WITH HIS FATHER (GENESIS 37:1-4)

Joseph's story begins in **Genesis 37**, where we are introduced to him as the **beloved son** of his father **Jacob** (also known as Israel). Joseph was Jacob's favorite son, born to him in his old age by his beloved wife **Rachel**. Because of this special favor, Jacob gave Joseph a **richly ornamented robe** (often referred to as a coat of many colors), a symbol of his love and preference for Joseph over his other sons. This favor, however, led to deep **resentment** and **jealousy** among Joseph's brothers.

A. The Father's Love for the Son: A Type of the Father's Love for Christ

The **special love** that Jacob had for Joseph foreshadows the **unique relationship** between God the Father and His Son, **Jesus Christ**. Just as Joseph was his father's **beloved son**, so too is Jesus the **beloved Son of God**. In **Matthew 3:17**, at Jesus' baptism, a voice from heaven declares, "This is my **beloved Son**, with whom I am well pleased."

The coat of many colors that Jacob gave to Joseph symbolizes the **honor** and **favor** that Joseph had in his father's eyes, much like the **divine glory** that Jesus possesses as the **Son of God**. Joseph's favored status with his father sets the stage for the **conflict** and **betrayal** that would follow, just as Jesus' divine status led to **opposition** and **betrayal** during His earthly ministry.

1. The Beloved Son Rejected

Just as Joseph was loved by his father but **rejected** by his brothers, **Jesus** was also rejected by those He came to save. **John 1:11** says, "He came to His own, and His own people did not receive Him." This theme of rejection runs throughout the gospel narrative, as Jesus, though sinless and sent from the Father, was rejected by the very people He came to redeem.

II. JOSEPH'S DREAMS AND HIS BROTHERS' HATRED (GENESIS 37:5-11)

Joseph's early life is marked by two **prophetic dreams**, in which he envisions his brothers and even his parents bowing down to him. In the first dream, Joseph sees sheaves of grain representing his brothers bowing down to his sheaf. In the second dream, he sees the sun, moon, and eleven stars bowing down to him. These dreams clearly foretold Joseph's future **exaltation** and **leadership**, but they further fueled the **jealousy** and **hatred** of his brothers.

A. Joseph's Dreams: A Foreshadowing of Christ's Exaltation

The **dreams** that Joseph had are a type of **Christ's future exaltation**. Just as Joseph was given a vision of his future rule over his brothers, so too was Jesus given the role of **ruler** and **King of kings**. In **Philippians 2:9-10**, Paul writes, "Therefore God has highly exalted Him and bestowed on Him the name that is above every name, so that at the name of Jesus every knee should bow, in heaven and on earth and under the earth."

Joseph's dreams foretold the **future submission** of his brothers, just as Christ's exaltation will result in the **universal submission** of all creation. However, just as Joseph's dreams were met with **hostility** from his brothers, Jesus' claim to kingship was also met with **opposition** from the religious leaders of His day.

1. The Revelation of Future Glory

Joseph's dreams represent a **revelation** of future glory, both for himself and for Christ. In the case of Joseph, the dreams signified his eventual rise to **power** in Egypt, where he would save his family from famine. In the case of Jesus, His future glory is revealed through His **resurrection** and **ascension**, where He is seated at the right hand of the Father.

2. The Response of Hostility

Joseph's brothers responded to his dreams with **hatred**, much like the religious leaders of Jesus' day responded to His claims with **hostility**. In **John 15:24-25**, Jesus says, "If I had not done among them the works that no one else did, they would not be guilty of sin; but now they have seen and hated both Me and My Father. But the word that is written in their Law must be fulfilled: 'They hated Me without a cause.'"

This parallel highlights the **injustice** and **unwarranted hatred** that both Joseph and Jesus faced as a result of their **divine revelations**.

III. JOSEPH'S BETRAYAL AND SALE INTO SLAVERY (GENESIS 37:12-28)

Joseph's brothers, driven by **jealousy** and **hatred**, conspired to kill him. However, instead of killing him, they threw him into a **pit** and later sold him to a caravan of **Ishmaelite traders** for **twenty pieces of silver**. The traders took Joseph to **Egypt**, where he was sold into **slavery**. This act of betrayal mirrors the **betrayal** of **Christ**, who was sold for **thirty pieces of silver** by one of His own disciples, **Judas Iscariot**.

A. Joseph's Betrayal: A Type of Christ's Betrayal

The betrayal of Joseph by his brothers serves as a **type** of **Christ's betrayal** by Judas. Both Joseph and Jesus were **betrayed** by those closest to them—Joseph by his own brothers, and Jesus by one of His twelve disciples. The act of betrayal in both stories leads to their **suffering** and **humiliation**, but ultimately serves to fulfill God's **sovereign plan** for salvation.

1. Sold for Pieces of Silver

The price for which Joseph was sold—**twenty pieces of silver**—foreshadows the price for which Jesus was betrayed—**thirty pieces of silver**. In both cases, the **betrayal** was motivated by **self-interest** and **greed**. In **Matthew 26:15**, Judas asks the chief priests, "What will you give me if I deliver Him over to you?" And they paid him thirty pieces of silver. This direct parallel underscores the **prophetic nature** of Joseph's story as a type of Christ's betrayal.

2. Stripped of His Robe

Before selling Joseph into slavery, his brothers **stripped him of his robe**, the symbol of his father's favor. This act of stripping Joseph of his robe parallels the **stripping of Christ** during His crucifixion. In **Matthew 27:28**, we read that the Roman soldiers "stripped Him and put a scarlet robe on Him." Just as Joseph's robe was a sign of his father's love, Christ's garment became a symbol of His **humiliation** and **mockery** at the hands of His captors.

IV. JOSEPH'S TIME IN EGYPT: A FORESHADOWING OF CHRIST'S HUMILIATION AND EXALTATION (GENESIS 39-41)

After being sold into slavery, Joseph was taken to Egypt and sold to **Potiphar**, an officer of Pharaoh. Despite his status as a slave, Joseph rose to a position of **trust** in Potiphar's household, but he was soon falsely accused by **Potiphar's wife** and thrown into **prison**. Even in prison, Joseph found favor with the prison warden, and eventually, his ability to **interpret dreams** brought him to the attention of **Pharaoh**.

Joseph's **humiliation** in prison and his subsequent **exaltation** to a position of power in Egypt mirrors the **humiliation** and **exaltation** of **Christ**, who suffered **death** on a cross before being **raised** to glory.

A. Joseph's Suffering and Christ's Suffering

Joseph's time in **prison** represents a period of **suffering** and **injustice**, much like the **suffering** of Christ during His **trial** and **crucifixion**. Both Joseph and Jesus endured **unjust treatment**, yet both trusted in God's sovereign plan for their lives.

1. Falsely Accused

Joseph was falsely accused of attempting to assault Potiphar's wife, just as Jesus was falsely accused of **blasphemy** and of being a threat to the Roman Empire. In both cases, these false accusations led to **unjust punishment**. However, these moments of **injustice** were part of God's **larger plan** to bring about **redemption**.

2. Trusting in God's Plan

Throughout his time in Egypt, Joseph continued to trust in God, even in the midst of his suffering. His faith in God's plan is evident when he interprets Pharaoh's dreams and attributes the ability to do so to God alone. In **Genesis 41:16**, Joseph says, "It is not in me; God will give Pharaoh a favorable answer." This faith in God's plan foreshadows Christ's **obedience** to the Father's will, even unto death. **Philippians 2:8** states, "And being found in human form, He humbled Himself by becoming obedient to the point of death, even death on a cross."

V. JOSEPH'S EXALTATION AND ROLE AS SAVIOR (GENESIS 41:38-57)

After interpreting **Pharaoh's dreams**, which foretold seven years of **plenty** followed by seven years of **famine**, Joseph was **exalted** to a position of power as the **second-in-command** in Egypt. Pharaoh put Joseph in charge of the entire land, and Joseph oversaw the collection and storage of grain during the years of plenty, which enabled Egypt to survive the famine. Joseph's rise to power and his role in saving **many lives** during the famine serves as a type of **Christ's exaltation** and His role as the **Savior** of the world.

A. Joseph as a Type of Christ the Savior

Joseph's role in saving Egypt and the surrounding nations from **famine** is a clear foreshadowing of **Christ's role** as the **Savior** of the world. Just as Joseph was **exalted** after his time of suffering and became the **provider** for those in need, Jesus was **exalted** after His resurrection and became the **source of salvation** for all who believe in Him.

1. Exalted to a Position of Power

Joseph's **exaltation** to a position of power in Egypt parallels Christ's **ascension** to the right hand of the Father. In **Genesis 41:40-41**, Pharaoh says to Joseph, "You shall be over my house, and all my people shall order themselves as you command. Only as regards the throne will I be greater than you." This echoes the exaltation of Christ described in **Philippians 2:9**, where Paul writes, "Therefore God has highly exalted Him and bestowed on Him the name that is above every name."

2. The Bread of Life

Joseph's role in providing **grain** during the famine can be seen as a type of Christ's role as the **Bread of Life**. In **John 6:35**, Jesus declares, "I am the bread of life; whoever comes to Me shall not hunger, and whoever believes in Me shall never thirst." Just as Joseph provided physical sustenance to save lives during the famine, Jesus provides **spiritual sustenance** to save souls from **eternal death**.

VI. JOSEPH'S RECONCILIATION WITH HIS BROTHERS: A PICTURE OF FORGIVENESS AND RESTORATION (GENESIS 45)

After years of separation, Joseph's brothers came to Egypt seeking **grain** during the famine. They did not recognize Joseph at first, but eventually, he revealed his identity to them. Instead of seeking **revenge** for their betrayal, Joseph forgave his brothers and recognized that God had used their evil actions for a **greater purpose**. In **Genesis 45:5**, Joseph says, "And now do not be distressed or angry with yourselves because you sold me here, for God sent me before you to preserve life."

A. Joseph's Forgiveness as a Type of Christ's Forgiveness

Joseph's **forgiveness** of his brothers serves as a powerful type of **Christ's forgiveness** of sinners. Just as Joseph forgave those who had wronged him, Jesus extends **forgiveness** to all who have sinned against Him. On the cross, Jesus prayed for those who crucified Him, saying, "Father, forgive them, for they know not what they do" (**Luke 23:34**).

1. Forgiving Those Who Betrayed Him

Joseph's ability to forgive his brothers mirrors Christ's willingness to forgive **Judas**, **Peter**, and all who have **betrayed** Him through sin. Just as Joseph saw God's **sovereign plan** at work through his betrayal, Jesus understood that His betrayal and crucifixion were part of God's **redemptive plan** for the world.

2. Restoration and Reconciliation

Joseph's reunion with his brothers also represents the **restoration** and **reconciliation** that Christ brings to all who come to Him in faith. Through His death and resurrection, Jesus reconciles sinners to God, restoring the broken relationship caused by sin. **2 Corinthians 5:18** declares, "All this is from God, who through Christ reconciled us to Himself and gave us the ministry of reconciliation."

VII. JOSEPH'S ROLE IN PRESERVING LIFE: A FORESHADOWING OF CHRIST'S ROLE AS THE GIVER OF ETERNAL LIFE (GENESIS 50:19-21)

In the final chapter of Genesis, Joseph reassures his brothers that he has truly forgiven them and that he will continue to provide for them and their families. In **Genesis 50:20**, Joseph famously says, "As for you, you meant evil against me, but God meant it for good, to bring it about that many people should be kept alive, as they are today." This statement highlights the **sovereignty of God** in using Joseph's suffering to bring about **salvation** for many.

A. Joseph's Preservation of Life as a Type of Christ's Gift of Eternal Life

Joseph's role in preserving physical life during the famine is a type of Christ's role in providing **eternal life** through His death and resurrection. Just as Joseph's suffering ultimately led to the salvation of many lives, Christ's suffering on the cross brings **salvation** to all who believe in Him.

1. God's Sovereign Plan

Joseph's statement in **Genesis 50:20** reflects the **sovereign plan of God** in turning **evil** into **good**. This theme is echoed in **Romans 8:28**, which says, "And we know that in all things God works for the good of those who love Him, who have been called according to His purpose." Just as God used Joseph's suffering to save many lives, He used Christ's suffering to bring about the **salvation of the world**.

2. The Giver of Life

Joseph's provision of grain during the famine points to **Christ's role** as the **giver of life**. Through His death and resurrection, Jesus offers **eternal life** to all who believe in Him. **John 10:28** says, "I give them eternal life, and they will never perish, and no one will snatch them out of My hand." Just as Joseph provided for his family and the nations during a time of great need, Jesus provides **eternal life** and **salvation** for all who come to Him in faith.

Fun Fact: Joseph's Name in Egyptian Culture

Interestingly, Joseph was given the Egyptian name **Zaphenath-paneah** by Pharaoh when he was exalted to a position of power in Egypt (**Genesis 41:45**). While the exact meaning of this name is debated, many scholars believe it means "God speaks, and He lives" or "the savior of the world." This title is fitting for Joseph, who acted as a **savior** during the famine, and it also points forward to **Christ**, who is the **true Savior of the world**.

Joseph as a Type of Christ

From the Tabernacle to Solomon's Temple to the Second Temple, the progression of God's dwelling among His people points toward a final and eternal fulfillment in Christ. The tearing of the temple veil at Jesus' crucifixion signifies the end of separation between God and humanity, and the beginning of the Church as the living temple, indwelt by the Spirit.

Solomon's Temple was the physical dwelling place of God among His people, where the Ark of the Covenant resided. As magnificent as it was, it served as a shadow of a greater reality. The destruction of this temple symbolized the passing of the old covenant system, pointing forward to the time when God's presence would dwell fully in Christ, the true Temple. The physical structure of the temple was temporary, but it laid the foundation for the spiritual temple found in Christ.

The Second Temple, rebuilt after the exile, held great significance for the Jewish people. It was the site of Jesus' ministry, and although it lacked the glory of Solomon's Temple, it still foreshadowed a greater fulfillment in Christ. The destruction of the Second Temple, as prophesied by Jesus, marks the end of the old sacrificial system and the transition to a new covenant where God's presence is no longer confined to a building but resides in Christ and His Church. Jesus, the ultimate Temple, fulfills what the Second Temple could only symbolize.

The story of **Joseph** is rich with **typological significance**, offering a powerful foreshadowing of the **life, death, and resurrection of Jesus Christ**. From his betrayal by his brothers to his rise to power and his role in saving many lives, Joseph's life mirrors the **gospel narrative** and points us to the **redemptive work** of Christ. Through Joseph's suffering and exaltation, we see a picture of

Christ's own suffering on the cross and His subsequent **exaltation** as the risen Lord and Savior.

Just as Joseph forgave his brothers and provided for their needs, Jesus offers **forgiveness** and **eternal life** to all who come to Him in faith. Joseph's story reminds us that God's **sovereign plan** is at work even in the midst of suffering and betrayal, and that He can turn **evil** into **good** for the salvation of many.

Ultimately, the story of Joseph points us to the **greater Joseph, Jesus Christ**, who was betrayed, crucified, and exalted, and who now offers salvation to the **world**. Through the lens of **typology**, Joseph's life becomes a **prophetic picture** of the **gospel**, illustrating the profound truth that God's **redemptive purposes** are fulfilled in **Christ**.

CHAPTER 13: THE SACRIFICE OF ISAAC: A TYPE OF CHRIST'S SACRIFICE

The story of **Abraham and Isaac** in **Genesis 22** stands as one of the most profound and poignant moments in the Old Testament. Known as the **Binding of Isaac**, or the **Akedah** in Hebrew, it recounts the moment when God commanded Abraham to offer his beloved son Isaac as a **sacrifice** on Mount Moriah. This act of faith, obedience, and divine intervention serves as a powerful **type** of **Christ's sacrificial death**, pointing toward the moment when God would offer **His only Son, Jesus**, as the ultimate sacrifice for the sins of the world.

In this chapter, we will delve into the details of **Genesis 22**, examining the typological significance of Isaac's near-sacrifice and its parallels to **Christ's crucifixion**. By exploring the themes of **faith**, **sacrifice**, and **redemption**, we will see how Abraham's willingness to offer Isaac foreshadows God's offering of Jesus on the cross. Through the lens of **typology**, the story of Abraham and Isaac reveals profound insights into the nature of **God's love**, the **substitutionary atonement** of Christ, and the ultimate fulfillment of God's plan for the **salvation of humanity**.

I. ABRAHAM'S TEST OF FAITH (GENESIS 22:1-2)

The story begins with God testing Abraham's faith by commanding him to offer his only son, Isaac, as a **burnt offering**. In **Genesis 22:1-2**, God says to Abraham, "Take your son, your only son Isaac, whom you love, and go to the land of Moriah, and offer him there as a burnt offering on one of the mountains of which I shall tell you." This command was both shocking and heartbreaking, as Isaac was the **child of promise**—the son through whom God had promised to fulfill His covenant with Abraham.

A. Isaac as the Beloved Son: A Type of Christ

Isaac's role as the **beloved son** of Abraham foreshadows **Jesus Christ**, the **beloved Son of God**. The language used in Genesis 22 is strikingly similar to the way the New Testament speaks of Jesus as God's beloved Son. In **Matthew 3:17**, at Jesus' baptism, a voice from heaven declares, "This is my **beloved Son**, with whom I am well pleased."

The emphasis on Isaac as Abraham's **only son** also parallels Jesus as God's **only begotten Son**. Although Abraham had another son, Ishmael, Isaac was the son of **promise**—the son through whom God's covenant would be fulfilled. Similarly, Jesus is the **fulfillment** of God's promise to redeem humanity. **John 3:16** declares, "For God so loved the world, that He gave His **only Son**, that whoever believes in Him should not perish but have eternal life."

1. The Promise and the Sacrifice

Isaac's birth was the result of a divine promise, just as Jesus' birth was the fulfillment of God's **promise of salvation**. In both cases, the **beloved son** is offered as a **sacrifice**, highlighting the parallel between Isaac's near-sacrifice and Christ's crucifixion.

2. The Journey to the Place of Sacrifice

Abraham's journey to the **land of Moriah**, where Isaac was to be sacrificed, prefigures **Christ's journey** to the cross. Both Isaac and Jesus traveled willingly to the place of their sacrifice, trusting in their fathers. The journey itself is a symbol of **obedience** and **faith**, as both Isaac and Jesus submitted to their fathers' will, even in the face of death.

II. ABRAHAM'S OBEDIENCE AND FAITH (GENESIS 22:3-6)

In response to God's command, Abraham immediately obeys. He rises early in the morning, saddles his donkey, and takes Isaac and two of his servants on the journey to **Mount Moriah**. The journey lasts for **three days**, during which Abraham's faith is tested as he prepares to offer his son.

A. Abraham's Faith as a Model of Trust in God

Abraham's **faith** in God's promise is central to the story. Despite the fact that God had promised to make a great nation through Isaac, Abraham trusted that God would somehow **provide** a solution. **Hebrews 11:17-19** offers insight into Abraham's mindset, explaining that Abraham believed that God could even **raise Isaac from the dead** if necessary: "By faith Abraham, when he was tested, offered up Isaac... He considered that God was able even to raise him from the dead, from which, figuratively speaking, he did receive him back."

This **resurrection motif** foreshadows Christ's own death and resurrection. Just as Abraham believed that Isaac could be raised from the dead, so too did **Jesus rise** from the dead after three days in the tomb. The **three-day journey** to Mount Moriah mirrors the **three days** that Jesus spent in the grave before His resurrection.

1. The Willingness to Sacrifice

Abraham's willingness to offer Isaac as a sacrifice prefigures God's willingness to offer His own Son, Jesus, as a **sacrifice for sin**. In both cases, the father is called to **give up** his beloved son, highlighting the **cost** of redemption. This act of obedience and faith reveals the depth of God's love for humanity, as He was willing to sacrifice His own Son for the salvation of the world.

2. Trusting in God's Provision

As Abraham and Isaac journeyed to Mount Moriah, Abraham trusted that God would somehow provide a **substitute** for Isaac. This foreshadows the **substitutionary atonement** of Christ, where Jesus becomes the **Lamb of God**, offered in our place. **Genesis 22:8** records Abraham's response to Isaac's question about the sacrifice: "God will provide for Himself the lamb for a burnt offering, my son." This statement is prophetic, pointing to the ultimate provision of Jesus as the Lamb of God who takes away the sins of the world (**John 1:29**).

III. THE SACRIFICIAL ACT: ISAAC AS A WILLING PARTICIPANT (GENESIS 22:6-10)

When Abraham and Isaac reach the appointed place on Mount Moriah, Abraham builds an altar, arranges the wood, and binds Isaac to the altar. The text is silent about any **resistance** from Isaac, suggesting that he willingly submitted to his father's will, just as **Jesus** willingly submitted to the will of His Father.

A. Isaac's Willingness: A Type of Christ's Obedience

Isaac's **willing submission** to his father's will prefigures **Christ's obedience** to the Father. In **Philippians 2:8**, Paul writes, "And being found in human form, He humbled Himself by becoming **obedient to the point of death**, even death on a cross." Just as Isaac trusted his father and allowed himself to be bound and placed on the altar, so too did Jesus trust His Father's will and willingly went to the cross.

1. The Silent Lamb

Isaac's silence throughout the sacrificial act is reminiscent of the **prophetic description** of the suffering servant in **Isaiah 53:7**: "He was oppressed, and He was afflicted, yet He opened not His mouth; like a lamb that is led to the slaughter, and like a sheep that before its shearers is silent, so He opened not His mouth." This description of the **Messiah** as a silent lamb points directly to **Jesus' silent suffering** during His trial and crucifixion, and Isaac's quiet submission to Abraham prefigures this.

2. The Binding of Isaac and the Cross

Isaac's **binding** to the altar can be seen as a type of **Christ's crucifixion**. Just as Isaac was bound to the wood of the altar, Jesus was bound to the **wood of the cross**. The image of Isaac being laid on the altar foreshadows Christ's ultimate sacrifice, where He was nailed to the cross and offered as the **atoning sacrifice** for sin.

IV. Divine Intervention: The Ram as a Substitute (Genesis 22:11-14)

As Abraham raises the knife to sacrifice his son, the **Angel of the Lord** calls out to him and stops him from carrying out the act. God then provides a **ram** caught in a thicket by its horns, which Abraham sacrifices in place of Isaac. This moment of divine intervention is key to understanding the **substitutionary nature** of the atonement.

A. The Ram as a Substitute: A Type of Christ's Sacrifice

The **ram** that is provided as a substitute for Isaac is a powerful **type of Christ**. Just as the ram took Isaac's place on the altar, **Jesus** takes our place on the cross. **Isaiah 53:5** declares, "But He was pierced for our transgressions; He was crushed for our iniquities; upon Him was the chastisement that brought us peace, and with His wounds we are healed." Jesus is the **substitute**, the one who bears the **penalty** for our sins, just as the ram bore the penalty in place of Isaac.

1. God's Provision of the Lamb

The ram caught in the thicket represents **God's provision** of a **sacrificial substitute**. Abraham had earlier declared that God would provide the lamb, and here we see that provision fulfilled in the form of the ram. This points forward to **Jesus Christ**, the **Lamb of God**, who is provided by God as the ultimate sacrifice for sin. **John 1:29** records John the Baptist's proclamation: "Behold, the Lamb of God, who takes away the sin of the world!"

2. The Doctrine of Substitutionary Atonement

The concept of **substitutionary atonement** is central to the Christian understanding of **Christ's sacrifice**. Just as the ram was sacrificed in Isaac's place, **Jesus** was sacrificed in our place. **2 Corinthians 5:21** explains, "For our sake He made Him to be sin who knew no sin, so that in Him we might become the righteousness of God." Through His death, Jesus bears the **penalty of sin** on behalf of humanity, allowing us to be reconciled to God.

V. THE SIGNIFICANCE OF MOUNT MORIAH: A FORESHADOWING OF CALVARY (GENESIS 22:14)

After the sacrifice of the ram, Abraham names the place **Jehovah Jireh**, meaning "The Lord will provide." This location, Mount Moriah, is significant because it is traditionally believed to be the same location where **Jerusalem** would later be built and where **Calvary**, the site of Christ's crucifixion, would stand.

A. Mount Moriah as a Type of Calvary

Mount Moriah, the place where Abraham was willing to offer his son Isaac, is often seen as a **type** of **Calvary**, the place where God offered His Son, Jesus. Just as Abraham was willing to offer Isaac on Mount Moriah, God the Father offered His Son on the cross at **Calvary**. The **geographical and theological connection** between these two events highlights the continuity of **God's redemptive plan** from the Old Testament to the New Testament.

1. The Lamb Provided on the Same Mountain

The traditional identification of Mount Moriah as the future site of **Jerusalem** and **Calvary** suggests that the **Lamb of God**—Jesus—was provided on the very same mountain where God provided the ram for Abraham. This connection emphasizes the **prophetic significance** of the sacrifice of Isaac as a **foreshadowing** of Christ's sacrifice.

2. The Ultimate Fulfillment of God's Promise

When Abraham names the place "The Lord will provide," it not only refers to the immediate provision of the ram but also to the **future provision** of Christ as the **Savior of the world**. God's promise to provide a substitute reaches its **ultimate fulfillment** in Jesus, the **Lamb of God**, who is sacrificed on **Calvary** for the sins of humanity.

VI. THE BLESSING OF ABRAHAM'S OBEDIENCE (GENESIS 22:15-18)

After the near-sacrifice of Isaac, God reaffirms His **covenant promises** to Abraham, declaring that because of Abraham's obedience, He will bless him and make his descendants as numerous as the stars in the sky and the sand on the seashore. This blessing, however, extends beyond Abraham's immediate family and points to the **Messianic fulfillment** in Christ.

A. The Blessing Through Isaac: A Type of Christ's Blessing to All Nations

The blessing that God promises through Isaac foreshadows the **blessing of salvation** that comes through **Jesus Christ**. In **Genesis 22:18**, God tells Abraham, "And in your offspring shall all the nations of the earth be blessed, because you have obeyed my voice." This promise finds its ultimate fulfillment in Christ, the **offspring of Abraham**, through whom the **blessing of salvation** is extended to **all nations**.

1. The Fulfillment in Christ

The **Apostle Paul** makes this connection clear in **Galatians 3:16**, where he writes, "Now the promises were made to Abraham and to his offspring. It does not say, 'And to offsprings,' referring to many, but referring to one, 'And to your offspring,' who is Christ." Jesus is the promised **offspring** through whom the blessings of God's covenant are realized, not just for the descendants of Abraham, but for all who come to faith in Christ.

2. The Blessing of Salvation to All Nations

Through Jesus, the **blessing of salvation** is extended to **all nations**, fulfilling the promise made to Abraham in **Genesis 12:3**: "In you all the families of the earth shall be blessed." The sacrifice of Christ on the cross brings the **blessing of forgiveness** and **eternal life** to all who believe, regardless of their nationality or background.

VII. ISAAC AS A TYPE OF CHRIST'S RESURRECTION (HEBREWS 11:17-19)

Although Isaac was not actually sacrificed, the **Apostle Paul** in **Hebrews 11:17-19** describes the event as a **type** of **resurrection**. Paul writes, "By faith Abraham, when he was tested, offered up Isaac... He considered that God was able even to raise him from the dead, from which, figuratively speaking, he did receive him back."

A. Isaac's Near-Sacrifice as a Picture of Christ's Death and Resurrection

Isaac's near-sacrifice and subsequent **deliverance** serve as a type of **Christ's death and resurrection**. Just as Isaac was figuratively raised from the dead when God intervened, **Jesus** was literally raised from the dead after His crucifixion. The **resurrection of Christ** is the cornerstone of the Christian faith, and Isaac's deliverance points toward the **victory over death** that Jesus achieved through His resurrection.

1. The Foreshadowing of Resurrection

Isaac's deliverance from death prefigures the **resurrection** of Christ, showing that God has power over life and death. Through Jesus' resurrection, believers are given the **hope of eternal life**. **Romans 6:4** declares, "We were buried therefore with Him by baptism into death, in order that, just as Christ was raised from the dead by the glory of the Father, we too might walk in newness of life."

2. The Hope of Resurrection for Believers

The story of Isaac points forward to the **resurrection hope** that all believers have in Christ. Just as Isaac was spared from death and figuratively received back from the dead, Christians have the promise of **eternal life** through Christ's resurrection. **1 Corinthians 15:20** declares, "But in fact Christ has been raised from the dead, the firstfruits of those who have fallen asleep." Through Christ, death is **defeated**, and eternal life is offered to all who believe.

Fun Fact: The Ram's Horn and the Shofar

One interesting detail in the story of the **Binding of Isaac** is the ram caught by its **horns** in the thicket. In Jewish tradition, the **ram's horn** became the basis for the **shofar**, a musical instrument made from a ram's horn that is used in Jewish religious ceremonies, particularly during **Rosh Hashanah** (the Jewish New Year) and **Yom Kippur** (the Day of Atonement). The shofar's sound is a call to **repentance** and a reminder of God's provision and mercy, much like the ram provided in place of Isaac.

The Sacrifice of Isaac as a Type of Christ's Sacrifice

From the Tabernacle to Solomon's Temple to the Second Temple, the progression of God's dwelling among His people points toward a final and eternal fulfillment in Christ. The tearing of the temple veil at Jesus' crucifixion signifies the end of separation between God and humanity, and the beginning of the Church as the living temple, indwelt by the Spirit.

Solomon's Temple was the physical dwelling place of God among His people, where the Ark of the Covenant resided. As magnificent as it was, it served as a shadow of a greater reality. The destruction of this temple symbolized the passing of the old covenant system, pointing forward to the time when God's presence would dwell fully in Christ, the true Temple. The physical structure of the temple was temporary, but it laid the foundation for the spiritual temple found in Christ.

The Second Temple, rebuilt after the exile, held great significance for the Jewish people. It was the site of Jesus' ministry, and although it lacked the glory of Solomon's Temple, it still foreshadowed a greater fulfillment in Christ. The destruction of the Second Temple, as prophesied by Jesus, marks the end of the old sacrificial system and the transition to a new covenant where God's presence is no longer confined to a building but resides in Christ and His Church. Jesus, the ultimate Temple, fulfills what the Second Temple could only symbolize.

    The story of **Abraham and Isaac** in **Genesis 22** is one of the most powerful and significant **types** of **Christ's sacrifice** in the Old Testament. Through the lens of typology, Isaac's near-sacrifice foreshadows the **death, burial, and resurrection** of **Jesus Christ**, the **Lamb of God** who takes away the sin of the world. Abraham's faith, Isaac's willingness, and God's provision of the ram all point to the **greater sacrifice** that would come through **Jesus**, the **beloved Son** of God.

    In both stories, we see the themes of **faith, obedience**, and **sacrifice** intertwined with God's **redemptive plan**. Just as Abraham was willing to offer his son, God was willing to offer His Son for the **salvation of humanity**. Just as Isaac was spared through the provision of a substitute, we are spared from the penalty of sin through **Christ's substitutionary atonement**.

    The story of Isaac's near-sacrifice also points forward to the **hope of resurrection**, as Isaac was figuratively raised from the dead when God intervened. This points to the **literal resurrection** of Christ, who conquered death and offers eternal life to all who believe in Him. Through Isaac's story, we are reminded of the **depth of God's love**, the **cost of redemption**, and the **hope of resurrection** that we have in Jesus Christ, the **greater Isaac**, who was offered once for all as the perfect sacrifice for sin.

CHAPTER 14: THE SABBATH: A TYPE OF THE ETERNAL REST IN CHRIST

Just as the Sabbath prefigures the eternal rest believers will experience in Christ, Solomon's Temple—dedicated as a house of peace and rest—served as a shadow of the true rest found in Jesus. The temple, in its grandeur, was not an end but pointed toward the greater temple, Christ, in whom we find perfect rest.

Solomon's Temple was the physical dwelling place of God among His people, where the Ark of the Covenant resided. As magnificent as it was, it served as a shadow of a greater reality. The destruction of this temple symbolized the passing of the old covenant system, pointing forward to the time when God's presence would dwell fully in Christ, the true Temple. The physical structure of the temple was temporary, but it laid the foundation for the spiritual temple found in Christ.

The **Sabbath** has been one of the most profound and enduring institutions in biblical history. First established at the culmination of **creation**, the Sabbath is introduced as the **seventh day** on which God **rested** after His work. More than just a day of rest, the Sabbath stands as a **type** of the **eternal rest** that believers enter through their faith in **Christ**. The Sabbath offers deep spiritual significance, symbolizing not only **physical cessation** from labor but also **spiritual peace** and **completion** through Christ's redemptive work.

In this chapter, we will explore the Sabbath as a **type** of the **eternal rest** that believers find in Jesus, delving into its theological roots, its significance in both the **Old** and **New Testaments**, and how it points forward to the **eternal rest** that awaits in the **kingdom of God**. By understanding the Sabbath in light of **Christ's work**, we can appreciate its profound meaning and its invitation to enter into a **relationship** of trust and **spiritual peace** with God.

I. THE ESTABLISHMENT OF THE SABBATH IN CREATION (GENESIS 2:2-3)

The origin of the Sabbath is found in the **creation account** in **Genesis 1-2**. After six days of creation, where God brought forth the heavens, the earth, and all living things, **Genesis 2:2-3** tells us that on the **seventh day**, God finished His work and **rested**: "And on the seventh day God finished His work that He had done, and He rested on the seventh day from all His work that He had done. So God blessed the seventh day and made it holy, because on it God rested from all His work that He had done in creation."

A. God's Rest: A Foreshadowing of Eternal Rest

God's **rest** on the seventh day serves as a **foreshadowing** of the **eternal rest** that believers will one day experience in **Christ**. It is important to note that God did not rest because He was tired, for God is omnipotent and never grows weary (**Isaiah 40:28**). Instead, God's rest symbolizes the **completion** of His creative work and His **satisfaction** in what He had made.

1. The Sabbath as a Symbol of Completion

The Sabbath rest signifies that **creation was finished**. Everything that needed to be done had been completed, and God looked upon His creation and declared it "very good" (**Genesis 1:31**). This idea of **completion** foreshadows the work of **Christ**, who, through His death and resurrection, brought the work of **salvation** to its full and final completion. On the cross, Jesus proclaimed, "**It is finished**" (**John 19:30**), signaling that the work of redeeming humanity from sin had been fully accomplished. Just as God rested on the seventh day after completing creation, Christ **entered His rest** after completing the work of **redemption**.

2. The Blessing and Sanctification of the Seventh Day

The fact that God **blessed** and **sanctified** the seventh day sets it apart as **holy**. In doing so, God established the Sabbath as a **sign** of His **covenant** with His people. This sanctification points forward to the **eternal rest** that believers will enjoy in Christ. **Hebrews 4:9-10** speaks of this rest: "So then, there remains a **Sabbath rest** for the people of God, for whoever has entered God's rest has also rested from his works as God did from His."

II. THE SABBATH COMMANDMENT IN THE MOSAIC LAW (EXODUS 20:8-11)

The Sabbath was later incorporated into the **Mosaic Law** as one of the **Ten Commandments**, which God gave to Israel through Moses at Mount Sinai. **Exodus 20:8-11** lays out the fourth commandment, which instructs the Israelites to remember the Sabbath day and to keep it holy: "Remember the Sabbath day, to keep it holy. Six days you shall labor, and do all your work, but the seventh day is a Sabbath to the Lord your God. On it you shall not do any work."

A. The Purpose of the Sabbath in the Law

In the Mosaic Law, the Sabbath was given as a **day of rest** for the people of Israel. It was a time for them to cease from their labors and to focus on **worship** and **fellowship** with God. The Sabbath served as a **weekly reminder** of God's **creative power** and His **covenant faithfulness** to His people.

1. The Sabbath as a Sign of the Covenant

In **Exodus 31:13**, God declares that the Sabbath is a **sign** between Him and the people of Israel: "You are to speak to the people of Israel and say, 'Above all you shall keep My Sabbaths, for this is a **sign** between Me and you throughout your generations, that you may know that I, the Lord, sanctify you.'" The Sabbath was a **marker** of Israel's identity as God's chosen people, set apart to worship and serve Him.

2. The Sabbath as a Day of Rest and Renewal

The Sabbath was intended to be a day of **physical rest** and **spiritual renewal**. By resting from their work, the Israelites were reminded of their **dependence** on God, who provides for their needs. The Sabbath was a time to reflect on God's **goodness**, **faithfulness**, and **provision**, pointing forward to the **eternal rest** that God would one day provide through **Christ**.

III. THE SABBATH AS A TYPE OF ETERNAL REST IN CHRIST (HEBREWS 4:1-10)

The **New Testament** reveals the deeper spiritual significance of the Sabbath, showing that it is a **type** of the **eternal rest** that believers enter through **faith in Christ**. In **Hebrews 4:1-10**, the author explains that the rest God promised His people is not merely a physical rest but a **spiritual rest** that comes through faith in **Jesus Christ**.

A. Entering God's Rest Through Faith in Christ

The book of **Hebrews** draws a parallel between the **rest** that the Israelites were promised in the **Promised Land** and the **spiritual rest** that believers enter through faith in **Christ**. Just as the Israelites were called to enter the Promised Land, which was described as a place of **rest** from their wanderings, Christians are called to enter into the **spiritual rest** that Christ provides.

1. The Failure of the Israelites to Enter God's Rest

In **Hebrews 4:2**, the author warns that the Israelites failed to enter God's rest because of their **disobedience** and lack of faith: "For good news came to us just as to them, but the message they heard did not benefit them, because they were not united by faith with those who listened." The **rest** that God had promised them in the **Promised Land** was a **shadow** of the greater rest that would come through

Christ. Their failure to enter that rest points to the need for **faith** and **obedience** in order to experience the rest that God offers.

2. The Sabbath Rest for the People of God

In **Hebrews 4:9-10**, the author concludes that there remains a **Sabbath rest** for the people of God: "So then, there remains a Sabbath rest for the people of God, for whoever has entered God's rest has also rested from his works as God did from His." This Sabbath rest is not merely about ceasing from physical labor but about **ceasing from striving** to achieve salvation through human effort. It is the **rest of grace**, where believers rely on the finished work of Christ for their **salvation** and find **peace** in His presence.

IV. JESUS AS THE LORD OF THE SABBATH (MATTHEW 12:1-8)

In the **Gospels**, Jesus makes a bold statement about His authority over the Sabbath. In **Matthew 12:1-8**, when the Pharisees accuse Jesus' disciples of breaking the Sabbath by picking grain, Jesus responds by declaring that He is the **Lord of the Sabbath**: "For the Son of Man is Lord of the Sabbath" (**Matthew 12:8**).

A. Jesus Fulfills the Sabbath

By declaring Himself the **Lord of the Sabbath**, Jesus is revealing that He is the **fulfillment** of the Sabbath's true meaning. The Sabbath was always meant to point to the **rest** that would come through Jesus. As the Lord of the Sabbath, Jesus brings **spiritual rest** to all who come to Him in faith. He fulfills the **Sabbath law** by providing the ultimate rest that the Sabbath symbolized.

1. Rest in Christ

In **Matthew 11:28-30**, Jesus invites all who are weary to come to Him and find rest: "Come to Me, all who labor and are heavy laden, and I will give you rest. Take My yoke upon you, and learn from Me, for I am gentle and lowly in heart, and you will find rest for your souls." This **rest** that Jesus offers is not merely a rest from physical labor but a **deep spiritual rest**—a rest from the burdens of **sin, guilt,** and **self-righteousness**. It is an invitation to **trust** in Him and find peace in His **finished work** on the cross.

2. The End of Striving

Through His death and resurrection, Jesus has accomplished everything needed for our **salvation**. As believers, we no longer need to strive to earn God's favor through works or rituals. The Sabbath, in this sense, becomes a symbol of **ceasing from works** and resting in the **grace of God. Hebrews 4:10** explains that just as God rested from His works, so too do believers rest from their own works, trusting in what Christ has done.

V. THE ESCHATOLOGICAL FULFILLMENT OF THE SABBATH: ETERNAL REST IN THE NEW CREATION

The ultimate fulfillment of the Sabbath is found in the **eternal rest** that believers will experience in the **new creation**. Just as God rested on the seventh day after completing His work of creation, believers will enter into **eternal rest** after the completion of their **earthly journey**.

A. The New Heavens and the New Earth as the Eternal Sabbath

The **Sabbath rest** that remains for the people of God points to the future reality of the **new heavens** and the **new earth**, where believers will enjoy **eternal rest** in the presence of God. **Revelation 21:1-4** describes the new creation, where there will be no more death, mourning, crying, or pain, for the old order of things has passed away. This is the **ultimate Sabbath rest**—a place of perfect peace, joy, and **communion** with God.

1. The Restoration of Creation

In the new creation, the **restoration** of all things will be complete, and believers will experience the **fullness** of God's presence. Just as God rested after His work of creation, we too will enter into a **state of rest**, free from the burdens of **sin, suffering**, and **death**. The new creation represents the **culmination** of God's redemptive plan and the fulfillment of the Sabbath's promise of **rest**.

2. Eternal Fellowship with God

The eternal rest that believers will experience is more than just the cessation of labor—it is the beginning of an **eternal fellowship** with God. In **Revelation 22:3-4**, we read that the people of God will serve Him and see His face, and His name will be on their foreheads. This is the **ultimate rest**, where believers will enjoy **unbroken communion** with God forever.

VI. THE SABBATH AS A FORETASTE OF HEAVEN

In this life, the **Sabbath** serves as a **foretaste** of the **eternal rest** that awaits believers in the **kingdom of God**. Each week, as we set aside time to rest and worship, we are reminded of the **greater rest** that is to come. The Sabbath is a **gift** from God, designed to help us remember His **faithfulness, provision**, and the **hope** of eternal life.

A. The Weekly Sabbath as a Spiritual Practice

The practice of observing the **Sabbath** serves as a reminder of our **dependence** on God and our need for **spiritual renewal**. By ceasing from our labors and focusing on **worship**, we are reminded of the **finished work** of Christ and the **rest** that He offers. The Sabbath is a time to reflect on God's **goodness** and to anticipate the **eternal rest** that awaits in the **new creation**.

1. A Day of Worship and Reflection

For Christians, the Sabbath can be seen as a day to **worship** God, **reflect** on His Word, and experience the **refreshment** that comes from His presence. In the midst of the busyness of life, the Sabbath offers an opportunity to **pause** and remember that our ultimate hope is in **Christ**.

2. The Sabbath as a Witness to the World

In a world that often values **productivity** and **achievement** above all else, the practice of observing the Sabbath can serve as a **witness** to the world of the **peace** and **rest** that comes from trusting in God. By setting aside time for rest and worship, Christians bear witness to the fact that **true rest** is found in **Christ alone**.

VII. THE SABBATH AND THE RESURRECTION: A NEW DAY OF REST

For Christians, the **resurrection of Jesus** on the **first day of the week** marked the beginning of a **new creation** and a **new day of rest**. While the Jewish Sabbath was observed on the **seventh day** (Saturday), the early Christians began to gather for worship on the **first day of the week** (Sunday) in honor of Christ's resurrection.

A. The Lord's Day: A New Sabbath Rest

The **Lord's Day** (Sunday) became the day of Christian worship and rest, symbolizing the **new creation** that began with Christ's resurrection. **Revelation 1:10** refers to **Sunday** as the "Lord's Day," and from the early church onward, it became the primary day of Christian worship and **celebration** of Christ's victory over sin and death.

1. A Day of Resurrection Celebration

By gathering on the **Lord's Day**, Christians celebrate the **resurrection** of Christ and the **rest** that He provides. Just as the **Sabbath** commemorates God's rest after creation, the **Lord's Day** commemorates Christ's **rest** after His work of redemption.

2. The New Creation and the Eternal Rest

The shift from the seventh day (Saturday) to the first day (Sunday) also reflects the reality that the **new creation** has begun in Christ. Believers now live in the **already but not yet** tension of the **kingdom of God**. While we await the fullness of God's kingdom in the **new heavens and the new earth**, we experience the **firstfruits** of that eternal rest each time we gather to worship on the **Lord's Day**.

Fun Fact: The Significance of the Number Seven in Scripture

The **number seven** is often associated with **completion** and **perfection** in Scripture. The seven days of creation culminate in the Sabbath, which symbolizes **completion** and **rest**. Interestingly, the number seven appears frequently throughout the Bible, particularly in the **book of Revelation**, where it is used to signify the **completeness** of God's work. For example, there are seven churches, seven seals, seven trumpets, and seven bowls of judgment. The **Sabbath**, as the **seventh day**, points to the **complete rest** that believers will experience in the **eternal kingdom**.

The Sabbath as a Type of Eternal Rest in Christ

From the Tabernacle to Solomon's Temple to the Second Temple, the progression of God's dwelling among His people points toward a final and eternal fulfillment in Christ. The tearing of the temple veil at Jesus' crucifixion signifies the end of separation between God and humanity, and the beginning of the Church as the living temple, indwelt by the Spirit.

Solomon's Temple was the physical dwelling place of God among His people, where the Ark of the Covenant resided. As magnificent as it was, it served as a shadow of a greater reality. The destruction of this temple symbolized the passing of the old covenant system, pointing forward to the time when God's presence would dwell fully in Christ, the true Temple. The physical structure of the temple was temporary, but it laid the foundation for the spiritual temple found in Christ.

The Second Temple, rebuilt after the exile, held great significance for the Jewish people. It was the site of Jesus' ministry, and although it lacked the glory of Solomon's Temple, it still foreshadowed a greater fulfillment in Christ. The destruction of the Second Temple, as prophesied by Jesus, marks the end of the old sacrificial system and the transition to a new covenant where God's presence is no longer confined to a building but resides in Christ and His Church. Jesus, the ultimate Temple, fulfills what the Second Temple could only symbolize.

The **Sabbath** is much more than just a day of rest—it is a profound **type** of the **eternal rest** that believers enter through **faith in Christ**. From its establishment at creation to its fulfillment in Christ, the Sabbath points to the **completion** of God's redemptive work and the **spiritual rest** that is found in Him. Through the lens of **typology**, we see that the Sabbath serves as a **shadow** of the **greater reality** of eternal rest that awaits believers in the **new creation**.

As we reflect on the meaning of the Sabbath, we are reminded of the **peace** and **rest** that Christ offers to all who come to Him in faith. Just as God rested on the seventh day after completing His work of creation, we are invited to **cease from our striving** and find **rest in Christ**, trusting in His **finished work** on the cross.

The **eternal Sabbath** that awaits believers in the **new heavens** and the **new earth** is a time of **perfect fellowship** with God, where we will experience **unbroken communion** with Him and enjoy the fullness of His **presence** forever. Until that day, the **weekly Sabbath** serves as a **foretaste** of the **eternal rest** that is to come—a reminder of God's faithfulness, provision, and the **hope of eternal life** in His kingdom.

In Christ, we find **rest for our souls**, for He is the **Lord of the Sabbath**, and through Him, we enter into the **eternal rest** that God has prepared for His people.

CHAPTER 15: MELCHIZEDEK: A TYPE OF CHRIST'S ETERNAL PRIESTHOOD

The figure of **Melchizedek** emerges mysteriously in the biblical narrative, appearing only briefly in **Genesis 14:18-20**, yet his significance spans the entire biblical canon, culminating in the **book of Hebrews**, where he is recognized as a **type** of **Christ's eternal priesthood**. Melchizedek, whose name means "King of Righteousness" and who is also identified as the **King of Salem** (a word meaning peace), holds the dual office of **king** and **priest**—a role that foreshadows the **Messianic work** of Jesus Christ. Without a recorded genealogy, beginning, or end, Melchizedek symbolizes an **eternal priesthood**, pointing to the eternal nature of Christ's **kingship** and **priesthood**.

This chapter will explore the biblical account of **Melchizedek** and the rich typological connection to **Christ**, focusing on the implications of Jesus' role as the **eternal High Priest**. We will delve into the theological significance of the **order of Melchizedek** and examine how it transcends the **Levitical priesthood**, establishing Jesus as the **supreme** and **eternal mediator** between God and humanity. By understanding the typology of Melchizedek, we gain deeper insights into Christ's unique and enduring role as both **King** and **Priest**.

I. THE MYSTERIOUS INTRODUCTION OF MELCHIZEDEK (GENESIS 14:18-20)

The first appearance of **Melchizedek** occurs in **Genesis 14**, following Abraham's victory over a coalition of kings. After Abraham rescues his nephew **Lot** and defeats the invading forces, he is met by **Melchizedek**, who brings bread and wine and offers a blessing over Abraham. **Genesis 14:18-20** records:

"And Melchizedek king of Salem brought out bread and wine. (He was priest of God Most High.) And he blessed him and said, 'Blessed be Abram by God Most High, Possessor of heaven and earth; and blessed be God Most High, who has delivered your enemies into your hand!' And Abram gave him a tenth of everything."

A. The Priest-King of Salem: A Dual Role

Melchizedek is identified as both the **King of Salem** and a **priest of God Most High**. This combination of roles—**king** and **priest**—is significant because in ancient Israel, the offices of king and priest were usually separate. However, Melchizedek holds both offices, prefiguring the **Messianic role** of **Christ**, who is also both **King** and **High Priest**.

1. King of Salem: A Foreshadowing of Christ's Kingship

As the King of **Salem** (which many scholars identify as an ancient name for **Jerusalem**), Melchizedek's reign points to Christ's future reign as the **King of Kings** and **Prince of Peace**. The name "Salem" comes from the Hebrew root **shalom**, meaning peace. Just as Melchizedek was the King of Salem (peace), Jesus is the true **King of Peace** who brings reconciliation between God and humanity.

2. Priest of God Most High: A Foreshadowing of Christ's Priesthood

Melchizedek's priesthood is unique because it predates the establishment of the **Levitical priesthood** by several centuries. He is described as a "priest of God Most High" (in Hebrew, **El Elyon**), a title that emphasizes the **universality** of his priesthood. Melchizedek is not limited to serving a particular nation or people; his priesthood serves the **Most High God**, foreshadowing Christ's universal priesthood, which extends to **all nations** and **all people**.

II. THE SIGNIFICANCE OF MELCHIZEDEK'S GENEALOGY (HEBREWS 7:1-3)

One of the most remarkable features of Melchizedek's appearance in **Genesis 14** is the absence of any mention of his **genealogy**. Unlike other priests or kings in the Bible, who are identified by their lineage, Melchizedek appears without any recorded **beginning** or **end**. This absence of genealogy is later emphasized in the **book of Hebrews**, where Melchizedek is described as "without father or mother or genealogy, having neither beginning of days nor end of life" (**Hebrews 7:3**).

A. Melchizedek's Timelessness: A Type of Christ's Eternal Priesthood

The lack of recorded genealogy for Melchizedek serves as a **type** of the **eternal priesthood** of Christ. Just as Melchizedek's priesthood is not tied to a specific **ancestry** or **lineage**, Christ's priesthood is not based on the **Levitical** order, which required priests to be descended from **Aaron**. Instead, Christ's priesthood is based on the **order of Melchizedek**, an eternal and **superior priesthood** that transcends the limitations of human lineage.

1. Christ's Eternal Nature

The description of Melchizedek as "without beginning of days or end of life" points directly to Christ's **eternality**. Jesus, as the **Son of God**, is **eternal**, without beginning or end. In **Revelation 1:8**, Jesus declares, "I am the Alpha and the Omega, the beginning and the end." This eternal nature is critical to understanding Christ's role as the **eternal High Priest**, who offers a sacrifice that is once for all and never needs to be repeated.

2. A Priesthood Not Based on Genealogy

Unlike the Levitical priests, whose authority was based on their descent from Aaron, Christ's priesthood is based on the **power**

of an indestructible life (Hebrews 7:16). This is why the author of Hebrews emphasizes that Christ is a priest **forever**, in the **order of Melchizedek (Hebrews 7:17)**. Melchizedek's lack of genealogy foreshadows Christ's superior priesthood, which is eternal and not subject to the limitations of human ancestry.

III. THE BLESSING OF ABRAHAM (GENESIS 14:19-20)

One of the key elements of Melchizedek's encounter with Abraham is the **blessing** that he offers. Melchizedek blesses both Abraham and **God Most High**, acknowledging that it was God who delivered Abraham's enemies into his hand. In return, Abraham gives Melchizedek a **tenth of everything** (a **tithe**), signifying Abraham's recognition of Melchizedek's authority and his role as a **priest**.

A. The Greater Blessing the Lesser: A Type of Christ's Superiority

In **Hebrews 7:7**, the author makes a theological point about this blessing: "It is beyond dispute that the inferior is blessed by the superior." The fact that Melchizedek blessed Abraham indicates that Melchizedek held a **superior position** to Abraham, the father of the nation of Israel. This superiority points to the **superior priesthood** of **Christ**, who, like Melchizedek, is greater than Abraham and the Levitical priesthood that descended from him.

1. The Blessing of God's Covenant

Melchizedek's blessing of Abraham foreshadows the **blessing** that comes through Christ, who is the **mediator** of the **New Covenant**. Just as Melchizedek blessed Abraham in acknowledgment of God's victory, Christ blesses all believers through His **sacrifice**, securing their **victory** over sin and death. The **New Covenant** in Christ's blood brings the ultimate blessing of **eternal life** and **reconciliation** with God.

2. Abraham's Response of Worship

Abraham's response to Melchizedek's blessing—giving a **tithe** of everything—represents an act of **worship** and **acknowledgment** of God's provision. This mirrors the response of believers to Christ's priesthood. As our **High Priest**, Christ intercedes on our behalf and offers the ultimate sacrifice for our sins. In return, we are called to offer our lives as a **living sacrifice**, holy and pleasing to God (**Romans 12:1**).

IV. MELCHIZEDEK AND THE LEVITICAL PRIESTHOOD (HEBREWS 7:4-10)

The **book of Hebrews** elaborates on the significance of Melchizedek's priesthood, particularly in comparison to the **Levitical priesthood**. The Levitical priests, who descended from **Levi**, were responsible for offering sacrifices on behalf of the people of Israel. However, their priesthood was **limited** by death, and their sacrifices had to be offered **repeatedly**.

In contrast, the **Melchizedekian priesthood**, as described in **Hebrews 7**, is **eternal** and **superior** to the Levitical priesthood. The author of Hebrews points out that even **Levi**, through Abraham, paid a **tithe** to Melchizedek, demonstrating Melchizedek's superiority over the Levitical order.

A. The Superiority of the Melchizedekian Priesthood

The argument made in **Hebrews 7:4-10** is that Melchizedek is **greater** than the Levitical priests because Abraham, the ancestor of Levi, paid tithes to him. Since Levi was still in the body of his ancestor Abraham, it is as if the **Levitical priesthood** itself paid tithes to Melchizedek. This establishes the **superiority** of the Melchizedekian priesthood over the Levitical priesthood.

1. A Priesthood Not Dependent on the Law

The **Levitical priesthood** was established under the **Mosaic Law**, and its authority was based on **genealogy**. In contrast, the Melchizedekian priesthood is not based on the **Law** but on the **power of an indestructible life (Hebrews 7:16)**. This points to the **eternal** and **unchanging** nature of Christ's priesthood, which does not rely on human ancestry or legal requirements.

2. The Limitations of the Levitical Priesthood

The **Levitical priests** were limited in their ability to provide **true atonement** for sin. Their sacrifices had to be offered continually, and they themselves were subject to **death**. In contrast, Christ's priesthood, in the order of Melchizedek, is **eternal**, and His sacrifice was offered **once for all (Hebrews 7:27)**. This demonstrates the superiority of Christ's priesthood and the **complete sufficiency** of His sacrifice.

V. CHRIST AS THE ETERNAL HIGH PRIEST IN THE ORDER OF MELCHIZEDEK (HEBREWS 7:11-28)

The **central theme** of **Hebrews 7** is the declaration that Christ is the **eternal High Priest** in the **order of Melchizedek**. The **Levitical priesthood**, while divinely instituted, was **imperfect** and could not bring about the **full redemption** of humanity. Therefore, a **new priesthood** was needed—one that would be **perfect, eternal**, and **able to save completely**.

A. A Perfect Priesthood

Christ's priesthood, like Melchizedek's, is **eternal** and **perfect**. Unlike the Levitical priests, who had to offer sacrifices for their own sins, Christ is the **sinless** High Priest who offered **Himself** as the perfect sacrifice. **Hebrews 7:26-27** states: "For it was indeed fitting that we should have such a high priest, holy, innocent, unstained, separated from sinners, and exalted above the heavens. He has no need, like those high priests, to offer sacrifices daily, first for His own sins and then for those of the people, since He did this once for all when He offered up Himself."

1. The Once-for-All Sacrifice

The **once-for-all** nature of Christ's sacrifice is central to the argument of **Hebrews 7**. Whereas the Levitical priests had to offer sacrifices **repeatedly**, Christ's sacrifice was **sufficient** for all time. This demonstrates the **superiority** of His priesthood and the **complete efficacy** of His atoning work.

2. An Eternal Intercession

In addition to offering the perfect sacrifice, Christ, as the eternal High Priest, continues to **intercede** for believers. **Hebrews 7:25** declares, "Consequently, He is able to save to the uttermost those who draw near to God through Him, since He always lives to make intercession for them." This ongoing intercession is possible because Christ's priesthood is **eternal**. Just as Melchizedek's priesthood is described as without end, so too is Christ's priesthood, ensuring that He is always able to mediate on behalf of those who come to Him.

VI. THE KING-PRIEST ROLE OF MELCHIZEDEK AND CHRIST

One of the unique aspects of Melchizedek's priesthood is that he was both a **king** and a **priest**. In ancient Israel, the roles of **king** and **priest** were typically separate, with the king ruling over the people and the priest serving as the mediator between the people and God. However, Melchizedek holds both offices, prefiguring Christ, who is both **King** and **High Priest**.

A. Christ as the King-Priest

In the **New Testament**, Christ is revealed as both **King** and **Priest**. He is the **King of Kings** who rules over all creation and the **eternal High Priest** who offers the perfect sacrifice for sin and intercedes for His people. This dual role is essential to understanding Christ's **Messianic mission**. As **King**, Jesus reigns with **authority** and **justice**, and as **High Priest**, He brings **reconciliation** between God and humanity.

1. The Kingship of Christ

Christ's kingship is evident throughout Scripture, but it is particularly emphasized in the **book of Revelation**, where Jesus is described as the **King of Kings and Lord of Lords (Revelation 19:16)**. His reign is eternal, and He exercises divine authority over all creation. This kingship fulfills the **Davidic covenant**, which promised that one of David's descendants would reign forever (**2 Samuel 7:12-16**).

2. The Priesthood of Christ

Christ's **priesthood** is equally significant. As the eternal High Priest in the order of Melchizedek, Jesus offers the perfect sacrifice for sin and provides **eternal redemption** for all who believe. His priesthood is unique in that it is both **eternal** and **universal**, transcending the limitations of the Levitical priesthood and bringing **salvation** to all people.

VII. THE NEW COVENANT AND THE PRIESTHOOD OF MELCHIZEDEK

The **book of Hebrews** connects Christ's priesthood in the order of Melchizedek to the establishment of the **New Covenant**. Under the **Old Covenant**, the Levitical priests offered sacrifices that could never fully atone for sin. However, under the **New Covenant**,

Christ's **once-for-all sacrifice** provides complete forgiveness and **eternal salvation**.

A. The Mediator of a Better Covenant

Christ, as the eternal High Priest, is the **mediator** of the **New Covenant**, which is established on **better promises. Hebrews 8:6** explains, "But as it is, Christ has obtained a ministry that is as much more excellent than the old as the covenant He mediates is better, since it is enacted on better promises." This New Covenant is characterized by **forgiveness of sins** and **reconciliation** with God, made possible through Christ's perfect sacrifice.

1. The Fulfillment of the Old Covenant

The **Old Covenant**, with its system of animal sacrifices and Levitical priests, was a **shadow** of the greater reality that would come in Christ. The **Levitical priesthood** and the sacrificial system were temporary measures that pointed to the need for a **greater priest** and a **better sacrifice**. In Christ, the Old Covenant is **fulfilled**, and the **New Covenant** is established, bringing eternal redemption and reconciliation with God.

2. The Eternal Nature of the New Covenant

The **eternal priesthood** of Christ ensures that the **New Covenant** is eternal. Unlike the **Levitical priests**, who were limited by death, Christ's priesthood is **unending**, and His sacrifice is **eternally effective**. This means that those who are in Christ are **eternally secure**, and their salvation is guaranteed by His ongoing intercession.

VIII. THE BREAD AND WINE OF MELCHIZEDEK: A FORESHADOWING OF THE EUCHARIST

When Melchizedek meets Abraham, he brings out **bread and wine**, offering them as part of his priestly blessing. This act of offering bread and wine has been seen by many theologians as a **foreshadowing** of the **Eucharist** or **Lord's Supper**, where **Christ** offers His **body** and **blood** in the form of bread and wine.

A. The Bread and Wine as Symbols of Christ's Sacrifice

In the **Last Supper**, Jesus takes bread and wine and declares them to be His **body** and **blood**, symbolizing the **new covenant** in His blood. Just as Melchizedek offered bread and wine to Abraham, Jesus offers His body and blood as the **means of salvation. Matthew 26:26-28** records Jesus' words: "Take, eat; this is My body... Drink of it, all of you, for this is My blood of the covenant, which is poured out for many for the forgiveness of sins."

1. The Eucharist as Participation in Christ's Sacrifice

The **Eucharist** is not merely a remembrance of Christ's sacrifice but a **participation** in it. When believers partake of the bread and wine, they are participating in the **New Covenant** and receiving the benefits of Christ's sacrifice. This act of communion is a reminder of the **eternal priesthood** of Christ, who continues to intercede for His people and offer the benefits of His sacrifice to all who believe.

2. The Connection to Melchizedek's Priesthood

The offering of **bread and wine** by Melchizedek can be seen as a **type** of the **Eucharist**, where Christ, the eternal High Priest, offers His body and blood for the **salvation of humanity**. Just as Melchizedek's priesthood transcends the **Levitical order**, so too does the Eucharist transcend the **sacrificial system** of the Old Covenant, offering believers a direct **participation** in the sacrifice of Christ.

Fun Fact: Melchizedek in Jewish Tradition

In **Jewish tradition**, Melchizedek is a figure shrouded in mystery, and there are various interpretations of his identity. Some early Jewish commentators believed that Melchizedek was actually **Shem**, the son of Noah, while others saw him as a **heavenly figure** or even an **angelic being**. While the **New Testament** identifies Melchizedek as a type of Christ, Jewish tradition has continued to explore the significance of his role as both **king** and **priest**, recognizing him as a unique figure in the biblical narrative.

Melchizedek as a Type of Christ's Eternal Priesthood

From the Tabernacle to Solomon's Temple to the Second Temple, the progression of God's dwelling among His people points toward a final and eternal fulfillment in Christ. The tearing of the temple veil at Jesus' crucifixion signifies the end of separation between God and humanity, and the beginning of the Church as the living temple, indwelt by the Spirit.

Solomon's Temple was the physical dwelling place of God among His people, where the Ark of the Covenant resided. As magnificent as it was, it served as a shadow of a greater reality. The destruction of this temple symbolized the passing of the old covenant system, pointing forward to the time when God's presence would dwell fully in Christ, the true Temple. The physical structure of the temple was temporary, but it laid the foundation for the spiritual temple found in Christ.

The Second Temple, rebuilt after the exile, held great significance for the Jewish people. It was the site of Jesus' ministry, and although it lacked the glory of Solomon's Temple, it still foreshadowed a greater fulfillment in Christ. The destruction of the Second Temple, as prophesied by Jesus, marks the end of the old sacrificial system and the transition to a new covenant where God's presence is no longer confined to a building but resides in Christ and His Church. Jesus, the ultimate Temple, fulfills what the Second Temple could only symbolize.

The **mysterious figure** of **Melchizedek** stands as one of the most profound **types** of **Christ's eternal priesthood** in the Bible. His appearance in **Genesis 14**, though brief, carries deep theological significance, pointing to the **eternal kingship** and **priesthood** of Jesus Christ. Melchizedek's dual role as **king** and **priest**, his lack of genealogy, and his offering of bread and wine all prefigure the **Messianic work** of Christ, who is both **King of Kings** and **eternal High Priest**.

Through the **lens of typology**, Melchizedek serves as a foreshadowing of Christ, whose priesthood is **superior** to the Levitical priesthood and whose **once-for-all sacrifice** secures **eternal salvation** for all who believe. Just as Melchizedek blessed Abraham and received a tithe from him, Christ blesses His people and intercedes for them as their **eternal High Priest**.

Ultimately, the priesthood of **Melchizedek** points to the **New Covenant** in Christ, where believers find **rest**, **forgiveness**, and **eternal life** through His sacrifice. As the eternal High Priest, Jesus continues to intercede for His people, ensuring that they are forever reconciled to God. The story of Melchizedek, though enigmatic, reveals the profound truth of **God's redemptive plan**, which finds its fulfillment in the **person and work** of Jesus Christ.

CHAPTER 16: THE EXODUS PLAGUES: A TYPE OF JUDGMENT AND DELIVERANCE

The **Ten Plagues of Egypt** found in **Exodus 7-12** stand as one of the most dramatic and powerful demonstrations of God's sovereignty, judgment, and deliverance in the entire Bible. These plagues were not merely random acts of devastation, but carefully orchestrated judgments that revealed God's power over the false gods of Egypt, while at the same time paving the way for the **deliverance** of His people, Israel, from slavery. The plagues also serve as a **type** or foreshadowing of **God's ultimate judgment** on sin and the **final deliverance** of believers, as detailed in the **book of Revelation**.

This chapter will explore the **ten plagues of Egypt** as a **type of judgment and deliverance**, highlighting their symbolic meaning in biblical theology. The plagues serve not only as God's response to the **hardness of Pharaoh's heart** but also as a representation of His ultimate judgment on the **forces of evil**. We will examine the specific **plagues**, their impact, and their **typological significance** in relation to **end-time judgments** and the **deliverance** of God's people, culminating in the **Lamb's victory** and the **final restoration** of creation.

I. THE PURPOSE OF THE TEN PLAGUES (EXODUS 7:1-5)

The story of the ten plagues begins with God's clear intent to reveal His **power** and **sovereignty** over Egypt and its gods. **Exodus 7:1-5** introduces the purpose behind the plagues, as God tells Moses:

"See, I have made you like God to Pharaoh, and your brother Aaron shall be your prophet... But I will harden Pharaoh's heart, and though I multiply My signs and wonders in the land of Egypt, Pharaoh will not listen to you. Then I will lay My hand on Egypt and bring My hosts, My people the children of Israel, out of the land of Egypt by great acts of judgment. The Egyptians shall know that I am the Lord, when I stretch out My hand against Egypt and bring out the people of Israel from among them."

In this passage, God clearly states His twofold purpose for sending the plagues: **judgment** on Egypt and its gods, and **deliverance** for Israel. This same pattern of judgment and deliverance will later be seen in the **final judgments** of Revelation, where God will judge the **wicked** while rescuing His people from **spiritual bondage** and bringing them into the **eternal kingdom**.

A. The Hardening of Pharaoh's Heart

Throughout the narrative of the plagues, we see a repeated phrase: God will **harden Pharaoh's heart**. This hardening of Pharaoh's heart serves to highlight the **stubbornness of sin** and the consequences of **resisting God's will**. Despite the increasingly severe judgments, Pharaoh refuses to repent, demonstrating the **hardness of human nature** in the face of divine revelation.

1. Pharaoh as a Symbol of Human Rebellion

Pharaoh represents the **arrogance** and **rebellion** of humanity that rejects God's rule. His stubborn refusal to release the Israelites, despite overwhelming evidence of God's power, mirrors the **rebellion** of those who reject Christ even in the face of divine judgment. This typifies the resistance of **sinful humanity** to God's authority, a resistance that will ultimately culminate in the final judgment described in **Revelation**.

2. God's Purpose in Judgment

God's hardening of Pharaoh's heart and the subsequent plagues were part of His divine plan to **reveal His glory** and **execute judgment** on Egypt's gods and idols. Each plague is aimed at undermining the Egyptians' belief in their gods and showing that **Yahweh alone is God**. This foreshadows the final judgments in

Revelation, where God's wrath is poured out to **vindicate His holiness** and establish His eternal rule over all creation.

II. THE FIRST PLAGUE: WATER TURNED TO BLOOD (EXODUS 7:14-24)

The first plague strikes at the heart of Egypt's lifeblood—the **Nile River**. The Nile was central to Egyptian civilization, providing water for drinking, agriculture, and transportation. In the first plague, God turned the waters of the Nile into **blood**, causing the fish to die and making the water undrinkable.

A. Symbol of Judgment on Life-Sustaining Forces

The Nile River was regarded as a **divine source of life** by the Egyptians, closely associated with the god **Hapi**, the god of the Nile. By turning the Nile into blood, God was declaring His superiority over the Egyptian gods and demonstrating that **He alone** is the source of life.

1. Blood as a Symbol of Judgment

The turning of water into blood represents **judgment**—specifically, the **death** that comes as a result of **sin**. Blood in the Bible is often associated with **life** and **sacrifice**, but here it signifies the **curse of death**. This foreshadows the **plagues of Revelation**, where the waters are turned to blood as a symbol of God's judgment on **sinful humanity (Revelation 16:4-6)**.

2. The Powerlessness of False Gods

This plague also reveals the **powerlessness** of Egypt's gods. The Egyptian priests and magicians attempted to replicate the miracle but could only mimic the appearance of turning water into blood on a small scale. They could not reverse the plague or restore the Nile, showing that the **gods of Egypt** were impotent in the face of **Yahweh's power**. This points forward to the **futility** of idolatry and the **supremacy** of God's kingdom over all false gods and systems.

III. THE SECOND PLAGUE: FROGS (EXODUS 8:1-15)

The second plague brings an overwhelming swarm of **frogs** throughout Egypt, filling houses, bedrooms, and even the ovens and kneading bowls. Frogs were associated with the Egyptian goddess **Heqet**, who was believed to have the form of a frog and was considered a symbol of **fertility** and **birth**.

A. Overwhelming Judgment and the Reversal of Creation

This plague highlights the **chaos** and **disorder** that result when God's creation is turned against itself. Instead of a controlled natural world, where animals serve their intended purposes, the plague of frogs symbolizes **creation gone awry**, with the creatures overtaking human spaces and causing discomfort and chaos.

1. Judgment on Egypt's Idols of Fertility

The abundance of frogs was a **judgment** on Egypt's worship of **fertility gods** like Heqet. God's power over creation is on full display, as He uses the very symbols of their false worship to bring them **discomfort** and **suffering**. The frogs, once revered, became a **curse**. This mirrors how **idolatry** ultimately leads to destruction and chaos, with the very objects of worship becoming instruments of **judgment**.

2. Foreshadowing of Judgment in Revelation

The plague of frogs also foreshadows the **unclean spirits** that proceed from the mouth of the **dragon, the beast, and the false prophet** in **Revelation 16:13-14**. Just as frogs plagued Egypt, these **demonic spirits** will gather the world's kings for the final battle of **Armageddon**, indicating the spiritual warfare that underlies both the plagues of Egypt and the end-time judgments.

IV. THE THIRD PLAGUE: GNATS (EXODUS 8:16-19)

The third plague brings an infestation of **gnats** (or lice), which come from the **dust of the earth**. This plague directly attacks the **priests of Egypt**, whose rituals of cleanliness are interrupted by the infestation, making it impossible for them to carry out their duties.

A. A Judgment on Egypt's Religious System

The gnats, emerging from the **dust**, are reminiscent of God's creation of **humanity** from the dust of the earth in **Genesis 2:7**. By using dust as the source of the plague, God demonstrates His power over life and creation, reminding both Egypt and Israel that He alone is the **Creator**.

1. The Failure of Egyptian Magicians

Unlike the previous plagues, the Egyptian magicians are unable to replicate the third plague. They recognize the **finger of God** in this judgment, admitting defeat before Moses and acknowledging that this plague comes from **Yahweh (Exodus 8:19)**. This demonstrates the **superiority** of God's power over the **limited abilities** of the magicians and their gods.

2. Symbol of Spiritual Uncleanliness

The plague of gnats also symbolizes **spiritual uncleanliness**, as the tiny creatures covered the land, making it impossible for the Egyptians to maintain ritual purity. This foreshadows the **plagues of Revelation**, where the **uncleanness** of the world will be exposed and judged by God.

V. The Fourth Plague: Flies (Exodus 8:20-32)

The fourth plague brings a swarm of **flies**, which fill the houses and land of Egypt, but notably, this plague does not affect the region of **Goshen**, where the Israelites live. This distinction marks the beginning of God's **separation** between the Egyptians and the Israelites, showing that His **judgment** will fall on Egypt but not on His **chosen people**.

A. The Separation of God's People from Judgment

The fact that **Goshen** is spared from the plague of flies serves as a powerful symbol of God's **protection** over His people. While Egypt suffers from the consequences of their sin and rebellion, Israel remains untouched, signifying the **covenant** relationship between God and His people.

1. A Shadow of Divine Protection

This distinction between Egypt and Israel points forward to the **final judgment**, where God will **protect** His people from the **wrath** that falls on the world. Just as the Israelites were spared from the plague of flies, believers are promised protection from the **judgment** that will come upon the earth during the **end times**.

2. Deliverance Through Judgment

The plague of flies also highlights the theme of **deliverance through judgment**. While God's judgment falls on Egypt, His people are preserved and protected, demonstrating that God's **wrath** against sin is always accompanied by His **mercy** toward those who belong to Him. This theme will reach its ultimate fulfillment in the **deliverance of believers** at the end of the age, as described in **Revelation 7:3**, where God's people are sealed and protected during the outpouring of His wrath.

VI. THE FIFTH PLAGUE: DEATH OF LIVESTOCK (EXODUS 9:1-7)

In the fifth plague, God sends a **pestilence** that strikes the **livestock** of Egypt, killing horses, donkeys, camels, cattle, and sheep. This plague once again spares the livestock of the Israelites, emphasizing the separation between **God's people** and the Egyptians.

A. Judgment on Egypt's Economy and Livelihood

The death of Egypt's livestock represents a **severe blow** to their economy and livelihood. Livestock were not only a source of food but also essential for transportation, agriculture, and trade. By striking down the livestock, God was demonstrating His power over Egypt's wealth and resources, showing that their **economic stability** was subject to His judgment.

1. The Powerlessness of Egypt's Gods

This plague was likely a direct judgment against the Egyptian gods associated with **livestock**, such as **Apis**, the bull god, and **Hathor**, the goddess of fertility and cattle. The death of the livestock demonstrated the **powerlessness** of these gods to protect their domain, underscoring Yahweh's supremacy over all creation.

2. A Symbol of God's Judgment on the Earth's Wealth

The plague of livestock foreshadows the **economic judgments** seen in the book of Revelation, where God's wrath will be poured out on the **wealth** and **materialism** of the world. In **Revelation 18**, the fall of **Babylon** represents the collapse of the world's corrupt economic systems, symbolizing the futility of trusting in **earthly wealth** instead of **God's provision**.

VII. THE SIXTH PLAGUE: BOILS (EXODUS 9:8-12)

The sixth plague brings **boils** that break out on the bodies of the Egyptians and their animals. The **painful sores** cover the people, and once again, the magicians are powerless to stop or replicate the plague. In fact, they are afflicted by the boils themselves, further demonstrating their **inability** to stand against God's power.

A. Judgment on the Body and Health

The plague of boils represents God's judgment on **human health** and the **frailty** of the human body. The Egyptians, who prided themselves on their **ritual cleanliness** and bodily health, were reduced to **suffering** and **sickness**, highlighting their vulnerability in the face of God's power.

1. The Suffering of Egypt's Priests and Magicians

The fact that the **magicians** and **priests** of Egypt were afflicted by the boils is particularly significant. These figures, who were supposed to mediate between the gods and the people, were rendered **powerless** by the plague, showing that they could not protect themselves or the people from **Yahweh's judgment**.

2. A Foreshadowing of the Final Judgments

The plague of boils foreshadows the **plague of sores** in **Revelation 16:2**, where those who worship the **beast** and take his mark are afflicted with **painful sores**. This connection between the Exodus plagues and the final judgments in Revelation reveals the **universal scope** of God's judgment on sin and the **inescapability** of His justice.

VIII. THE SEVENTH PLAGUE: HAIL (EXODUS 9:13-35)

The seventh plague brings a devastating storm of **hail**, accompanied by **lightning** and **thunder**, that destroys crops, livestock, and property across Egypt. This plague is unprecedented in its severity, and God explicitly warns the Egyptians to take cover before the storm strikes.

A. Judgment on Egypt's Agriculture and Food Supply

The plague of hail targets Egypt's **agriculture**, which was vital to their **food supply** and economy. The destruction of crops and livestock further weakens Egypt's stability and shows God's power over the forces of **nature**.

1. A Call to Repentance

Before sending the hail, God gives Pharaoh and the Egyptians a **warning**, telling them to seek shelter and protect their animals and servants. This warning demonstrates God's **mercy** even in judgment, as He offers the Egyptians an opportunity to **repent** and take action to avoid the full brunt of the plague.

2. A Type of the Final Plagues in Revelation

The plague of hail mirrors the **hailstones** that fall during the **final judgments** in **Revelation 16:21**, where **hailstones weighing about a hundred pounds** fall from heaven, signaling the **severity** and **inevitability** of God's final judgment on the earth. The **destruction** caused by the hail in Egypt foreshadows the **global destruction** that will come upon the **unrepentant** in the last days.

IX. THE EIGHTH PLAGUE: LOCUSTS (EXODUS 10:1-20)

The eighth plague brings a swarm of **locusts** that devour what little remains of Egypt's crops after the hail. The locusts cover the land, consuming every green plant and tree, leaving Egypt in **total desolation**.

A. Judgment on Egypt's Abundance

The plague of locusts represents God's judgment on Egypt's **abundance** and **prosperity**. Egypt, which was known for its fertile land and agricultural wealth, is brought to a state of **desolation** as the locusts consume everything in their path.

1. The Devouring Judgment of God

The locusts symbolize God's ability to **consume** and **destroy** the material wealth of those who refuse to acknowledge His sovereignty. This plague highlights the **futility** of trusting in **earthly riches** and serves as a warning to those who place their hope in the **things of this world**.

2. A Foreshadowing of the Final Judgments

The plague of locusts also foreshadows the **demonic locusts** in **Revelation 9:1-11**, which are released during the **fifth trumpet judgment**. These locusts, unlike their counterparts in Egypt, are **demonic beings** that torment the unrepentant. The connection between the locusts of Egypt and the locusts of Revelation highlights the **spiritual dimension** of God's judgments and the **torment** that awaits those who reject Him.

X. THE NINTH PLAGUE: DARKNESS (EXODUS 10:21-29)

The ninth plague brings **darkness** over the land of Egypt for three days, a **thick darkness** that can be felt. During this time, the Egyptians are unable to see or move, but the Israelites in **Goshen** have light.

A. Judgment on Egypt's Sun God

The plague of darkness is a direct attack on **Ra**, the Egyptian **sun god**, who was considered the most powerful of all their deities. By plunging the land into **darkness**, God demonstrates that He alone controls the forces of **light** and **darkness**, further exposing the **powerlessness** of Egypt's gods.

1. Spiritual Darkness and the Judgment of God

The physical darkness in Egypt represents a deeper **spiritual darkness** that had fallen over the nation. This plague symbolizes the **blindness** and **ignorance** of those who reject God's truth, foreshadowing the **eternal separation** from God that will come upon the unrepentant in the final judgment.

2. A Foreshadowing of the Final Judgment

The plague of darkness foreshadows the **plague of darkness** in **Revelation 16:10-11**, where the kingdom of the **beast** is plunged into darkness, and the people gnaw their tongues in **agony**. The connection between the darkness of Egypt and the darkness in Revelation points to the **ultimate judgment** that will come upon the kingdom of this world, which is ruled by **spiritual darkness**.

XI. THE TENTH PLAGUE: THE DEATH OF THE FIRSTBORN (EXODUS 11-12)

The tenth and final plague brings the **death of the firstborn** in Egypt, from the firstborn of Pharaoh to the firstborn of the cattle. This plague is the climax of God's judgment on Egypt and leads directly to the **Exodus**, as Pharaoh finally relents and allows the Israelites to leave.

A. Judgment and Deliverance Through the Passover

The tenth plague also marks the institution of the **Passover**, where the Israelites are instructed to **sacrifice a lamb** and spread its **blood** on their doorposts. When the **destroying angel** passes through

Egypt, the houses with the **blood of the lamb** are spared, while the firstborn in the unmarked houses are struck down.

1. The Passover as a Type of Christ's Sacrifice

The **Passover lamb** is a clear **type** of **Christ**, who is called the **Lamb of God** in **John 1:29**. Just as the blood of the Passover lamb protected the Israelites from the plague of death, the **blood of Christ** protects believers from **eternal death** and **judgment**. The death of the firstborn in Egypt serves as a **shadow** of the **death** and **resurrection** of Jesus, the **firstborn of all creation** (**Colossians 1:15**).

2. A Foreshadowing of the Final Judgment

The death of the firstborn in Egypt foreshadows the **final judgment** in Revelation, where the **unrepentant** will face **eternal separation** from God. Just as the Egyptians experienced the ultimate judgment for their **hardness of heart**, those who reject Christ will face the **second death** described in **Revelation 20:14**.

XII. THE TYPOLOGICAL SIGNIFICANCE OF THE PLAGUES IN REVELATION

The ten plagues of Egypt are not only historical events but also **types** that point forward to the **end-time judgments** described in the **book of Revelation**. The **parallels** between the plagues of Egypt and the plagues of Revelation are striking, revealing a **theological pattern** of **judgment** and **deliverance** that spans the entire Bible.

A. The Final Judgments of Revelation

The plagues in Revelation serve the same dual purpose as the plagues of Egypt: they are God's **judgment** on the **wicked** and His **deliverance** of His people. Just as God judged Egypt for its **idolatry**, **oppression**, and **rebellion**, He will judge the world for its **sin** and **rejection** of Christ. And just as He delivered the Israelites from slavery in Egypt, He will deliver His people from the **bondage of sin** and bring them into the **eternal kingdom**.

1. Judgment on the False Gods of This World

The plagues of Revelation, like those of Egypt, target the **false gods** and **idols** of this world. Whether it is the **economic system** of Babylon, the **political power** of the beast, or the **deceptive influence** of the false prophet, God's judgments in Revelation expose the **futility** of trusting in anything other than **Him**.

2. Deliverance Through the Lamb

The **Lamb** who was slain in the Passover becomes the **victorious Lamb** in Revelation. **Revelation 7:9-10** describes a great multitude standing before the throne, clothed in white robes and holding palm branches, proclaiming, "Salvation belongs to our God who sits on the throne, and to the **Lamb**!" Just as the Israelites were delivered through the blood of the Passover lamb, believers are delivered through the blood of **Jesus**, the Lamb of God.

Fun Fact: The Plagues and Ancient Egyptian Gods

Each of the ten plagues was a **direct assault** on the Egyptian **pantheon of gods**. For example, the first plague, turning the Nile to blood, challenged **Hapi**, the god of the Nile, while the ninth plague, darkness, challenged **Ra**, the sun god. The plagues were not random acts of destruction but were specifically designed to demonstrate the **powerlessness** of Egypt's gods in the face of **Yahweh**, the one true God. This systematic dismantling of Egypt's belief system highlights the **spiritual warfare** that underpins the biblical narrative and serves as a reminder that **God alone is sovereign** over all powers and principalities.

The Exodus Plagues as a Type of Judgment and Deliverance

From the Tabernacle to Solomon's Temple to the Second Temple, the progression of God's dwelling among His people points toward a final and eternal fulfillment in Christ. The tearing of the temple veil at Jesus' crucifixion signifies the end of separation between God and humanity, and the beginning of the Church as the living temple, indwelt by the Spirit.

Solomon's Temple was the physical dwelling place of God among His people, where the Ark of the Covenant resided. As magnificent as it was, it served as a shadow of a greater reality. The destruction of this temple symbolized the passing of the old covenant system, pointing forward to the time when God's presence would dwell fully in Christ, the true Temple. The physical structure of the temple was temporary, but it laid the foundation for the spiritual temple found in Christ.

The Second Temple, rebuilt after the exile, held great significance for the Jewish people. It was the site of Jesus' ministry, and although it lacked the glory of Solomon's Temple, it still foreshadowed a greater fulfillment in Christ. The destruction of the Second Temple, as prophesied by Jesus, marks the end of the old sacrificial system and the transition to a new covenant where God's presence is no longer confined to a building but resides in Christ and His Church. Jesus, the ultimate Temple, fulfills what the Second Temple could only symbolize.

The **ten plagues of Egypt** serve as a profound **type** of **God's judgment** on sin and **deliverance** of His people. Through these plagues, God demonstrated His **sovereignty** over the false gods of Egypt, revealing the **powerlessness** of idolatry and the **certainty** of His judgment. At the same time, the plagues served as a means of **deliverance** for the Israelites, who were set free from slavery and led into the **Promised Land**.

This pattern of **judgment and deliverance** is repeated in the **book of Revelation**, where the **end-time plagues** serve as God's final judgment on the world, while believers are delivered through the blood of the **Lamb**. The plagues of Egypt and the plagues of Revelation together reveal the ultimate **victory of God** over the forces of **evil** and the **eternal salvation** of His people.

In both the **Exodus** and the **end times**, God's people are called to **trust** in His **deliverance** and to remain faithful in the face of **judgment**. The plagues remind us that God's **wrath** against sin is real, but so too is His **mercy** and **deliverance** for those who put their faith in Him. Through the **blood of the Lamb**, we are spared from judgment and brought into the **eternal kingdom**, where we will dwell with God forever in **peace** and **righteousness**.

CHAPTER 17: BOAZ AND RUTH: A TYPE OF CHRIST AS THE KINSMAN-REDEEMER

The story of **Boaz** and **Ruth** in the **Book of Ruth** stands as a profound illustration of God's **redemptive love**. Set during the time of the judges, the narrative begins with a tale of hardship, loss, and destitution, but it transforms into a beautiful testimony of **grace**, **redemption**, and **hope**. **Boaz**, a wealthy relative of Naomi's late husband, emerges as the **kinsman-redeemer** for Ruth, a Moabite widow. His actions not only restore Ruth and her mother-in-law **Naomi** to security but also prefigure **Christ's redemptive work** for His **bride**, the Church.

This chapter explores the story of **Boaz and Ruth** as a **type** of **Christ's role as the kinsman-redeemer**. The typology of Boaz points forward to Jesus, who **redeems** His people and takes the **Church** as His **bride** through His sacrifice. By examining the customs of the **kinsman-redeemer** in ancient Israel, the role of **Boaz** in Ruth's life, and the parallels between Boaz's actions and Christ's redemptive work, we gain a deeper understanding of God's **grace** and **faithfulness**.

I. THE BACKGROUND OF RUTH AND THE ROLE OF THE KINSMAN-REDEEMER

The **Book of Ruth** opens with a scene of tragedy. **Elimelech**, his wife **Naomi**, and their two sons, **Mahlon** and **Chilion**, leave **Bethlehem** due to a famine and settle in **Moab**, where the two sons marry Moabite women, **Orpah** and **Ruth**. However, Elimelech and his two sons die, leaving Naomi, Orpah, and Ruth as widows. Faced with destitution, Naomi decides to return to Bethlehem, urging her daughters-in-law to remain in Moab. Ruth, however, refuses to leave Naomi and famously declares, "**Where you go I will go, and where you lodge I will lodge. Your people shall be my people, and your God my God**" (Ruth 1:16).

A. The Kinsman-Redeemer in Israelite Law (Leviticus 25:25)

In ancient Israel, the **kinsman-redeemer** (Hebrew: **go'el**) played a crucial role in **preserving** and **restoring** family lines and property. According to **Leviticus 25:25**, if an Israelite man died and left his widow without a male heir, it was the duty of the **nearest male relative** to marry the widow and redeem the family's property. This practice ensured the continuation of the deceased man's lineage and provided for the **economic welfare** of the widow.

1. Redeeming the Land and the Family Name

The role of the kinsman-redeemer involved two primary responsibilities:

- **Redeeming the land** that had been sold or lost by a relative due to financial hardship.
- **Marrying the widow** of a deceased relative to produce offspring and continue the deceased's family name.

The concept of **redemption** in Israelite culture went beyond mere legal or financial obligation. It symbolized the **preservation of life**, lineage, and inheritance, aligning with God's **covenantal promise** to Israel

2. Typology of the Kinsman-Redeemer: A Shadow of Christ's Redemption

The role of the **kinsman-redeemer** in ancient Israel serves as a **type** of Christ's role as the **Redeemer** of His people. Just as the kinsman-redeemer restored property, lineage, and dignity to the family in need, **Christ redeems His people** from sin and restores them to a **right relationship** with God. In this sense, the **kinsman-redeemer** is a picture of the **greater redemption** that would come through Jesus, the **true Redeemer** of both **Jew** and **Gentile**.

II. BOAZ ENTERS THE SCENE: A MAN OF INTEGRITY AND KINDNESS (RUTH 2)

The narrative introduces **Boaz** in **Ruth 2**, where Ruth goes to glean in the fields to provide for herself and Naomi. Boaz is described as a "worthy man" of Bethlehem, a man of great character, wealth, and influence (**Ruth 2:1**). When Boaz notices Ruth gleaning in his field, he inquires about her, and upon learning that she is the Moabite widow who has shown great loyalty to Naomi, he extends his protection and provision to her.

A. Boaz's Grace and Protection Toward Ruth

Boaz's actions toward Ruth are filled with **grace** and **kindness**. He tells Ruth to remain in his field, assuring her that she will be safe and well cared for. Boaz also instructs his workers to allow Ruth to glean among the **sheaves** and to **leave extra grain** for her, ensuring that she and Naomi will have plenty to eat.

1. Boaz's Compassion as a Type of Christ's Grace

Boaz's actions toward Ruth reflect **Christ's compassion** for His people. Just as Boaz provided **protection** and **provision** for Ruth, Christ extends His grace to those who come to Him in **faith**. Boaz's care for Ruth, a **foreigner** and **widow**, mirrors Christ's love for the **outcast** and **marginalized**. In the same way, Christ offers **redemption** and **grace** to all, regardless of their background or status.

2. Ruth's Humility and Gratitude

Ruth responds to Boaz's kindness with **humility** and **gratitude**, asking, "**Why have I found favor in your eyes, that you should take notice of me, since I am a foreigner?**" (**Ruth 2:10**). This reflects the attitude of believers who recognize that their salvation is an act of **God's grace** and not something they have earned. Ruth's humility is a model of the **humility** that believers are called to exhibit in response to God's grace.

III. THE PROPOSAL AT THE THRESHING FLOOR: RUTH SEEKS REDEMPTION (RUTH 3)

In **Ruth 3**, Naomi instructs Ruth to approach Boaz at the **threshing floor** and essentially propose marriage. This act is culturally significant because it demonstrates Ruth's **request** for Boaz to act as her **kinsman-redeemer**. After Boaz finishes working and falls asleep at the threshing floor, Ruth lies at his feet, a gesture of submission and humility. When Boaz wakes, Ruth asks him to "**spread your wings over your servant, for you are a redeemer**" (**Ruth 3:9**).

A. The Symbolism of the Threshing Floor

The setting of this encounter is the **threshing floor**, a place where grain is separated from the chaff. In biblical imagery, the threshing floor often symbolizes **judgment**, **separation**, and **provision**. The threshing floor serves as the location where Boaz, the redeemer, agrees to redeem Ruth, pointing to the **spiritual redemption** that Christ provides.

1. Ruth's Bold Request for Redemption

Ruth's request for Boaz to act as her redeemer is bold but reflects her **trust** in Boaz's **character** and **kindness**. By asking Boaz to "spread his wings" over her, Ruth is invoking imagery of

protection and **marriage**, essentially asking Boaz to take her under his care as her **husband** and **redeemer**.

2. The Willingness of the Redeemer

Boaz responds to Ruth's request with **grace** and a willingness to fulfill the role of kinsman-redeemer, but he notes that there is a **closer relative** who has the first right to redeem her (**Ruth 3:12-13**). Boaz's commitment to follow the proper legal channels reflects his **integrity** and **desire to do what is right**. This willingness to redeem Ruth mirrors **Christ's willingness** to offer Himself as the **redeemer** of His people.

IV. BOAZ REDEEMS RUTH: THE LEGAL TRANSACTION (RUTH 4:1-10)

In **Ruth 4**, Boaz goes to the **city gate**, the place where legal matters are settled, to meet with the **nearer kinsman-redeemer** and the elders of the city. Boaz presents the case to the nearer relative, offering him the opportunity to redeem the land that belonged to Naomi's husband, **Elimelech**. Initially, the relative is willing to redeem the land, but when Boaz explains that redeeming the land also involves **marrying Ruth**, the relative declines, fearing that it will jeopardize his own inheritance.

A. Boaz's Role as the Willing Redeemer

After the nearer kinsman-redeemer steps aside, Boaz formally declares his intention to redeem the land and marry Ruth. In the presence of the elders and witnesses, Boaz states, "**I have bought from the hand of Naomi all that belonged to Elimelech and all that belonged to Chilion and Mahlon. Also Ruth the Moabite, the widow of Mahlon, I have bought to be my wife, to perpetuate the name of the dead in his inheritance**" (Ruth 4:9-10).

1. The Legal Act of Redemption

Boaz's act of redemption is **legal**, public, and witnessed by the elders of the city, signifying the **binding nature** of his commitment. In the same way, Christ's redemption of His people is **legal** in the sense that it fulfills the **requirements of the law**. Through His **sacrifice** on the cross, Christ fulfills the demands of God's justice, paying the **penalty for sin** and securing **eternal life** for His people.

2. The Willingness of Christ to Redeem

Just as Boaz was willing to redeem Ruth and take her as his wife, Christ is willing to **redeem His bride**, the Church. **Ephesians 5:25-27** describes Christ's love for the Church, stating, "**Husbands, love your wives, as Christ loved the church and gave Himself up for her, that He might sanctify her, having cleansed her by the washing of water with the word, so that He might present the church to Himself in splendor, without spot or wrinkle or any such thing, that she might be holy and without blemish.**" Christ's **sacrifice** is the ultimate act of redemption, securing the **salvation** and **sanctification** of His people.

V. BOAZ MARRIES RUTH: A PICTURE OF CHRIST'S UNION WITH THE CHURCH (RUTH 4:13-17)

Following the legal transaction, Boaz marries Ruth, and she bears a son, **Obed**, who becomes the father of **Jesse**, the father of **David**. The birth of Obed not only restores Naomi's **family line** but also places Ruth in the **genealogy of Jesus Christ**. This union between Boaz and Ruth is a picture of the **union between Christ and His Church**.

A. The Bride of Christ

Ruth, a **Gentile** widow, is brought into the family of Israel through her marriage to Boaz, just as the **Church** (comprised of both

Jew and Gentile) is brought into the family of God through **Christ's redemptive work**. The marriage of Boaz and Ruth is a **type** of the **union** between Christ and His bride, the Church.

1. The Inclusion of the Gentiles

Ruth's inclusion in the **genealogy of Christ** is a powerful reminder of the **inclusion of the Gentiles** in God's plan of redemption. Just as Ruth, a Moabite, was welcomed into the covenant community of Israel, Christ's redemption extends to all people, regardless of ethnicity or background. **Galatians 3:28** declares, **"There is neither Jew nor Greek, there is neither slave nor free, there is no male and female, for you are all one in Christ Jesus."**

2. The Bride of Christ in the New Testament

The imagery of the Church as the **bride of Christ** is a recurring theme in the New Testament. **Revelation 19:7** proclaims, **"Let us rejoice and exult and give Him the glory, for the marriage of the Lamb has come, and His Bride has made herself ready."** Just as Boaz took Ruth as his bride, Christ will return for His **bride**, the Church, and there will be a **wedding feast** in heaven.

VI. THE LEGACY OF BOAZ AND RUTH: A LINEAGE OF KINGS AND THE MESSIAH

The union of Boaz and Ruth leads to the birth of **Obed**, who becomes the grandfather of **King David**. This places Ruth, a **Moabite widow**, in the direct lineage of the **Messiah**, Jesus Christ. The significance of this cannot be overstated, as it demonstrates God's ability to use unlikely people and circumstances to fulfill His **redemptive plan**.

A. The Line of David

The birth of Obed is celebrated as the **restoration** of Naomi's family line. The women of the town declare, **"Blessed be the Lord,** who has not left you this day without a redeemer, and may his name be renowned in Israel! He shall be to you a restorer of life and a nourisher of your old age, for your daughter-in-law who loves you, who is more to you than seven sons, has given birth to him" (**Ruth 4:14-15**). Through Obed, Naomi's family is redeemed, and through Obed's descendants, the **kingdom of Israel** is established.

1. The Davidic Covenant

The birth of Obed ultimately leads to the birth of **David**, the great king of Israel, through whom God would establish the **Davidic covenant**. God promises David that one of his descendants would reign on his throne **forever (2 Samuel 7:12-16)**, a promise fulfilled in **Jesus Christ**, the **Son of David**.

2. Christ, the Ultimate King and Redeemer

Christ, the **Son of David**, is the **ultimate King** and **Redeemer**. Just as Boaz redeemed Ruth and restored Naomi's family line, Christ redeems His people and restores them to a **right relationship** with God. The **lineage of Boaz and Ruth** points directly to Christ, demonstrating that God's plan of redemption was unfolding even in the seemingly small and personal story of a **Moabite widow** and a **Bethlehem farmer**.

VII. THE TYPOLOGY OF BOAZ: A SHADOW OF CHRIST'S REDEMPTIVE WORK

The story of Boaz and Ruth serves as a powerful **type** of Christ's redemptive work. Boaz's actions as the **kinsman-redeemer** foreshadow Christ's role as the **Redeemer of His people**, and the entire narrative points to the **greater redemption** that would come through **Jesus**.

A. Boaz's Willingness to Redeem

One of the key aspects of Boaz's character is his **willingness** to redeem Ruth. Despite the fact that Ruth is a **Moabite** and a **widow**, Boaz is willing to marry her and redeem her family's inheritance. This mirrors Christ's willingness to **redeem sinful humanity**, despite our unworthiness. **Romans 5:8** declares, "**But God shows His love for us in that while we were still sinners, Christ died for us.**"

1. The Cost of Redemption

Boaz's redemption of Ruth comes at a cost—he must marry her and take on the responsibility of her family's inheritance. Similarly, Christ's redemption of His people came at the **ultimate cost**—His own life. **1 Peter 1:18-19** states, "**You were ransomed from the futile ways inherited from your forefathers, not with perishable things such as silver or gold, but with the precious blood of Christ, like that of a lamb without blemish or spot.**"

2. The Legal and Public Nature of Redemption

Boaz's redemption of Ruth is not a secretive or hidden act; it is done **publicly** at the city gate, witnessed by the elders of the community. This public nature of redemption reflects the **legal** and **binding** aspect of Christ's work on the cross. Through His death and resurrection, Christ legally secured the **salvation** of His people, satisfying the demands of **God's justice** and providing **eternal life** for all who believe.

VIII. THE SPIRITUAL LESSONS OF BOAZ AND RUTH

The story of Boaz and Ruth offers numerous **spiritual lessons** for believers, particularly regarding the themes of **redemption**, **faithfulness**, and **God's sovereignty**.

A. God's Sovereign Plan

One of the most remarkable aspects of the Book of Ruth is the way that God's **sovereign hand** is at work behind the scenes. What begins as a story of **loss** and **tragedy**—with Naomi and Ruth facing destitution—ends with **restoration** and **joy**. God is working through every circumstance to bring about His plan, even when it is not immediately visible.

1. From Tragedy to Redemption

Naomi's journey from **bitterness** to **joy** serves as a reminder that God can bring **redemption** out of even the most difficult circumstances. Just as God redeemed Naomi and Ruth through Boaz, He redeems His people through Christ, transforming **sorrow** into **joy** and **despair** into **hope**.

2. Trusting in God's Providence

Ruth's story teaches us the importance of **trusting in God's providence**, even when we don't understand what He is doing. Ruth's faithfulness to Naomi and her willingness to follow God's leading ultimately result in her being redeemed and becoming part of the **Messianic line**. This is a reminder that God's plan is always **perfect**, and we can trust Him to work all things together for **good** (**Romans 8:28**).

Fun Fact: Ruth's Place in the Genealogy of Jesus

Ruth, a Moabite, is one of only five women mentioned in the **genealogy of Jesus** in **Matthew 1**. The inclusion of Ruth, a **foreigner**, in the lineage of the **Messiah** highlights God's **inclusive plan of salvation** for both Jew and Gentile. This demonstrates that God's **grace** extends to all people, regardless of their background or nationality, and that He can use anyone, no matter how unlikely, to fulfill His **redemptive purposes**.

Boaz and Ruth as a Type of Christ and the Church

From the Tabernacle to Solomon's Temple to the Second Temple, the progression of God's dwelling among His people points toward a final and eternal fulfillment in Christ. The tearing of the temple veil at Jesus' crucifixion signifies the end of separation between God and humanity, and the beginning of the Church as the living temple, indwelt by the Spirit.

Solomon's Temple was the physical dwelling place of God among His people, where the Ark of the Covenant resided. As magnificent as it was, it served as a shadow of a greater reality. The destruction of this temple symbolized the passing of the old covenant system, pointing forward to the time when God's presence would dwell fully in Christ, the true Temple. The physical structure of the temple was temporary, but it laid the foundation for the spiritual temple found in Christ.

The Second Temple, rebuilt after the exile, held great significance for the Jewish people. It was the site of Jesus' ministry, and although it lacked the glory of Solomon's Temple, it still foreshadowed a greater fulfillment in Christ. The destruction of the Second Temple, as prophesied by Jesus, marks the end of the old sacrificial system and the transition to a new covenant where God's presence is no longer confined to a building but resides in Christ and His Church. Jesus, the ultimate Temple, fulfills what the Second Temple could only symbolize.

The story of **Boaz and Ruth** is not just a love story; it is a **theological masterpiece** that points to the **redemption** that would come through **Jesus Christ**. Boaz, as the **kinsman-redeemer**, is a type of Christ, who **redeems His bride**, the Church, through His **sacrifice**. The marriage of Boaz and Ruth foreshadows the **union** of Christ and His people, and the birth of their son, Obed, points forward to the **Messianic line** that would culminate in the birth of **Jesus**, the ultimate **Redeemer**.

Through the lens of **typology**, the story of Boaz and Ruth reveals profound truths about God's **grace**, **faithfulness**, and **sovereignty**. It teaches us that God is always at work, even in the midst of **tragedy**, and that His plan for **redemption** is far greater than we can imagine. Just as Boaz redeemed Ruth and restored her family's inheritance, Christ redeems His people and restores them to a right relationship with God, securing for them an **eternal inheritance** in His kingdom.

The story of **Boaz and Ruth** reminds us that God's **redemptive plan** is unfolding in every detail of our lives, and that through **faith in Christ**, we are **redeemed**, restored, and brought into the **family of God**.

CHAPTER 18: THE TABERNACLE'S VEIL: A TYPE OF CHRIST'S FLESH

The **Tabernacle** was central to Israel's worship and relationship with God during their wilderness journey and before the construction of Solomon's Temple. Within the Tabernacle stood the **Holy of Holies**, the most sacred space where God's presence dwelled. Separating this space from the rest of the Tabernacle was a thick **veil**, a curtain that symbolized the separation between a holy God and sinful humanity. However, this separation was not meant to last forever. In the New Testament, this veil becomes a profound **type** or symbol of **Christ's flesh**. When Christ died on the cross and His flesh was torn, the veil in the Temple was miraculously torn from top to bottom, symbolizing that through His **sacrifice**, believers now have direct access to God.

In this chapter, we will explore the **typology** of the veil in the **Tabernacle**, its significance in both the Old and New Testaments, and how it points to **Christ's death** on the cross. By understanding the veil as a **type** of Christ's flesh, we gain a deeper appreciation of how Jesus' death opened the way for us to enter into the presence of God. We will also reflect on how this act of divine grace profoundly changed the nature of our relationship with God, from one of **separation** to one of **intimacy**.

I. The Tabernacle: God's Dwelling Place Among His People (Exodus 25-31)

The **Tabernacle** was the place where God dwelled among His people in the wilderness. Designed according to the specific instructions given by God to **Moses** on Mount Sinai, the Tabernacle was a mobile sanctuary where the Israelites could offer sacrifices and meet with God. Its construction, detailed in **Exodus 25-31**, was meant to reflect the **holiness** and **majesty** of God, while also illustrating the need for a **mediator** to bridge the gap between God and humanity.

A. The Structure of the Tabernacle

The Tabernacle was divided into two main sections: the **Holy Place** and the **Holy of Holies** (also known as the Most Holy Place). The Holy Place contained the **lampstand**, the **table of showbread**, and the **altar of incense**, while the Holy of Holies housed the **Ark of the Covenant**, which represented the very **presence of God**.

1. The Holy Place

The first section, the Holy Place, was where the **priests** performed their daily duties, such as offering incense and maintaining the lampstand. This space was accessible to the priests, but not to the general population of Israel.

2. The Holy of Holies

The Holy of Holies, however, was the innermost sanctuary where only the **high priest** could enter, and only once a year on the **Day of Atonement**. It was here that the high priest would sprinkle the blood of the sacrifice on the **mercy seat** of the Ark of the Covenant to atone for the sins of the people.

II. THE VEIL IN THE TABERNACLE: A BARRIER BETWEEN GOD AND MAN (EXODUS 26:31-35)

The **veil** that separated the Holy Place from the Holy of Holies was a massive and intricately designed curtain. **Exodus 26:31-35** provides the description of the veil:

"You shall make a veil of blue and purple and scarlet yarns and fine twined linen. It shall be made with cherubim skillfully worked into it. And you shall hang it on four pillars of acacia overlaid with gold, with hooks of gold, on four bases of silver. And you shall hang the veil from the clasps, and bring the Ark of the Testimony in there within the veil. And the veil shall separate for you the Holy Place from the Most Holy."

The veil was not just a decorative feature; it was a **physical barrier** that symbolized the **separation** between a holy and perfect God and sinful humanity. This veil stood as a reminder that access to God's presence was limited and could only be achieved through a **mediator**.

A. The Design of the Veil

The veil's design was rich with **symbolism**. It was made of blue, purple, and scarlet yarn, colors that represented **heaven**, **royalty**, and **sacrifice**. The fine linen emphasized **purity**, and the cherubim woven into the fabric pointed to the **guardian angels** that protect God's holiness. These details foreshadowed the person of **Christ**, who would one day **tear down** the barrier between God and man through His death.

1. Cherubim and the Protection of God's Holiness

The cherubim embroidered on the veil recall the **cherubim** stationed at the entrance to the **Garden of Eden** after Adam and Eve's fall (**Genesis 3:24**). Their role was to prevent humanity from re-entering the Garden and accessing the **Tree of Life**. Similarly, the cherubim on the veil symbolized the **guardianship of God's holiness**, barring unholy people from entering His presence.

2. The Weight and Strength of the Veil

Historically, the veil is believed to have been a **thick and heavy** curtain, possibly several inches thick. Its strength represented the **impossibility** of humanity tearing the veil through its own efforts. Only God could provide a way through the barrier, which would be accomplished in the person of **Christ**.

B. The Purpose of the Veil

The veil's purpose was to emphasize the **separation** caused by sin. Even though Israel was God's chosen people, they could not approach Him directly. Only the **high priest**, after extensive purification rituals, could pass through the veil to offer sacrifices for the people's sins. This separation was not intended to be permanent but served as a **temporary measure** until God's ultimate plan of redemption through **Jesus Christ**.

III. THE VEIL AS A TYPE OF CHRIST'S FLESH (HEBREWS 10:19-20)

The **New Testament** reveals the deeper meaning of the veil, connecting it directly to the **flesh of Christ**. **Hebrews 10:19-20** explains that the tearing of the veil represents the tearing of Christ's flesh, through which believers are granted access to God's presence:

> "Therefore, brothers, since we have confidence to enter the holy places by the blood of Jesus, by the new and living way that He opened for us through the curtain, that is, through His flesh."

A. The Tearing of the Veil and Christ's Death (Matthew 27:50-51)

The moment of **Christ's death** is marked by the **supernatural tearing** of the veil in the Temple. **Matthew 27:50-51** records this event:

> "And Jesus cried out again with a loud voice and yielded up His spirit. And behold, the curtain of the temple was torn in two, from top to bottom. And the earth shook, and the rocks were split."

This tearing of the veil was not a random occurrence but a direct **sign** from God that the **barrier** between humanity and God had been removed. Just as Christ's flesh was **torn** on the cross, the veil in the Temple was torn, symbolizing that access to God was now available to all through **Jesus Christ**.

1. Torn from Top to Bottom

The fact that the veil was torn from **top to bottom** is significant. This detail indicates that it was **God**, not man, who tore the veil. It was a divine act, showing that the **way to God** had been opened by God Himself through the **sacrifice of His Son**. No longer would there be a need for a **high priest** to mediate between God and man, because Christ had fulfilled that role once and for all.

2. The End of the Old Covenant

The tearing of the veil also signaled the **end of the Old Covenant** and the **beginning of the New Covenant**. Under the Old Covenant, access to God was limited and mediated through priests and sacrifices. But through Christ's death, the sacrificial system was fulfilled, and believers now have **direct access** to God through Christ, who serves as both the **sacrifice** and the **high priest**.

B. Christ's Flesh as the New Veil

In **Hebrews 10:20**, the author explicitly identifies **Christ's flesh** with the veil. Just as the veil in the Tabernacle and later in the Temple separated the people from the **presence of God**, Christ's flesh became the veil that was **torn** to open the way for believers to enter into God's presence. Through His death, Jesus became the **new and living way** by which we can confidently approach the **throne of grace**.

IV. THE SIGNIFICANCE OF THE TEARING OF THE VEIL: ACCESS TO GOD

The tearing of the veil has profound **theological implications** for the believer. Under the Old Covenant, the separation between God and humanity was made clear by the existence of the veil, which only the high priest could pass through. With the tearing of the veil, the **barrier of sin** that separated humanity from God was removed, and believers now have **direct access** to the presence of God.

A. Access to the Presence of God

One of the most significant outcomes of the tearing of the veil is the **access to God's presence** that believers now enjoy. No longer is access restricted to the high priest once a year; instead, every believer has the privilege of coming **boldly** before God's throne:

> "Let us then with confidence draw near to the throne of grace, that we may receive mercy and find grace to help in time of need." (Hebrews 4:16)

1. The Priesthood of All Believers

The tearing of the veil also signifies the **priesthood of all believers**. In the Old Testament, only the high priest could enter the Holy of Holies, but under the New Covenant, all believers are considered **priests** who can approach God directly. **1 Peter 2:9** affirms this, saying, "**But you are a chosen race, a royal priesthood, a holy nation, a people for His own possession...**" As priests, believers now have the **responsibility** and **privilege** of offering **spiritual sacrifices** to God.

2. A Personal Relationship with God

Before the tearing of the veil, God's presence was something distant and accessible only through intermediaries. But Christ's death changes that. Now, believers can enjoy a **personal relationship** with God. They are no longer separated from Him by their sin, because Christ's death has made atonement and opened the way for **intimacy** with God.

V. THE VEIL AND THE CONCEPT OF ATONEMENT

The tearing of the veil is deeply connected to the **concept of atonement** in both the Old and New Testaments. In the Old Covenant, atonement was made through the **blood of animals**, but it was always **temporary** and **imperfect**. The **Day of Atonement** was a yearly event, and each year the high priest had to enter the Holy of Holies to offer sacrifices for the sins of the people. However, these sacrifices could never truly **remove sin**; they could only **cover** it for a time.

A. Atonement Through the Blood of Christ

In contrast, Christ's sacrifice on the cross provided **perfect atonement**. Unlike the animal sacrifices of the Old Testament, which were limited in their effectiveness, Christ's sacrifice was **once for all**, completely sufficient to atone for the sins of humanity:

> "But when Christ appeared as a high priest of the good things that have come, then through the greater and more perfect tent (not made with hands, that is, not of this creation) He entered once for all into the holy places, not by means of the blood of goats and calves but by means of His own blood, thus securing an eternal redemption." (Hebrews 9:11-12)

1. The Finality of Christ's Sacrifice

The tearing of the veil symbolizes the **finality** of Christ's sacrifice. No longer would there be a need for **repeated sacrifices**; Christ's death accomplished what the sacrificial system could not. Through His blood, He secured **eternal redemption**, and the veil's tearing marked the end of the old way of approaching God.

2. The Fulfillment of the Day of Atonement

Christ's death on the cross fulfilled the **Day of Atonement**. Just as the high priest would sprinkle the blood of the sacrifice on the **mercy seat** in the Holy of Holies, Christ's blood was shed to make atonement for the sins of the world. By tearing the veil, God declared that the **final atonement** had been made, and now, through Christ's blood, we can enter into the **Holy of Holies**—into God's very presence.

B. The Role of the High Priest

The **high priest** played a central role in the Old Testament sacrificial system, acting as the mediator between God and the people. He alone could enter the Holy of Holies to make atonement for the nation's sins. However, with the tearing of the veil, Christ Himself became the **Great High Priest** who mediates between God and humanity.

1. Christ as the Eternal High Priest

Hebrews 7:23-24 describes Christ's priesthood as **eternal** and **unchanging**:

> "The former priests were many in number, because they were prevented by death from continuing in office, but He holds His priesthood permanently, because He continues forever."

Christ's priesthood is superior to the Levitical priesthood because He is not subject to death, and His **sacrifice** was once for all. As the eternal High Priest, Christ continuously **intercedes** for His people, ensuring that they have **ongoing access** to God's grace and mercy.

2. The Role of Intercession

One of the primary functions of the high priest in the Old Testament was to **intercede** on behalf of the people. In the New Covenant, Christ fulfills this role as our **intercessor**. **Romans 8:34** states, "**Who is to condemn? Christ Jesus is the one who died—more than that, who was raised—who is at the right hand of God, who indeed is interceding for us.**" As the one who has torn the veil, Christ now stands as the eternal **mediator**, guaranteeing that believers have continual access to God's presence.

VI. THE VEIL AND THE NEW COVENANT

The tearing of the veil marked the inauguration of the **New Covenant**, which was prophesied in the Old Testament and fulfilled in the New. The **Old Covenant** was based on the **Law of Moses**, which emphasized external rituals, sacrifices, and regulations that highlighted the separation between God and humanity. But the **New Covenant**, established through Christ's blood, brings about a new way of relating to God—one based on **grace**, **faith**, and **intimacy**.

A. The Promise of the New Covenant (Jeremiah 31:31-34)

The prophet **Jeremiah** foretold the coming of the New Covenant, in which God would establish a new relationship with His people:

> "Behold, the days are coming, declares the Lord, when I will make a new covenant with the house of Israel and the house of Judah... For this is the covenant that I will make with the house of Israel after those days, declares the Lord: I will put My law within them, and I will write it on their hearts. And I will be their God, and they shall be My people." (Jeremiah 31:31, 33)

The New Covenant would no longer rely on external rituals and sacrifices but would be based on an **internal transformation** of the heart. The tearing of the veil signifies that the **Old Covenant** has been fulfilled and that the **New Covenant** has begun.

1. The Internalization of God's Law

Under the New Covenant, God's law is no longer written on tablets of stone but is written on the **hearts** of His people. This internalization of God's law is made possible through the work of the **Holy Spirit**, who indwells believers and empowers them to live in **obedience** to God.

2. A Personal Relationship with God

The New Covenant also emphasizes a **personal relationship** with God. No longer is access to God mediated through priests and sacrifices; instead, every believer has the privilege of knowing God intimately. **Jeremiah 31:34** promises, "**And no longer shall each one teach his neighbor and each his brother, saying, 'Know the Lord,' for they shall all know Me, from the least of them to the greatest, declares the Lord. For I will forgive their iniquity, and I will remember their sin no more.**"

B. The Blood of the Covenant

The New Covenant was established through the **blood of Christ**. During the **Last Supper**, Jesus declared that His blood would be the **blood of the covenant**, poured out for the forgiveness of sins:

> "And He took a cup, and when He had given thanks He gave it to them, saying, 'Drink of it, all of you, for this is My blood of the covenant, which is poured out for many for the forgiveness of sins.'" (Matthew 26:27-28)

The tearing of the veil symbolizes the **fulfillment** of this covenant. Through the shedding of His blood, Christ inaugurated the New Covenant, providing **complete forgiveness** and **restoration** to all who believe in Him.

VII. THE SIGNIFICANCE OF THE VEIL FOR CHRISTIAN WORSHIP AND SPIRITUAL LIFE

The tearing of the veil has profound implications for **Christian worship** and **spiritual life**. In the Old Covenant, worship was highly regulated, with specific rituals, sacrifices, and festivals that emphasized the separation between God and His people. But in the New Covenant, worship is characterized by **freedom**, **intimacy**, and **spiritual communion** with God.

A. Worship in Spirit and Truth

Jesus spoke of the new kind of worship that would characterize the New Covenant during His conversation with the **Samaritan woman** at the well. In **John 4:23-24**, He declares:

> "But the hour is coming, and is now here, when the true worshipers will worship the Father in spirit and truth, for the Father is seeking such people to worship Him. God is spirit, and those who worship Him must worship in spirit and truth."

Because the veil has been torn, believers now have direct access to God, and worship is no longer confined to a specific place or ritual. Instead, it is a **spiritual** act, where believers can worship God in **truth**, experiencing **communion** with Him through the **Holy Spirit**.

1. The Role of the Holy Spirit in Worship

The tearing of the veil opened the way for believers to experience the indwelling of the **Holy Spirit**, who enables them to worship God in spirit and truth. The Holy Spirit transforms worship from an **external ritual** to an **internal reality**, where believers experience the **presence of God** in their hearts.

2. A Personal Experience of God's Presence

In the New Covenant, worship is not merely an obligation; it is a **personal experience** of God's presence. Believers no longer need to rely on **priests** or **mediators** to bring them into the presence of God. Instead, they can approach God **boldly** and enjoy an **intimate relationship** with Him.

VIII. FUN FACT: THE VEIL'S SYMBOLISM IN EARLY CHRISTIAN ART

In **early Christian art**, the image of the **torn veil** became a powerful symbol of **salvation** and **access to God**. In many early churches, depictions of the torn veil were placed in prominent positions, often near the altar, to remind worshipers that through Christ's death, the way to God had been opened. The image of the torn veil was also used in early Christian writings to emphasize the **transition** from the **Old Covenant** to the **New Covenant**, highlighting the superiority of Christ's priesthood and sacrifice.

The Tabernacle's Veil as a Type of Christ's Flesh

From the Tabernacle to Solomon's Temple to the Second Temple, the progression of God's dwelling among His people points toward a final and eternal fulfillment in Christ. The tearing of the temple veil at Jesus' crucifixion signifies the end of separation between God and humanity, and the beginning of the Church as the living temple, indwelt by the Spirit.

Solomon's Temple was the physical dwelling place of God among His people, where the Ark of the Covenant resided. As magnificent as it was, it served as a shadow of a greater reality. The destruction of this temple symbolized the passing of the old covenant system, pointing forward to the time when God's presence would dwell fully in Christ, the true Temple. The physical structure of the temple was temporary, but it laid the foundation for the spiritual temple found in Christ.

The Second Temple, rebuilt after the exile, held great significance for the Jewish people. It was the site of Jesus' ministry, and although it lacked the glory of Solomon's Temple, it still foreshadowed a greater fulfillment in Christ. The destruction of the Second Temple, as prophesied by Jesus, marks the end of the old sacrificial system and the transition to a new covenant where God's presence is no longer confined to a building but resides in Christ and His Church. Jesus, the ultimate Temple, fulfills what the Second Temple could only symbolize.

The **veil** in the Tabernacle, which separated the **Holy of Holies** from the rest of the sanctuary, served as a constant reminder of the **separation** between God and humanity due to sin. But with the death of **Christ**, the **ultimate High Priest**, the veil was torn, signifying the removal of that separation and the **opening of the way** for believers to enter into God's presence.

The veil, as a **type of Christ's flesh**, symbolizes the **atoning work** of Jesus, whose **sacrifice** on the cross provided the **perfect** and **final** way to God. Through His death, Christ fulfilled the role of both the **high priest** and the **sacrifice**, bringing an end to the old system of worship and establishing the **New Covenant**.

The tearing of the veil reminds us that we now have **direct access** to God, and that through Christ's blood, we are **redeemed**, forgiven, and restored to a **right relationship** with Him. As we worship God in **spirit and truth**, we can approach Him boldly, knowing that the barrier of sin has been removed and that we are now **welcome** in His presence.

The story of the **veil** is not just an ancient tradition, but a powerful reminder of the **love** and **sacrifice** of Christ, who made a way for us to be in **fellowship** with God forever. Through His torn flesh, we are granted the privilege of **drawing near** to the **throne of grace**, where we can find **mercy**, **forgiveness**, and **eternal life**.

CHAPTER 19: JOSHUA: A TYPE OF JESUS LEADING GOD'S PEOPLE INTO REST

The **story of Joshua** leading the Israelites into the Promised Land serves as a profound **type** or **foreshadowing** of **Jesus Christ** leading believers into **eternal rest**. Joshua, the successor to Moses, is tasked with bringing God's people into the land promised to their forefathers. However, the narrative of Joshua is much more than just a historical account of military conquests. It is a **theological masterpiece** that points toward the **spiritual rest** that Christ offers to all who believe.

Joshua's Hebrew name, **Yehoshua** (or **Yeshua**), is the same name as **Jesus** in the New Testament. This connection is not accidental. Just as Joshua led the Israelites into the **physical Promised Land, Jesus leads believers into the eternal rest** of salvation and the **heavenly Promised Land**. By studying the life and actions of Joshua, we gain insight into the **redemptive work of Christ**, who is the **ultimate deliverer** and **leader** of God's people.

This chapter will explore the life of Joshua as a **type of Christ**, highlighting the parallels between Joshua's leadership of Israel and Jesus' role as the **Savior of the world**. We will also delve into the concept of **rest**—both the temporary rest that Joshua brought to the Israelites and the **eternal rest** that Jesus provides for believers. Through this typology, we will see how Joshua's life and leadership prefigure the **greater work of Christ**, who brings His people into **complete peace** and **rest** in the presence of God.

I. THE LIFE OF JOSHUA: GOD'S CHOSEN LEADER FOR ISRAEL (JOSHUA 1)

Joshua, the son of **Nun**, first appears in the **Exodus** narrative as a young man chosen by **Moses** to lead Israel's army in the battle against the **Amalekites (Exodus 17:9-13)**. From the very beginning, Joshua is portrayed as a man of **courage, faith,** and **obedience** to God. Later, he serves as **Moses' assistant**, accompanying him partway up **Mount Sinai** when Moses received the **Ten Commandments (Exodus 24:13)**. Joshua also demonstrated his faithfulness when he, along with **Caleb**, brought back a positive report after spying out the Promised Land, despite the majority of the spies discouraging the people from entering **(Numbers 14:6-9)**.

A. Joshua as the Successor to Moses

After Moses' death, God appoints Joshua as the leader who will bring the Israelites into the **Promised Land**. **Joshua 1:1-2** begins with God's command to Joshua:

> "After the death of Moses the servant of the Lord, the Lord said to Joshua the son of Nun, Moses' assistant, 'Moses my servant is dead. Now therefore arise, go over this Jordan, you and all this people, into the land that I am giving to them, to the people of Israel.'"

Joshua's appointment as the successor to Moses marks a significant turning point in Israel's history. Whereas Moses led the people **out of Egypt** and through the wilderness, Joshua's mission is to lead them **into the Promised Land**. This transition mirrors the shift from the **Old Covenant** under the law, represented by Moses, to the **New Covenant** of grace, represented by Jesus.

1. A New Generation and a New Leader

One of the key themes in Joshua's leadership is the idea of a **new generation** entering into **God's promises**. The generation that left Egypt under Moses' leadership failed to enter the Promised Land due to their **disobedience** and **unbelief**. Now, under Joshua's leadership, a new generation is prepared to enter the land of **Canaan**.

This parallels the **new life** that Jesus brings to believers. Just as Joshua leads a new generation into the Promised Land, Jesus leads believers into a **new life of faith** and **eternal rest**.

2. The Promise of God's Presence

God's promise to be with Joshua as He was with Moses underscores the importance of **God's presence** in achieving His purposes. In **Joshua 1:5**, God assures Joshua:

> "No man shall be able to stand before you all the days of your life. Just as I was with Moses, so I will be with you. I will not leave you or forsake you."

This promise is significant because it echoes the **Great Commission** given by Jesus to His disciples in **Matthew 28:20**, where Jesus promises, "**I am with you always, to the end of the age.**" Just as Joshua could not succeed without God's presence, believers cannot fulfill their mission without the **presence of Christ**. This promise of God's presence points to the **Holy Spirit**, who empowers believers to live the Christian life and enter into God's rest.

II. CROSSING THE JORDAN RIVER: A TYPE OF BAPTISM AND NEW LIFE (JOSHUA 3-4)

One of the first challenges Joshua faces as Israel's new leader is crossing the **Jordan River**, which stood as a natural barrier between the Israelites and the Promised Land. In **Joshua 3**, God miraculously parts the waters of the Jordan, allowing the Israelites to cross on dry ground. This event is reminiscent of the **parting of the Red Sea**, where God delivered Israel from **Egyptian bondage** through Moses.

A. The Jordan Crossing as a Type of Baptism

The crossing of the Jordan River serves as a **type** of **baptism**, symbolizing the **transition** from the old life of wandering in the wilderness to the **new life** of living in the Promised Land. In Christian theology, **baptism** represents the believer's identification with the **death, burial, and resurrection** of Jesus Christ. Just as the Israelites crossed from the wilderness into the Promised Land, baptism marks the believer's transition from **spiritual death** to **spiritual life**.

1. Death to the Old Life

When the Israelites crossed the Jordan, they left behind the **wilderness**, a place of wandering and uncertainty, and entered into the **land of promise**. Similarly, when believers are baptized, they leave behind their **old life of sin** and are raised to walk in **newness of life** through Christ. **Romans 6:4** states:

> "We were buried therefore with Him by baptism into death, in order that, just as Christ was raised from the dead by the glory of the Father, we too might walk in newness of life."

2. Entering into God's Promises

Crossing the Jordan also symbolizes **entering into God's promises**. For the Israelites, the Promised Land was the fulfillment of God's covenant with **Abraham**, **Isaac**, and **Jacob**. For believers, baptism represents the beginning of a **life of faith**, where we claim the promises of God through **Jesus Christ**. Just as Joshua led the Israelites into the land promised to their forefathers, Jesus leads believers into the **fullness of life** that God has prepared for them.

B. The Memorial Stones: Remembering God's Faithfulness

After the Israelites crossed the Jordan, Joshua instructed them to take **twelve stones** from the riverbed and set them up as a **memorial** at **Gilgal**. These stones were meant to serve as a reminder to future generations of what God had done for Israel. **Joshua 4:6-7** explains:

> "That this may be a sign among you. When your children ask in time to come, 'What do those stones mean to you?' then you shall tell them that the waters

of the Jordan were cut off before the ark of the covenant of the Lord. When it passed over the Jordan, the waters of the Jordan were cut off. So these stones shall be to the people of Israel a memorial forever."

1. A Memorial of God's Deliverance

The **memorial stones** serve as a reminder of God's **faithfulness** in delivering His people and bringing them into the Promised Land. Similarly, believers are called to **remember** God's faithfulness in delivering them from **sin** and bringing them into a relationship with Him. The **Lord's Supper** (communion) serves as a memorial of Christ's death and resurrection, reminding believers of the **sacrifice** He made to redeem them.

2. Passing on Faith to the Next Generation

The memorial stones also highlight the importance of **passing on faith** to future generations. Just as the Israelites were instructed to tell their children about God's mighty works, believers are called to pass on the message of the **gospel** to the next generation. **Psalm 78:4** says:

> "We will not hide them from their children, but tell to the coming generation the glorious deeds of the Lord, and His might, and the wonders that He has done."

III. THE BATTLE OF JERICHO: VICTORY THROUGH FAITH AND OBEDIENCE (JOSHUA 6)

The first major challenge the Israelites faced after crossing the Jordan was the fortified city of **Jericho**. Jericho was a **stronghold** that stood in the way of Israel's conquest of the Promised Land. However, God had a specific plan for how the Israelites were to conquer the city, one that required **faith** and **obedience** rather than conventional military strategy.

A. God's Unconventional Battle Plan

Instead of instructing Joshua and the Israelites to attack the city walls directly, God gave them a very unusual battle plan. They were to march around the city once a day for **six days**, with the **priests** carrying the **Ark of the Covenant** and blowing trumpets. On the seventh day, they were to march around the city seven times, and after the priests blew their trumpets, the people were to shout, and the walls of Jericho would fall down.

1. Faith and Obedience

The conquest of Jericho required the Israelites to **trust** in God's plan, even though it seemed illogical from a human perspective. **Hebrews 11:30** highlights the faith of the Israelites in this event:

> "By faith the walls of Jericho fell down after they had been encircled for seven days."

The victory at Jericho demonstrates that **faith** and **obedience** to God's word are essential for experiencing His promises. Just as Joshua and the Israelites trusted in God's plan, believers are called to trust in **Jesus Christ** and follow Him in **faith**.

2. The Role of the Ark of the Covenant

The **Ark of the Covenant**, which represented God's presence, played a central role in the conquest of Jericho. The priests carried the Ark as they marched around the city, symbolizing that the victory was not won by human strength but by the **power of God**. In the same way, Christ's **presence** in the life of the believer is the source of victory over sin and spiritual strongholds. **2 Corinthians 10:4** reminds us that "the weapons of our warfare are not of the flesh but have divine power to destroy strongholds."

B. Jericho as a Type of Spiritual Strongholds

Jericho can be seen as a **type** of the **spiritual strongholds** that stand in the way of believers entering into the fullness of God's promises. Just as the walls of Jericho were a physical barrier that needed to be removed, there are **spiritual barriers**—such as sin, unbelief, and fear—that must be overcome for believers to experience **victory** and **rest** in Christ.

1. Overcoming Spiritual Strongholds Through Christ

Believers are called to trust in the **power of Christ** to tear down the spiritual strongholds in their lives. Just as Joshua led the Israelites in obedience to God's plan to bring down the walls of Jericho, Jesus leads believers in the **spiritual battle** against the forces of darkness. Through Christ's **death and resurrection**, the ultimate victory over sin and death has been won, and believers are empowered to live in freedom.

2. Entering Into Spiritual Rest

The fall of Jericho opened the way for the Israelites to enter more fully into the Promised Land, which symbolized **rest** from their enemies. In the same way, believers are invited to enter into **spiritual rest** through faith in Christ. This rest is not just the absence of conflict but the **presence of peace** and **security** in God's promises.

IV. JOSHUA AND THE CONCEPT OF REST: A FORESHADOWING OF ETERNAL REST (HEBREWS 4:8-9)

The **Promised Land** was often referred to as a place of **rest** for the Israelites, a land flowing with milk and honey where they would no longer be oppressed by their enemies. However, the **rest** that Joshua brought to Israel was only a **temporary** and **incomplete** rest. **Hebrews 4:8-9** makes it clear that the rest Joshua provided was not the **ultimate rest** that God intended for His people:

> "For if Joshua had given them rest, God would not have spoken of another day later on. So then, there remains a Sabbath rest for the people of God."

The writer of Hebrews explains that the **physical rest** provided by Joshua in the Promised Land was a **foreshadowing** of the **spiritual and eternal rest** that comes through Jesus Christ.

A. The Temporary Rest of the Promised Land

While Joshua led the Israelites into the **Promised Land**, the rest they experienced there was **imperfect** and temporary. Israel continued to face challenges from their enemies, and their **disobedience** led to times of turmoil and unrest. The rest they sought was not fully realized in the physical land of Canaan.

1. Rest Interrupted by Disobedience

Throughout the **book of Judges**, we see that Israel's rest was constantly interrupted by their **disobedience** and failure to remain faithful to God. This cycle of rest and unrest points to the fact that true rest cannot be found in earthly circumstances but only in **God's presence**.

2. The Incomplete Nature of Earthly Rest

The rest that Joshua brought to the Israelites was incomplete because it was tied to their **obedience** and **faithfulness**. In contrast, the rest that Jesus offers is **complete** and **eternal** because it is based on His **finished work** on the cross. While Joshua's rest depended on the Israelites' ability to follow God's commandments, Jesus' rest is based on **grace**, and it is freely given to all who believe in Him.

B. The Eternal Rest Provided by Jesus (Hebrews 4:1-11)

Hebrews 4 contrasts the rest that Joshua provided with the **eternal rest** offered by Jesus. While Joshua's rest was tied to a specific land and time, Jesus' rest is **spiritual** and **eternal**, available to all who place their faith in Him.

1. The Invitation to Enter God's Rest

In **Hebrews 4:1**, the author invites believers to **enter into God's rest**, warning them not to fall short through **unbelief**:

"Therefore, while the promise of entering His rest still stands, let us fear lest any of you should seem to have failed to reach it."

This rest is not just about physical relaxation but about **spiritual peace** and **security** in God's presence. Through faith in Christ, believers can experience this rest **now** and look forward to its **complete fulfillment** in eternity.

2. Sabbath Rest and the Work of Christ

The concept of **Sabbath rest** is central to understanding the rest that Jesus provides. Just as God rested on the **seventh day** after creating the world, believers are invited to **rest** in the **finished work** of Christ. **Hebrews 4:10** explains:

"For whoever has entered God's rest has also rested from his works as God did from His."

This rest is not about ceasing from physical labor but about ceasing from the **works-based righteousness** that characterized the Old Covenant. Through Jesus, believers enter into a state of **grace**, where they no longer strive to earn God's favor but rest in the **salvation** that has already been accomplished through Christ.

V. JOSHUA AND JESUS: PARALLELS BETWEEN THEIR ROLES AS DELIVERERS

The parallels between Joshua and Jesus go beyond their shared name. Both figures serve as **deliverers** of God's people, leading them into a place of **rest** and **promise**. However, while Joshua's deliverance was **physical** and tied to a specific place and time, Jesus' deliverance is **spiritual** and **eternal**.

A. The Name "Joshua" (Yeshua) and Its Meaning

The name **Joshua** in Hebrew is **Yehoshua** or **Yeshua**, which means **"Yahweh is salvation."** This is the same name as **Jesus** in the New Testament. The connection between their names highlights their roles as **saviors** or **deliverers**. Just as Joshua delivered Israel from their enemies and led them into the Promised Land, Jesus delivers believers from **sin** and leads them into the **eternal Promised Land** of heaven.

1. Joshua's Deliverance from Physical Enemies

Joshua's role as Israel's leader was to deliver them from the **Canaanite nations** that inhabited the Promised Land. Through a series of military victories, Joshua secured the land for the Israelites, allowing them to settle and experience rest from their enemies. However, this deliverance was **temporary**, as Israel continued to face challenges and conflicts in the years that followed.

2. Jesus' Deliverance from Sin and Death

In contrast, Jesus' deliverance is **spiritual** and **eternal**. Through His death and resurrection, Jesus delivers believers from the **power of sin** and **death**. While Joshua's victories were won through physical battles, Jesus won the ultimate victory over sin through His **sacrificial death** on the cross. **Colossians 2:15** explains that Jesus "disarmed the rulers and authorities and put them to open shame, by triumphing over them in Him." This victory ensures that believers are no longer enslaved to sin but are free to experience **eternal life** in Christ.

B. Leading God's People Into Rest

Both Joshua and Jesus are responsible for leading God's people into **rest**. However, while Joshua led the Israelites into a **temporary** rest in the Promised Land, Jesus leads believers into an **eternal** rest in the presence of God.

1. The Temporary Nature of Joshua's Rest

As we have already explored, the rest that Joshua provided in the Promised Land was incomplete. It was a **shadow** of the greater rest that would come through Christ. The Israelites' rest in Canaan was interrupted by their **disobedience**, and they continued to face challenges from their enemies. This imperfection in Joshua's rest points to the need for a **greater deliverer** who could provide a **perfect** and **eternal** rest.

2. The Eternal Nature of Jesus' Rest

Jesus, the **greater Joshua**, offers a rest that is **permanent** and **eternal**. His rest is not tied to a specific geographical location but is found in a **relationship with God**. Through faith in Christ, believers enter into **spiritual rest**—a rest that is marked by **peace**, **assurance**, and **intimacy** with God. **Matthew 11:28-30** captures Jesus' invitation to this rest:

> "Come to me, all who labor and are heavy laden, and I will give you rest. Take my yoke upon you, and learn from me, for I am gentle and lowly in heart, and you will find rest for your souls. For my yoke is easy, and my burden is light."

Jesus' rest is not just about **freedom from physical enemies** but about **freedom from the burden of sin** and the **weight of trying to earn salvation**. In Christ, believers find **true rest** for their souls, a rest that will culminate in **eternal life** with God.

VI. FUN FACT: THE BATTLE OF AI AND THE PRINCIPLE OF OBEDIENCE

In the **book of Joshua**, after the victory at Jericho, the Israelites experienced a temporary defeat at **Ai** because of one man's **disobedience—Achan**. Despite the clear instructions to destroy all the spoils of Jericho, Achan took some of the **devoted things** for himself, bringing **God's judgment** on the entire nation (**Joshua 7**). After this disobedience was addressed, God allowed the Israelites to defeat Ai.

This story serves as a **reminder** of the importance of **obedience** in the life of a believer. Just as Israel could not experience rest until the sin of Achan was dealt with, believers cannot experience the **fullness of God's rest** until they address areas of **disobedience** in their lives. This principle highlights the importance of living in **faithful obedience** to God's word in order to fully experience His promises.

Joshua as a Type of Christ and the Promise of Eternal Rest

From the Tabernacle to Solomon's Temple to the Second Temple, the progression of God's dwelling among His people points toward a final and eternal fulfillment in Christ. The tearing of the temple veil at Jesus' crucifixion signifies the end of separation between God and humanity, and the beginning of the Church as the living temple, indwelt by the Spirit.

Solomon's Temple was the physical dwelling place of God among His people, where the Ark of the Covenant resided. As magnificent as it was, it served as a shadow of a greater reality. The destruction of this temple symbolized the passing of the old covenant system, pointing forward to the time when God's presence would dwell fully in Christ, the true Temple. The physical structure of the temple was temporary, but it laid the foundation for the spiritual temple found in Christ.

The Second Temple, rebuilt after the exile, held great significance for the Jewish people. It was the site of Jesus' ministry, and although it lacked the glory of Solomon's Temple, it still foreshadowed a greater fulfillment in Christ. The destruction of the Second Temple, as prophesied by Jesus, marks the end of the old sacrificial system and the transition to a new covenant where God's presence is no longer confined to a building but resides in Christ and His Church. Jesus, the ultimate Temple, fulfills what the Second Temple could only symbolize.

The story of Joshua is a profound **foreshadowing** of the greater deliverance and rest that would come through **Jesus Christ**. As Joshua led the Israelites into the Promised Land, providing them with temporary rest from their enemies, Jesus leads believers into the **eternal rest** of salvation. Through His death and resurrection, Jesus has torn down the **spiritual barriers** that once separated humanity from God and has opened the way for believers to experience **true rest** in His presence.

Joshua's leadership, victories, and challenges point to the **greater work of Christ**, who not only delivers us from the power of sin but also invites us to enter into a **relationship** with God that is characterized by **peace**, **security**, and **eternal life**. Just as Joshua's name means "Yahweh is salvation," Jesus is the one who brings the **ultimate salvation** and rest to God's people.

The **Promised Land** that Joshua led the Israelites into was a temporary reflection of the **heavenly Promised Land** that awaits all who place their faith in Christ. As believers, we are called to trust in **Jesus**, our **greater Joshua**, and to follow Him into the **eternal rest** that He has prepared for us. Through Christ, we can rest from our works and find **complete peace** in His finished work on the cross. This is the true and lasting rest that Joshua's life pointed to—a rest that is available to all who believe and follow Jesus.

CHAPTER 20: THE CITIES OF REFUGE: A TYPE OF CHRIST AS OUR REFUGE

In the Old Testament, **God** established **Cities of Refuge** within Israel as safe havens for individuals who accidentally killed someone, protecting them from the avenger of blood until a proper trial could be held. These cities, introduced in **Numbers 35:6-34**, serve as a type and foreshadowing of **Jesus Christ**, who is the ultimate refuge for sinners fleeing from the judgment of **sin** and **death**. Just as these cities provided safety for those in danger, Christ provides **spiritual refuge** for all who come to Him for protection and salvation.

The **Cities of Refuge** offer profound theological insights into God's justice, mercy, and the provision He has made for sinners through Christ. This chapter explores the **typology** of the Cities of Refuge, emphasizing how these Old Testament institutions prefigure **Christ** as the **safe haven** for all who seek refuge from the **wrath of God**. We will also examine the **practical** and **spiritual** implications of seeking refuge in Christ and how these cities highlight the **grace** and **justice** of God.

I. THE ESTABLISHMENT OF THE CITIES OF REFUGE (NUMBERS 35:6-34)

The Cities of Refuge were designated places in **ancient Israel** where individuals who had accidentally killed someone could flee for safety. God gave Moses specific instructions to establish these cities when the Israelites entered the **Promised Land**. The purpose of these cities was to provide **protection** from the **avenger of blood**—usually a close relative of the deceased who sought to avenge the death. This protection was not an escape from justice but rather a means to ensure that **justice** was carried out fairly, preventing a **blood feud** or personal vengeance before a proper trial could take place.

A. The Purpose of the Cities of Refuge

The key purpose of the Cities of Refuge was to ensure **due process** and **justice** in cases of accidental manslaughter. In ancient societies, it was common for the nearest relative of a murder victim to act as the **avenger of blood**, seeking vengeance for the deceased. Without the Cities of Refuge, individuals who accidentally caused the death of another person would be subject to immediate revenge, even if the death was unintentional.

In **Numbers 35:12**, God commands that these cities should be a place of protection, stating:

> "The cities shall be for you a refuge from the avenger, that the manslayer may not die until he stands before the congregation for judgment."

These cities were not meant to shelter murderers or those who committed **premeditated** acts of violence. Instead, they were specifically for those who killed someone **unintentionally** or through **negligence**, without malicious intent. This distinction was vital to preserving the **justice** of the legal system in Israel.

1. Six Cities of Refuge

There were six designated Cities of Refuge—three on each side of the **Jordan River**. This ensured that no matter where someone lived in Israel, they would have reasonable access to one of these cities. **Deuteronomy 19:2-3** highlights the importance of accessibility:

> "You shall set apart three cities for yourselves in the land that the Lord your God is giving you to possess... You shall measure the distances and divide into three parts the area of the land that the Lord your God gives you as a possession, so that any manslayer can flee to them."

These six cities were: **Kedesh**, **Shechem**, **Hebron** (on the west side of the Jordan), and **Bezer**, **Ramoth**, and **Golan** (on the east side of the Jordan). They were well-distributed to ensure that anyone who needed to flee could do so quickly.

2. Temporary Shelter Until Judgment

Once the accused manslayer reached a City of Refuge, they were granted protection until their case could be heard by the **congregation**. If the killing was found to be accidental, the individual could remain in the city safely until the death of the **high priest**. At that point, they would be free to return to their home without fear of retribution. However, if the killing was found to be **premeditated**, the individual would be handed over to the avenger of blood and executed.

The key here is that the Cities of Refuge provided a **temporary** haven, allowing time for **justice** to be properly administered. This temporary nature is significant because it points to a **greater refuge** that would come through **Jesus Christ**—a refuge that is **permanent** and based on the **grace** of God.

II. THE CITIES OF REFUGE AS A TYPE OF CHRIST (HEBREWS 6:18)

In the New Testament, the **author of Hebrews** connects the concept of **refuge** to Christ, describing Him as the **ultimate refuge** for believers who seek safety from the **wrath of God**. Hebrews 6:18 states:

> "So that by two unchangeable things, in which it is impossible for God to lie, we who have fled for refuge might have strong encouragement to hold fast to the hope set before us."

Here, the writer draws on the imagery of fleeing to a **place of refuge** to illustrate the **security** and **assurance** that believers have in Christ. Just as those who accidentally killed someone in Israel could flee to a City of Refuge, sinners can flee to Christ, who provides **safety** from the judgment that sin deserves.

A. The Need for Refuge from Judgment

The Bible makes it clear that all of humanity stands guilty before a **holy God. Romans 3:23** declares, "for all have sinned and fall short of the glory of God," and **Romans 6:23** adds, "for the wages of sin is death." This means that every person is deserving of **judgment** for their sin, and without a **refuge**, there is no escape from God's wrath.

However, in His mercy, God has provided a **refuge** in the person of **Jesus Christ**. Just as the Cities of Refuge offered protection to those who sought safety, Christ offers protection to those who **repent** and **believe** in Him. He shields them from the **penalty** of their sin through His **sacrifice** on the cross.

1. Jesus as Our Safe Haven

Jesus is described throughout the New Testament as the **only way** to escape the judgment of sin. **John 14:6** records Jesus saying, "I am the way, and the truth, and the life. No one comes to the Father except through me." Christ's **atoning work** on the cross made it possible for sinners to be **justified** before God, allowing them to enter into His presence without fear of condemnation.

2. Eternal Refuge Versus Temporary Refuge

While the Cities of Refuge provided **temporary** safety until the death of the high priest, Christ's **refuge** is **eternal**. Those who come to Him are **fully justified** and no longer have to fear the **second death**—eternal separation from God in **hell**. In Christ, believers find **permanent security**, not just temporary shelter from judgment.

III. THE REQUIREMENTS FOR FLEEING TO A CITY OF REFUGE: A PICTURE OF FAITH IN CHRIST

Fleeing to a City of Refuge required the individual to take **decisive action**. They had to recognize their need for protection and run to the city as quickly as possible. This serves as a **picture** of the faith that is required to come to Christ for salvation. Just as the manslayer could not delay in seeking refuge, sinners must recognize their need for **forgiveness** and **run to Christ** for safety.

A. Acknowledging the Need for Refuge

The first step in fleeing to a City of Refuge was **recognizing** the danger one was in. The individual had to acknowledge that the **avenger of blood** was pursuing them and that they needed to seek protection. Similarly, sinners must first **recognize** their **sinful condition** and their need for a Savior. **Romans 3:10** states, "None is righteous, no, not one," and **Romans 6:23** adds, "For the wages of sin is death." Until a person acknowledges their sin, they will not seek refuge in Christ.

1. The Urgency of Fleeing

In the Old Testament, there was an **urgency** in fleeing to a City of Refuge. The manslayer could not afford to delay, as the **avenger of blood** could overtake them if they hesitated. This urgency mirrors the need for individuals to come to Christ without delay. **Hebrews 3:15** warns, "Today, if you hear His voice, do not harden your hearts." The offer of refuge is extended to all, but it must be received with **urgency** and **faith**.

2. Faith in the Promise of Refuge

The manslayer fleeing to the City of Refuge had to **trust** that the city would provide protection as God had promised. In the same way, sinners must place their **faith** in Christ, trusting that He will provide the refuge and salvation that God has promised. **Ephesians 2:8** teaches that salvation comes through **faith**: "For by grace you have been saved through faith. And this is not your own doing; it is the gift of God."

B. Entering the City for Safety

Once the manslayer reached the City of Refuge, they were **safe** as long as they remained within the city's walls. This illustrates the **security** that believers have when they are **in Christ**. Those who come to Christ are **safe** from the wrath of God, and as long as they remain in Him, they cannot be touched by judgment. **John 10:28-29** speaks of this **eternal security**, with Jesus saying:

> "I give them eternal life, and they will never perish, and no one will snatch them out of My hand. My Father, who has given them to Me, is greater than all, and no one is able to snatch them out of the Father's hand."

Just as the manslayer was safe within the City of Refuge, believers are safe in **Christ**, who shields them from **condemnation**.

IV. THE HIGH PRIEST AND THE RELEASE OF THE REFUGEE: A TYPE OF CHRIST'S PRIESTHOOD

One of the most unique aspects of the Cities of Refuge was that the manslayer was required to remain in the city until the death of the **high priest**. Once the high priest died, the manslayer was free to leave the city and return home without fear of retribution. This aspect of the Cities of Refuge serves as a type of **Christ's priesthood**, showing how Jesus, our **Great High Priest**, has secured **eternal freedom** for us through His death.

A. The Role of the High Priest in the Cities of Refuge

The high priest's death served as a **legal turning point** for the individual seeking refuge. The high priest represented the **nation of Israel** before God, and his death symbolized a **new beginning** for the manslayer. This aspect of the law was unique in that it linked the **release of the refugee** to the death of the high priest, further emphasizing the **substitutionary** role of the priesthood in Israel's legal system.

1. The High Priest's Death as a Release

The death of the high priest signified that the debt of **bloodshed** had been satisfied, even in the case of accidental manslaughter. The individual who had fled to the City of Refuge was no longer under the threat of the avenger of blood, because the high priest's death had **fulfilled the legal requirement** for their release.

2. Christ's High Priesthood and Our Release

This aspect of the Cities of Refuge points directly to **Jesus Christ**, who is described in **Hebrews 7:24-25** as our eternal **High Priest**:

> "But He holds His priesthood permanently, because He continues forever. Consequently, He is able to save to the uttermost those who draw near to God through Him, since He always lives to make intercession for them."

Just as the high priest's death in Israel secured the release of the refugee, **Christ's death** secures the **eternal release** of believers from the penalty of sin. Through His **sacrifice**, Jesus has fulfilled the **legal requirements** of the law, and those who come to Him for refuge are set free from the **condemnation** of sin.

B. Christ as the Ultimate High Priest

The **book of Hebrews** presents Jesus as the **ultimate High Priest**, whose priesthood is far superior to that of the Levitical priesthood. **Hebrews 9:11-12** explains:

> "But when Christ appeared as a high priest of the good things that have come, then through the greater and more perfect tent (not made with hands, that is, not of this creation) He entered once for all into the holy places, not by means of the blood of goats and calves but by means of His own blood, thus securing an eternal redemption."

Christ's priesthood is not limited by **death**, as was the case with the high priests of Israel. His priesthood is **eternal**, and His death secures an **eternal redemption** for all who come to Him for refuge. Just as the manslayer was freed upon the death of the high priest, believers are freed from **sin** and **death** through the death and resurrection of Christ.

V. CHRIST AS OUR REFUGE: THE FULFILLMENT OF THE CITIES OF REFUGE

While the Cities of Refuge provided a **temporary** and **physical** place of safety, **Christ** offers an **eternal** and **spiritual** refuge for all who come to Him. The **gospel** presents Jesus as the **only refuge** for sinners, offering protection from the judgment that sin deserves.

A. The Assurance of Safety in Christ

Those who fled to a City of Refuge could be confident that they were safe as long as they remained within the city. Similarly, those who come to Christ for refuge can be **confident** that they are safe from the **wrath of God. Romans 8:1** declares, "There is therefore now no condemnation for those who are in Christ Jesus." Believers who have taken refuge in Christ are **secure** in His salvation and can rest in the knowledge that they are **protected** from God's judgment.

1. Christ's Refuge is Available to All

The Cities of Refuge were open to all Israelites and even to **foreigners** living among them. This inclusiveness points to the **universal offer of salvation** in Christ. Jesus offers refuge to **all people**, regardless of their background, ethnicity, or past sins. **John 6:37** records Jesus saying, "All that the Father gives me will come to me, and whoever comes to me I will never cast out."

2. The Urgency of Seeking Refuge in Christ

Just as the manslayer had to flee to the City of Refuge quickly, sinners are called to seek refuge in Christ with **urgency. 2 Corinthians 6:2** reminds us that "now is the day of salvation." The offer of refuge in Christ is available, but it must be received with **faith** and **repentance**.

B. Christ's Refuge is Permanent

Unlike the Cities of Refuge, where the manslayer could only remain temporarily until the death of the high priest, Christ's refuge is **permanent**. Those who take refuge in Him are **secure forever**. **John 10:28** emphasizes the eternal security that believers have in Christ:

> "I give them eternal life, and they will never perish, and no one will snatch them out of My hand."

This eternal security is the **fulfillment** of what the Cities of Refuge foreshadowed. In Christ, believers are not just temporarily protected from judgment—they are given **eternal life** and will never face condemnation.

VI. FUN FACT: THE SYMBOLISM OF THE CITY NAMES

The names of the six Cities of Refuge are rich with **symbolic meaning**, each pointing to different aspects of God's provision and character. For example:

- **Kedesh** means **"holy"** or **"set apart"**, reflecting God's holiness and the holiness required to approach Him.

- **Shechem** means **"shoulder"**, symbolizing strength and support, as Christ carries the burdens of those who come to Him.

- **Hebron** means **"fellowship"**, pointing to the intimate relationship believers have with God through Christ.

- **Bezer** means **"fortress"**, reflecting the protection and security found in Christ.

- **Ramoth** means **"heights"**, symbolizing the exalted position believers have in Christ.

- **Golan** means **"joy"**, reflecting the joy and peace that come from being in God's refuge.

These names highlight the **characteristics** of Christ as our refuge, providing not only safety but also **fellowship**, **strength**, and **joy** in His presence.

Christ, Our Eternal City of Refuge

From the Tabernacle to Solomon's Temple to the Second Temple, the progression of God's dwelling among His people points toward a final and eternal fulfillment in Christ. The tearing of the temple veil at Jesus' crucifixion signifies the end of separation between God and humanity, and the beginning of the Church as the living temple, indwelt by the Spirit.

Solomon's Temple was the physical dwelling place of God among His people, where the Ark of the Covenant resided. As magnificent as it was, it served as a shadow of a greater reality. The destruction of this temple symbolized the passing of the old covenant system, pointing forward to the time when God's presence would dwell fully in Christ, the true Temple. The physical structure of the temple was temporary, but it laid the foundation for the spiritual temple found in Christ.

The Second Temple, rebuilt after the exile, held great significance for the Jewish people. It was the site of Jesus' ministry, and although it lacked the glory of Solomon's Temple, it still foreshadowed a greater fulfillment in Christ. The destruction of the Second Temple, as prophesied by Jesus, marks the end of the old sacrificial system and the transition to a new covenant where God's presence is no longer confined to a building but resides in Christ and His Church. Jesus, the ultimate Temple, fulfills what the Second Temple could only symbolize.

The **Cities of Refuge** in ancient Israel were a divine provision of **mercy** and **justice**, ensuring that those who accidentally caused harm could find safety from vengeance. However, these cities were merely a **shadow** of the greater refuge that would come through **Jesus Christ**. As the **ultimate refuge**, Christ offers **protection**, **forgiveness**, and **eternal life** to all who come to Him in faith.

Just as the manslayer had to flee to the City of Refuge to escape the avenger of blood, sinners must flee to **Christ** to escape the **judgment** their sins deserve. In Christ, we find **perfect security**, for He is the **Great High Priest** who has offered His own life as the **sacrifice** for our sins. Through His death and resurrection, we are set free from the **penalty of sin** and are granted **eternal refuge** in Him.

The **typology** of the Cities of Refuge points to the **gospel message**—that **Jesus is our refuge**. In Him, we are safe from the judgment of sin, secure in the **love of God**, and assured of **eternal life**. This is the hope of the gospel, and it is the hope that every believer can cling to as they find their refuge in **Christ alone**.

CHAPTER 21: THE ROCK IN THE WILDERNESS: A TYPE OF CHRIST THE LIVING WATER

In the vast and challenging wilderness of the **Exodus**, the people of Israel often found themselves in need of miraculous provision from God. One of the most striking examples of this divine provision occurs when **Moses**, at God's command, strikes a **rock**, and **water** flows out, quenching the thirst of the **Israelites**. This event, recorded in **Exodus 17:6**, is a profound display of God's faithfulness, but it is also rich in **symbolism** that points forward to **Jesus Christ** as the **Rock** who was struck to provide **living water** for His people.

The **Apostle Paul** in **1 Corinthians 10:4** explicitly connects this event to Christ, stating that the rock which followed the Israelites in the wilderness was Christ. This connection reveals the deeper spiritual meaning behind the physical event: just as the rock was struck to provide **life-giving water**, Christ was **struck** (crucified) to provide the **living water** of the **Holy Spirit** to all who believe in Him.

In this chapter, we will explore the **typology** of the **rock in the wilderness** as a type of **Christ**, drawing out the theological richness of this symbolism and examining how the **Old Testament** narrative points forward to the **salvation** that Christ brings. We will also consider how the **living water** that flows from Christ is essential to the **spiritual life** of every believer. Additionally, we will incorporate a **fun fact** about how the desert terrain of the **Sinai Peninsula** contributes to the importance of water in biblical typology.

I. THE CONTEXT OF THE ROCK IN THE WILDERNESS (EXODUS 17:1-7)

The event of **Moses striking the rock** takes place during Israel's journey through the wilderness, shortly after their **exodus from Egypt**. After witnessing numerous miracles—such as the parting of the **Red Sea** and the provision of **manna** from heaven—the Israelites find themselves in a region called **Rephidim**, where there is no water for them to drink.

A. Israel's Grumbling and God's Response

Despite having witnessed God's faithfulness time and again, the people of Israel **grumble** against Moses, complaining that they have been brought out of Egypt only to die of thirst in the wilderness. Their complaint reveals not only their physical need for water but also their **spiritual short-sightedness** and lack of faith in God's provision.

Exodus 17:2-3 captures their frustration:

"Therefore the people quarreled with Moses and said, 'Give us water to drink.' And Moses said to them, 'Why do you quarrel with me? Why do you test the Lord?' But the people thirsted there for water, and the people grumbled against Moses and said, 'Why did you bring us up out of Egypt, to kill us and our children and our livestock with thirst?'"

Rather than responding to their complaints with anger, God provides a **gracious solution**. He instructs Moses to take his staff—the same staff used to part the Red Sea—and strike a **rock** at **Horeb**. When Moses strikes the rock, **water** will flow out, providing for the needs of the people.

1. Moses Strikes the Rock

Following God's instructions, Moses strikes the rock, and **water** miraculously flows out, quenching the thirst of the entire nation of Israel. This act not only meets their immediate physical need but also serves as a **divine reminder** that God is the provider of life, even in the most barren places.

2. The Significance of Water in the Wilderness

In the desert context of the **Sinai Peninsula**, water was not only a basic necessity for survival but also a powerful symbol of **life** and **divine provision**. The Israelites' dependence on God for water highlighted their total reliance on Him for **sustenance** and **life itself**. This reliance on water as a symbol of life becomes a key theme throughout the Bible, culminating in Jesus' declaration that He is the source of **living water**.

B. The Naming of the Place: Massah and Meribah

Following the miraculous provision of water, Moses names the place **Massah** (which means **testing**) and **Meribah** (which means **quarreling**), reflecting the attitude of the Israelites during this event. These names serve as a reminder of the people's **lack of faith** and the way they tested the Lord. Yet, in the midst of their grumbling and doubt, God demonstrates His **grace** by providing for their needs.

This theme of **testing** and **quarreling** is significant because it points to the broader spiritual realities of humanity's struggle with faith and God's continual offer of **grace** and **provision**, even in the face of our **doubt**.

II. THE ROCK AS A TYPE OF CHRIST (1 CORINTHIANS 10:4)

The **Apostle Paul** provides a clear connection between the **rock** in the wilderness and **Jesus Christ** in his letter to the **Corinthians**. In **1 Corinthians 10:1-4**, Paul recounts the story of Israel's journey through the wilderness and states that the Israelites "all drank the same spiritual drink. For they drank from the spiritual Rock that followed them, and the Rock was Christ."

By making this connection, Paul emphasizes that the **rock** in the wilderness was not just a source of physical water but also a **spiritual symbol** pointing to the ultimate **source of life**—Jesus Christ.

A. The Striking of the Rock as a Picture of Christ's Sacrifice

One of the most important aspects of this typology is the fact that the **rock** was **struck** in order to provide water. This act of striking prefigures the **crucifixion of Christ**, where He was "struck" for our transgressions. Just as the rock was struck to bring forth life-giving water for the Israelites, Christ was struck (crucified) to bring forth the **living water** of the **Holy Spirit** to all who believe.

1. Isaiah's Prophecy of the Suffering Servant

The image of Christ being struck is vividly prophesied in **Isaiah 53:4-5**, which describes the **Suffering Servant** who would be **wounded** for our sins:

> "Surely he has borne our griefs and carried our sorrows; yet we esteemed him stricken, smitten by God, and afflicted. But he was pierced for our transgressions; he was crushed for our iniquities; upon him was the chastisement that brought us peace, and with his wounds we are healed."

Just as the rock in the wilderness was **struck** to provide water, Christ was **pierced** to provide the spiritual sustenance needed for eternal life. The **striking of the rock** is therefore a vivid foreshadowing of the **atoning work** of Christ on the cross.

2. The Water as a Symbol of the Holy Spirit

In the **New Testament**, water is often used as a symbol of the **Holy Spirit**. In **John 7:37-39**, Jesus speaks of the **living water** that will flow from Him, referring to the **Holy Spirit** who would be given to believers after His death and resurrection:

> "On the last day of the feast, the great day, Jesus stood up and cried out, 'If anyone thirsts, let him come to me and drink. Whoever believes in me, as the Scripture has said, "Out of his heart will flow rivers of living water."' Now this he said about the Spirit, whom those who believed in him were to receive, for as yet the Spirit had not been given, because Jesus was not yet glorified."

Just as the physical water from the rock sustained the Israelites in the wilderness, the **living water** of the Holy Spirit sustains believers spiritually, bringing **life** and **refreshment** to their souls. The water that flows from Christ is not just temporary relief but **eternal life**.

B. Christ, the Rock of Our Salvation

The Bible frequently uses the imagery of a **rock** to describe God's **steadfastness**, **strength**, and **reliability**. In the **Old Testament**, God is often referred to as a **Rock**—a place of refuge and strength for His people.

- **Psalm 18:2**: "The Lord is my rock and my fortress and my deliverer, my God, my rock, in whom I take refuge, my shield, and the horn of my salvation, my stronghold."

This language finds its fulfillment in **Jesus Christ**, who is the **Rock** of our salvation. Just as the physical rock in the wilderness provided life-giving water, Jesus, the **spiritual Rock**, provides the water of **eternal life**. In Him, we find **refuge**, **strength**, and **salvation**.

III. THE REBELLION AT MERIBAH: A SECOND STRIKING OF THE ROCK (NUMBERS 20:1-13)

Later in Israel's wilderness journey, a similar situation arises in **Numbers 20**. Once again, the people are without water, and they grumble against Moses and Aaron. However, this time, when Moses seeks God's guidance, God instructs him to **speak** to the rock rather than strike it.

A. Moses' Disobedience

In a moment of frustration with the people, Moses **strikes** the rock instead of speaking to it as God commanded. Although water still flows from the rock, Moses' disobedience leads to serious consequences. God tells Moses and Aaron that because they did not trust Him and did not **sanctify** Him before the people, they would not lead the Israelites into the Promised Land (**Numbers 20:12**).

This act of disobedience on Moses' part disrupts the **symbolism** of the rock as a type of Christ. The **rock** had already been struck once (in Exodus 17), symbolizing Christ's crucifixion. Striking the rock a second time was unnecessary, just as Christ's sacrifice on the cross is **once for all**—there is no need for Christ to be "struck" again.

1. The Sufficiency of Christ's Sacrifice

Moses' disobedience at Meribah underscores the **sufficiency** of Christ's sacrifice. Just as Moses was only meant to strike the rock once, Christ's death on the cross is a **once-for-all** sacrifice. **Hebrews 9:26-28** makes this clear:

> "But as it is, he has appeared once for all at the end of the ages to put away sin by the sacrifice of himself... so Christ, having been offered once to bear the sins of many, will appear a second time, not to deal with sin but to save those who are eagerly waiting for him."

The **living water** that flows from Christ is the result of His single, sufficient sacrifice. Once the rock was struck in **Exodus 17**, there was no need for it to be struck again—just as Christ's one act of atonement is sufficient for all time.

2. Speaking to the Rock: A Picture of Faith

In contrast to striking the rock, God's instruction for Moses to **speak** to the rock in **Numbers 20** represents a shift from the need for sacrifice to the **role of faith** in accessing the blessings of God. After Christ's sacrifice, believers are no longer required to "strike" Christ or perform any further works for salvation. Instead, they are called to **speak** to Him in **faith**, trusting that the **living water** He provides is freely available to all who believe.

This act of **speaking** to the rock mirrors the simplicity of the **gospel message**: salvation comes through **faith** in the finished work of Christ, not through our own efforts. The **living water** of the Holy Spirit is available to all who come to Christ in faith, asking for the **refreshment** and **life** that only He can give.

IV. THE LIVING WATER: CHRIST'S PROMISE OF THE HOLY SPIRIT (JOHN 7:37-39)

One of the most powerful New Testament passages linking **water** to **Christ** is found in **John 7:37-39**, where Jesus stands up during the **Feast of Tabernacles** and offers a remarkable invitation to the people:

> "On the last day of the feast, the great day, Jesus stood up and cried out, 'If anyone thirsts, let him come to me and drink. Whoever believes in me, as the Scripture has said, "Out of his heart will flow rivers of living water."' Now this he said about the Spirit, whom those who believed in him were to receive, for as yet the Spirit had not been given, because Jesus was not yet glorified."

A. The Feast of Tabernacles and Water Imagery

The context of Jesus' statement is significant. The **Feast of Tabernacles** was a celebration that commemorated Israel's wilderness journey, and one of its central features was the **water-drawing ceremony**, in which water was drawn from the **Pool of Siloam** and poured out at the altar, symbolizing God's provision of water in the wilderness and the future outpouring of God's Spirit.

In this context, Jesus stands up and declares that **He** is the source of **living water**. Just as the rock in the wilderness provided water for the Israelites, Jesus offers the **Holy Spirit** as the living water that will sustain and refresh the souls of all who believe in Him.

1. The Holy Spirit as Living Water

The **living water** that Jesus speaks of refers to the **Holy Spirit**, who would be given to believers after Jesus' glorification (His death, resurrection, and ascension). The **Holy Spirit** is the one who brings **life**, **renewal**, and **refreshment** to the believer's soul. Just as water is essential for physical life, the Holy Spirit is essential for **spiritual life**.

The **Apostle Paul** affirms this in **Titus 3:5-6**, describing the Holy Spirit's work of regeneration and renewal:

> "He saved us, not because of works done by us in righteousness, but according to his own mercy, by the washing of regeneration and renewal of the Holy Spirit, whom he poured out on us richly through Jesus Christ our Savior."

2. Rivers of Living Water Flowing from Believers

Jesus not only promises that those who believe in Him will receive the **living water** of the Holy Spirit, but He also declares that this living water will flow out of them to others. This imagery of **rivers of living water** flowing from the believer's heart suggests that the **Holy Spirit** not only fills and satisfies the believer but also enables them to be a source of **life** and **blessing** to others.

This powerful image of the **Holy Spirit** flowing from believers highlights the **transformative** work of the Spirit in the lives of those who trust in Christ. As believers are filled with the **living water**, they become vessels through which God's grace, love, and life flow out to others, bringing refreshment and renewal to the world.

V. THE SPIRITUAL SIGNIFICANCE OF WATER IN BIBLICAL TYPOLOGY

Throughout the Bible, **water** is used as a powerful symbol of **life**, **cleansing**, and **renewal**. From the waters of **creation** in **Genesis** to the **river of life** flowing from the throne of God in **Revelation**, water plays a central role in illustrating God's provision for both physical and spiritual life.

A. Water as a Symbol of Life and Sustenance

In the **Sinai wilderness**, water was a precious commodity, and its scarcity made it all the more valuable. For the Israelites wandering in the desert, water was not just a physical necessity but also a symbol of **God's provision** and **faithfulness**. The miracle of water flowing from the rock emphasized that God was the **source of life** and sustenance for His people, even in the most barren places.

Similarly, in the New Testament, **Jesus** is presented as the source of **spiritual life**. Just as physical water sustains the body, the **Holy Spirit** sustains the soul, bringing **life** and **refreshment** to those who are spiritually thirsty.

1. Baptism as a Symbol of Cleansing

In addition to symbolizing life and sustenance, water is also a symbol of **cleansing** in the Bible. The **ritual washings** of the Old Testament, as well as **Christian baptism**, use water to represent **purification** from sin and a **new beginning**. **Titus 3:5** speaks of the **"washing of regeneration"** by the Holy Spirit, linking the imagery of water to the spiritual renewal that comes through faith in Christ.

2. The River of Life in Revelation

The imagery of **water** reaches its climax in the book of **Revelation**, where the **river of life** flows from the throne of God and the Lamb:

> "Then the angel showed me the river of the water of life, bright as crystal, flowing from the throne of God and of the Lamb." (Revelation 22:1)

This vision represents the **eternal life** and **refreshment** that will flow from God's presence in the new creation, fulfilling all the symbolic meanings of water throughout the Bible. In the same way that the rock in the wilderness provided water for the Israelites, **Christ**, the **Lamb of God**, will provide the **living water** that sustains His people forever.

VI. FUN FACT: THE DESERT TERRAIN AND THE IMPORTANCE OF WATER

The **Sinai Peninsula**, where the Israelites wandered for 40 years, is an arid desert region with scarce water resources. The

miracle of water flowing from a rock in this context is even more remarkable because of the **barren** and **inhospitable** nature of the landscape. In the ancient Near East, water was considered a **divine blessing** and a symbol of **life**, which is why so many biblical narratives emphasize God's provision of water in the wilderness.

The **Sinai wilderness** remains one of the most **water-scarce** places on earth, making the miracle of **water flowing from a rock** all the more significant. This not only highlights the **supernatural** nature of the event but also reinforces the message that God is the **source** of life, even in the most difficult and barren circumstances.

Christ, the Rock of Our Salvation and the Source of Living Water

From the Tabernacle to Solomon's Temple to the Second Temple, the progression of God's dwelling among His people points toward a final and eternal fulfillment in Christ. The tearing of the temple veil at Jesus' crucifixion signifies the end of separation between God and humanity, and the beginning of the Church as the living temple, indwelt by the Spirit.

Solomon's Temple was the physical dwelling place of God among His people, where the Ark of the Covenant resided. As magnificent as it was, it served as a shadow of a greater reality. The destruction of this temple symbolized the passing of the old covenant system, pointing forward to the time when God's presence would dwell fully in Christ, the true Temple. The physical structure of the temple was temporary, but it laid the foundation for the spiritual temple found in Christ.

The Second Temple, rebuilt after the exile, held great significance for the Jewish people. It was the site of Jesus' ministry, and although it lacked the glory of Solomon's Temple, it still foreshadowed a greater fulfillment in Christ. The destruction of the Second Temple, as prophesied by Jesus, marks the end of the old sacrificial system and the transition to a new covenant where God's presence is no longer confined to a building but resides in Christ and His Church. Jesus, the ultimate Temple, fulfills what the Second Temple could only symbolize.

The story of **Moses striking the rock** in the wilderness is not just an account of **God's provision** of water for the Israelites; it is a profound **foreshadowing** of the **living water** that Christ would provide through His death and resurrection. Just as the rock was struck to provide life-giving water, Christ was struck to provide the **living water** of the **Holy Spirit**.

In Christ, we find the **source** of **eternal life**, the one who quenches our spiritual thirst and brings **renewal** to our souls. The **living water** that flows from Him is available to all who come to Him in **faith**, and it not only sustains us but also transforms us into vessels of **blessing** for others.

The typology of the **rock in the wilderness** teaches us that God's provision is **abundant**, **miraculous**, and **eternal**. Just as the Israelites depended on the water from the rock for their survival, we depend on **Christ** for our spiritual life. And just as the rock was struck once to provide water, Christ's sacrifice on the cross was **once for all**, providing the **living water** of the Holy Spirit to all who believe.

As we drink deeply from the **living water** that Christ offers, we are refreshed, renewed, and empowered to share that water with a world that is **spiritually thirsty**.

CHAPTER 22: THE SCAPEGOAT: A TYPE OF CHRIST BEARING OUR SINS

The concept of a **scapegoat**—a creature bearing the sins of a community and taking those sins away—comes directly from the **Day of Atonement** ritual in the Old Testament, specifically in **Leviticus 16**. In this solemn event, the **high priest** symbolically placed the sins of **Israel** on the head of a goat, which was then sent into the wilderness, carrying away the nation's iniquities. This action was a profound illustration of the removal of sin, foreshadowing the work of **Jesus Christ**, who bore the sins of the world and took them away through His death on the cross.

The **scapegoat** serves as one of the most striking **types** of **Christ** in the Old Testament. While the sacrificial system of ancient Israel involved multiple elements to atone for sins, the imagery of the scapegoat highlights the crucial concept of **substitution**—an innocent being bearing the guilt and punishment of others. Jesus is the **ultimate scapegoat**, taking upon Himself the sins of humanity and removing them once and for all.

This chapter will explore the **typology** of the scapegoat in the **Day of Atonement** as a **prefiguration** of Christ's sacrificial work on the cross. We will examine how the rituals surrounding the scapegoat reflect the deeper theological themes of **atonement, forgiveness**, and **the removal of sin**. Additionally, we will explore the significance of Christ as the **Lamb of God** who takes away the sins of the world and how the scapegoat points to the **gospel** message of salvation.

I. THE DAY OF ATONEMENT: A PICTURE OF CHRIST'S WORK (LEVITICUS 16)

The **Day of Atonement** (known in Hebrew as **Yom Kippur**) was the most important day in the Jewish calendar and was observed annually to atone for the **sins of the entire nation** of Israel. It was the one day of the year when the **high priest** entered the **Holy of Holies**, the innermost part of the **Tabernacle** (and later the **Temple**), to offer sacrifices for the sins of the people.

A. The Two Goats: One for Sacrifice, One for the Scapegoat

The ritual of the Day of Atonement involved **two goats**, each playing a different role in the atonement process. One goat was sacrificed, and its blood was sprinkled on the **mercy seat** of the **Ark of the Covenant** inside the Holy of Holies, symbolizing the **atonement** for the people's sins. This goat represents the **death** necessary for sin to be forgiven, as **Leviticus 17:11** says, "for it is the blood that makes atonement by the life."

The second goat, known as the **scapegoat**, was not sacrificed but was sent into the wilderness, symbolically carrying the sins of Israel away from the camp. The high priest laid his hands on the head of this goat and confessed over it all the **iniquities** and **transgressions** of the Israelites, transferring the **guilt** of the people onto the goat. The goat was then led into the wilderness by a designated person, never to return, signifying the **removal** of the people's sins from their presence.

1. The Significance of the Scapegoat

The **scapegoat** played a crucial role in the Day of Atonement because it emphasized not only the **forgiveness** of sin but also its **removal**. While the blood of the sacrificial goat atoned for the sins of Israel, the scapegoat visually illustrated that those sins had been **taken away**—removed from the community, just as the psalmist declares in **Psalm 103:12**:

> "As far as the east is from the west, so far does he remove our transgressions from us."

2. The Wilderness as a Symbol of Separation

The fact that the scapegoat was led into the wilderness is significant. The **wilderness** in the Bible often represents a place of **separation** and **abandonment**, far removed from the presence of God and His people. By sending the scapegoat into the wilderness, Israel symbolically sent their sins far away from them, never to return. This act foreshadows the **complete separation** of believers from their sins through the work of Christ.

B. The Role of the High Priest in the Day of Atonement

The **high priest** played a vital role in the Day of Atonement, acting as the **mediator** between God and the people. He alone was permitted to enter the Holy of Holies, where God's presence dwelled above the Ark of the Covenant. His actions on this day symbolized the **cleansing** of the people and the **removal** of their sins, preparing them to continue in fellowship with God for another year.

The **book of Hebrews** makes it clear that the high priest's work on the Day of Atonement was a **shadow** of the greater priestly work that Christ would accomplish. As **Hebrews 9:11-12** states:

> "But when Christ appeared as a high priest of the good things that have come, then through the greater and more perfect tent (not made with hands, that is, not of this creation) He entered once for all into the holy places, not by means of the blood of goats and calves but by means of His own blood, thus securing an eternal redemption."

The high priest's actions with the scapegoat prefigured Christ's role as the one who would **bear** the sins of the people and **remove** them forever.

II. THE SCAPEGOAT AS A TYPE OF CHRIST BEARING OUR SINS

The imagery of the **scapegoat** in Leviticus 16 provides a vivid picture of how Christ would one day bear the **sins of the world** and take them away through His death on the cross. Just as the high priest laid the sins of Israel on the scapegoat, so too were the sins of **humanity** laid upon **Jesus**, the perfect Lamb of God.

A. The Transfer of Sins to the Scapegoat (Isaiah 53:6)

One of the most crucial elements of the scapegoat ritual was the **transfer of sin**. By laying his hands on the goat and confessing the sins of Israel, the high priest symbolically transferred the **guilt** of the people onto the goat, which then carried those sins away. This act of transferring guilt points to the **substitutionary** nature of Christ's atonement.

The **prophet Isaiah** foretold this transfer of sin in his famous **Suffering Servant** passage. **Isaiah 53:6** declares:

> "All we like sheep have gone astray; we have turned—every one—to his own way; and the Lord has laid on Him the iniquity of us all."

Here, Isaiah speaks of the **Messiah**, the one who would bear the sins of the people and take their punishment upon Himself. Just as the scapegoat carried the sins of Israel into the wilderness, Christ carried the **sins of humanity** to the cross, where He bore the **wrath of God** in our place.

1. Christ as the Sin-Bearer

The idea of **Christ as the sin-bearer** is central to the doctrine of the atonement. In **1 Peter 2:24**, the Apostle Peter emphasizes this truth:

> "He Himself bore our sins in His body on the tree, that we might die to sin and live to righteousness. By His wounds you have been healed."

Christ's role as the ultimate **sin-bearer** is what distinguishes Him from the scapegoats of the Old Testament. While the scapegoats of Israel temporarily removed the people's sins for a year, Christ's sacrifice **once for all** removed the sins of the world, providing **eternal forgiveness** and **reconciliation** with God.

2. The Burden of Sin

Just as the scapegoat carried the **burden of Israel's sins**, Christ carried the **burden of our sins**. This burden was not only physical but also spiritual, as Jesus bore the weight of God's **righteous judgment** against sin. In the **Garden of Gethsemane**, we see a glimpse of the immense burden Christ would bear on the cross, as He prayed:

> "My soul is very sorrowful, even to death. Remain here and watch with me." (Matthew 26:38)

The burden of sin was so great that Christ sweat **drops of blood** as He anticipated the coming **judgment** that He would endure on behalf of humanity.

B. The Removal of Sin: As Far as the East is from the West (Psalm 103:12)

The scapegoat's journey into the wilderness is symbolic of the **complete removal** of sin from the people. Once the goat was led away, the sins it carried were considered **gone**—removed from the community and never to return. This imagery foreshadows the **total forgiveness** and **removal of sin** that Christ offers to those who place their faith in Him.

Psalm 103:12 captures the essence of this truth:

> "As far as the east is from the west, so far does He remove our transgressions from us."

In Christ, our sins are not merely covered or temporarily set aside—they are **completely removed**. Through His sacrificial death, Christ has taken our sins away, so that they are no longer counted against us.

1. The Wilderness as a Place of Separation

The wilderness into which the scapegoat was sent symbolizes a place of **separation** and **abandonment**. In biblical imagery, the wilderness is often associated with **isolation** and **estrangement** from God's presence. By sending the scapegoat into the wilderness, Israel's sins were symbolically **separated** from the people, never to return.

Christ's atonement accomplishes the same reality for believers. Through His death, He removes our sins, carrying them away so that we are no longer under the **guilt** or **condemnation** of sin. **Hebrews 10:17** affirms this, quoting God's promise:

> "I will remember their sins and their lawless deeds no more."

2. Total Forgiveness in Christ

The **scapegoat** ritual points to the **total forgiveness** available in Christ. When we place our faith in Jesus, our sins are not just **forgiven** in the sense that God no longer holds them against us—they are also **forgotten**, removed entirely from His sight. This total forgiveness is part of the **new covenant** that Christ established through His blood, as foretold in **Jeremiah 31:34**:

> "For I will forgive their iniquity, and I will remember their sin no more."

This truth gives believers assurance that their sins are truly **gone**, no longer held against them, and that they are fully reconciled to God through Christ's atoning work.

III. THE LAMB OF GOD WHO TAKES AWAY THE SINS OF THE WORLD (JOHN 1:29)

The **scapegoat** imagery in the Old Testament directly foreshadows **Christ's work** as the **Lamb of God** who takes away the sins of the world. In **John 1:29**, **John the Baptist** identifies Jesus as the **Lamb of God**, using sacrificial language that would have been familiar to his Jewish audience:

> "Behold, the Lamb of God, who takes away the sin of the world!"

This declaration points to the fact that Jesus is both the **sacrificial lamb** and the **scapegoat**—the one who bears the sins of the world and takes them away.

A. The Dual Role of Christ: Sacrificial Lamb and Scapegoat

Christ fulfills both roles of the Day of Atonement ritual. As the **sacrificial lamb**, He sheds His blood to atone for the sins of humanity, satisfying the **righteous demands** of God's law. As the **scapegoat**, He carries those sins away, removing them from us and granting us forgiveness and freedom.

1. The Blood of the Lamb for Atonement

Just as the blood of the sacrificial goat on the Day of Atonement made atonement for Israel's sins, so too does the blood of Christ make **atonement** for the sins of humanity. **Hebrews 9:22** states that "without the shedding of blood there is no forgiveness of sins." Christ's blood, shed on the cross, serves as the **final sacrifice**, fulfilling the sacrificial system of the Old Testament and providing **eternal redemption**.

2. The Removal of Sin by the Scapegoat

While the sacrificial lamb deals with the **payment** for sin, the scapegoat illustrates the **removal** of sin. Christ not only pays the price for sin through His blood, but He also **removes** the guilt of sin from those who believe in Him. Through His death and resurrection, Christ ensures that sin no longer has power over those who are in Him.

B. The Fulfillment of Isaiah's Prophecy

The **Suffering Servant** passage in **Isaiah 53** finds its ultimate fulfillment in Christ, who bears the sins of the world and takes them away. Isaiah's prophecy vividly describes the **substitutionary** nature of Christ's atonement, highlighting the fact that He would be pierced for our transgressions and crushed for our iniquities.

Isaiah 53:6 encapsulates the role of the scapegoat:

"All we like sheep have gone astray; we have turned—every one—to his own way; and the Lord has laid on Him the iniquity of us all."

Christ, the **sinless Lamb of God**, takes upon Himself the sins of the world and bears the punishment that we deserve. Through His sacrifice, we are **justified, cleansed**, and **reconciled** to God.

IV. THE THEOLOGY OF SUBSTITUTIONARY ATONEMENT

The **scapegoat** ritual provides a powerful illustration of the doctrine of **substitutionary atonement**, which lies at the heart of the **gospel** message. In this doctrine, Christ takes the place of sinners, bearing the **penalty** for their sins so that they might receive **forgiveness** and **reconciliation** with God.

A. Christ as Our Substitute

The concept of **substitution** is central to the **atonement**. Just as the scapegoat took the place of Israel and carried away their sins, Christ takes the place of humanity, bearing the punishment for sin in our stead. **2 Corinthians 5:21** beautifully expresses this truth:

> "For our sake He made Him to be sin who knew no sin, so that in Him we might become the righteousness of God."

Christ, the sinless Son of God, became the **substitute** for sinners, taking upon Himself the **wrath** of God that we deserved. In exchange, we receive His **righteousness** and are justified before God.

1. The Wrath of God Satisfied

Through His sacrificial death, Christ satisfied the **wrath of God** against sin. The **scapegoat** imagery emphasizes the seriousness of sin and the need for **atonement**. God's justice demanded that sin be dealt with, and Christ took that punishment upon Himself, enduring the **separation** from God that sin brings.

2. The Exchange of Sin and Righteousness

The doctrine of **imputed righteousness** teaches that Christ's righteousness is credited to believers, just as their sins were credited to Him on the cross. This exchange—our sins for His righteousness—is the heart of the gospel. As **Romans 3:24-25** explains, we are "justified by His grace as a gift, through the redemption that is in Christ Jesus, whom God put forward as a propitiation by His blood, to be received by faith."

B. The Perfection of Christ's Sacrifice

Unlike the scapegoat, which had to be repeated every year on the Day of Atonement, Christ's sacrifice was **once for all**. **Hebrews 10:14** declares:

> "For by a single offering He has perfected for all time those who are being sanctified."

The **perfection** of Christ's sacrifice means that His atoning work is **complete** and **sufficient** for all who believe. There is no need for repeated sacrifices, as Christ has fulfilled the sacrificial system and provided **eternal redemption**.

V. THE SCAPEGOAT AND THE GOSPEL MESSAGE

The **scapegoat** typology is a powerful tool for understanding and communicating the **gospel message**. At its core, the gospel is about **substitution**—Christ taking the place of sinners and bearing their sins so that they can be reconciled to God.

A. The Offer of Forgiveness and Freedom

Just as the scapegoat symbolically carried away the sins of Israel, Christ offers to carry away the sins of all who place their **faith** in Him. The gospel is the message of **forgiveness** and **freedom** from the guilt and penalty of sin. **John 1:29** captures this truth:

> "Behold, the Lamb of God, who takes away the sin of the world!"

Through His death and resurrection, Christ removes the burden of sin from believers, granting them **forgiveness** and **eternal life**.

1. Freedom from the Guilt of Sin

The imagery of the scapegoat highlights the **freedom** that comes from having one's sins removed. Just as the people of Israel were freed from the guilt of their sins through the scapegoat, believers are freed from **guilt** and **condemnation** through Christ. **Romans 8:1** proclaims:

> "There is therefore now no condemnation for those who are in Christ Jesus."

2. Freedom from the Power of Sin

In addition to freeing us from the guilt of sin, Christ also frees us from the **power** of sin. Through His atoning work, believers are no longer enslaved to sin but are empowered to live **righteously** through the Holy Spirit. **Romans 6:6-7** declares:

> "We know that our old self was crucified with Him in order that the body of sin might be brought to nothing, so that we would no longer be enslaved to sin. For one who has died has been set free from sin."

B. The Call to Faith in the Ultimate Scapegoat

The scapegoat typology invites individuals to place their **faith** in **Jesus Christ**, the ultimate scapegoat who bore the sins of the world. Just as the Israelites depended on the scapegoat to carry away their sins, so too must individuals today depend on **Christ** for their **salvation**.

The gospel calls all people to **confess** their sins and trust in Christ's atoning work. As the **Apostle Paul** wrote in **Romans 10:9-10**:

> "If you confess with your mouth that Jesus is Lord and believe in your heart that God raised Him from the dead, you will be saved. For with the heart one believes and is justified, and with the mouth one confesses and is saved."

VI. FUN FACT: THE TRADITION OF THE SCAPEGOAT IN ANCIENT JEWISH HISTORY

In ancient Jewish tradition, the scapegoat ritual involved not only sending the goat into the wilderness but also ensuring that it never returned to the community. The goat was often led to a remote location and pushed off a cliff to ensure that it could not find its way back to the camp. This action reinforced the idea that the sins of the people were **gone for good**, never to return.

This tradition adds a deeper layer to the scapegoat imagery, as it emphasizes the **total separation** of the people from their sins. In Christ, we have the assurance that our sins are **completely removed** and will never be held against us again.

Christ, the Ultimate Scapegoat, and the Removal of Our Sins

From the Tabernacle to Solomon's Temple to the Second Temple, the progression of God's dwelling among His people points toward a final and eternal fulfillment in Christ. The tearing of the temple veil at Jesus' crucifixion signifies the end of separation between God and humanity, and the beginning of the Church as the living temple, indwelt by the Spirit.

Solomon's Temple was the physical dwelling place of God among His people, where the Ark of the Covenant resided. As magnificent as it was, it served as a shadow of a greater reality. The destruction of this temple symbolized the passing of the old covenant system, pointing forward to the time when God's presence would dwell fully in Christ, the true Temple. The physical structure of the temple was temporary, but it laid the foundation for the spiritual temple found in Christ.

The Second Temple, rebuilt after the exile, held great significance for the Jewish people. It was the site of Jesus' ministry, and although it lacked the glory of Solomon's Temple, it still foreshadowed a greater fulfillment in Christ. The destruction of the Second Temple, as prophesied by Jesus, marks the end of the old sacrificial system and the transition to a new covenant where God's presence is no longer confined to a building but resides in Christ and His Church. Jesus, the ultimate Temple, fulfills what the Second Temple could only symbolize.

The **scapegoat** on the Day of Atonement provides a powerful **foreshadowing** of **Christ's work** as the ultimate **sin-bearer**. Through His death on the cross, Christ takes upon Himself the sins of the world and removes them as far as the east is from the west. Just as the scapegoat carried the sins of Israel into the wilderness, Christ bears the **guilt** and **punishment** of our sins, providing **forgiveness** and **freedom** for all who trust in Him.

In Christ, we find not only **atonement** for our sins but also the **removal** of those sins, ensuring that they will never be counted against us again. As we reflect on the scapegoat imagery, we are reminded of the **incredible grace** and **mercy** of God, who provided His Son as the perfect **substitute** for sinners. Through faith in Christ, we are freed from the **guilt** and **power** of sin and are given the gift of **eternal life**.

This chapter highlights the profound theological truths embedded in the scapegoat ritual and how they point to the **gospel message** of salvation. In Christ, we have the ultimate scapegoat—the one who bears our sins and removes them forever. **Hallelujah! What a Savior!**

CHAPTER 23: THE FEASTS OF ISRAEL: TYPES OF CHRIST'S MINISTRY AND THE CHURCH

The Feast of Tabernacles not only recalled Israel's time in temporary shelters but also pointed to the future, where God would dwell permanently among His people. While Solomon's Temple stood as a physical representation of God's presence, it foreshadowed the true and eternal temple—Christ, whose body is the ultimate tabernacle.

The **Feasts of Israel**, ordained by God in the **Old Testament**, served as annual celebrations and memorials of His faithfulness and provision for His people. However, these feasts were not only historical commemorations; they were also rich in **prophetic symbolism**, each one foreshadowing significant aspects of **Christ's ministry** and the role of the **Church** in God's redemptive plan.

The Feast of Tabernacles not only recalled Israel's time in temporary shelters but also pointed to the future, where God would dwell permanently among His people. While Solomon's Temple stood as a physical representation of God's presence, it foreshadowed the true and eternal temple—Christ, whose body is the ultimate tabernacle.

In this chapter, we will explore three key feasts: the **Feast of Unleavened Bread**, the **Feast of Firstfruits**, and the **Feast of Weeks** (also known as **Pentecost**). Each of these feasts reveals a different dimension of Christ's life, death, resurrection, and the birth of the Church. By examining these feasts in the context of **biblical typology**, we can gain a deeper understanding of how the **Old Testament** points forward to the fulfillment of God's redemptive plan in the **New Testament**, particularly in the ministry of Christ and the establishment of His Church.

I. THE FEAST OF UNLEAVENED BREAD: A TYPE OF CHRIST'S SINLESS LIFE AND THE CHURCH'S CALL TO PURITY

The **Feast of Unleavened Bread**, instituted in **Leviticus 23:6**, is celebrated immediately after the **Passover** and lasts for seven days. During this feast, the Israelites were commanded to eat bread made without **leaven** (yeast), symbolizing the removal of **sin** from their lives. Leaven, in biblical typology, often represents **sin** or **corruption**, and the removal of leaven during this feast symbolized the need for **holiness** and **purity** in the lives of God's people.

A. The Sinless Life of Christ

The **Feast of Unleavened Bread** is a powerful type of **Christ's sinless life**. Just as the Israelites were commanded to remove all leaven from their homes, Christ came into the world as the **sinless Lamb of God**, free from the corruption of sin. In **John 8:46**, Jesus challenges His opponents by asking, "Which one of you convicts me of sin?" This rhetorical question emphasizes His sinless nature—He was without fault, the perfect sacrifice who would take away the sins of the world.

1. Leaven as a Symbol of Sin

Throughout Scripture, **leaven** often serves as a metaphor for **sin** and **moral corruption**. Jesus Himself used leaven to symbolize the corrupting influence of the **Pharisees** and **Sadducees**, warning His disciples to beware of their teachings (**Matthew 16:6**). In the context of the Feast of Unleavened Bread, the absence of leaven highlights the need for **purity** and **holiness** before God. Just as leaven quickly spreads through dough, sin has a pervasive effect on the human heart, leading to moral decay.

In contrast, **Christ's sinlessness** stands as a testimony to His perfect **obedience** and **righteousness**. He fulfilled the **law** perfectly and remained untainted by the sin that affects all of humanity. His life of perfect obedience to the Father made Him the perfect sacrifice, the **unblemished Lamb**, who could atone for the sins of the world.

2. Christ, the Unleavened Bread of Life

Jesus declared Himself to be the **bread of life** in **John 6:35**, saying, "I am the bread of life; whoever comes to me shall not hunger, and whoever believes in me shall never thirst." In this declaration, Jesus reveals that He is the **spiritual sustenance** for all who believe in Him. Just as the Israelites ate **unleavened bread** during this feast, symbolizing the removal of sin, believers are called to partake in Christ, the **sinless bread**, who gives **eternal life** and sustains them spiritually.

The sinless nature of Christ as the **unleavened bread** reminds us that our salvation is based on His **righteousness**, not our own. He lived a life of perfect **obedience** to the Father, and through His sacrifice, He offers that same righteousness to us.

B. The Church's Call to Purity

The **Feast of Unleavened Bread** also speaks to the **Church's call to purity**. Just as the Israelites were commanded to remove all leaven from their homes, the **Church** is called to live in **holiness** and **purity**, free from the corruption of sin. The Apostle Paul makes this connection in **1 Corinthians 5:7-8**, where he writes:

> "Cleanse out the old leaven that you may be a new lump, as you really are unleavened. For Christ, our Passover lamb, has been sacrificed. Let us therefore celebrate the festival, not with the old leaven, the leaven of malice and evil, but with the unleavened bread of sincerity and truth."

Paul urges the Corinthian believers to **purge** themselves of sin, using the imagery of leaven to represent the **moral decay** that can spread through the Church. The Church is to be a **holy** and **pure** people, set apart for God, just as Israel was commanded to be.

1. Sanctification and the Church

The call to **holiness** in the Church is closely tied to the process of **sanctification**—the ongoing work of the **Holy Spirit** in the life of a believer, conforming them to the image of Christ. Just as the Israelites observed the Feast of Unleavened Bread each year, remembering their **deliverance** from Egypt and their call to holiness, believers are called to live in continual **repentance** and **purity**, relying on the Holy Spirit to **sanctify** them.

The removal of leaven from the home symbolizes the believer's need to continually examine their life for **sin** and to **repent**. The Church, as the **bride of Christ**, is called to be pure and spotless, ready for the return of her **Bridegroom**.

2. Christ's Work of Cleansing His Bride

Christ's sinless life not only serves as a model for believers but also as the means by which the Church is made **holy**. **Ephesians 5:25-27** describes Christ's love for the Church and His work of **sanctification**:

> "Christ loved the church and gave himself up for her, that he might sanctify her, having cleansed her by the washing of water with the word, so that he might present the church to himself in splendor, without spot or wrinkle or any such thing, that she might be holy and without blemish."

Just as the Israelites were called to remove leaven from their homes, Christ is at work in His Church, **cleansing** and **sanctifying** her through the power of His Word and the **Holy Spirit**, preparing her to be presented to Him in **holiness** and **purity**.

II. THE FEAST OF FIRSTFRUITS: A TYPE OF CHRIST'S RESURRECTION AND THE RESURRECTION OF BELIEVERS

The **Feast of Firstfruits**, celebrated on the **day after the Sabbath** following the Passover, is detailed in **Leviticus 23:10**. This feast marked the **beginning** of the **harvest season**, when the Israelites would bring the **first sheaf** of their crops to the priest as an offering to the Lord. This offering symbolized their **gratitude** for God's provision and served as a promise of the **full harvest** to come.

In the **New Testament**, the **Feast of Firstfruits** is understood as a **type** of **Christ's resurrection**, as well as the **resurrection** of believers. Just as the firstfruits of the harvest were offered to God as a sign of the full harvest to come, Christ's resurrection is the **firstfruits** of the resurrection that all believers will experience at His return.

A. Christ, the Firstfruits of the Resurrection (1 Corinthians 15:20-23)

The Apostle Paul explicitly connects the **Feast of Firstfruits** to **Christ's resurrection** in **1 Corinthians 15:20-23**:

> "But in fact Christ has been raised from the dead, the firstfruits of those who have fallen asleep. For as by a man came death, by a man has come also the resurrection of the dead. For as in Adam all die, so also in Christ shall all be made alive. But each in his own order: Christ the firstfruits, then at his coming those who belong to Christ."

Paul's use of the term **firstfruits** here is significant. Just as the first sheaf of the harvest was a **pledge** of the full harvest to come, Christ's resurrection is the **guarantee** of the future resurrection of all believers. His victory over **death** is the assurance that those who belong to Him will also be raised to eternal life.

1. The Importance of the Resurrection

The resurrection of Christ is the **cornerstone** of the Christian faith. Without the resurrection, Paul argues, the Christian faith would be in vain, and believers would still be in their sins (**1 Corinthians 15:17**). The resurrection not only validates Christ's identity as the **Son of God** but also confirms that His sacrifice was **accepted** by the Father as the perfect atonement for sin.

The **Feast of Firstfruits** symbolizes the **new life** that comes through Christ's resurrection. Just as the firstfruits of the harvest represent the **beginning** of new growth, Christ's resurrection marks the beginning of the **new creation**, where death is defeated, and eternal life is secured for all who believe in Him.

2. The Guarantee of the Full Harvest

Christ's resurrection as the **firstfruits** also serves as a **guarantee** of the **full harvest**—the resurrection of all believers at the end of the age. Paul emphasizes this point in **1 Corinthians 15:23**, stating that "each in his own order" will be raised: first Christ, and then those who belong to Him.

This assurance of future resurrection provides **hope** for believers, knowing that **death** is not the end. Just as Christ was raised from the dead, so too will all who have placed their faith in Him experience **resurrection** and **eternal life** in the presence of God. The **Feast of Firstfruits** points forward to this glorious hope, reminding us that the best is yet to come.

B. The Resurrection of Believers: The Full Harvest

The **resurrection of believers** is the culmination of God's redemptive plan, the **full harvest** that follows Christ's resurrection as the firstfruits. In **Romans 8:11**, Paul speaks of the **Holy Spirit** as the agent of this future resurrection:

> "If the Spirit of him who raised Jesus from the dead dwells in you, he who raised Christ Jesus from the dead will also give life to your mortal bodies through his Spirit who dwells in you."

The promise of resurrection is not just a distant hope; it is a **present reality** for believers, guaranteed by the **indwelling Holy Spirit**. Just as the firstfruits of the harvest guaranteed the full harvest, the presence of the Holy Spirit in the life of a believer guarantees the **resurrection** and **eternal life** to come.

1. The New Creation

The resurrection of believers is part of God's plan for the **new creation**. Just as Christ's resurrection marks the beginning of the **new creation**, so too does the future resurrection of believers represent the **renewal** of all things. **Revelation 21:4** describes the **new heavens and new earth**, where **death**, **sorrow**, and **pain** will be no more.

Believers look forward to this **future reality**, where they will be raised in **glorified bodies**, free from the effects of sin and death. The **Feast of Firstfruits** reminds us that, just as God provided the firstfruits of the harvest, He has provided the firstfruits of the **resurrection** in Christ, guaranteeing the full harvest of eternal life for His people.

2. Living in the Hope of Resurrection

The promise of resurrection shapes how believers live in the present. Just as the Israelites offered the firstfruits of their harvest in **gratitude** and **faith** that God would provide the full harvest, believers are called to live in **faith** and **hope**, trusting that God will bring about the **fullness** of His promises.

This hope empowers believers to live with an **eternal perspective**, knowing that **death** is not the end and that **eternal life** awaits those who belong to Christ.

III. THE FEAST OF WEEKS (PENTECOST): A TYPE OF THE COMING OF THE HOLY SPIRIT AND THE BIRTH OF THE CHURCH

The **Feast of Weeks**, also known as **Pentecost**, is the **second major harvest festival** in the Jewish calendar and is celebrated **fifty days** after the Feast of Firstfruits. The **Feast of Weeks** marked the **end** of the grain harvest and was a time of **thanksgiving** for God's provision.

In the **New Testament**, **Pentecost** takes on a new significance as the day on which the **Holy Spirit** was poured out on the disciples, marking the **birth of the Church**. This event, recorded in **Acts 2**, fulfills the prophetic symbolism of the Feast of Weeks and inaugurates a new era in **salvation history**.

A. The Historical Significance of Pentecost (Acts 2)

The day of **Pentecost** in the New Testament is the day when the **Holy Spirit** descended upon the disciples, empowering them to preach the **gospel** and inaugurating the **Church**. **Acts 2:1-4** describes the event:

> "When the day of Pentecost arrived, they were all together in one place. And suddenly there came from heaven a sound like a mighty rushing wind, and it filled the entire house where they were sitting. And divided tongues as of fire appeared to them and rested on each one of them. And they were all filled with the Holy Spirit and began to speak in other tongues as the Spirit gave them utterance."

The outpouring of the Holy Spirit on **Pentecost** fulfilled Jesus' promise to send the **Comforter** and marks the beginning of the **Church Age**. The disciples, once fearful and unsure, were empowered by the Holy Spirit to boldly proclaim the gospel, and **three thousand people** were added to the Church on that day (**Acts 2:41**).

1. Pentecost as the Birth of the Church

The **Feast of Weeks** celebrated the **harvest** in the Old Testament, and at Pentecost, we see the **firstfruits of the spiritual harvest**—the birth of the Church. Just as the Israelites celebrated the **ingathering** of the grain harvest, Pentecost represents the beginning of the **spiritual harvest**, where people from every tribe and nation would come to faith in Christ.

The outpouring of the **Holy Spirit** on Pentecost also fulfills the promise of the **new covenant**, in which God would put His Spirit within His people, empowering them to live according to His will. This event marked a **new era** in God's relationship with His people, where the **Holy Spirit** would dwell within believers, guiding, teaching, and empowering them for ministry.

2. The Universal Reach of the Gospel

The **tongues of fire** and the disciples' ability to speak in different languages on the day of Pentecost symbolized the **universal reach** of the gospel. The **Feast of Weeks** was one of the major pilgrimage feasts, and Jews from all over the **Roman Empire** were present in **Jerusalem** for the celebration. When the disciples began to speak in various languages, these visitors heard the gospel in their own tongues, a powerful demonstration of God's desire for the gospel to reach **all nations**.

Pentecost signifies the **global mission** of the Church, as the **Holy Spirit** empowers believers to proclaim the gospel to the **ends of the earth**. The **Feast of Weeks** points to this **spiritual harvest**, where people from every nation, tribe, and tongue are gathered into the kingdom of God through the preaching of the gospel.

B. The Holy Spirit as the Firstfruits of the Full Harvest

The **Holy Spirit** given at Pentecost is described in the New Testament as the **firstfruits** of the full **inheritance** that believers will receive in Christ. **Romans 8:23** speaks of the **Holy Spirit** as the firstfruits of our **redemption**:

> "And not only the creation, but we ourselves, who have the firstfruits of the Spirit, groan inwardly as we wait eagerly for adoption as sons, the redemption of our bodies."

The **Holy Spirit** is the **down payment** or **guarantee** of the **future inheritance** that believers will receive when Christ returns. Just as the firstfruits of the harvest guaranteed the full harvest, the presence of the Holy Spirit in the life of a believer guarantees the full realization of their **salvation**—eternal life in the presence of God.

1. The Work of the Holy Spirit in the Church

The **Holy Spirit** plays a central role in the life of the **Church**, empowering believers to carry out the mission of Christ. At Pentecost, the disciples were filled with the Holy Spirit and began to proclaim the gospel with **boldness** and **power**. This same Holy Spirit continues to **empower** the Church today, equipping believers for ministry, guiding them into truth, and transforming them into the image of Christ.

The **Feast of Weeks** points to the ongoing work of the Holy Spirit in the **Church Age**, as the gospel continues to spread, and the **spiritual harvest** continues to grow. The **outpouring** of the Holy Spirit at Pentecost marked the beginning of this **spiritual harvest**, and believers today are called to continue the work of proclaiming the gospel, empowered by the same Spirit.

2. The Spirit of Unity and Diversity

The events of Pentecost also highlight the **unity** and **diversity** of the Church. As people from different nations heard the gospel in their own languages, the **Holy Spirit** demonstrated that the message of salvation was not limited to one **ethnic group** or **nation**. The Church, born at Pentecost, would be a **global body** made up of people from every nation and culture, united by their faith in Christ and empowered by the Holy Spirit.

Ephesians 4:4-6 emphasizes the unity of the Church:

"There is one body and one Spirit—just as you were called to the one hope that belongs to your call—one Lord, one faith, one baptism, one God and Father of all, who is over all and through all and in all."

At the same time, the Church is made up of people with diverse **gifts** and **callings**, all empowered by the Holy Spirit for the purpose of building up the body of Christ. The **Feast of Weeks** and Pentecost point to the **diverse unity** of the Church, where believers from every nation are united in their mission to proclaim the gospel and make disciples of all nations.

IV. FUN FACT: THE AGRICULTURAL SIGNIFICANCE OF THE FEASTS

The **Feasts of Israel** were closely tied to the **agricultural cycle** of the land. The **Feast of Unleavened Bread**, the **Feast of Firstfruits**, and the **Feast of Weeks** all corresponded to different stages of the harvest. The **Feast of Unleavened Bread** took place during the **barley harvest**, the **Feast of Firstfruits** marked the **beginning** of the grain harvest, and the **Feast of Weeks** celebrated the **end** of the grain harvest. These agricultural feasts not only reminded the Israelites of God's provision but also foreshadowed the **spiritual harvest** that would come through Christ and the Church.

The Feast of Tabernacles not only recalled Israel's time in temporary shelters but also pointed to the future, where God would dwell permanently among His people. While Solomon's Temple stood as a physical representation of God's presence, it foreshadowed the true and eternal temple—Christ, whose body is the ultimate tabernacle.

In the **New Testament**, Jesus often used **agricultural imagery** to describe the **kingdom of God**. For example, in **John 4:35**, Jesus says:

> "Look, I tell you, lift up your eyes, and see that the fields are white for harvest."

The **Feasts of Israel** serve as a reminder that the **harvest** of souls is ongoing, and believers are called to participate in the **spiritual harvest** by sharing the gospel and making disciples.

The Feast of Tabernacles not only recalled Israel's time in temporary shelters but also pointed to the future, where God would dwell permanently among His people. While Solomon's Temple stood as a physical representation of God's presence, it foreshadowed the true and eternal temple—Christ, whose body is the ultimate tabernacle.

Christ's Ministry and the Church in the Feasts of Israel

The Feast of Tabernacles not only recalled Israel's time in temporary shelters but also pointed to the future, where God would dwell permanently among His people. While Solomon's Temple stood as a physical representation of God's presence, it foreshadowed the true and eternal temple—Christ, whose body is the ultimate tabernacle.

From the Tabernacle to Solomon's Temple to the Second Temple, the progression of God's dwelling among His people points toward a final and eternal fulfillment in Christ. The tearing of the temple veil at Jesus' crucifixion signifies the end of separation between God and humanity, and the beginning of the Church as the living temple, indwelt by the Spirit.

Solomon's Temple was the physical dwelling place of God among His people, where the Ark of the Covenant resided. As magnificent as it was, it served as a shadow of a greater reality. The destruction of this temple symbolized the passing of the old covenant system, pointing forward to the time when God's presence would dwell fully in Christ, the true Temple. The physical structure of the temple was temporary, but it laid the foundation for the spiritual temple found in Christ.

The Second Temple, rebuilt after the exile, held great significance for the Jewish people. It was the site of Jesus' ministry, and although it lacked the glory of Solomon's Temple, it still foreshadowed a greater fulfillment in Christ. The destruction of the Second Temple, as prophesied by Jesus, marks the end of the old sacrificial system and the transition to a new covenant where God's presence is no longer confined to a building but resides in Christ and His Church. Jesus, the ultimate Temple, fulfills what the Second Temple could only symbolize.

The **Feasts of Israel** were not merely religious observances for the Jewish people; they were **prophetic shadows** of the **ministry of Christ** and the **birth of the Church**. The **Feast of Unleavened Bread** points to Christ's **sinless life** and the Church's call to **holiness**. The **Feast of Firstfruits** foreshadows Christ's **resurrection** and the future resurrection of all believers. The **Feast of Weeks** (Pentecost) marks the outpouring of the **Holy Spirit** and the beginning of the **spiritual harvest** in the Church Age.

The Feast of Tabernacles not only recalled Israel's time in temporary shelters but also pointed to the future, where God would dwell permanently among His people. While Solomon's Temple stood as a physical representation of God's presence, it foreshadowed the true and eternal temple—Christ, whose body is the ultimate tabernacle.

As believers, we are called to live in light of these **truths**, participating in the ongoing **spiritual harvest** and trusting in the **promises** of resurrection and eternal life. The **Feasts of Israel** remind us that God's plan of redemption, begun in the **Old Testament**, finds its **fulfillment** in **Jesus Christ** and continues through the work of the **Holy Spirit** in the Church today. Just as the Israelites celebrated God's provision through the **harvest**, we celebrate the **spiritual harvest** that Christ has inaugurated and look forward to the day when the full **harvest** of souls will be gathered into His eternal kingdom.

The Feast of Tabernacles not only recalled Israel's time in temporary shelters but also pointed to the future, where God would dwell permanently among His people. While Solomon's Temple stood as a physical representation of God's presence, it foreshadowed the true and eternal temple—Christ, whose body is the ultimate tabernacle.

CHAPTER 24: SAMSON: A TYPE OF CHRIST'S SACRIFICIAL STRENGTH

Samson, a judge of Israel, is one of the most enigmatic and complex figures in the Old Testament. His story, detailed in the **Book of Judges**, is filled with feats of **superhuman strength**, impulsive actions, and moments of apparent failure. However, despite his flaws, Samson is also a **type of Christ**, particularly in his **sacrificial death**, which brought deliverance to the people of Israel. His life offers a rich exploration of **redemption, sacrifice**, and the ultimate victory over **sin** and **death**.

This chapter delves into the life of **Samson**, examining how his strength and final act of **self-sacrifice** foreshadow the work of **Jesus Christ**. While Samson's life is marked by moral and spiritual struggles, his **sacrificial death** in **Judges 16:29-30** prefigures Christ's **ultimate sacrifice** on the cross. Both Samson and Jesus used their strength to defeat the enemies of God's people, but in different ways—Samson through physical might, and Jesus through the spiritual victory of the cross and resurrection. By analyzing these parallels, we gain deeper insights into the **nature of Christ's sacrifice** and the **hope of salvation** He offers to His people.

Additionally, we will explore the **typological connections** between Samson and Christ, focusing on how Samson's life serves as both a **cautionary tale** and a **prophetic foreshadowing** of Christ's perfect fulfillment of God's redemptive plan. The life of Samson is a testament to the complex interplay of **human weakness** and **divine strength**, ultimately pointing to the **true source of salvation—Jesus Christ**.

I. THE BIRTH OF SAMSON AND HIS NAZARITE VOW: A TYPE OF CHRIST'S HOLY CALLING

Samson's story begins with a divine announcement of his birth, which parallels the **announcements of miraculous births** found elsewhere in Scripture, including the birth of Jesus. In **Judges 13**, the angel of the Lord appears to Samson's mother, who had been **barren**, and announces that she will give birth to a son who would begin to **deliver Israel from the Philistines**. Samson's birth was therefore seen as the beginning of God's **deliverance** for Israel, just as the birth of Christ was the dawn of God's **redemption** for all humanity.

A. The Announcement of Samson's Birth (Judges 13:2-5)

The announcement of Samson's birth carries significant weight, as it echoes the divine promises made to figures such as **Abraham and Sarah** and **Zechariah and Elizabeth**. **Judges 13:2-5** records the angel's message:

> "There was a certain man of Zorah, of the tribe of the Danites, whose name was Manoah. And his wife was barren and had no children. And the angel of the Lord appeared to the woman and said to her, 'Behold, you are barren and have not borne children, but you shall conceive and bear a son. Therefore be careful and drink no wine or strong drink, and eat nothing unclean, for behold, you shall conceive and bear a son. No razor shall come upon his head, for the child shall be a Nazarite to God from the womb, and he shall begin to save Israel from the hand of the Philistines.'"

The birth of Samson is not merely the arrival of another judge in Israel's history, but the **fulfillment of a divine promise**. Samson's life is marked by his **Nazarite vow**, which was a symbol of his **consecration to God**. According to **Numbers 6**, a Nazarite vow involved three key restrictions: abstaining from wine, avoiding contact with the dead, and not cutting one's hair. Samson's strength, given to him by God, was tied to his **obedience** to these vows.

1. Samson's Birth as a Parallel to Christ's Birth

Like Samson, **Jesus' birth** was also foretold by an angel, specifically the angel **Gabriel**. In **Luke 1:31-33**, Gabriel announces to the Virgin Mary that she will conceive and bear a son who will be called **Jesus**, and that He will **save His people** from their sins. Both Samson and Jesus were born under **divine mandate** to save their people, though the scope of their salvation differed—Samson delivered Israel from physical oppression, while Christ delivered humanity from **spiritual bondage**.

The parallel between Samson and Christ is evident in the **miraculous nature of their births**, both of which heralded the beginning of a new chapter in God's plan for His people. While Samson's birth was a moment of **hope** for Israel, it was only a **shadow** of the **ultimate hope** found in Christ, whose birth ushered in the **salvation of the world**.

2. The Nazarite Vow and Holiness

Samson's **Nazarite vow** set him apart as **holy to the Lord** from birth, which was a foreshadowing of Christ's own **holiness** and **dedication** to God's will. While Samson struggled to live up to the demands of his vow, often breaking it through his choices and actions, Jesus perfectly fulfilled His holy calling. Christ lived a life of **complete obedience** to the Father, fulfilling every aspect of the law and remaining **sinless**.

In this way, Samson serves as a **type** of Christ in his consecration to God, but he also serves as a **contrast** to Christ's perfect obedience. Where Samson failed in his **Nazarite vow**, Christ succeeded in living a life of perfect **righteousness** and **holiness**.

B. Samson's Strength as a Gift from God

Samson's **supernatural strength** was a gift from God, given to him to accomplish the **deliverance of Israel** from their enemies. Throughout his life, Samson's strength is seen as a **sign of God's favor** and a symbol of the **power of God** working through a flawed individual. However, Samson's strength was not his own—it was dependent on his **faithfulness** to his Nazarite vow, particularly the vow regarding his hair.

In many ways, Samson's strength is a **foreshadowing** of Christ's divine power. While Samson's strength was physical, Christ's strength was **spiritual**, and through His strength, He defeated **sin**, **death**, and **Satan** on behalf of His people.

II. SAMSON'S FAILURES AND WEAKNESSES: A CONTRAST TO CHRIST'S PERFECT OBEDIENCE

Though Samson was chosen by God to deliver Israel, his life is marked by repeated **failures** and **moral weaknesses**. His **impulsive nature**, **poor choices**, and eventual betrayal by **Delilah** all reveal the **brokenness** of humanity and the need for a **perfect Savior**. In contrast to Samson, who frequently succumbed to his **fleshly desires**, Christ lived a life of **perfect obedience** and **self-control**, never wavering from His mission to save humanity.

A. Samson's Moral Weaknesses and Failures

Despite his consecration as a **Nazarite**, Samson repeatedly violated his vows and made poor decisions that ultimately led to his downfall. Some of the key failures in Samson's life include his **relationships with Philistine women**, his **revenge-driven actions**, and his eventual betrayal by **Delilah**. These episodes highlight Samson's **human weaknesses** and serve as a reminder that even those chosen by God can fall short.

1. Samson's Relationship with Delilah

One of the most famous stories in Samson's life is his relationship with **Delilah**, a Philistine woman who ultimately betrays him. In **Judges 16**, Delilah is approached by the **Philistine rulers**, who offer her a large sum of money to discover the secret of Samson's strength. After several failed attempts to learn the secret, Samson finally reveals that his strength is tied to his **hair**, a key element of his Nazarite vow.

Delilah arranges for Samson's hair to be cut while he sleeps, and when he awakens, he finds that his **strength has left him**. The Philistines capture Samson, gouge out his eyes, and imprison him. This moment marks the **lowest point** in Samson's life—a man once endowed with **great strength** is now weak, blind, and imprisoned.

Samson's relationship with Delilah serves as a warning against the dangers of **compromise** and **moral failure**. His downfall came not through a lack of physical strength but through a lack of **spiritual discernment** and obedience to God.

2. The Consequences of Disobedience

Samson's disobedience to his Nazarite vow and his moral failures had **devastating consequences**. Not only did he lose his physical strength, but he also lost his **freedom** and his **sight**. Samson's story serves as a **cautionary tale** about the consequences of living according to one's **fleshly desires** rather than in **obedience to God**.

In contrast, Jesus Christ never succumbed to **temptation** or moral failure. Throughout His life, Jesus remained **faithful** to His calling and was **obedient** to the Father's will, even to the point of death on the cross. Where Samson failed, Christ succeeded, offering **salvation** to all who place their trust in Him.

B. The Contrast Between Samson and Christ

Samson's life, marked by **failure** and **weakness**, stands in stark contrast to the life of **Jesus Christ**, who lived in perfect obedience to God's will. While Samson was **chosen** by God to deliver Israel, he frequently fell short of his calling due to his **moral weaknesses**. In contrast, Christ perfectly fulfilled His mission, living a life of **sinless obedience** and ultimately offering Himself as the perfect **sacrifice** for the sins of the world.

1. Samson's Strength vs. Christ's Strength

While Samson's strength was **physical**, Christ's strength was **spiritual**. Samson relied on his **God-given physical abilities** to defeat Israel's enemies, while Christ used His **spiritual strength** to defeat the ultimate enemies of humanity—**sin**, **death**, and **Satan**. Through His death and resurrection, Christ accomplished what no human strength could—He brought **eternal salvation** to His people.

2. Samson's Sacrifice vs. Christ's Sacrifice

In the final moments of Samson's life, he made the ultimate **sacrifice**, giving his life to defeat the enemies of Israel. While Samson's sacrifice was a **physical act** of strength, Christ's sacrifice was a **spiritual act** of strength that brought **eternal salvation** to humanity. Samson's death, while significant, pales in comparison to the **cosmic significance** of Christ's sacrificial death on the cross.

III. Samson's Sacrificial Death: A Type of Christ's Sacrifice

The most significant parallel between Samson and Christ is found in their **sacrificial deaths**. In **Judges 16:29-30**, after being captured by the Philistines, **Samson prays to God** for the return of his strength so that he can destroy the Philistine temple and defeat Israel's enemies. In an act of **self-sacrifice**, Samson pulls down the pillars of the temple, killing himself and the Philistines gathered there. His death brought **deliverance** to Israel, though it cost him his life.

This act of sacrificial strength is a **type** of Christ's **sacrifice** on the cross. Just as Samson gave his life to defeat Israel's enemies, Christ gave His life to **defeat sin and death**, bringing **salvation** to His people.

A. Samson's Prayer for Strength and His Final Act of Deliverance

After being captured and humiliated by the Philistines, Samson is brought to their temple as a spectacle. In his **blindness** and **weakness**, Samson turns to God in prayer, asking for the return of his strength one final time. **Judges 16:28** records Samson's prayer:

> "Then Samson called to the Lord and said, 'O Lord God, please remember me and please strengthen me only this once, O God, that I may be avenged on the Philistines for my two eyes.'"

God grants Samson's request, and with his restored strength, Samson pulls down the pillars of the Philistine temple, killing more of his enemies in his death than he had during his life. This final act of strength is both a moment of **triumph** and **tragedy**—Samson's life ends in **self-sacrifice**, but it also brings **deliverance** to Israel.

1. Samson's Death as a Type of Christ's Sacrifice

Samson's sacrificial death foreshadows the **ultimate sacrifice** made by Christ on the cross. Just as Samson gave his life to defeat the Philistines, Christ gave His life to defeat the **forces of sin**, **death**, and **Satan**. Both Samson and Christ used their **strength** to bring deliverance to their people, but Christ's sacrifice was far greater in scope—it brought **eternal salvation** to all who believe.

While Samson's death was a **physical act** of strength, Christ's death was a **spiritual act** of love and obedience to the Father's will. In His sacrifice, Christ bore the **sins of humanity**, taking the punishment we deserved so that we might be reconciled to God.

2. The Victory of Samson's Death

In death, Samson achieved a great **victory** over Israel's enemies. The Philistines had long been a thorn in Israel's side, oppressing them and leading them away from God. Through his death, Samson destroyed a significant portion of the Philistine leadership and brought **temporary deliverance** to Israel. This victory, however, was only a **shadow** of the greater victory that Christ would achieve through His death and resurrection.

Christ's victory on the cross was not just over **earthly enemies** but over the **spiritual enemies** of humanity. Through His death, Christ defeated **sin** and **death**, providing **eternal deliverance** for His people. As **Hebrews 2:14-15** explains:

> "Since therefore the children share in flesh and blood, He Himself likewise partook of the same things, that through death He might destroy the one who

has the power of death, that is, the devil, and deliver all those who through fear of death were subject to lifelong slavery."

Christ's death was the ultimate act of **sacrificial strength**, and through it, He brought **eternal salvation** to His people.

B. Christ's Sacrificial Death and the Defeat of Sin and Death

The death of Jesus on the cross was the **pinnacle** of His mission to bring **salvation** to the world. Unlike Samson, whose sacrifice was primarily **physical** and brought **temporary deliverance**, Christ's sacrifice was **spiritual** and brought **eternal deliverance** to all who believe. Through His death, Christ defeated the powers of **sin**, **death**, and **Satan**, ensuring the ultimate victory of His people.

1. The Finality of Christ's Sacrifice

One of the most significant aspects of Christ's sacrifice is its **finality**. While Samson's death brought a temporary reprieve from Israel's enemies, Christ's death on the cross brought a **once-for-all** victory over the powers of darkness. As **Hebrews 9:26** explains, Christ's sacrifice was sufficient to atone for the sins of humanity:

> "But as it is, He has appeared once for all at the end of the ages to put away sin by the sacrifice of Himself."

Christ's death was not merely a temporary solution but a **permanent victory** over sin and death. Through His resurrection, He proved His victory, and believers now share in that victory, knowing that death no longer has the final say.

2. The Defeat of Satan and the Powers of Darkness

Through His death, Christ not only atoned for sin but also **defeated Satan** and the powers of darkness. **Colossians 2:15** describes this victory:

> "He disarmed the rulers and authorities and put them to open shame, by triumphing over them in Him."

Samson's death, while significant in its own right, is a **type** of the far greater victory won by Christ. Samson's physical strength could only defeat Israel's enemies for a time, but Christ's spiritual strength defeated **sin**, **death**, and **Satan** for all eternity. His victory is complete, and through Him, believers are freed from the **fear of death** and the **power of sin**.

IV. FUN FACT: SAMSON'S STRENGTH AND THE ANCIENT WORLD'S FASCINATION WITH HEROES

Throughout history, many cultures have been fascinated with the idea of **heroes** who possess **superhuman strength**. In ancient mythology, figures like **Hercules** in Greek mythology and **Gilgamesh** in Mesopotamian legend were celebrated for their extraordinary abilities. These heroes were often seen as **semi-divine** beings who used their strength to accomplish great feats and overcome **formidable challenges**.

Samson, as a biblical figure, shares similarities with these mythological heroes in that he possesses **supernatural strength** and is called to defeat Israel's enemies. However, unlike these mythological heroes, Samson's strength is not his own but is given to him by **God**. Samson's story demonstrates that **true strength** comes from **God** alone, and his life serves as a reminder of the **divine power** that can work through even the most flawed individuals.

Moreover, Samson's story points to the **ultimate hero—Jesus Christ**—whose strength was not physical but **spiritual**. While mythological heroes like Hercules were celebrated for their physical prowess, Christ's true heroism was in His **self-sacrifice** and **victory over sin and death**. Christ's victory is greater than any mythological hero's because it brings **eternal life** and **salvation** to all who believe.

Samson as a Type of Christ and the Sacrificial Strength of the Savior

From the Tabernacle to Solomon's Temple to the Second Temple, the progression of God's dwelling among His people points toward a final and eternal fulfillment in Christ. The tearing of the temple veil at Jesus' crucifixion signifies the end of separation between God and humanity, and the beginning of the Church as the living temple, indwelt by the Spirit.

Solomon's Temple was the physical dwelling place of God among His people, where the Ark of the Covenant resided. As magnificent as it was, it served as a shadow of a greater reality. The destruction of this temple symbolized the passing of the old covenant system, pointing forward to the time when God's presence would dwell fully in Christ, the true Temple. The physical structure of the temple was temporary, but it laid the foundation for the spiritual temple found in Christ.

The Second Temple, rebuilt after the exile, held great significance for the Jewish people. It was the site of Jesus' ministry, and although it lacked the glory of Solomon's Temple, it still foreshadowed a greater fulfillment in Christ. The destruction of the Second Temple, as prophesied by Jesus, marks the end of the old sacrificial system and the transition to a new covenant where God's presence is no longer confined to a building but resides in Christ and His Church. Jesus, the ultimate Temple, fulfills what the Second Temple could only symbolize.

Samson's life, filled with moments of great **strength** and deep **weakness**, ultimately serves as a **foreshadowing** of the greater **Savior to come—Jesus Christ**. While Samson was chosen by God to deliver Israel from their physical enemies, his life was marred by **moral failures** and **disobedience**. In contrast, Christ lived a life of **perfect obedience** and offered Himself as the perfect sacrifice for the sins of the world.

Samson's **sacrificial death** in the temple of the Philistines serves as a **type** of Christ's ultimate sacrifice on the cross. Just as Samson used his strength to bring deliverance to Israel, Christ used His strength to defeat the powers of **sin**, **death**, and **Satan**. Through

His death and resurrection, Christ secured **eternal salvation** for all who believe in Him.

In reflecting on Samson's life, we are reminded of both the **weakness** of humanity and the **strength** of God's **redemptive plan**. Samson's story points us to the need for a **Savior** who is greater than any earthly hero—one who can truly defeat the enemies of **sin** and **death** and bring **eternal life** to His people. That Savior is **Jesus Christ**, the ultimate **sacrificial strength**, whose victory on the cross has brought deliverance to all who place their faith in Him.

CHAPTER 25: THE MANNA AND QUAIL: A TYPE OF GOD'S PROVISION IN CHRIST

The story of **manna and quail** from **Exodus 16** stands as one of the most powerful illustrations of God's faithful provision to His people during their time in the wilderness. After the **Israelites' exodus** from Egypt, they wandered in the desert, where food and water were scarce. In their complaints and fears, God responded by miraculously providing **manna from heaven** and **quail** as sustenance. This daily provision ensured the survival of the nation of Israel during their 40 years in the wilderness and taught them to **trust** in God's ongoing care.

Beyond its immediate significance, the provision of **manna and quail** serves as a **type** that points forward to the **ultimate provision** in **Jesus Christ**. In the **New Testament**, Jesus identifies Himself as the **true Bread of Life**, the **spiritual sustenance** that believers require to maintain their relationship with God. The connection between the manna in the Old Testament and Christ in the New Testament underscores the idea that **God's provision** is not only for our physical needs but also for our **spiritual sustenance** and eternal life.

This chapter will explore the **typology** of the manna and quail as a **foreshadowing** of Christ's provision for His people. It will delve into the nature of **God's daily provision**, the **lessons** that the Israelites learned through their dependence on manna, and the significance of Jesus being the true **Bread of Life**. By understanding these biblical connections, we will gain a deeper appreciation for God's provision throughout history and how Christ ultimately fulfills all that the manna symbolized.

I. THE CONTEXT OF THE MANNA AND QUAIL IN THE WILDERNESS (EXODUS 16)

The Israelites had only recently been **delivered from Egypt**, experiencing the **miracle** of the parting of the **Red Sea** and their safe passage to freedom. However, shortly after their deliverance, the **harsh reality** of wilderness life set in. The people soon found themselves without food and began to **grumble** against Moses and Aaron, questioning why they had been brought out of Egypt to die in the wilderness.

A. The Israelites' Complaint and God's Response

In **Exodus 16:2-3**, the Israelites expressed their fear and dissatisfaction:

> "And the whole congregation of the people of Israel grumbled against Moses and Aaron in the wilderness, and the people of Israel said to them, 'Would that we had died by the hand of the Lord in the land of Egypt, when we sat by the meat pots and ate bread to the full, for you have brought us out into this wilderness to kill this whole assembly with hunger.'"

Despite the miraculous works God had already performed on their behalf, the Israelites struggled with **trusting** Him for their **daily needs**. Rather than remembering God's faithfulness, they looked back with **nostalgia** at their life in Egypt, where, although they were slaves, they at least had access to food.

In response to their complaints, God showed His **compassion** and **faithfulness** by promising to provide for their needs. He assured them that He would **rain bread from heaven**, and He did so in the form of **manna**. Additionally, He provided **quail** for meat, ensuring that they had both **bread** and **protein** for sustenance.

God's provision of manna and quail teaches a key lesson about **trust**—His people are to rely on Him for their **daily bread**, trusting that He will supply their needs day by day.

B. THE MIRACLE OF MANNA AND QUAIL

God's provision came in the form of two miraculous food sources: **manna**, which was described as a fine, flaky substance that appeared on the ground each morning, and **quail**, which were birds that came in large numbers to the Israelite camp in the evening.

In **Exodus 16:4**, God said to Moses:

> "Behold, I am about to rain bread from heaven for you, and the people shall go out and gather a day's portion every day, that I may test them, whether they will walk in my law or not."

The provision of manna was not just about feeding the Israelites—it was also a **test** of their **faith** and **obedience**. God commanded that they gather only as much as they needed for each day, except on the sixth day when they were to gather enough for two days in order to observe the **Sabbath rest** on the seventh day. This requirement to gather just enough for each day was intended to teach the Israelites to **trust in God's daily provision** and not to hoard or rely on their own strength.

The quail, meanwhile, were provided in the evening to give the people meat. In **Exodus 16:12**, God spoke to Moses:

> "I have heard the grumbling of the people of Israel. Say to them, 'At twilight you shall eat meat, and in the morning you shall be filled with bread. Then you shall know that I am the Lord your God.'"

Through these daily miracles, God not only provided for the physical needs of His people but also reminded them that He was their **source** and **provider**. The Israelites were to learn that **man does not live by bread alone**, but by every word that comes from the mouth of God—a lesson that would become even more significant in the context of Jesus' ministry.

1. The Nature of Manna

The **manna** that appeared each morning was described as being like **coriander seed**, white in color, and tasting like wafers made with **honey (Exodus 16:31)**. It was a **heavenly bread**, unlike anything the Israelites had seen before, and it became their **daily sustenance** for 40 years in the wilderness. The miraculous nature of manna was clear: it could not be stored or hoarded, as any attempt to keep it overnight (except before the Sabbath) would result in it **rotting** and becoming **inedible**.

The limitations God placed on the gathering and storage of manna were intended to teach the Israelites **dependence** on Him. Each day they were reminded that their survival was not dependent on their own efforts but on God's **ongoing provision**.

2. The Quail for Meat

While the **manna** was the primary food source for the Israelites during their time in the wilderness, God also provided **quail** on certain occasions to give them meat. In **Numbers 11**, we see a further account of God providing quail to the Israelites after they complained again about their food. Quail would descend on the camp in the evening, providing enough meat for the entire nation.

Together, the **manna and quail** served as a powerful demonstration of God's **faithfulness** and His ability to meet the needs of His people, even in the most barren and desolate circumstances.

II. MANNA AS A TYPE OF CHRIST, THE BREAD OF LIFE (JOHN 6:32-35)

While the manna provided **physical sustenance** to the Israelites in the wilderness, it also served as a **foreshadowing** of the **true bread from heaven—Jesus Christ**, who provides **spiritual sustenance** for all who believe in Him. Jesus made this connection explicit in **John 6**, where He identifies Himself as the **Bread of Life** and explains that just as God provided manna to sustain the Israelites in the wilderness, He Himself is the **true bread** that gives **eternal life**.

A. Jesus, the True Bread from Heaven

In **John 6:32-35**, Jesus addresses the crowd that had followed Him after He miraculously fed the 5,000 with five loaves and two fish. The people, having experienced this miraculous provision of food, sought more signs and more bread. Jesus, however, pointed them to the **deeper meaning** behind His miracles:

> "Jesus then said to them, 'Truly, truly, I say to you, it was not Moses who gave you the bread from heaven, but my Father gives you the true bread from heaven. For the bread of God is He who comes down from heaven and gives life to the world.' They said to Him, 'Sir, give us this bread always.' Jesus said to them, 'I am the bread of life; whoever comes to me shall not hunger, and whoever believes in me shall never thirst.'"

Jesus reveals that the **manna** in the wilderness was a **type** of the **true provision** that God was offering through Him. While the manna fed the Israelites' bodies for a time, it could not give them **eternal life**. In contrast, Jesus is the **true bread** who came down from heaven, and all who partake in Him will receive **eternal sustenance** and **spiritual nourishment** that leads to everlasting life.

1. The Superiority of Christ's Provision

The manna that God provided to the Israelites was a **temporary provision**—it sustained them during their wilderness journey, but it could not grant them **eternal life**. In fact, the Israelites who ate the manna eventually died, as Jesus pointed out in **John 6:49**:

> "Your fathers ate the manna in the wilderness, and they died."

In contrast, Jesus offers something far greater. As the **Bread of Life**, He provides **eternal sustenance**—those who believe in Him will **never hunger** or **thirst** spiritually. In **John 6:51**, Jesus declares:

> "I am the living bread that came down from heaven. If anyone eats of this bread, he will live forever. And the bread that I will give for the life of the world is my flesh."

This statement emphasizes the **superiority** of Christ's provision over the manna in the wilderness. While the manna was a **miracle** in its own right, it pointed forward to the **greater miracle** of God's provision in Christ. Jesus' **incarnation**, His coming down from heaven, and His **sacrificial death** on the cross are the ultimate expressions of God's provision for humanity's deepest need—**salvation** and **eternal life**.

2. The Spiritual Significance of Bread

Bread has long been a symbol of **sustenance** and **life** in many cultures, and in the biblical narrative, it represents God's provision for His people. In the wilderness, manna served as **daily bread** for the Israelites, meeting their immediate needs. However, bread also has a **spiritual dimension**, as it symbolizes the **Word of God** and the **life** that God offers to His people.

In **Deuteronomy 8:3**, Moses reminded the Israelites of the deeper lesson behind the manna:

> "He humbled you and let you hunger and fed you with manna, which you did not know, nor did your fathers know, that He might make you know that man does not live by bread alone, but man lives by every word that comes from the mouth of the Lord."

Jesus echoed this truth when He was tempted by Satan in the wilderness. In **Matthew 4:4**, He quoted this verse to emphasize that **spiritual sustenance** is more important than physical sustenance:

> "It is written, 'Man shall not live by bread alone, but by every word that comes from the mouth of God.'"

By identifying Himself as the **Bread of Life**, Jesus was not only pointing to His role as the one who **nourishes** and **sustains** His people spiritually but also to the fact that He is the **living Word of God**—the **ultimate revelation** of God's will and provision for humanity.

B. The Call to Believe in Christ, the Bread of Life

Throughout **John 6**, Jesus repeatedly emphasizes the necessity of **believing** in Him to receive the **life-giving bread** that He offers. Just as the Israelites had to gather and eat the manna each day, so too must individuals **come to Christ** and **believe in Him** to receive **eternal life**.

In **John 6:35**, Jesus makes a powerful statement about the spiritual satisfaction that comes from believing in Him:

> "I am the bread of life; whoever comes to me shall not hunger, and whoever believes in me shall never thirst."

This invitation to **come** and **believe** is central to the gospel message. Just as the Israelites depended on the manna for their **daily**

sustenance, believers must depend on Christ for their **spiritual sustenance**. Faith in Jesus is the means by which we partake of the **Bread of Life** and receive the **eternal nourishment** that only He can provide.

1. The Necessity of Daily Dependence

The daily gathering of manna in the wilderness teaches us an important spiritual principle: **daily dependence** on God's provision. The Israelites could not hoard manna or rely on yesterday's portion to sustain them for today. Each day, they had to go out and **trust God** for that day's provision. In the same way, believers are called to **daily trust** in Christ for their **spiritual sustenance**.

Jesus emphasizes this principle in the **Lord's Prayer**, where He instructs His disciples to pray, **"Give us this day our daily bread"** (**Matthew 6:11**). This prayer is not just about physical bread but also about the **spiritual sustenance** we need each day to remain **faithful** and **dependent** on God.

2. Partaking in Christ by Faith

In **John 6:53-58**, Jesus uses **symbolic language** to describe the necessity of **partaking** in Him by faith. He speaks of **eating His flesh** and **drinking His blood**, which refers to the need for believers to **fully trust** in His **sacrifice** for their salvation:

> "Truly, truly, I say to you, unless you eat the flesh of the Son of Man and drink His blood, you have no life in you. Whoever feeds on my flesh and drinks my blood has eternal life, and I will raise him up on the last day. For my flesh is true food, and my blood is true drink."

This passage points to the **sacrificial nature** of Christ's work on the cross and the need for believers to **appropriate** that sacrifice by faith. Just as the Israelites had to physically eat the manna to be sustained, believers must **spiritually partake** of Christ by placing their **faith** in Him and trusting in His **atoning work** for their salvation.

III. THE LESSONS OF MANNA AND QUAIL: TRUST, OBEDIENCE, AND GRATITUDE

The story of manna and quail in **Exodus 16** offers more than just a record of God's miraculous provision—it also provides valuable **lessons** about the nature of **trust, obedience**, and **gratitude**. These lessons were not only important for the Israelites but also for believers today as we seek to **depend** on God's provision in every area of our lives.

A. Trusting in God's Daily Provision

The **daily nature** of the manna highlights the importance of **trusting God** for our needs one day at a time. The Israelites were not allowed to gather more than they needed for a single day (except before the Sabbath), and any attempt to do so resulted in the manna **spoiling**. This forced them to **rely on God** day by day, trusting that He would provide what they needed for each day.

This principle of **daily trust** is just as relevant for believers today. While we often want to have **security** and **control** over our future, God calls us to live in **dependence** on Him, trusting that He will provide what we need each day. As Jesus taught in the **Sermon on the Mount**, we are not to worry about tomorrow, for **each day has enough trouble of its own (Matthew 6:34)**.

1. A Test of Faith

God's provision of manna was also a **test of faith** for the Israelites. In **Exodus 16:4**, God explicitly states that the daily gathering of manna was a way to test whether the people would **walk in His law**. Would they trust Him enough to gather only what they needed for the day, or would they try to **take matters into their own hands** by hoarding food for the future?

This test of faith is one that believers still face today. We are often tempted to **rely on ourselves** or seek **security** in things other than God's provision. Yet, like the Israelites, we are called to **trust** in God's faithfulness and believe that He will provide for us day by day.

2. Learning Contentment

The **quail** that God provided in the wilderness also teaches an important lesson about **contentment**. The Israelites were not content with the manna alone—they wanted **meat** as well, and God granted their request by sending quail. However, their **grumbling** and lack of contentment eventually led to **judgment**, as we see in **Numbers 11**, where many Israelites died as a result of their **greed**.

This episode serves as a reminder of the danger of **discontentment** and the importance of being grateful for what God provides. **Philippians 4:11-12** teaches us the value of **contentment** in every circumstance:

> "I have learned in whatever situation I am to be content. I know how to be brought low, and I know how to abound. In any and every circumstance, I have learned the secret of facing plenty and hunger, abundance and need."

B. The Call to Obedience

The gathering of manna also required **obedience** on the part of the Israelites. They were commanded to gather the manna each day according to their needs, and they were forbidden from gathering on the **Sabbath**. Those who disobeyed these instructions by gathering too much or by attempting to gather on the Sabbath found that the manna either **spoiled** or was not available.

This call to **obedience** was a way for the Israelites to demonstrate their **trust** in God. By following His commands regarding the manna, they showed that they believed in His ability to provide for them. In the same way, believers today are called to **obey** God's Word, trusting that His commands are for our **good** and that He will provide for our needs as we walk in **faithful obedience**.

Fun Fact: Manna's Mysterious Nature and Modern Interpretations

The nature of manna has fascinated both theologians and scientists alike. Described in **Exodus 16:14-15** as **fine, flake-like** and tasting like **wafers made with honey**, manna was unlike any other food the Israelites had encountered. While manna's exact composition remains a mystery, some scholars have suggested that it may have been a natural substance produced by insects or plants in the desert, while others view it as a **supernatural provision** unique to that time.

Interestingly, some regions of the Middle East still produce a **substance** that is sometimes referred to as "manna." For example, in parts of **Iran** and **Iraq**, certain insects secrete a sweet, flake-like substance that resembles the biblical description of manna. However, these natural phenomena do not fully explain the **miraculous nature** of the manna in the Bible, which was provided daily for 40 years and ceased as soon as the Israelites entered the Promised Land.

Whether natural or supernatural in origin, the story of manna continues to capture the **imagination** of scholars and believers alike, pointing to the **mystery** and **miracle** of God's provision for His people.

Christ, the Bread of Life, and God's Eternal Provision

From the Tabernacle to Solomon's Temple to the Second Temple, the progression of God's dwelling among His people points toward a final and eternal fulfillment in Christ. The tearing of the temple veil at Jesus' crucifixion signifies the end of separation between God and humanity, and the beginning of the Church as the living temple, indwelt by the Spirit.

Solomon's Temple was the physical dwelling place of God among His people, where the Ark of the Covenant resided. As magnificent as it was, it served as a shadow of a greater reality. The destruction of this temple symbolized the passing of the old covenant system, pointing forward to the time when God's presence would dwell fully in Christ, the true Temple. The physical structure of the temple was temporary, but it laid the foundation for the spiritual temple found in Christ.

The Second Temple, rebuilt after the exile, held great significance for the Jewish people. It was the site of Jesus' ministry, and although it lacked the glory of Solomon's Temple, it still foreshadowed a greater fulfillment in Christ. The destruction of the Second Temple, as prophesied by Jesus, marks the end of the old sacrificial system and the transition to a new covenant where God's presence is no longer confined to a building but resides in Christ and His Church. Jesus, the ultimate Temple, fulfills what the Second Temple could only symbolize.

The story of **manna and quail** in the wilderness serves as a powerful reminder of **God's faithfulness** and His ability to provide for the needs of His people. As the Israelites journeyed through the barren wilderness, God provided **daily sustenance** in the form of manna and quail, teaching them to **trust in His provision** and to walk in **obedience**.

More importantly, the manna is a **type of Christ**, the true **Bread of Life** who provides **eternal sustenance** to all who believe in Him. While the manna in the wilderness could only sustain the Israelites temporarily, Christ offers **eternal life** and **spiritual nourishment** that will never fade. Through His death and resurrection, Christ has become the ultimate **provision** for humanity's deepest need—**salvation** and reconciliation with God.

As believers, we are called to **come to Christ** daily, trusting in Him for our **spiritual sustenance** and relying on His provision in every area of our lives. Just as the Israelites had to gather manna each day, so too must we **depend on Christ** each day, knowing that He is the **source of life** and the **sustainer of our souls**.

In the story of **manna and quail**, we see the **faithfulness** of God, the **importance of trust**, and the **superiority of Christ's provision**. As we continue our journey of faith, may we always look to Christ, the **Bread of Life**, and find our satisfaction in Him alone.

CHAPTER 26: THE DELIVERANCE FROM BABYLON: A TYPE OF SPIRITUAL REDEMPTION

The **deliverance of Israel from Babylonian captivity** is one of the most significant events in the **Old Testament**, representing the fulfillment of God's promises to restore His people after a period of judgment. The **Babylonian exile** was a time of great sorrow and disillusionment for Israel, as the people of God were removed from their land and taken to a foreign nation. Yet, in their captivity, there was also a message of **hope**: God had not abandoned His people. He had a plan to restore them and bring them back to the **Promised Land**. The **return from exile** was a **physical deliverance**, but it also carried deep **spiritual significance** as a **type** of the greater spiritual redemption that would come through **Jesus Christ**.

This chapter will explore the **deliverance from Babylon** as a type of **spiritual redemption**, examining the ways in which Israel's **return from exile** foreshadows the **spiritual deliverance** that Christ brings to those who are **captives** of sin and the **world system**. We will delve into the **historical context** of the Babylonian exile, the **significance** of the return under leaders like **Ezra** and **Nehemiah**, and the **theological lessons** that emerge from this period of Israel's history. Additionally, we will look at how **Babylon** functions as a **symbol** in **Scripture**, representing the world's opposition to God and His people, and how Christ calls believers to come out of this **spiritual Babylon**, just as He called the Israelites to return from physical Babylon.

By examining the deliverance from Babylon as a **type** of spiritual redemption, we can gain a deeper understanding of how **God's plan** for Israel's restoration points forward to His ultimate plan of **salvation** and **deliverance** for all humanity through Christ. This chapter will also emphasize the ongoing relevance of these themes for believers today, as we live in a world that often mirrors the **spiritual captivity** represented by Babylon.

I. THE HISTORICAL CONTEXT OF THE BABYLONIAN CAPTIVITY

To fully understand the **spiritual typology** of Israel's deliverance from Babylon, it is important to first explore the **historical context** of the **Babylonian exile**. The exile was a direct result of Israel's persistent **disobedience** to God, particularly their refusal to follow His **covenant** and their **idolatrous practices**. After centuries of warnings from the prophets, God allowed the **Babylonians** to conquer **Judah** and take the people into **captivity** as a form of divine judgment.

A. The Fall of Jerusalem and the Beginning of the Exile

The **Babylonian Empire**, under the leadership of **King Nebuchadnezzar**, was the dominant power in the ancient Near East during the late 7th and early 6th centuries BC. In **586 BC**, Nebuchadnezzar's army laid siege to **Jerusalem**, destroyed the **Temple**, and carried the people of Judah into **exile**. This event marked the **end** of the **Davidic monarchy** and the loss of the **Promised Land**—a devastating blow to the identity and faith of the people of Israel.

The **prophet Jeremiah** had foreseen this catastrophe, warning the people that their continued **rebellion** against God would result in destruction and exile. In **Jeremiah 25:11-12**, he prophesied that the exile would last for **seventy years**:

> "This whole land shall become a ruin and a waste, and these nations shall serve the king of Babylon seventy years. Then after seventy years are completed, I will punish the king of Babylon and that nation, the land of the Chaldeans, for their iniquity, declares the Lord, making the land an everlasting waste."

The **Babylonian captivity** was a period of deep **sorrow** and **lament** for the Israelites, as they found themselves in a foreign land, far from the **Temple** where they had worshiped God. **Psalm 137** captures the heartache of this time:

> "By the waters of Babylon, there we sat down and wept, when we remembered Zion." (Psalm 137:1)

The exile was a period of both **judgment** and **refinement**, as the Israelites were forced to confront the consequences of their **idolatry** and **unfaithfulness**. Yet, even in the midst of their captivity, there was a **promise of restoration**—a promise that God would one day bring His people back to their land.

B. The Role of Prophets During the Exile

During the Babylonian exile, God raised up **prophets** to speak words of hope and comfort to the exiled people. **Isaiah**, **Jeremiah**, and **Ezekiel** all delivered prophecies that pointed to a future **restoration** for Israel, even as they called the people to **repentance** and **faithfulness**.

One of the most significant prophecies of deliverance came from **Isaiah**, who foretold the rise of **Cyrus the Great**, the king of **Persia**, who would overthrow Babylon and allow the Israelites to return to their land. In **Isaiah 45:1-4**, God calls Cyrus His **anointed** and declares that he will be the one to set Israel free:

> "Thus says the Lord to his anointed, to Cyrus, whose right hand I have grasped, to subdue nations before him and to loose the belts of kings, to open doors before him that gates may not be closed... For the sake of my servant Jacob, and Israel my chosen, I call you by your name, I name you, though you do not know me."

This prophecy highlights the **sovereignty of God** over the nations and His ability to use even foreign rulers to accomplish His purposes. Cyrus would become the instrument of Israel's **physical deliverance**, but this deliverance would also point to a greater **spiritual redemption** that God would accomplish through Christ.

II. THE RETURN FROM BABYLON: A TYPE OF SPIRITUAL DELIVERANCE

After seventy years in exile, the Israelites were finally given the opportunity to **return to their land**. This moment of **deliverance** marked the **end** of their captivity and the beginning of a new chapter in their relationship with God. The return from Babylon was a **physical event**, but it also serves as a **type** of the **spiritual deliverance** that Christ offers to all who are **captives** of sin and the **world system**.

A. The Decree of Cyrus and the Return of the Exiles (Ezra 1-2)

The return from Babylon was made possible by a **decree** from **Cyrus the Great**, the Persian king who had conquered Babylon in **539 BC**. In **Ezra 1:1-3**, we read about this decree:

> "In the first year of Cyrus king of Persia, that the word of the Lord by the mouth of Jeremiah might be fulfilled, the Lord stirred up the spirit of Cyrus king of Persia, so that he made a proclamation throughout all his kingdom and also put it in writing: 'Thus says Cyrus king of Persia: The Lord, the God of heaven, has given me all the kingdoms of the earth, and he has charged me to build him a house at Jerusalem, which is in Judah. Whoever is among you of all his people, may his God be with him, and let him go up to Jerusalem, which is in Judah, and rebuild the house of the Lord, the God of Israel—he is the God who is in Jerusalem.'"

This decree allowed the Israelites to **return to their land** and begin the process of **rebuilding** the **Temple** in Jerusalem. Under the leadership of **Zerubbabel, Ezra**, and **Nehemiah**, the exiles began the work of **restoration**, both physically and spiritually. They rebuilt the **Temple** and the **walls of Jerusalem**, reestablished the **worship of God**, and recommitted themselves to **obeying the Law**.

The return from Babylon marked the **end of exile** and the **restoration of Israel** as God's people in the land He had promised them. However, this event also serves as a **type** of the greater **spiritual deliverance** that Christ would accomplish for His people.

1. The Symbolism of Returning to the Land

The return from Babylon was not just a political or geographical event—it was a **spiritual homecoming**. For the Israelites, the **Promised Land** was a symbol of God's **covenant faithfulness** and His desire to **dwell** with His people. The **land of Israel** represented the **blessings** of God's covenant, and their return to the land was a sign of His **mercy** and **forgiveness**.

In the same way, the **spiritual redemption** that Christ offers involves a return to **fellowship with God**. Sin separates humanity from God, just as the exile separated Israel from the land. Through Christ, believers are **restored** to **relationship** with God and brought into the **kingdom of heaven**, which is the **true Promised Land** for those who belong to Him.

2. The Rebuilding of the Temple

One of the first tasks the returning exiles undertook was the **rebuilding of the Temple** in Jerusalem. The Temple was the **center** of Israel's religious life, and its destruction by the Babylonians had been a devastating blow. The rebuilding of the Temple was a sign that God's **presence** would once again dwell with His people.

In the New Testament, **Jesus** is revealed as the true **Temple of God**. In **John 2:19-21**, Jesus says:

> "Destroy this temple, and in three days I will raise it up." The Jews then said, "It has taken forty-six years to build this temple, and will you raise it up in three days?" But He was speaking about the temple of His body.

Jesus' **death** and **resurrection** fulfilled the **typology** of the Temple, showing that He is the **place where God's presence** dwells and the means by which people can come into **communion** with God. Just as the Israelites returned from exile to rebuild the physical Temple, so too are believers **called out of spiritual exile** to become the **Temple of the Holy Spirit**.

B. Babylon as a Symbol of Spiritual Captivity

In Scripture, **Babylon** is not only a historical empire but also a **symbol** of **spiritual captivity** and the **world system** that stands in opposition to God. Throughout the **Bible**, Babylon represents **human pride, idolatry**, and **rebellion** against God's authority. In the **book of Revelation**, Babylon is portrayed as the **great harlot**, symbolizing the corrupt world system that entices people away from God.

In **Revelation 18:4**, a voice from heaven calls out to God's people:

> "Come out of her, my people, lest you take part in her sins, lest you share in her plagues."

This call to **come out of Babylon** is a **spiritual parallel** to the call for the Israelites to return from Babylonian exile. Just as God called the Israelites to leave physical Babylon and return to the **Promised Land**, He calls believers to **come out of spiritual Babylon** and enter into the **kingdom of God**.

1. Babylon as a Metaphor for the World System

In **Revelation**, Babylon represents the **world system** that opposes God's kingdom. This system is characterized by **materialism, idolatry**, and **moral corruption**. Just as ancient Babylon was a center of **wealth** and **power**, the Babylon of **Revelation** symbolizes the seductive allure of the world's values, which are at odds with the values of God's kingdom.

Believers are called to **come out of Babylon**, meaning that they are to **reject** the ways of the world and live in **holiness** and **obedience** to God. **Romans 12:2** emphasizes this call to be separate from the world:

> "Do not be conformed to this world, but be transformed by the renewal of your mind, that by testing you may discern what is the will of God, what is good and acceptable and perfect."

2. Spiritual Captivity and Deliverance in Christ

Just as the Israelites were captives in **physical Babylon**, so too are all people **spiritual captives** to **sin** and the **world system** until they are delivered by Christ. The **Apostle Paul** describes this captivity in **Ephesians 2:1-3**, where he writes:

"And you were dead in the trespasses and sins in which you once walked, following the course of this world, following the prince of the power of the air, the spirit that is now at work in the sons of disobedience—among whom we all once lived in the passions of our flesh, carrying out the desires of the body and the mind, and were by nature children of wrath, like the rest of mankind."

In this passage, Paul explains that before coming to faith in Christ, all people are **enslaved** to sin and to the ways of the world. This spiritual **captivity** mirrors the Israelites' physical captivity in Babylon. However, just as God delivered Israel from Babylon, Christ delivers believers from the **captivity of sin** and brings them into the **freedom** of His kingdom.

Galatians 5:1 declares:

"For freedom Christ has set us free; stand firm therefore, and do not submit again to a yoke of slavery."

Through Christ's **death** and **resurrection**, believers are **set free** from the power of sin and the influence of the world system. They are no longer captives in **Babylon** but are citizens of the **heavenly Jerusalem**, the **kingdom of God**.

III. THE SPIRITUAL LESSONS OF THE RETURN FROM BABYLON

The return from Babylon is rich with **spiritual lessons** that are applicable to believers today. The **physical deliverance** of Israel serves as a **type** of the **spiritual deliverance** that Christ offers, and the challenges the Israelites faced during their return to the land mirror the challenges believers face in their **walk of faith**.

A. Restoration and Renewal

One of the central themes of the return from Babylon is the idea of **restoration** and **renewal**. The **Israelites** returned to a land that had been devastated by war, with a **Temple** that had been destroyed and **walls** that had been torn down. Yet, under the leadership of **Ezra**, **Nehemiah**, and **Zerubbabel**, they undertook the work of **rebuilding** the Temple and the walls of **Jerusalem**.

This work of **restoration** parallels the **spiritual restoration** that occurs in the lives of believers. Just as the Israelites rebuilt the physical structures of their land, so too are believers called to engage in the work of **spiritual renewal**. **2 Corinthians 5:17** reminds us:

> "Therefore, if anyone is in Christ, he is a new creation. The old has passed away; behold, the new has come."

In Christ, believers experience **spiritual renewal**, where the **old self**—which was enslaved to sin—is replaced by the **new self**, which is empowered by the Holy Spirit to live a life of **holiness** and **obedience**.

1. The Importance of Rebuilding the Temple

The **rebuilding of the Temple** was a crucial aspect of the return from Babylon. The Temple represented the **presence of God** among His people, and its destruction had symbolized the **broken relationship** between Israel and God. By rebuilding the Temple, the Israelites were symbolically restoring their **relationship** with God and reestablishing their identity as His people.

In the same way, the **work of spiritual renewal** involves the **restoration** of our relationship with God. **Sin** separates us from God, but through **repentance** and **faith** in Christ, we are able to **rebuild** that relationship. As believers, we are called to be the **Temple of the Holy Spirit**, and we must continually work to ensure that our lives are places where God's **presence** can dwell.

2. Rebuilding the Walls of Jerusalem

In addition to rebuilding the Temple, the Israelites also rebuilt the **walls of Jerusalem**, which had been destroyed by the Babylonians. The walls represented **protection** and **security**, and their reconstruction was essential for the safety and stability of the city.

For believers, the rebuilding of the walls serves as a metaphor for the importance of **spiritual boundaries**. Just as the walls of

Jerusalem protected the city from external threats, so too must believers establish **boundaries** that protect them from the **influence** of the world and the **temptations** of sin. **Proverbs 4:23** instructs us:

> "Keep your heart with all vigilance, for from it flow the springs of life."

By establishing **spiritual boundaries** and guarding our hearts, we can protect ourselves from the **spiritual captivity** that Babylon represents and remain faithful to God's calling.

B. The Call to Holiness

Another key lesson from the return from Babylon is the call to **holiness** and **separation** from the surrounding nations. The Israelites were tempted to **compromise** their faith by intermarrying with the pagan nations around them, which would have led to **idolatry** and unfaithfulness to God's covenant. In response, leaders like **Ezra** and **Nehemiah** called the people to **repentance** and a renewed commitment to **holiness**.

In the same way, believers today are called to **separate themselves** from the **world system** represented by Babylon. **1 Peter 1:15-16** emphasizes the call to holiness:

> "But as He who called you is holy, you also be holy in all your conduct, since it is written, 'You shall be holy, for I am holy.'"

Holiness involves not only **moral purity** but also **faithfulness** to God's Word and a commitment to **live differently** from the world. Believers are called to **come out of Babylon** by rejecting the values and practices of the world and living according to the values of **God's kingdom**.

1. The Danger of Compromise

One of the greatest challenges the Israelites faced during their return from Babylon was the temptation to **compromise** with the surrounding nations. This temptation is mirrored in the spiritual lives of believers today, as we are constantly faced with the allure of **worldly values** and **practices** that stand in opposition to God's will.

Romans 12:2 warns us not to be **conformed** to this world, but to be **transformed** by the renewal of our minds. This transformation requires a daily commitment to **holiness** and a rejection of the **compromise** that would lead us away from God.

2. The Call to Repentance and Renewal

Just as the Israelites were called to **repentance** and renewal under the leadership of Ezra and Nehemiah, so too are believers called to live in a state of **continual repentance**. Sin can easily creep into our lives, just as the pagan influences threatened the Israelites. However, through **repentance** and **confession**, we can continually restore our relationship with God and remain **faithful** to Him.

Fun Fact: Babylon in Popular Culture

Babylon has captured the **imagination** of people for centuries, and its name has become synonymous with **wealth**, **corruption**, and **oppression**. In popular culture, Babylon is often depicted as a symbol of **decadence** and **moral decline**. The phrase "the fall of Babylon" is used metaphorically to describe the downfall of corrupt powers or regimes.

For example, in the **Rastafarian movement**, Babylon represents the **oppressive systems** of Western society, and the call to "come out of Babylon" is interpreted as a call to **resist** the injustices of the world and return to a life of **spiritual purity** and connection with **God**.

In **music**, **art**, and **literature**, Babylon is often used as a symbol of the **tension** between **good** and **evil**, **corruption** and **redemption**—a tension that is ultimately resolved in the **biblical narrative** through the **redemptive work of Christ**.

Deliverance from Babylon as a Type of Spiritual Redemption

From the Tabernacle to Solomon's Temple to the Second Temple, the progression of God's dwelling among His people points toward a final and eternal fulfillment in Christ. The tearing of the temple veil at Jesus' crucifixion signifies the end of separation between God and humanity, and the beginning of the Church as the living temple, indwelt by the Spirit.

Solomon's Temple was the physical dwelling place of God among His people, where the Ark of the Covenant resided. As magnificent as it was, it served as a shadow of a greater reality. The destruction of this temple symbolized the passing of the old covenant system, pointing forward to the time when God's presence would dwell fully in Christ, the true Temple. The physical structure of the temple was temporary, but it laid the foundation for the spiritual temple found in Christ.

The Second Temple, rebuilt after the exile, held great significance for the Jewish people. It was the site of Jesus' ministry, and although it lacked the glory of Solomon's Temple, it still foreshadowed a greater fulfillment in Christ. The destruction of the Second Temple, as prophesied by Jesus, marks the end of the old sacrificial system and the transition to a new covenant where God's presence is no longer confined to a building but resides in Christ and His Church. Jesus, the ultimate Temple, fulfills what the Second Temple could only symbolize.

The **deliverance of Israel** from Babylonian captivity serves as a profound **type** of the **spiritual redemption** that Christ offers to all who are **enslaved** by sin and the world system. Just as God delivered the Israelites from the physical captivity of Babylon and brought them back to their **Promised Land**, Christ delivers believers from the **captivity of sin** and brings them into the **kingdom of God**.

Through the story of **Israel's return** from Babylon, we learn important lessons about **trusting in God's deliverance**, engaging in the work of **spiritual renewal**, and maintaining **holiness** in the face of the **world's temptations**. We are reminded that, just as God was faithful to His people in the past, He remains faithful to us today, calling us to **come out of Babylon** and live as **citizens** of His **heavenly kingdom**.

As we reflect on the deliverance from Babylon, we are encouraged to see the **parallels** between Israel's physical journey and our own **spiritual journey**. Just as the Israelites returned to rebuild their **Temple** and their **city**, we are called to **build our lives** on the foundation of Christ, the **true Temple**. Through His **death** and **resurrection**, Christ has freed us from the **powers of sin and death**, and in Him, we find our **ultimate redemption**.

CHAPTER 27: DAVID AS A TYPE OF CHRIST THE KING

David, the shepherd boy who became **King of Israel**, is one of the most significant figures in the Bible. His life, described in **1 Samuel 16 to 2 Samuel 24**, is marked by moments of **courage, faith,** and **humility**, as well as by **sin, repentance,** and **restoration**. David is often seen as a **type of Christ**, especially in his role as **king** and **shepherd** over Israel. David's reign points forward to the reign of **Jesus Christ**, the **ultimate Shepherd-King**, who will rule over all creation in **eternal peace**.

In this chapter, we will explore the **typological connections** between David and Christ, focusing on how David's life and reign as king serve as a **shadow** of the **greater kingship** of Christ. From David's humble beginnings as a shepherd to his establishment as king over Israel, his battles against Israel's enemies, his failures, and ultimately, the **covenant** God made with him, each aspect of David's life reflects something about the **person** and **work** of Christ.

We will examine key moments in David's life and reign, such as his **anointing**, his battles against **Goliath** and other enemies, his **sin** with Bathsheba, and God's **covenant** with him. Throughout these events, David's role as a **type of Christ** becomes clear. In addition, we will look at **New Testament passages** that draw direct parallels between David and Christ, such as Jesus' identification as the **Son of David** and His role as the **Good Shepherd** who lays down His life for the sheep.

By understanding David as a type of Christ, we can gain deeper insights into the **nature of Jesus' kingship**, His role as our **Shepherd-King**, and His ultimate **reign of peace** that will be established when He returns. This chapter will also explore how believers today are called to live under the **reign of Christ**, the **King of kings**, and how David's life serves as both a **foreshadowing** and a **lesson** for those who follow Christ.

I. DAVID'S ANOINTING AS A TYPE OF CHRIST'S KINGSHIP

David's story begins with his **anointing** by the prophet **Samuel**. In **1 Samuel 16**, God rejects **Saul** as king over Israel because of his **disobedience** and sends Samuel to the house of **Jesse** to anoint a new king. David, the youngest of Jesse's sons, is chosen by God to be the next king of Israel. This moment of anointing marks the beginning of David's journey toward kingship, though he would not take the throne until years later.

A. David's Anointing by Samuel (1 Samuel 16:1-13)

David's anointing is significant because it demonstrates that God does not choose leaders based on **outward appearances** or human standards. When Samuel arrives at Jesse's house, he initially assumes that one of David's older brothers—tall and impressive in appearance—must be the one God has chosen. However, God rejects all of David's brothers and chooses David, the youngest and seemingly least significant, to be the next king of Israel.

1 Samuel 16:7 captures the heart of God's choice:

> "But the Lord said to Samuel, 'Do not look on his appearance or on the height of his stature, because I have rejected him. For the Lord sees not as man sees: man looks on the outward appearance, but the Lord looks on the heart.'"

David's anointing points forward to **Christ**, the **Messiah** (which means "Anointed One"), who would also come in **humility** rather than in worldly grandeur. Like David, Jesus did not fit the expectations of the people who were looking for a **conquering king** or **military leader**. Instead, Jesus came as a **servant**, born in a humble manger, and He lived a life of **obedience** to the Father, culminating in His sacrificial death on the cross.

1. David's Humble Beginnings and Christ's Humility

David was a **shepherd boy**, tending his father's flocks in the fields when Samuel came to anoint him. His humble occupation and his seemingly insignificant position in his family reflect the **humility of Christ**, who also came as a **shepherd**—the **Good Shepherd** who lays down His life for His sheep.

In **John 10:11**, Jesus identifies Himself as the Good Shepherd:

> "I am the good shepherd. The good shepherd lays down his life for the sheep."

David's role as a shepherd not only prefigures Christ's shepherding ministry but also points to the way in which God chooses those who are **humble** and **faithful** to lead His people. Just as David was chosen not because of his outward appearance but because of his **heart**, so too was Christ chosen as the **Savior** of the world because of His **perfect obedience** and **righteousness**.

2. Anointed by the Spirit

After Samuel anointed David with oil, the **Spirit of the Lord** came upon David **from that day forward (1 Samuel 16:13)**. This anointing by the Spirit is a significant moment in David's life, as it empowered him for the task of kingship. Similarly, Jesus was **anointed by the Holy Spirit** at His baptism, marking the beginning of His **public ministry**.

In **Luke 3:21-22**, we read about Jesus' baptism and the descent of the Holy Spirit:

> "Now when all the people were baptized, and when Jesus also had been baptized and was praying, the heavens were opened, and the Holy Spirit descended on Him in bodily form, like a dove; and a voice came from heaven, 'You are my beloved Son; with you I am well pleased.'"

Both David and Jesus were anointed by the Spirit, signifying God's **favor** and **empowerment** for their respective roles. David's anointing points forward to the **greater anointing** of Christ, who was filled with the **Holy Spirit** and empowered to bring about the **kingdom of God** on earth.

II. DAVID'S VICTORY OVER GOLIATH: A TYPE OF CHRIST'S VICTORY OVER SIN AND DEATH

One of the most well-known stories in the Bible is David's **defeat of Goliath**, the giant Philistine warrior who defied the armies of Israel. This story, found in **1 Samuel 17**, serves as a powerful metaphor for Christ's victory over the **giants** of **sin**, **death**, and **Satan**. Just as David, the unlikely hero, defeated Goliath with **faith** and a **simple stone**, so too did Christ defeat the powers of darkness through His **death** and **resurrection**.

A. David's Faith and Trust in God

When David arrived at the battlefield, he was not a trained soldier but a **young shepherd** bringing provisions to his brothers. Yet, when he heard Goliath mocking the armies of Israel and **defying God**, David was filled with **righteous indignation**. He could not believe that the men of Israel, including King Saul, were afraid to face the Philistine giant. David's faith in God's power to deliver His people was unwavering, and he volunteered to fight Goliath.

In **1 Samuel 17:37**, David expressed his trust in God's ability to deliver him:

> "The Lord who delivered me from the paw of the lion and from the paw of the bear will deliver me from the hand of this Philistine."

David's faith and **dependence on God** are key aspects of his role as a type of Christ. Just as David trusted in God's strength to defeat Goliath, so too did Christ trust in the Father's plan as He faced the **giant of sin** and **death** on behalf of humanity. Christ's **victory** on the cross was not achieved through **worldly power** or **military strength**, but through **obedience**, **humility**, and **faith** in the Father's will.

1. The Defeat of the Giant

David's battle with Goliath was not a **fair fight** in the eyes of the world. Goliath was a **seasoned warrior**, towering over David and armed with **heavy weapons** and **armor**. David, on the other hand, went into battle with only a **sling** and five **smooth stones**. However, it was not David's physical strength or weapons that won the battle, but his **faith** in God.

In **1 Samuel 17:45-47**, David declared:

> "You come to me with a sword and with a spear and with a javelin, but I come to you in the name of the Lord of hosts, the God of the armies of Israel, whom you have defied. This day the Lord will deliver you into my hand... For the battle is the Lord's, and He will give you into our hand."

David's victory over Goliath is a type of **Christ's victory** over the **giant enemies** of sin and death. Just as David defeated Goliath with a single stone, Christ defeated sin and death through His **sacrificial death** on the cross and His **resurrection** from the dead. The battle was not fought with **human strength** or **worldly weapons**, but with the **power of God**.

2. Christ's Victory Over Sin and Death

The **giant of Goliath** represents the **forces of evil** and the **fear** that can overwhelm the people of God. Just as Goliath taunted and threatened the armies of Israel, **Satan** and the forces of darkness seek to **ensnare** and **defeat** humanity through **sin** and **death**. However, just as David stepped forward to **defend Israel** and fight on their behalf, Christ stepped forward to fight on behalf of all humanity, defeating **Satan**, **sin**, and **death** through His victory on the cross.

In **1 Corinthians 15:54-57**, Paul celebrates Christ's victory over death:

> "When the perishable puts on the imperishable, and the mortal puts on immortality, then shall come to pass the saying that is written: 'Death is swallowed up in victory.' 'O death, where is your victory? O death, where is your sting?' The sting of death is sin, and the power of sin is the law. But thanks be to God, who gives us the victory through our Lord Jesus Christ."

David's victory over Goliath points forward to the **greater victory** of Christ, who has conquered death and offers eternal life to all who believe in Him.

III. DAVID AS THE SHEPHERD-KING: A TYPE OF CHRIST, THE GOOD SHEPHERD

David is often referred to as the **shepherd-king** because he began his life as a **shepherd** tending his father's flocks and later became the **king of Israel**, shepherding the nation under God's guidance. This dual role of shepherd and king serves as a powerful **type** of Christ, who is both the **Good Shepherd** and the **King of kings**. David's care for his flock and his **protection** of Israel as king mirror Christ's care for His people and His role as the **eternal Shepherd-King**.

A. David's Early Life as a Shepherd

Before David was anointed king, he was a **shepherd**, caring for his father's sheep in the fields of **Bethlehem**. As a shepherd, David learned the skills of **protection**, **guidance**, and **sacrifice**, which would later serve him well as king. Shepherding required **vigilance** and **courage**, as David had to protect his flock from **predators** like lions and bears. His experience as a shepherd prepared him to become the protector of **Israel**, God's flock.

In **1 Samuel 17:34-36**, David recounts his experience as a shepherd to King Saul:

> "Your servant used to keep sheep for his father. And when there came a lion, or a bear, and took a lamb from the flock, I went after him and struck him and delivered it out of his mouth. And if he arose against me, I caught him by his beard and struck him and killed him. Your servant has struck down both lions and bears, and this uncircumcised Philistine shall be like one of them, for he has defied the armies of the living God."

David's willingness to risk his life for his sheep foreshadows **Christ's sacrificial love** for His people. In the **New Testament**, Jesus describes Himself as the **Good Shepherd** who lays down His life for the sheep. This imagery of the shepherd who is willing to give everything for the protection and care of the flock points directly to **Jesus' mission** on earth.

1. Christ, the Good Shepherd

In **John 10:11-14**, Jesus makes one of the most profound statements about His identity and His relationship with His people:

> "I am the good shepherd. The good shepherd lays down his life for the sheep. He who is a hired hand and not a shepherd, who does not own the sheep, sees the wolf coming and leaves the sheep and flees, and the wolf snatches them and scatters them. He flees because he is a hired hand and cares nothing for the sheep. I am the good shepherd. I know my own and my own know me."

Christ's identification as the **Good Shepherd** reveals His deep **care** and **sacrifice** for His people. Just as David was willing to fight lions and bears to protect his flock, so too was Christ willing to face **Satan**, **sin**, and **death** to protect and redeem His people. Christ's love for His sheep is so great that He was willing to lay down His **life** on the cross to secure their **eternal salvation**.

David's role as a **shepherd-king** points forward to the ultimate **Shepherd-King**, Jesus Christ, who not only leads and protects His people but also offers **eternal life** to those who follow Him.

2. The Shepherd-King as Protector and Guide

As king, David continued to act as a **shepherd**, guiding the nation of Israel with **wisdom**, **compassion**, and **strength**. His reign brought **peace** and **stability** to the land, and he was known for his **care** for the people. In the same way, Christ, as the Shepherd-King, leads His people with **gentleness** and **love**, guiding them through the challenges of life and bringing them into the safety of His kingdom.

Psalm 23, one of the most beloved psalms attributed to David, beautifully captures the imagery of God as the **shepherd** who leads His people:

> "The Lord is my shepherd; I shall not want. He makes me lie down in green pastures. He leads me beside still waters. He restores my soul. He leads me in paths of righteousness for His name's sake." (Psalm 23:1-3)

David's experience as a shepherd shaped his understanding of **God's care** for His people, and this psalm reflects his deep trust in God as the **ultimate Shepherd**. Christ fulfills this role as the **Good**

Shepherd, leading His people beside **still waters** and restoring their souls.

IV. THE DAVIDIC COVENANT: A TYPE OF CHRIST'S ETERNAL KINGSHIP

One of the most significant moments in David's life is the **covenant** that God made with him, known as the **Davidic Covenant**. In **2 Samuel 7**, God promises David that his **kingdom** will endure forever and that one of his **descendants** will sit on the throne for eternity. This covenant points directly to **Jesus Christ**, the **Son of David**, who is the **fulfillment** of God's promise of an eternal kingdom.

A. God's Promise to David (2 Samuel 7:12-16)

In **2 Samuel 7:12-16**, God speaks to David through the prophet **Nathan**, making a series of promises that would have profound significance for Israel and for the world:

> "When your days are fulfilled and you lie down with your fathers, I will raise up your offspring after you, who shall come from your body, and I will establish his kingdom. He shall build a house for my name, and I will establish the throne of his kingdom forever. I will be to him a father, and he shall be to me a son... And your house and your kingdom shall be made sure forever before me. Your throne shall be established forever."

This promise of an **eternal throne** is fulfilled in **Jesus Christ**, who is both the **descendant of David** and the **eternal King**. While David's immediate son, **Solomon**, would build the **Temple** and continue David's dynasty, it is ultimately through **Jesus** that God's promise of an **eternal kingdom** is fulfilled.

1. Christ, the Son of David

Throughout the **New Testament**, Jesus is repeatedly referred to as the **Son of David**, emphasizing His role as the **fulfillment** of the Davidic Covenant. In the **Gospel of Matthew**, Jesus' genealogy is traced through **David**, highlighting His **royal lineage**:

> "The book of the genealogy of Jesus Christ, the son of David, the son of Abraham." (Matthew 1:1)

Jesus' identity as the Son of David is a key aspect of His messianic role. As the **rightful heir** to David's throne, Jesus is the **King of kings** who will reign forever. His kingdom is not limited to **earthly rule** but extends to the entire **universe**, and His reign will never end.

In **Revelation 19:16**, Jesus is described as the **King of kings and Lord of lords**:

> "On His robe and on His thigh He has a name written, King of kings and Lord of lords."

Christ's reign is the **ultimate fulfillment** of God's promise to David. Through Jesus, the **throne of David** is established forever, and His kingdom will never be shaken.

2. The Eternal Kingdom of Christ

The **Davidic Covenant** points to the **eternal nature** of Christ's kingdom. While David's reign brought **peace** and **prosperity** to Israel for a time, it was only a **shadow** of the **eternal peace** and **righteousness** that Christ would bring through His reign. Christ's kingdom is not based on **earthly power** or **military might**, but on the **justice**, **righteousness**, and **love** of God.

In **Isaiah 9:6-7**, the prophet foretells the coming of the **Messiah** and His eternal reign:

> "For to us a child is born, to us a son is given; and the government shall be upon His shoulder, and His name shall be called Wonderful Counselor, Mighty God, Everlasting Father, Prince of Peace. Of the increase of His government and of peace there will be no end, on the throne of David and over His kingdom, to establish it and to uphold it with justice and with righteousness from this time forth and forevermore. The zeal of the Lord of hosts will do this."

Christ's kingdom is marked by **peace, justice**, and **righteousness**, and His reign will bring about the **restoration** of all creation. As believers, we are called to live as **citizens** of this **eternal kingdom**, following the **Shepherd-King** who leads us in paths of righteousness.

V. DAVID'S SIN AND REPENTANCE: A TYPE OF CHRIST'S PERFECT OBEDIENCE

While David's life is often seen as a **type of Christ**, it is important to recognize that David, unlike Christ, was not **sinless**. One of the most well-known stories in David's life is his **sin** with **Bathsheba** and the subsequent consequences of his actions. This episode, found in **2 Samuel 11-12**, serves as a stark reminder of **human frailty** and the need for **repentance**. However, it also highlights the **contrast** between David's **failures** and Christ's **perfect obedience**.

A. David's Sin with Bathsheba (2 Samuel 11)

In **2 Samuel 11**, we read the account of David's **adultery** with **Bathsheba**, the wife of **Uriah the Hittite**. David's **lust** for Bathsheba led him to commit **adultery** and then arrange for Uriah's **death** in battle to cover up the sin. This series of events represents one of the **darkest moments** in David's life, and it had **far-reaching consequences** for his reign and his family.

David's sin with Bathsheba serves as a reminder that even those chosen by God can **fall** into sin. However, it also points to the need for **repentance** and **restoration**.

B. Nathan's Confrontation and David's Repentance (2 Samuel 12)

In **2 Samuel 12**, the prophet **Nathan** confronts David about his sin, using a **parable** to reveal the **gravity** of his actions. When David realizes the depth of his sin, he is filled with **remorse** and **repents** before God.

David's **psalm of repentance**, **Psalm 51**, is a powerful expression of his **sorrow** and desire for **restoration**:

"Have mercy on me, O God, according to your steadfast love; according to your abundant mercy blot out my transgressions. Wash me thoroughly from my iniquity, and cleanse me from my sin." (Psalm 51:1-2)

David's repentance stands in contrast to Christ's **perfect obedience**. While David, like all humans, was prone to sin, **Jesus** remained **sinless** throughout His life. Christ's **perfect righteousness** and **obedience** to the Father are what qualify Him to be the **ultimate Shepherd-King** and the **Savior** of the world.

Fun Fact: David's Legacy in Jewish and Christian Tradition

David holds a central place not only in **Christian tradition** but also in **Jewish tradition**. In Judaism, David is revered as the greatest **king** of Israel, and his **psalms** form a core part of **Jewish worship**. The **Star of David**, a symbol often associated with **Judaism**, is named after him.

In **Christianity**, David's legacy is most prominently seen in his role as a **type of Christ**. The **Messianic title** "Son of David" is used throughout the **Gospels** to emphasize Jesus' fulfillment of the **Davidic Covenant** and His role as the **eternal king**. Additionally, David's **psalms** are widely used in Christian **liturgy** and **worship**, and they continue to inspire believers today in their personal and corporate expressions of faith.

David as a Type of Christ the King

From the Tabernacle to Solomon's Temple to the Second Temple, the progression of God's dwelling among His people points toward a final and eternal fulfillment in Christ. The tearing of the temple veil at Jesus' crucifixion signifies the end of separation between God and humanity, and the beginning of the Church as the living temple, indwelt by the Spirit.

Solomon's Temple was the physical dwelling place of God among His people, where the Ark of the Covenant resided. As magnificent as it was, it served as a shadow of a greater reality. The destruction of this temple symbolized the passing of the old covenant system, pointing forward to the time when God's presence would dwell fully in Christ, the true Temple. The physical structure of the temple was temporary, but it laid the foundation for the spiritual temple found in Christ.

The Second Temple, rebuilt after the exile, held great significance for the Jewish people. It was the site of Jesus' ministry, and although it lacked the glory of Solomon's Temple, it still foreshadowed a greater fulfillment in Christ. The destruction of the Second Temple, as prophesied by Jesus, marks the end of the old sacrificial system and the transition to a new covenant where God's presence is no longer confined to a building but resides in Christ and His Church. Jesus, the ultimate Temple, fulfills what the Second Temple could only symbolize.

    David's life as **shepherd**, **king**, and **warrior** points forward to the **greater King**, **Jesus Christ**, who is the **Shepherd-King** over all creation. Through David's **anointing**, his **victory over Goliath**, his role as **shepherd**, and the **Davidic Covenant**, we see glimpses of Christ's **perfect kingship**, His **victory over sin and death**, and His eternal reign of **peace**.

    While David was a **flawed human being** who experienced moments of failure and repentance, his life still serves as a **shadow** of the **Messiah** who would come. Christ, the **Son of David**, is the **fulfillment** of all that David represented. He is the **Good Shepherd** who lays down His life for the sheep, the **victorious King** who conquers death, and the **Eternal King** who will reign forever in righteousness and peace.

    As believers, we are called to follow the **Shepherd-King**, placing our **faith** and **trust** in His rule, and living as **citizens** of His eternal kingdom. David's life reminds us of the importance of **faith**, **obedience**, and **repentance**, while Christ's life and reign offer us the promise of **eternal peace** and **victory** in His kingdom.

CHAPTER 28: MOSES AS A MEDIATOR: A TYPE OF CHRIST THE MEDIATOR

Moses stands as one of the most significant figures in the Old Testament, known for his leadership, his deep connection with God, and his role as the **mediator** between God and the people of Israel. Moses' unique position as **mediator** is highlighted in moments such as his **intercession** for Israel after the **golden calf incident** in **Exodus 32**, where he pleads with God not to destroy His people for their disobedience. This act of intercession sets Moses apart as a **type** of the ultimate **mediator—Jesus Christ**, who intercedes on behalf of humanity and reconciles us to God.

In this chapter, we will explore the **typology** of Moses as a **mediator**, focusing on how his role in the Old Testament foreshadows the **mediating work of Christ** in the New Testament. We will delve into key moments in Moses' life, such as his **calling at the burning bush**, his leadership during the **Exodus**, and his **intercession** for the Israelites. These moments not only define Moses' role as a leader but also provide insight into how Christ would later act as the **perfect Mediator** between God and humanity.

Additionally, we will examine the **theological significance** of Moses' mediating role and how it points to the **necessity of a mediator** in the relationship between a **holy God** and **sinful humanity**. Christ's work as the **ultimate Mediator** fulfills and surpasses the mediation of Moses, offering a **permanent reconciliation** between God and humanity through His **sacrificial death** and **ongoing intercession**.

By understanding Moses' role as a mediator, we gain a deeper appreciation for the work of Christ, who stands as our **Advocate** before the Father and who, through His atoning work, makes it possible for us to **enter into a relationship with God**.

I. MOSES AS A MEDIATOR IN THE OLD TESTAMENT

Throughout the **Old Testament**, Moses is presented as the **mediator** between God and the people of Israel. His position as mediator is unique, as he is not only the leader of the Israelites but also the one through whom God delivers His **laws**, His **commands**, and His **judgment**. Moses often stands in the gap between a **holy God** and a **rebellious people**, pleading for mercy and offering guidance.

A. Moses' Call as a Mediator (Exodus 3:1-10)

The first indication of Moses' role as a mediator comes in his **calling** at the **burning bush** in **Exodus 3**. After fleeing Egypt and spending forty years as a shepherd in **Midian**, Moses encounters God in a burning bush on **Mount Horeb**. Here, God calls Moses to return to Egypt and lead the Israelites out of **slavery**, establishing him as the one who would **mediate** between God and His people.

In **Exodus 3:7-10**, God reveals His plan for Moses:

> "Then the Lord said, 'I have surely seen the affliction of my people who are in Egypt, and have heard their cry because of their taskmasters. I know their sufferings, and I have come down to deliver them out of the hand of the Egyptians and to bring them up out of that land to a good and broad land, a land flowing with milk and honey... Come, I will send you to Pharaoh that you may bring my people, the children of Israel, out of Egypt.'"

This moment is significant because it sets Moses apart as God's chosen **instrument** to bring about the **deliverance** of Israel. Just as Moses was called to **deliver** the Israelites from physical bondage in Egypt, Christ would later be sent to deliver humanity from the **bondage of sin**. In this way, Moses' role as a mediator between God and Israel foreshadows Christ's work as the **ultimate Mediator** between God and all humanity.

1. Moses' Reluctance and God's Assurance

Despite the enormity of the task before him, Moses initially expresses **reluctance** and doubt about his ability to carry out God's plan. He questions his own qualifications and asks, **"Who am I that I should go to Pharaoh and bring the children of Israel out of Egypt?"** (**Exodus 3:11**). This moment of hesitation reflects Moses' **humility** and his awareness of his own limitations. Yet, God assures Moses that He will be with him, empowering him to fulfill his role as mediator.

In this way, Moses' **reluctance** and God's **empowerment** highlight the reality that **true mediation** between God and humanity requires God's **initiative** and **support**. Just as Moses needed God's presence to mediate on behalf of Israel, Christ's role as mediator is empowered by His divine nature and His **obedience** to the Father's will.

2. The Mediator's Connection to God

An important aspect of Moses' role as mediator is his unique **relationship with God**. Throughout his life, Moses enjoys an **intimacy with God** that few others in the Old Testament experience. In **Exodus 33:11**, we are told that **"the Lord used to speak to Moses face to face, as a man speaks to his friend."** This **direct communication** with God sets Moses apart as a mediator and establishes his authority to **lead** and **intercede** on behalf of the people.

This connection between Moses and God points forward to Christ, who has an even greater **intimacy** with the Father. In **John 1:18**, we are told that Christ, the **only Son**, is **"in the bosom of the Father"**, and He has made the Father known. Christ's **perfect relationship** with the Father qualifies Him to be the **ultimate Mediator**, capable of reconciling humanity to God in a way that Moses could not fully accomplish.

B. Moses' Intercession for Israel (Exodus 32:30-32)

One of the most profound examples of Moses' mediating role occurs in **Exodus 32**, during the **golden calf incident**. After receiving the **Ten Commandments** on **Mount Sinai**, Moses returns to the camp of Israel, only to find that the people have **rebelled** by creating and worshiping a golden calf. This act of **idolatry** enrages God, and He threatens to **destroy** the people and start over with Moses.

In this moment of crisis, Moses steps into his role as mediator, pleading with God to **spare** the Israelites despite their sin. In **Exodus 32:30-32**, Moses approaches God in **intercession**:

> "The next day Moses said to the people, 'You have sinned a great sin. And now I will go up to the Lord; perhaps I can make atonement for your sin.' So Moses returned to the Lord and said, 'Alas, this people has sinned a great sin. They have made for themselves gods of gold. But now, if you will forgive their sin, please do so. But if not, please blot me out of your book that you have written.'"

Moses' willingness to offer his own life in exchange for the forgiveness of Israel's sin highlights his **sacrificial role** as mediator. Although God ultimately **forgives** the people without taking Moses' life, this act of intercession points forward to the **greater sacrifice** that Christ would make on behalf of humanity. While Moses offered his life as a **symbolic gesture**, Christ actually **gave His life** on the cross to atone for the sins of the world.

1. The Nature of Intercession

Moses' intercession on behalf of Israel demonstrates the **essential role** of a mediator in standing between **God's holiness** and **human sinfulness**. The Israelites had violated God's covenant by worshiping the golden calf, and they deserved God's **judgment**. Yet, through Moses' intercession, they were granted **mercy**.

This act of intercession reflects Christ's role as the **ultimate Mediator** who continually intercedes for His people. In **1 Timothy 2:5**, Paul writes:

> "For there is one God, and there is one mediator between God and men, the man Christ Jesus."

Christ's intercession goes beyond Moses' temporary mediation; through His **sacrifice**, Christ has made a **permanent atonement** for sin, and He continually pleads on behalf of believers before the Father. As the **perfect Mediator**, Christ stands in the gap between a **holy God** and **sinful humanity**, ensuring that those who trust in Him are forgiven and reconciled to God.

2. A Willingness to Sacrifice

Moses' willingness to offer his own life for the sake of the people points to the **sacrificial love** that Christ would demonstrate on the cross. While Moses could not actually offer his life as an atonement for Israel's sin, Christ's **death on the cross** fulfilled this role perfectly. In **John 15:13**, Jesus says:

> "Greater love has no one than this, that someone lay down his life for his friends."

Christ's **sacrificial death** on the cross is the ultimate expression of His role as Mediator. Through His death, He **bore the penalty** for sin that humanity deserved and **satisfied** the demands of God's justice. In this way, Christ's mediation surpasses that of Moses, providing a **once-for-all atonement** for sin and securing **eternal life** for those who believe in Him.

II. CHRIST AS THE ULTIMATE MEDIATOR

While Moses served as a mediator for the people of Israel, his mediation was **limited** and **temporary**. In contrast, Christ's mediation is **universal**, applying to all humanity, and it is **eternal**, providing a **permanent reconciliation** between God and humanity. In this section, we will explore the ways in which Christ fulfills and surpasses Moses' role as mediator, focusing on His **sacrificial death**, His **ongoing intercession**, and His role as the **High Priest** who mediates on behalf of believers.

A. The Sacrificial Death of Christ

At the heart of Christ's mediating work is His **sacrificial death** on the cross. While Moses could intercede for the people and plead for God's mercy, he could not **atone** for their sins. Only through the **shedding of blood** could sin be atoned for, as stated in **Hebrews 9:22**:

> "Without the shedding of blood, there is no forgiveness of sins."

Christ's death on the cross fulfills this requirement for atonement. As the **Lamb of God**, Christ offered Himself as the perfect **sacrifice** to take away the sins of the world. In **John 1:29**, **John the Baptist** declares:

> "Behold, the Lamb of God, who takes away the sin of the world!"

Through His death, Christ accomplished what Moses could only point toward—**full and final atonement** for sin. His blood cleanses us from all unrighteousness and restores our relationship with God.

1. The Fulfillment of the Sacrificial System

In the **Old Testament**, Moses established the **sacrificial system** that God gave to Israel as a means of atoning for sin. The **priests** would offer sacrifices on behalf of the people, shedding the blood of **animals** to cover their sins. However, these sacrifices were **temporary** and had to be repeated year after year. They were a **shadow** of the greater sacrifice that was to come.

In **Hebrews 10:1-4**, the author explains the **limitations** of the Old Testament sacrifices:

> "For since the law has but a shadow of the good things to come instead of the true form of these realities, it can never, by the same sacrifices that are continually offered every year, make perfect those who draw near... For it is impossible for the blood of bulls and goats to take away sins."

Christ's death on the cross fulfills the **sacrificial system** once and for all. As the **perfect sacrifice**, Christ's blood does not merely **cover** sin but **takes it away** entirely. In **Hebrews 10:12**, we read:

> "But when Christ had offered for all time a single sacrifice for sins, He sat down at the right hand of God."

This **once-for-all sacrifice** is what makes Christ the ultimate Mediator. His death on the cross has **permanently** reconciled us to God, and there is no longer any need for repeated sacrifices. Through His **atoning work**, Christ has accomplished what Moses and the Old Testament priests could not—**eternal redemption** for all who believe in Him.

2. Christ as the Lamb of God

In the **Passover** celebration, which was instituted by Moses in **Exodus 12**, the Israelites were commanded to sacrifice a **lamb** and apply its blood to the doorposts of their houses. This act of faith protected them from the **judgment** of God and spared them from the **death** that came upon the firstborn of Egypt.

This Passover lamb was a **type** of the **Lamb of God**, Jesus Christ, whose blood would provide **ultimate protection** from the judgment of God. Just as the blood of the Passover lamb spared the Israelites from physical death, the blood of Christ spares believers from **spiritual death** and **eternal separation** from God.

In **1 Corinthians 5:7**, Paul declares:

"For Christ, our Passover lamb, has been sacrificed."

Through His **sacrificial death**, Christ has become the perfect Passover Lamb, offering eternal **life** and **salvation** to all who trust in Him. His blood protects us from the judgment of God and brings us into a new covenant relationship with Him.

B. Christ's Ongoing Intercession

While Christ's **death** on the cross accomplished the atonement for sin, His work as Mediator did not end there. Christ continues to serve as our **Advocate** and **Intercessor**, continually **pleading** on our behalf before the Father. In this way, Christ's mediation is **ongoing**, providing believers with the assurance that their **sins are forgiven** and that they are in a **right relationship** with God.

In **Romans 8:34**, Paul writes:

"Who is to condemn? Christ Jesus is the one who died—more than that, who was raised—who is at the right hand of God, who indeed is interceding for us."

Christ's ongoing intercession means that He continually **pleads** for His people, ensuring that their sins are forgiven and that they remain in the grace of God. Just as Moses interceded for the Israelites during the golden calf incident, Christ intercedes for believers, ensuring that they are not condemned but are accepted in the **presence of God**.

1. The Role of the High Priest

In the Old Testament, the **high priest** played a crucial role in mediating between God and the people. On the **Day of Atonement**, the high priest would enter the **Holy of Holies** and offer a sacrifice on behalf of the entire nation, seeking God's **forgiveness** for the sins of Israel. This act of mediation was necessary for maintaining the people's relationship with God.

Christ, however, is not only the **sacrifice** for sin but also the **High Priest** who offers that sacrifice. In **Hebrews 4:14-16**, we read about Christ's role as our **great High Priest**:

> "Since then we have a great high priest who has passed through the heavens, Jesus, the Son of God, let us hold fast our confession. For we do not have a high priest who is unable to sympathize with our weaknesses, but one who in every respect has been tempted as we are, yet without sin. Let us then with confidence draw near to the throne of grace, that we may receive mercy and find grace to help in time of need."

As our **High Priest**, Christ understands our weaknesses and continually **intercedes** for us before the Father. His intercession provides us with the confidence to approach God's throne, knowing that we will receive **mercy** and **grace** in our time of need.

2. Christ's Heavenly Ministry

After His **resurrection** and **ascension**, Christ entered into His **heavenly ministry** as our **eternal High Priest**. In **Hebrews 9:24**, we are told that Christ has entered **heaven itself**, now to appear in the **presence of God** on our behalf:

> "For Christ has entered, not into holy places made with hands, which are copies of the true things, but into heaven itself, now to appear in the presence of God on our behalf."

This passage highlights the **ongoing nature** of Christ's mediation. He is continually in the presence of the Father, **interceding** for us and ensuring that we remain in a right relationship with God. Through His **heavenly ministry**, Christ serves as the **bridge** between God and humanity, guaranteeing that those who trust in Him are **reconciled** to God.

III. THE NECESSITY OF A MEDIATOR

The role of a **mediator** is essential in the relationship between a **holy God** and **sinful humanity**. Without a mediator, there is no way for sinful people to approach God, as His **holiness** cannot tolerate sin. Moses' role as mediator in the Old Testament demonstrates the necessity of someone standing between God and His people, pleading for mercy and offering atonement.

In this section, we will explore why a **mediator** is necessary and how Christ fulfills this role perfectly. We will also examine the **difference** between Moses' mediation, which was **temporary** and **imperfect**, and Christ's mediation, which is **eternal** and **perfect**.

A. The Problem of Sin

The fundamental issue that necessitates a mediator is the problem of **sin**. Sin separates humanity from God and creates a **barrier** between us and Him. In **Isaiah 59:2**, we read:

> "But your iniquities have made a separation between you and your God, and your sins have hidden His face from you so that He does not hear."

This separation means that without a mediator, we cannot approach God or have a relationship with Him. Sin **alienates** us from God and brings His **judgment** upon us. The role of a mediator is to **reconcile** the two parties—God and humanity—and to remove the barrier of sin.

1. Moses as a Temporary Mediator

Moses' role as a mediator in the Old Testament was **limited** by his humanity and by the fact that the **sacrifices** he offered were **temporary**. While Moses could plead for the people and offer sacrifices for their sins, these sacrifices had to be repeated **year after year**, as they were insufficient to fully atone for sin.

In **Hebrews 10:1**, we read about the **temporary nature** of the Old Testament sacrifices:

"For since the law has but a shadow of the good things to come instead of the true form of these realities, it can never, by the same sacrifices that are continually offered every year, make perfect those who draw near."

Moses' mediation was a **foreshadowing** of the **greater mediation** that would come through Christ. While Moses could offer **temporary relief** from God's judgment, Christ provides **permanent reconciliation** through His once-for-all sacrifice.

2. The Need for a Perfect Mediator

Because of the **seriousness of sin** and the **holiness of God**, only a perfect mediator could truly reconcile humanity to God. This is where Christ's role as Mediator is **superior** to that of Moses. Christ, as both **fully God** and **fully man**, is uniquely qualified to bridge the gap between God and humanity. His **sinless life**, His **sacrificial death**, and His **resurrection** make Him the **perfect** and **eternal Mediator**.

In **1 Timothy 2:5-6**, Paul writes:

"For there is one God, and there is one mediator between God and men, the man Christ Jesus, who gave Himself as a ransom for all, which is the testimony given at the proper time."

Christ's **mediating work** is not limited to a specific time or place, as Moses' was. Instead, His mediation is **universal**, applying to all people, and it is **eternal**, offering a permanent solution to the problem of sin.

Fun Fact: Moses' Role in Other Religious Traditions

While Moses is most well-known as a central figure in **Judaism** and **Christianity**, he is also revered in **Islam** as a prophet and mediator. In Islam, Moses (known as **Musa**) is seen as one of the most important prophets, and his role as a mediator between God and the **Children of Israel** is emphasized in the **Qur'an**. However, while Islam recognizes Moses as a great prophet, it does not view him as a type of Christ in the same way that Christianity does.

Moses' role as a **mediator** has had a profound impact on religious traditions across the world, but it is in **Christianity** that his typological significance is fully realized. By understanding Moses as a type of Christ, Christians gain a deeper appreciation for the **mediating work of Jesus**, who fulfills and surpasses all that Moses represented.

Christ, the Perfect Mediator

From the Tabernacle to Solomon's Temple to the Second Temple, the progression of God's dwelling among His people points toward a final and eternal fulfillment in Christ. The tearing of the temple veil at Jesus' crucifixion signifies the end of separation between God and humanity, and the beginning of the Church as the living temple, indwelt by the Spirit.

Solomon's Temple was the physical dwelling place of God among His people, where the Ark of the Covenant resided. As magnificent as it was, it served as a shadow of a greater reality. The destruction of this temple symbolized the passing of the old covenant system, pointing forward to the time when God's presence would dwell fully in Christ, the true Temple. The physical structure of the temple was temporary, but it laid the foundation for the spiritual temple found in Christ.

The Second Temple, rebuilt after the exile, held great significance for the Jewish people. It was the site of Jesus' ministry, and although it lacked the glory of Solomon's Temple, it still foreshadowed a greater fulfillment in Christ. The destruction of the Second Temple, as prophesied by Jesus, marks the end of the old sacrificial system and the transition to a new covenant where God's presence is no longer confined to a building but resides in Christ and His Church. Jesus, the ultimate Temple, fulfills what the Second Temple could only symbolize.

Moses' role as a **mediator** in the Old Testament serves as a powerful **foreshadowing** of the **greater mediation** that would come through Jesus Christ. While Moses interceded for the people of Israel and sought to reconcile them to God, his mediation was **temporary** and **limited**. In contrast, Christ's mediation is **eternal**, offering a **once-for-all sacrifice** for sin and securing **permanent reconciliation** between God and humanity.

As the **ultimate Mediator**, Christ fulfills all that Moses pointed toward. His **sacrificial death** on the cross provides atonement for sin, and His **ongoing intercession** before the Father ensures that believers remain in a right relationship with God. Through Christ, the barrier of sin is removed, and we are able to approach God with confidence, knowing that we are forgiven and accepted.

In **Hebrews 7:25**, we are reminded of the power of Christ's mediating work:

> "Consequently, He is able to save to the uttermost those who draw near to God through Him, since He always lives to make intercession for them."

As believers, we are called to place our **faith** in Christ, the perfect Mediator, and to trust in His **atoning work** and **ongoing intercession**. Just as Moses stood in the gap for Israel, so too does Christ stand in the gap for us, ensuring that we are **reconciled to God** and that we enjoy the **blessings** of eternal life in His presence.

CHAPTER 29: ELIJAH AS A TYPE OF JOHN THE BAPTIST

The figure of **Elijah** in the Old Testament is one of profound power, drama, and divine authority. As a prophet, Elijah's mission was to call the people of **Israel** back to **repentance** and **faithfulness** to **God** during a time of rampant **idolatry** and **spiritual apostasy** under the reign of **King Ahab** and **Queen Jezebel**. His ministry, marked by dramatic encounters, miracles, and confrontations with false prophets, made him one of the most prominent and revered figures in Jewish history.

Yet Elijah's role extends beyond his immediate context as a prophet. In the biblical narrative, Elijah is also portrayed as a **type** of **John the Baptist**, the **forerunner** of **Jesus Christ**. Both Elijah and John the Baptist served as **preparatory figures**, heralding a call to repentance and preparing the way for **greater revelations** of God's will and purpose. Elijah's **fiery ministry** in the Old Testament is echoed in the **ministry of John the Baptist**, who came with the same spirit and power of Elijah to prepare the people for the coming of the **Messiah**.

This chapter will explore the **typological connections** between Elijah and John the Baptist, focusing on how Elijah's prophetic ministry foreshadowed the ministry of John the Baptist, who in turn **prepared the way** for Christ. By examining the key aspects of Elijah's life, such as his confrontations with King Ahab, his encounter on **Mount Carmel**, and his departure from earth, we can gain a deeper understanding of how these events prefigure the role of John the Baptist in the **New Testament**. We will also delve into the **New Testament passages** that explicitly connect Elijah and John the Baptist, such as **Malachi's prophecy** and Jesus' own statements about John.

Furthermore, this chapter will examine how the **mission** of both Elijah and John the Baptist carries forward into the present-day call for **repentance**, renewal, and preparation for the ultimate **return**

of Christ. The typology of Elijah and John the Baptist highlights the importance of **preparation** and the call to **return to God**, which remains relevant for believers today.

I. THE MINISTRY OF ELIJAH: A CALL TO REPENTANCE

Elijah's ministry, as described in **1 Kings 17 to 2 Kings 2**, is characterized by his bold confrontations with the **idolatry** and **wickedness** of Israel's leadership, particularly under **King Ahab** and **Queen Jezebel**. Ahab's reign was marked by the worship of **Baal**, a pagan deity, and the persecution of the prophets of the Lord. In this context, Elijah emerged as a **voice of righteousness**, calling the people of Israel to return to the **covenant** they had abandoned and to forsake their idolatrous practices.

A. Elijah's Confrontation with Ahab (1 Kings 17-18)

Elijah's first appearance in the biblical narrative is abrupt and dramatic. In **1 Kings 17:1**, Elijah is introduced as the prophet from **Tishbe** who boldly declares to King Ahab:

> "As the Lord, the God of Israel, lives, before whom I stand, there shall be neither dew nor rain these years, except by my word."

This declaration marks the beginning of a **severe drought** in Israel, which was a direct judgment from God due to the nation's **idolatry** and **apostasy**. Elijah's pronouncement of drought was not just a natural calamity; it was a divine warning designed to lead the people to **repentance**.

The **drought** is significant because it reflects the **spiritual drought** that had fallen over Israel during Ahab's reign. The people had turned away from the **true God** and were worshiping **Baal**, a fertility god associated with rain and agricultural abundance. Elijah's declaration of drought was a direct challenge to **Baal's supposed power** and a call for the people to recognize that **Yahweh** alone was the true source of life and sustenance.

1. The Role of Elijah as a Forerunner

Elijah's role as a forerunner is evident in his mission to **prepare** the people of Israel for a return to **faithfulness** and **covenant relationship** with God. His confrontations with Ahab and the prophets of Baal served as a dramatic call for the people to **repent** and turn back to God. In this sense, Elijah's ministry foreshadows the ministry of **John the Baptist**, who also came to prepare the way for a greater revelation of God's work.

John the Baptist's message was similar to Elijah's: a call for the people to **repent**, for the kingdom of God was at hand. In **Matthew 3:1-3**, John's mission is described in the same terms as that of Elijah:

> "In those days John the Baptist came preaching in the wilderness of Judea, 'Repent, for the kingdom of heaven is at hand.' For this is he who was spoken of by the prophet Isaiah when he said, 'The voice of one crying in the wilderness: Prepare the way of the Lord; make his paths straight.'"

Both Elijah and John the Baptist came during times of **spiritual darkness**, calling the people to return to **righteousness** and **obedience** to God's commands. Elijah's role as a forerunner to **national repentance** parallels John the Baptist's role as the forerunner to **Christ**, who would bring the ultimate **salvation** to the world.

2. The Spirit and Power of Elijah in John the Baptist

The connection between Elijah and John the Baptist is explicitly mentioned in the **New Testament**, where John is described as coming in the **spirit and power of Elijah**. In **Luke 1:16-17**, the angel Gabriel speaks to **Zechariah**, John the Baptist's father, about the role John would play in preparing the way for the Messiah:

> "And he will turn many of the children of Israel to the Lord their God, and he will go before Him in the spirit and power of Elijah, to turn the hearts of the fathers to the children, and the disobedient to the wisdom of the just, to make ready for the Lord a people prepared."

This passage draws a direct connection between **Elijah** and **John the Baptist**, highlighting how John's ministry would mirror Elijah's mission of calling the people to **repentance** and preparing them for a **divine visitation**. Both Elijah and John the Baptist were sent to confront **sin** and call the people back to God, laying the groundwork for a **greater revelation**—Elijah's for the renewal of Israel's covenant relationship with God and John's for the coming of the **Messiah**.

B. The Showdown on Mount Carmel (1 Kings 18:16-40)

One of the most dramatic and well-known events in Elijah's ministry is his confrontation with the **prophets of Baal** on **Mount Carmel**. In **1 Kings 18**, Elijah challenges the 450 prophets of Baal to a contest to prove who the **true God** is. The prophets of Baal were to prepare a sacrifice and call on their god to **send fire** from heaven to consume it, while Elijah would call on the **Lord** to do the same. Whichever deity answered with fire would be declared the true God.

The prophets of Baal called on their god from morning until noon, but **no fire** came. They **danced** and **cut themselves**, but still, there was no response. Elijah then took his turn, rebuilding the **altar of the Lord** with twelve stones, symbolizing the **twelve tribes of Israel**. He prepared the sacrifice, drenched it with water, and called on the Lord:

> "O Lord, God of Abraham, Isaac, and Israel, let it be known this day that you are God in Israel, and that I am your servant, and that I have done all these things at your word. Answer me, O Lord, answer me, that this people may know that you, O Lord, are God, and that you have turned their hearts back." (1 Kings 18:36-37)

Immediately, the **fire of the Lord** fell and consumed the sacrifice, the wood, the stones, and even the water in the trench. The people fell on their faces and declared, **"The Lord, He is God!"** The prophets of Baal were then seized and executed according to the law of Moses.

1. The Call to National Repentance

The showdown on Mount Carmel was more than just a dramatic display of **God's power**; it was a call to **national repentance**. Elijah's challenge to the people of Israel was clear: they could no longer **waver** between two opinions. They had to choose between **serving Baal** or **serving the Lord**. In **1 Kings 18:21**, Elijah confronts the people with this challenge:

> "How long will you go limping between two different opinions? If the Lord is God, follow Him; but if Baal, then follow him."

This call to **decisive action** and **repentance** mirrors John the Baptist's call for the people of Israel to **repent** and **prepare** for the coming of the **kingdom of God**. Just as Elijah confronted the people of Israel with their **idolatry** and called them to return to the **Lord**, John the Baptist called the people to turn from their **sins** and be **baptized** as a sign of their repentance and readiness for the coming **Messiah**.

In **Matthew 3:7-8**, John the Baptist's message to the religious leaders of his day echoes the urgency and decisiveness of Elijah's call:

> "But when he saw many of the Pharisees and Sadducees coming to his baptism, he said to them, 'You brood of vipers! Who warned you to flee from the wrath to come? Bear fruit in keeping with repentance.'"

Both Elijah and John the Baptist confronted the **spiritual complacency** of their respective generations and called for genuine **repentance** and a return to **faithfulness**.

2. The Role of Fire in Elijah's Ministry

Fire plays a significant role in the ministry of **Elijah**, symbolizing God's **judgment**, **purification**, and **divine presence**. The **fire from heaven** that consumes Elijah's sacrifice on Mount Carmel is a powerful display of God's **supremacy** over false gods and idols. This imagery of fire would later be associated with **John the Baptist**, who foretold the coming of **one** who would baptize with the **Holy Spirit** and **fire**.

In **Matthew 3:11**, John the Baptist speaks of the Messiah's coming in terms of fire:

> "I baptize you with water for repentance, but He who is coming after me is mightier than I, whose sandals I am not worthy to carry. He will baptize you with the Holy Spirit and fire."

Just as Elijah's fire from heaven demonstrated God's power and called the people to **repentance**, the fire of the **Holy Spirit** would later be poured out on the day of **Pentecost**, signifying the

purification and **empowerment** of the believers to carry out the mission of God. Elijah's fire was a **physical manifestation** of God's presence, while the **Holy Spirit's fire** in the New Testament represents the **spiritual renewal** and transformation that comes through Christ.

II. JOHN THE BAPTIST AS THE FULFILLMENT OF ELIJAH'S ROLE

The **New Testament** explicitly identifies **John the Baptist** as the **fulfillment** of the prophetic role of Elijah. Both **Malachi** and **Jesus** confirm that John the Baptist came in the **spirit and power of Elijah**, preparing the way for the **coming of Christ**. John's ministry was one of **preparation**, calling the people of Israel to **repentance** and **baptism** in anticipation of the arrival of the **Messiah**.

A. Malachi's Prophecy and the Return of Elijah (Malachi 4:5-6)

The connection between **Elijah** and **John the Baptist** is grounded in the prophecy found in **Malachi 4:5-6**, the final verses of the **Old Testament**:

> "Behold, I will send you Elijah the prophet before the great and awesome day of the Lord comes. And he will turn the hearts of fathers to their children and the hearts of children to their fathers, lest I come and strike the land with a decree of utter destruction."

This prophecy speaks of the return of **Elijah** before the **day of the Lord**, a time of **judgment** and **salvation**. The **Jewish people** believed that Elijah would literally return to prepare the way for the **Messiah**, which is why many asked if **John the Baptist** was the reincarnated Elijah. However, the **New Testament** clarifies that John came not as the literal Elijah but in the **spirit and power of Elijah**, fulfilling the **essence** of Elijah's mission.

In **Matthew 17:10-13**, after the **Transfiguration**, the disciples ask Jesus about the prophecy of Elijah's return. Jesus responds:

"And the disciples asked Him, 'Then why do the scribes say that first Elijah must come?' He answered, 'Elijah does come, and he will restore all things. But I tell you that Elijah has already come, and they did not recognize him, but did to him whatever they pleased. So also the Son of Man will certainly suffer at their hands.' Then the disciples understood that He was speaking to them of John the Baptist."

Jesus confirms that **John the Baptist** fulfilled the role of **Elijah**, preparing the way for the **Messiah** and calling the people to **repentance**. Just as Elijah called Israel to turn back to God, John the Baptist called the people to prepare their hearts for the coming of the Lord.

1. John the Baptist's Message of Repentance

Like Elijah, John the Baptist's central message was one of **repentance**. He called the people of Israel to turn from their sins and prepare for the coming of the **kingdom of God**. In **Matthew 3:1-2**, we read:

"In those days John the Baptist came preaching in the wilderness of Judea, 'Repent, for the kingdom of heaven is at hand.'"

John's baptism of **repentance** served as a symbolic cleansing, preparing the people for the arrival of the **Messiah**. His message was urgent and confrontational, echoing the **boldness** of Elijah's ministry. Just as Elijah confronted the false prophets and the corrupt leadership of his day, John the Baptist boldly confronted the **religious leaders** of Israel, calling them to **genuine repentance**.

In **Matthew 3:7-10**, John speaks to the **Pharisees** and **Sadducees** who came to observe his baptisms:

"But when he saw many of the Pharisees and Sadducees coming to his baptism, he said to them, 'You brood of vipers! Who warned you to flee from the wrath to come? Bear fruit in keeping with repentance. And do not presume to say to yourselves, 'We have Abraham as our father,' for I tell you, God is able from these stones to raise up children for Abraham. Even now the axe is laid to the root of the trees. Every tree therefore that does not bear good fruit is cut down and thrown into the fire.'"

John's message of repentance was **uncompromising**, just as Elijah's message to Israel had been. Both prophets called the people to turn away from **sin**, warning them of the **judgment** to come if they did not heed the call.

2. Baptism as a Symbol of Preparation

One of the key aspects of John the Baptist's ministry was his practice of **baptism**. While **baptism** was not unknown in the Jewish tradition—being used in certain **purification rituals**—John's baptism had a unique significance. It was a **baptism of repentance**, symbolizing the need for **spiritual cleansing** and preparation for the coming of the **Messiah**.

In **Mark 1:4**, we read:

> "John appeared, baptizing in the wilderness and proclaiming a baptism of repentance for the forgiveness of sins."

John's baptism was not the **final fulfillment** of salvation, but it was a **preparatory act**. Just as Elijah prepared the way for the **renewal** of Israel's relationship with God, John's baptism prepared the people for the **new covenant** that would be inaugurated through Christ's death and resurrection. John's role as a **preparatory figure** mirrors Elijah's mission, as both prophets served as **forerunners** who called the people to **prepare** for a greater divine intervention.

III. ELIJAH'S ASCENSION AND THE LEGACY OF JOHN THE BAPTIST

Elijah's ministry did not end with his death; rather, Elijah was taken up to heaven in a **whirlwind**, symbolizing his **eternal significance** and the continuation of his **prophetic mission**. This moment is filled with typological significance, especially when considered alongside the **legacy** of John the Baptist, whose ministry, though ending in his **martyrdom**, left a lasting impact in **preparing the way** for Christ.

A. Elijah's Ascension (2 Kings 2:1-12)

One of the most remarkable events in Elijah's life is his **departure** from earth. In **2 Kings 2**, Elijah is taken up to heaven in a **whirlwind** as his disciple **Elisha** looks on. Before his departure, Elijah asks Elisha if there is anything he can do for him. Elisha requests a **double portion** of Elijah's spirit, and Elijah promises that if Elisha sees him being taken up, his request will be granted.

In **2 Kings 2:11-12**, we read the dramatic account of Elijah's ascension:

> "And as they still went on and talked, behold, chariots of fire and horses of fire separated the two of them. And Elijah went up by a whirlwind into heaven. And Elisha saw it and he cried, 'My father, my father! The chariots of Israel and its horsemen!' And he saw him no more."

Elijah's ascension into heaven is significant for several reasons. First, it underscores Elijah's unique role as a **prophet** who did not taste death but was taken directly into God's presence. This mirrors the **eternal significance** of Elijah's ministry, which would be fulfilled in the person of **John the Baptist** and ultimately in **Christ**.

1. The Prophetic Legacy of Elijah

Elijah's ascension did not mark the end of his influence. His spirit was passed on to **Elisha**, who continued his prophetic work. This transfer of **prophetic authority** mirrors the way John the Baptist's mission was ultimately fulfilled in the person of **Jesus Christ**. Just as Elisha carried on the work of Elijah, Jesus fulfilled and surpassed the preparatory work of **John the Baptist**.

In **John 3:30**, John the Baptist himself acknowledges this transition:

> "He must increase, but I must decrease."

John's role as the **forerunner** was to prepare the way for Christ, and once Christ's ministry began, John's mission was complete. Just as Elijah's departure made way for Elisha's ministry, John's ministry made way for the **greater work** of Christ, who would bring about the **fullness of salvation**.

2. Elijah's Return in Eschatological Prophecy

Elijah's role as a **forerunner** is not only fulfilled in **John the Baptist**, but also carries eschatological significance. In **Jewish tradition**, it was believed that Elijah would return before the **Messiah** to **restore all things** and herald the coming of the **day of the Lord**. This belief is based on **Malachi's prophecy** and has continued to be an important part of **Jewish eschatology**.

Interestingly, in the **Book of Revelation**, two **witnesses** appear during the end times to prophesy and perform miracles, including the ability to **call down fire** from heaven (**Revelation 11:3-6**). Many scholars believe that one of these witnesses may represent **Elijah**, further emphasizing his role as a forerunner in both **John the Baptist** and **future eschatological** events.

B. The Martyrdom of John the Baptist (Matthew 14:1-12)

While Elijah was taken up to heaven in a **whirlwind**, **John the Baptist**'s earthly ministry ended in **martyrdom**. John's bold confrontation of **sin**—specifically, his public denunciation of **Herod Antipas** for his adulterous marriage to **Herodias**—led to his imprisonment and eventual execution. In **Matthew 14:3-12**, we read the account of John's death:

> "For Herod had seized John and bound him and put him in prison for the sake of Herodias, his brother Philip's wife, because John had been saying to him, 'It is not lawful for you to have her.' And though he wanted to put him to death, he feared the people, because they held him to be a prophet... So he sent and had John beheaded in the prison."

John's death marked the end of his **earthly ministry**, but his role as the forerunner of Christ was **complete**. Just as Elijah's departure made way for **Elisha**, John's death made way for the **greater work** of Christ, whose ministry would bring the **fullness of salvation** to the world.

1. John the Baptist's Legacy in the New Testament

Despite his death, John the Baptist's influence continued to shape the early Christian movement. His disciples, many of whom later became **followers of Jesus**, helped spread the message of repentance and **salvation**. John's emphasis on **preparation**, **repentance**, and **baptism** laid the groundwork for the **gospel message** that Jesus and His apostles would proclaim.

In **Acts 19:1-7**, we find an example of John's disciples who had not yet heard of **Jesus**, but who were later baptized in the name of the **Lord**. This passage underscores John's lasting influence and the way his ministry prepared people to receive the **Messiah**.

2. John the Baptist as a Model of Boldness and Humility

John the Baptist is often seen as a model of **boldness** and **humility**. Like Elijah, he was willing to **speak truth** to power, even at great personal cost. His confrontation with **Herod** ultimately led to his martyrdom, but he remained steadfast in his commitment to God's truth. At the same time, John demonstrated profound humility, recognizing that his role was to **prepare the way** for someone greater.

In **John 1:27**, John the Baptist says of Jesus:

> "Even He who comes after me, the strap of whose sandal I am not worthy to untie."

This combination of **boldness** and **humility** is a powerful example for believers today, reminding us of the importance of standing firm in the **truth** while also acknowledging our **dependence** on Christ.

FUN FACT: ELIJAH'S APPEARANCE IN THE TRANSFIGURATION

One of the most fascinating connections between **Elijah** and **John the Baptist** is found in the account of the **Transfiguration**. In **Matthew 17:1-3**, **Elijah** appears alongside **Moses** on the mountain when Jesus is **transfigured** before Peter, James, and John. This appearance signifies the fulfillment of the **Law** (represented by

Moses) and the **Prophets** (represented by Elijah) in the person of **Jesus**.

Elijah's presence at the Transfiguration highlights his enduring significance as a **prophetic figure** who, like **John the Baptist**, pointed to the coming of the **Messiah**. It also reinforces the connection between Elijah and John the Baptist, as both served as **forerunners** preparing the way for the **revelation of God's glory** in Christ.

Elijah and John the Baptist as Forerunners of Christ

From the Tabernacle to Solomon's Temple to the Second Temple, the progression of God's dwelling among His people points toward a final and eternal fulfillment in Christ. The tearing of the temple veil at Jesus' crucifixion signifies the end of separation between God and humanity, and the beginning of the Church as the living temple, indwelt by the Spirit.

Solomon's Temple was the physical dwelling place of God among His people, where the Ark of the Covenant resided. As magnificent as it was, it served as a shadow of a greater reality. The destruction of this temple symbolized the passing of the old covenant system, pointing forward to the time when God's presence would dwell fully in Christ, the true Temple. The physical structure of the temple was temporary, but it laid the foundation for the spiritual temple found in Christ.

The Second Temple, rebuilt after the exile, held great significance for the Jewish people. It was the site of Jesus' ministry, and although it lacked the glory of Solomon's Temple, it still foreshadowed a greater fulfillment in Christ. The destruction of the Second Temple, as prophesied by Jesus, marks the end of the old sacrificial system and the transition to a new covenant where God's presence is no longer confined to a building but resides in Christ and His Church. Jesus, the ultimate Temple, fulfills what the Second Temple could only symbolize.

The connection between **Elijah** and **John the Baptist** offers profound insights into the **continuity** of God's plan for **salvation**.

Both Elijah and John the Baptist served as **forerunners**, preparing the people for a greater revelation of **God's work**. Elijah called the nation of **Israel** to **repentance** and faithfulness to the **covenant**, while John the Baptist called the people to prepare their hearts for the coming of the **Messiah**.

In both cases, their ministries were marked by **boldness**, **confrontation**, and a call to **repentance**. Elijah's fiery ministry on **Mount Carmel** and John's baptism of **repentance** in the **Jordan River** both served as **preparatory acts**, pointing toward a **greater revelation** to come.

The typology of Elijah and John the Baptist reminds us that **preparation** is essential in our relationship with God. Just as the people of Israel were called to **repent** and turn back to God in the time of Elijah and John, so too are we called to prepare our hearts for the **return of Christ**, the **ultimate fulfillment** of all prophetic expectation.

Through the lives of Elijah and John the Baptist, we see the importance of **repentance**, **boldness**, and **humility** in our walk with God. Their ministries laid the groundwork for the **revelation of Christ**, and their legacy continues to inspire believers today as we seek to follow in their footsteps, preparing the way for the **Lord's return**.

CHAPTER 30: THE HIGH PRIEST'S GARMENTS: A TYPE OF CHRIST'S ROLE AS HIGH PRIEST

In the Old Testament, **the high priest** served a unique and essential role in the life of Israel's religious practices. The high priest acted as the **mediator** between God and the people, offering sacrifices on their behalf, interceding for them, and overseeing the rituals of the **tabernacle** and **temple**. One of the most profound aspects of the high priest's role was the significance of his **garments**, which were not merely ornamental but imbued with deep **symbolic meaning**. These garments represented the **holiness** and **intercession** required of the high priest in his duties, and they foreshadowed the ultimate fulfillment of the priestly role in **Jesus Christ**.

In **Exodus 28**, God gave detailed instructions for the creation of the **high priest's garments**, including the **ephod**, the **breastplate**, the **robe**, and other elements. Each piece of the high priest's attire carried spiritual significance, symbolizing the **holiness, intercession**, and **mediation** required in the relationship between God and His people. These garments served as a **type** of the ultimate High Priest, **Jesus Christ**, who would not only intercede for His people but also offer Himself as the **perfect sacrifice** for sin.

In this chapter, we will explore the **typological connection** between the high priest's garments and the high priestly role of Christ, examining how each aspect of the high priest's attire points forward to the **person and work of Christ**. By understanding the spiritual significance of these garments, we can gain a deeper appreciation of Christ's role as our **High Priest**, who intercedes for us and has made a once-for-all sacrifice to reconcile us to God.

I. THE HIGH PRIEST'S GARMENTS: AN OVERVIEW (EXODUS 28)

The instructions for the **high priest's garments** are found in **Exodus 28**, where God commands Moses to appoint **Aaron** and his sons as priests and provides detailed instructions for their sacred garments. The high priest's attire was designed to reflect the **holiness** of his office and to serve as a reminder of his unique role as the one who represented the people before God.

In **Exodus 28:2-4**, God gives a summary of the purpose of the high priest's garments:

> "And you shall make holy garments for Aaron your brother, for glory and for beauty. You shall speak to all the skillful, whom I have filled with a spirit of skill, that they make Aaron's garments to consecrate him for my priesthood. These are the garments that they shall make: a breastpiece, an ephod, a robe, a coat of checker work, a turban, and a sash. They shall make holy garments for Aaron your brother and his sons to serve me as priests."

The high priest's garments were not only practical but also **symbolic**, representing the high priest's role in **mediating** between God and Israel. These garments were made for **glory and beauty**, but they also served a deeper purpose in reflecting the **holiness** and **consecration** of the priestly office.

The high priest's garments included several key elements, each with its own spiritual significance:

- **The Ephod**
- **The Breastpiece**
- **The Robe of the Ephod**
- **The Turban and the Plate of Gold**
- **The Bells and Pomegranates**
- **The Linen Tunic, Sash, and Other Garments**

Each of these garments foreshadowed aspects of **Christ's high priestly role**, revealing how He would fulfill the **mediatorial** and

intercessory functions of the high priest through His work of redemption.

A. The Ephod: Bearing the Names of God's People

The **ephod** was one of the central garments of the high priest and was worn over the linen tunic and robe. It was made of **gold**, **blue**, **purple**, and **scarlet yarn**, intricately woven with fine linen. The ephod was fastened at the shoulders with two **onyx stones**, each engraved with the names of six of the **tribes of Israel**. The purpose of the ephod was to serve as a **memorial** of the people of Israel whenever the high priest entered the presence of God.

In **Exodus 28:12**, God explains the significance of the onyx stones:

> "And you shall set the two stones on the shoulder pieces of the ephod, as stones of remembrance for the sons of Israel. And Aaron shall bear their names before the Lord on his two shoulders for remembrance."

The ephod and the onyx stones symbolized the high priest's responsibility to **bear the people of Israel** on his shoulders whenever he came before God. This act of **bearing the names** of the people on his shoulders reflected the high priest's role as the one who **carried the burdens** of the people before God and interceded on their behalf.

1. The Typology of Christ Bearing Our Burdens

The imagery of the high priest bearing the names of the people on his shoulders foreshadows Christ's role as the one who **bears the burdens** of His people. Just as the high priest carried the names of the **twelve tribes of Israel** into the presence of God, so too does Christ carry the **sins** and **burdens** of His people, interceding for them before the Father.

In **Isaiah 53:4**, the prophet foretells Christ's work as the **suffering servant**, bearing the iniquities of His people:

> "Surely He has borne our griefs and carried our sorrows; yet we esteemed Him stricken, smitten by God, and afflicted."

Christ, our High Priest, took upon Himself the **burdens** of our sins, carrying them to the cross and offering Himself as the **atoning sacrifice**. His role as the **bearer of our burdens** surpasses that of the Old Testament high priest, as Christ not only intercedes for us but also removes the **guilt** and **weight** of sin through His sacrificial death.

2. The Shoulder Stones as a Sign of Christ's Advocacy

The onyx stones on the ephod also point to Christ's role as our **Advocate** before the Father. Just as the high priest bore the names of the tribes on his shoulders as a **memorial** before God, so too does Christ bear the **names** of His people in His ongoing ministry of **intercession**.

In **Hebrews 7:25**, we are told of Christ's continuing work as our High Priest:

> "Consequently, He is able to save to the uttermost those who draw near to God through Him, since He always lives to make intercession for them."

Christ's work as our **Advocate** is eternal and perfect. He continually presents the **names** of His people before the Father, advocating for them and ensuring their **salvation**. The onyx stones on the ephod serve as a reminder that Christ, our High Priest, continually bears us before God, interceding for us in a way that guarantees our reconciliation and eternal security.

B. The Breastpiece of Judgment: The Role of Intercession

One of the most important elements of the high priest's garments was the **breastpiece of judgment**, also known as the **breastplate**. This breastpiece was made of the same materials as the ephod—gold, blue, purple, and scarlet yarn—and was adorned with twelve **precious stones**, each engraved with the name of one of the **twelve tribes of Israel**. The breastpiece was worn over the high priest's heart and served as a symbol of his role as an **intercessor** for the people.

In **Exodus 28:29**, the purpose of the breastpiece is described:

> "So Aaron shall bear the names of the sons of Israel in the breastpiece of judgment on his heart, when he goes into the Holy Place, to bring them to regular remembrance before the Lord."

The high priest wore the breastpiece of judgment whenever he entered the Holy Place, bringing the names of the people before God as a **memorial**. The breastpiece was not only a symbol of the high priest's intercession but also a reminder of the **righteous judgment** that God executed through the **priestly office**.

1. Christ as the Perfect Intercessor

The **breastpiece of judgment** foreshadows Christ's role as the **perfect intercessor** for His people. Just as the high priest bore the names of the tribes of Israel on his heart, so too does Christ bear the names of His people in His **heart** as He intercedes for them before the Father. Christ's intercession, however, is far superior to that of the Old Testament high priest, as His intercession is based on His **perfect righteousness** and **sacrificial death**.

In **Romans 8:34**, Paul speaks of Christ's ongoing work of intercession:

> "Who is to condemn? Christ Jesus is the one who died—more than that, who was raised—who is at the right hand of God, who indeed is interceding for us."

Christ's intercession is rooted in His work as the **High Priest** who offered Himself as the perfect sacrifice for sin. His intercession is not merely a **reminder** of the people's sin, as the breastpiece of judgment was, but a **guarantee** of their forgiveness and acceptance before God.

2. The Stones of the Breastpiece as a Symbol of Christ's Love for His People

The twelve stones on the breastpiece, each engraved with the name of one of the tribes of Israel, symbolize the **love** and **concern** that the high priest bore for the people of God. By wearing the breastpiece over his heart, the high priest demonstrated his **commitment** to the people and his role as their **representative** before God.

This imagery of bearing the names of God's people on his heart finds its ultimate fulfillment in Christ, who bore the **burden of sin** and **death** out of His **love** for humanity. In **John 15:13**, Jesus speaks of the **greatest love**:

> "Greater love has no one than this, that someone lay down his life for his friends."

Christ's role as our **High Priest** is rooted in His love for His people. He bore our sins on the cross and continues to intercede for us because of His **deep love** and **commitment** to our salvation. The stones of the breastpiece serve as a reminder of Christ's **unceasing love** and His desire to see His people reconciled to God.

C. The Robe of the Ephod and the Bells of Holiness

The high priest also wore a **robe of the ephod**, a blue garment that was worn beneath the ephod and breastpiece. At the hem of the robe were alternating **golden bells** and **pomegranates**, which served both a symbolic and practical purpose. The bells were to be heard as the high priest entered the **Holy of Holies** on the **Day of Atonement**, signifying that he was entering the presence of God on behalf of the people.

In **Exodus 28:34-35**, the significance of the bells is described:

> "A golden bell and a pomegranate, a golden bell and a pomegranate, around the hem of the robe. And it shall be on Aaron when he ministers, and its sound shall be heard when he goes into the Holy Place before the Lord, and when he comes out, so that he does not die."

The bells symbolized the **holiness** and **authority** of the high priest, as well as the **seriousness** of his role in approaching God on behalf of the people. The high priest had to enter the Holy Place with **reverence** and **obedience**, lest he incur the judgment of God.

1. The Robe and Bells as a Type of Christ's Holiness

The **robe of the ephod** and the **bells of holiness** foreshadow Christ's role as the **holy and sinless High Priest**, who entered the **heavenly Holy of Holies** to offer Himself as the atoning sacrifice for sin. Unlike the Old Testament high priests, who were sinful and had to offer sacrifices for their own sins, Christ was **sinless** and entered the presence of God with **perfect holiness**.

In **Hebrews 4:15**, we are reminded of Christ's sinlessness:

> "For we do not have a high priest who is unable to sympathize with our weaknesses, but one who in every respect has been tempted as we are, yet without sin."

Christ's sinlessness qualified Him to be the perfect **sacrifice** for sin and the perfect **mediator** between God and humanity. The robe and bells worn by the high priest symbolized the **holiness** required to approach God, but Christ fulfilled this requirement perfectly, offering Himself as the **spotless Lamb**.

2. The Sound of the Bells: A Sign of Christ's Intercession

The **sound of the bells** on the high priest's robe was a reminder to the people that the high priest was **interceding** for them in the Holy Place. As the people heard the bells ringing, they knew that the high priest was standing before God on their behalf, making atonement for their sins.

This imagery points forward to Christ's **ongoing intercession** for His people. Just as the high priest's bells signaled his presence before God, so too does Christ's **heavenly ministry** signal His ongoing work of intercession. In **Hebrews 9:24**, we are told that Christ now appears before God on our behalf:

> "For Christ has entered, not into holy places made with hands, which are copies of the true things, but into heaven itself, now to appear in the presence of God on our behalf."

The sound of the bells serves as a reminder that Christ is always present before the Father, interceding for us and ensuring that we are continually accepted and forgiven.

II. CHRIST AS THE ULTIMATE HIGH PRIEST

The high priest's garments, with all their **symbolic meaning** and **spiritual significance**, were only a **shadow** of the greater **priestly role** that would be fulfilled in Christ. While the high priest in the Old Testament served as a **mediator** between God and the people, offering sacrifices and interceding on their behalf, his work was ultimately **incomplete** and **temporary**. The high priest had to offer sacrifices year after year, and his intercession could never fully reconcile the people to God.

In contrast, Christ's work as the **ultimate High Priest** is **perfect**, **complete**, and **eternal**. Through His **death**, **resurrection**, and **ongoing intercession**, Christ has fully reconciled humanity to God and secured eternal **salvation** for all who believe in Him.

A. The Once-for-All Sacrifice

One of the most significant aspects of Christ's high priestly work is His offering of a **once-for-all sacrifice** for sin. In the Old Testament, the high priest had to offer sacrifices continually, as the blood of animals could not fully atone for sin. These sacrifices were a **temporary measure**, pointing forward to the **perfect sacrifice** that Christ would offer on the cross.

In **Hebrews 10:11-14**, the writer of Hebrews contrasts the **repeated sacrifices** of the Old Testament with the **once-for-all sacrifice** of Christ:

> "And every priest stands daily at his service, offering repeatedly the same sacrifices, which can never take away sins. But when Christ had offered for all time a single sacrifice for sins, He sat down at the right hand of God... For by a single offering He has perfected for all time those who are being sanctified."

Christ's sacrifice on the cross was the **perfect fulfillment** of the **sacrificial system**. His death fully atoned for sin, making it unnecessary for any further sacrifices to be offered. As our High Priest, Christ offered not the blood of animals but **His own blood**, securing eternal **redemption** for His people.

1. The Veil Torn: Access to God Through Christ

When Christ offered Himself as the sacrifice for sin, the **veil of the temple** was torn in two, symbolizing the end of the **separation** between God and humanity. In the Old Testament, the high priest could only enter the **Holy of Holies** once a year, and only after offering a sacrifice for his own sins and the sins of the people. The veil in the temple represented the **barrier** between a **holy God** and **sinful humanity**.

In **Matthew 27:50-51**, we read of the moment when the veil was torn:

> "And Jesus cried out again with a loud voice and yielded up His spirit. And behold, the curtain of the temple was torn in two, from top to bottom."

The tearing of the veil signifies that, through Christ's sacrifice, the way to God has been **opened**. No longer is there a need for a high priest to mediate between God and the people; through Christ's death, we have **direct access** to the Father. As our High Priest, Christ has **removed the barrier** of sin and made it possible for us to **approach God** with confidence.

In **Hebrews 4:16**, we are encouraged to approach God's throne with boldness:

> "Let us then with confidence draw near to the throne of grace, that we may receive mercy and find grace to help in time of need."

Christ's sacrifice has made it possible for us to enter God's presence without fear, knowing that we are **accepted** and **forgiven** through His blood.

2. Christ's High Priestly Prayer

In addition to offering Himself as the perfect sacrifice, Christ also continues to intercede for His people as their High Priest. One of the most profound examples of Christ's **intercessory work** is found in **John 17**, where Jesus prays for His disciples and for all who will believe in Him.

In **John 17:9**, Jesus prays for those who belong to Him:

> "I am praying for them. I am not praying for the world but for those whom You have given me, for they are Yours."

This **High Priestly Prayer** reveals Christ's deep **concern** for His people and His desire to see them **sanctified** and protected. Just as the high priest in the Old Testament interceded for the people, so too does Christ continually pray for those who belong to Him, ensuring their **salvation** and **perseverance** in the faith.

B. Christ's Ongoing Intercession

Christ's work as High Priest did not end with His death and resurrection. He continues to **intercede** for His people, ensuring that they are continually forgiven and accepted by the Father. In **Hebrews 7:25**, we are reminded of Christ's ongoing intercession:

> "Consequently, He is able to save to the uttermost those who draw near to God through Him, since He always lives to make intercession for them."

Christ's intercession is not based on the **temporary sacrifices** of the Old Testament but on His **once-for-all sacrifice**. As our High Priest, Christ continually presents His **finished work** before the Father, ensuring that His people are fully and forever **reconciled** to God.

Fun Fact: The Colors of the High Priest's Garments

The **colors** used in the high priest's garments—**gold**, **blue**, **purple**, and **scarlet**—carry significant **symbolic meaning**. Each of these colors points to different aspects of the **character** and **work of Christ**:

- **Gold** represents **divinity** and **royalty**, pointing to Christ's status as the **Son of God** and **King of kings**.

- **Blue** symbolizes **heaven** and **eternity**, reminding us that Christ, our High Priest, came from heaven to bring salvation to the world.

- **Purple** represents **royalty** and **sovereignty**, pointing to Christ's role as the **King** who reigns over all creation.

- **Scarlet** represents **blood** and **sacrifice**, pointing to Christ's **atoning death** on the cross.

These colors, woven into the high priest's garments, foreshadow the **divine attributes** and **sacrificial work** of Christ, who is the ultimate High Priest and King.

The Fulfillment of the High Priest's Garments in Christ

From the Tabernacle to Solomon's Temple to the Second Temple, the progression of God's dwelling among His people points toward a final and eternal fulfillment in Christ. The tearing of the temple veil at Jesus' crucifixion signifies the end of separation between God and humanity, and the beginning of the Church as the living temple, indwelt by the Spirit.

Solomon's Temple was the physical dwelling place of God among His people, where the Ark of the Covenant resided. As magnificent as it was, it served as a shadow of a greater reality. The destruction of this temple symbolized the passing of the old covenant system, pointing forward to the time when God's presence would dwell fully in Christ, the true Temple. The physical structure of the temple was temporary, but it laid the foundation for the spiritual temple found in Christ.

The Second Temple, rebuilt after the exile, held great significance for the Jewish people. It was the site of Jesus' ministry, and although it lacked the glory of Solomon's Temple, it still foreshadowed a greater fulfillment in Christ. The destruction of the Second Temple, as prophesied by Jesus, marks the end of the old sacrificial system and the transition to a new covenant where God's presence is no longer confined to a building but resides in Christ and His Church. Jesus, the ultimate Temple, fulfills what the Second Temple could only symbolize.

The **high priest's garments**, with all their symbolic meaning and spiritual significance, were a **foreshadowing** of the **greater reality** that would be fulfilled in Christ. Each aspect of the high priest's attire—the ephod, the breastpiece, the robe, the turban—pointed to Christ's work as the **perfect High Priest**, who would offer

Himself as the **once-for-all sacrifice** for sin and continue to intercede for His people.

While the high priest in the Old Testament served as a temporary mediator between God and the people, Christ serves as the **eternal mediator**, ensuring that all who belong to Him are forever **reconciled** to God. Through His **death**, **resurrection**, and **ongoing intercession**, Christ has fulfilled the priestly role in a way that far surpasses the Old Testament system. He is the High Priest who has torn the veil, opened the way to God, and continually presents His finished work before the Father.

As believers, we can take great comfort in knowing that Christ is our **High Priest**, who bears our burdens, intercedes for us, and ensures our eternal salvation. The high priest's garments, once a symbol of holiness and mediation, find their ultimate fulfillment in the person and work of **Jesus Christ**, our Savior, and High Priest forever.

CHAPTER 31: THE GOLDEN LAMPSTAND: A TYPE OF CHRIST AS THE LIGHT OF THE WORLD

The **Golden Lampstand**, also known as the **Menorah**, is one of the most significant and symbolic items in the **Tabernacle** that God commanded Moses to build. As part of the **Holy Place**, the lampstand was designed to provide continuous **light** in the otherwise dark interior of the **Tabernacle**, illuminating the way for the **priests** to carry out their sacred duties. More than a functional object, the Golden Lampstand holds deep symbolic significance, serving as a **type of Christ**, who is the true **Light of the World**, bringing **spiritual illumination** to those living in **darkness**.

In this chapter, we will explore the **typology** of the Golden Lampstand in relation to Christ, examining its design, purpose, and spiritual significance. By understanding how the **lampstand's light** illuminated the **Holy Place**, we can better appreciate how **Christ's light** illuminates the **hearts of believers** and brings them into a saving relationship with God. We will also look at key passages in both the Old and New Testaments that connect the **lampstand's light** to the **person and work of Christ**.

Additionally, we will consider the **practical application** of this typology for modern believers. Just as the **lampstand** in the Tabernacle symbolized the **constant presence of light** in a dark place, so too does Christ's light shine in the **darkness of the world**, calling us to be **reflectors** of that light and to walk in His **illumination**.

I. THE GOLDEN LAMPSTAND: AN OVERVIEW (EXODUS 25:31-40)

The **Golden Lampstand** was one of the sacred objects located in the **Holy Place** of the Tabernacle. Positioned opposite the **Table of Showbread** and near the **Altar of Incense**, the lampstand played a crucial role in providing **light** for the priests as they ministered in the Holy Place. Unlike natural light, which would fade at night, the light of the lampstand was designed to burn continually, representing the **everlasting light** of God's presence.

In **Exodus 25:31-40**, God gives specific instructions for the construction of the lampstand:

> "You shall make a lampstand of pure gold. The lampstand shall be made of hammered work: its base, its stem, its cups, its calyxes, and its flowers shall be of one piece with it. And there shall be six branches going out of its sides, three branches of the lampstand out of one side of it and three branches of the lampstand out of the other side of it... And you shall make seven lamps for it. And the lamps shall be set up so as to give light on the space in front of it." (Exodus 25:31, 32, 37)

The **Golden Lampstand** was made of **pure gold** and was formed from a single piece of **hammered work**, emphasizing the unity and craftsmanship that went into its creation. The lampstand had a **central shaft** with three **branches** on each side, making a total of seven **lamps**. These lamps were filled with **olive oil** and were to burn **continually**, symbolizing God's ongoing presence and **illumination**.

A. The Purpose of the Lampstand

The primary function of the **Golden Lampstand** was to provide **light** in the Holy Place. Since the Tabernacle was a closed tent with no windows or natural light, the priests needed the lampstand to illuminate their way as they ministered before the Lord. This practical function, however, carried deep spiritual significance. The lampstand was not just a source of physical light; it was a symbol of **God's presence** and His role as the **source of spiritual light** for His people.

In **Leviticus 24:2-4**, God commanded that the lampstand's lamps be kept burning continually:

> "Command the people of Israel to bring you pure oil from beaten olives for the lamp, that a light may be kept burning regularly. Outside the veil of the testimony, in the tent of meeting, Aaron shall arrange it from evening to morning before the Lord regularly. It shall be a statute forever throughout your generations. He shall arrange the lamps on the lampstand of pure gold before the Lord regularly."

The **perpetual light** of the lampstand represented the **continual presence of God** among His people, illuminating their way and guiding them in the darkness. Just as the priests needed the lampstand to perform their duties, so too do we need the **light of Christ** to guide us in our spiritual walk.

1. The Symbolism of Light in Scripture

Throughout Scripture, **light** is used as a powerful metaphor for **God's presence**, **truth**, and **guidance**. From the very beginning of the Bible, light is associated with God's creative power and His ability to **dispel darkness**. In **Genesis 1:3**, God's first recorded words in creation are, **"Let there be light,"** and with this command, the darkness was dispelled, and creation was set in motion.

In a similar way, the **light of the lampstand** in the Tabernacle symbolized the **spiritual light** that comes from God, illuminating the path for His people and driving away the darkness of **sin** and **ignorance**. As we will see, this theme of **light** as a representation of God's presence and truth culminates in the person of **Jesus Christ**, who is the ultimate **Light of the World**.

2. The Seven Lamps: Symbol of Perfection and Completion

The **seven lamps** on the Golden Lampstand carry a significant symbolic meaning, as the number seven in the Bible often represents **perfection** and **completion**. The fact that there were seven lamps on the lampstand suggests that the light provided by the lampstand was **complete** and **perfect**, representing the **fullness of God's light**.

In the **Book of Revelation**, we see a connection between the number seven and the presence of God's **Spirit**. In **Revelation 4:5**, the **seven lamps of fire** are identified as the **seven spirits of God**:

> "From the throne came flashes of lightning, and rumblings and peals of thunder, and before the throne were burning seven torches of fire, which are the seven spirits of God."

This passage suggests that the **seven lamps** of the Golden Lampstand in the Tabernacle symbolized the **fullness of the Holy Spirit**, who illuminates the hearts and minds of believers and brings them into the **knowledge of God's truth**. The light of the seven lamps points forward to the **spiritual light** that Christ, through the Holy Spirit, brings into the world.

B. The Design of the Lampstand: A Symbol of Life and Growth

The design of the Golden Lampstand was rich in **botanical imagery**, featuring **cups shaped like almond blossoms**, along with **calyxes** and **flowers**. This design was not merely decorative but carried deep spiritual significance, symbolizing **life**, **growth**, and **fruitfulness**.

In **Exodus 25:33**, we read about the almond blossoms on the lampstand:

> "Three cups made like almond blossoms, each with calyx and flower, on one branch, and three cups made like almond blossoms, each with calyx and flower, on the other branch—so for the six branches going out of the lampstand."

The **almond blossom** was one of the first trees to bloom in the spring, symbolizing **new life** and **renewal**. By incorporating almond blossoms into the design of the lampstand, God was reminding the people of **His power** to bring **life** and **growth**. This imagery of **life and fruitfulness** is also a powerful **type** of Christ, who brings **spiritual life** to all who believe in Him.

1. Christ as the Source of Spiritual Life

The **botanical design** of the lampstand, with its almond blossoms and flowers, points forward to Christ as the **source of**

spiritual life. Just as the almond tree blossoms with new life in the spring, so too does Christ bring **new life** to those who trust in Him. In **John 15:5**, Jesus uses the metaphor of a **vine** to describe His role as the source of spiritual life and fruitfulness:

> "I am the vine; you are the branches. Whoever abides in me and I in him, he it is that bears much fruit, for apart from me you can do nothing."

Just as the branches of the lampstand were adorned with almond blossoms, symbolizing life and growth, so too are believers called to **abide in Christ** and bear spiritual fruit through their relationship with Him. Christ is the **light** that brings **life**, and without Him, we remain in spiritual darkness.

2. The Lampstand's Unity: A Type of Christ's Oneness with the Church

Another significant aspect of the **lampstand's design** is its **unity**. The lampstand was made from a single piece of hammered gold, with its central shaft and six branches forming one cohesive structure. This unity is a **type** of Christ's **oneness** with His people, the **Church**. Just as the lampstand had multiple branches but was still one unified object, so too are believers **one body** in Christ, though we are many members.

In **John 17:21**, Jesus prays for the **unity** of His followers:

> "That they may all be one, just as You, Father, are in me, and I in You, that they also may be in us, so that the world may believe that You have sent me."

The **unity of the lampstand** symbolizes the unity of Christ and His Church. Just as the lampstand provided light in the Holy Place, so too does Christ's **light** shine through the Church, illuminating the world and pointing people to the **truth of the Gospel**.

II. CHRIST AS THE LIGHT OF THE WORLD (JOHN 8:12)

The typology of the **Golden Lampstand** finds its ultimate fulfillment in the person of **Jesus Christ**, who declared Himself to be the **Light of the World**. In **John 8:12**, Jesus makes one of His most profound statements about His identity:

> "Again Jesus spoke to them, saying, 'I am the light of the world. Whoever follows me will not walk in darkness, but will have the light of life.'"

This declaration connects Jesus directly to the **symbolism of the lampstand** in the Tabernacle. Just as the lampstand provided light in the Holy Place, allowing the priests to serve in God's presence, so too does Christ provide **spiritual light**, enabling us to walk in **fellowship with God** and **serve** Him in truth.

A. The Significance of Light in the Ministry of Christ

Throughout His ministry, **light** played a central role in Jesus' teaching and in His identity as the **Messiah**. In the **Gospel of John**, Jesus is often referred to as the **Light**, emphasizing His role in bringing **spiritual illumination** to a world darkened by sin and ignorance. The **light of Christ** is not merely physical light; it is the light of **truth**, **holiness**, and **salvation**.

In **John 1:4-5**, John the Evangelist introduces Jesus as the light that dispels darkness:

> "In Him was life, and the life was the light of men. The light shines in the darkness, and the darkness has not overcome it."

The **light of Christ** is both **life-giving** and **victorious** over darkness. Just as the light of the lampstand shone in the **Holy Place**, providing illumination in an otherwise dark environment, so too does Christ's light shine in the **hearts** of believers, bringing them into a **saving relationship** with God and enabling them to walk in **truth**.

1. Christ's Light Reveals Truth and Exposes Darkness

One of the primary functions of light is to **reveal** what is hidden and to **expose** what is in darkness. In the spiritual sense, the **light of Christ** reveals the truth of God's Word and exposes the **sin** and **deception** that keep people in **spiritual blindness**. In **John 3:19-21**, Jesus explains the connection between light, truth, and judgment:

> "And this is the judgment: the light has come into the world, and people loved the darkness rather than the light because their works were evil. For everyone who does wicked things hates the light and does not come to the light, lest his works should be exposed. But whoever does what is true comes to the light, so that it may be clearly seen that his works have been carried out in God."

The **light of Christ** has the power to **reveal** the **true condition** of our hearts, exposing sin and leading us to **repentance** and **transformation**. Just as the lampstand's light enabled the priests to carry out their duties in the Holy Place, Christ's light enables us to walk in **obedience** and **holiness**, fully aware of God's truth and presence.

2. The Light of Life: Christ's Role in Salvation

In His declaration that He is the **Light of the World**, Jesus also promises that those who **follow Him** will not walk in darkness but will have the **light of life**. This promise speaks to Christ's role in **salvation**. Through His life, death, and resurrection, Jesus brings **spiritual life** to those who trust in Him, rescuing them from the **darkness of sin** and giving them the **light of eternal life**.

In **Colossians 1:13**, Paul describes the **deliverance** that Christ provides:

> "He has delivered us from the domain of darkness and transferred us to the kingdom of His beloved Son, in whom we have redemption, the forgiveness of sins."

The **light of Christ** is not just an abstract concept; it is the **life-giving power** that brings us into a **right relationship** with God. Just as the lampstand's light provided continual illumination in the Tabernacle, so too does Christ's light provide us with the **spiritual illumination** needed to walk in **fellowship** with God and experience the **fullness** of His salvation.

B. The Fulfillment of the Lampstand in Christ's Ministry

The **Golden Lampstand** in the Tabernacle served as a **type** of Christ's role as the **Light of the World**, and this typology is fulfilled in **Christ's earthly ministry**. Just as the lampstand provided **continuous light** in the Holy Place, so too did Christ's presence bring **spiritual light** to those living in darkness. Through His **teachings**, **miracles**, and ultimate sacrifice on the cross, Christ revealed the **light of God's truth** and opened the way for people to come into a saving relationship with Him.

1. Christ's Light as the Guide for Believers

One of the key functions of the **lampstand's light** was to guide the priests as they carried out their duties in the **Holy Place**. Without the light of the lampstand, the priests would be unable to see clearly, and their work would be hindered. In the same way, Christ's light serves as a guide for **believers**, helping us to walk in **truth** and **righteousness** as we serve God.

In **Psalm 119:105**, the psalmist declares:

> "Your word is a lamp to my feet and a light to my path."

This verse reminds us that God's Word, which is ultimately fulfilled in Christ, is the **light** that guides us in our daily walk with Him. Just as the priests needed the lampstand's light to carry out their work, we need the **light of Christ** to guide us in our spiritual journey and to help us discern God's will for our lives.

2. The Church as a Reflection of Christ's Light

While Christ is the ultimate **Light of the World**, He also calls **believers** to be **reflections** of His light, shining in the darkness and pointing others to Him. In **Matthew 5:14-16**, Jesus tells His followers that they are the **light of the world**:

> "You are the light of the world. A city set on a hill cannot be hidden. Nor do people light a lamp and put it under a basket, but on a stand, and it gives light to all in the house. In the same way, let your light shine before others, so that they may see your good works and give glory to your Father who is in heaven."

Just as the **lampstand's light** was meant to shine continually in the Holy Place, so too are we called to let our light shine in the world, reflecting the **light of Christ** and bringing glory to God. As believers, we are not the source of the light, but we are called to be **vessels** through which Christ's light shines, illuminating the darkness and leading others to the truth of the Gospel.

III. THE PRACTICAL APPLICATION OF CHRIST AS THE LIGHT

The **typology** of the **Golden Lampstand** as a type of **Christ's light** is not just a theological concept; it has practical implications for our daily lives as **believers**. Understanding that Christ is the **Light of the World** challenges us to walk in His light, to reflect His light in the world, and to live in a way that honors Him as our source of **spiritual illumination**.

A. Walking in the Light of Christ

One of the most important aspects of Christ's role as the **Light of the World** is His call for us to **walk in His light**. In **John 12:35-36**, Jesus urges His followers to live in the light while they have the opportunity:

> "So Jesus said to them, 'The light is among you for a little while longer. Walk while you have the light, lest darkness overtake you. The one who walks in the darkness does not know where he is going. While you have the light, believe in the light, that you may become sons of light.'"

To walk in the **light of Christ** means to live in **obedience** to His Word, to allow His light to **illuminate** our hearts and minds, and to turn away from the **darkness of sin**. Just as the priests relied on the lampstand's light to perform their sacred duties, we must rely on Christ's light to guide us in our spiritual walk and to help us live lives that are pleasing to God.

1. The Importance of Spiritual Discernment

Walking in the **light of Christ** also involves developing **spiritual discernment**, the ability to distinguish between **truth** and falsehood, **light** and **darkness**. In a world filled with **deception** and **spiritual darkness**, we need the **light of Christ** to help us discern **God's will** and to make wise choices in our lives.

In **Ephesians 5:8-10**, Paul encourages believers to walk as **children of light**:

> "For at one time you were darkness, but now you are light in the Lord. Walk as children of light (for the fruit of light is found in all that is good and right and true), and try to discern what is pleasing to the Lord."

As children of light, we are called to pursue what is **good**, **right**, and **true**, allowing the light of Christ to **illuminate** our path and help us live in a way that honors Him.

2. Turning Away from Darkness

Walking in the light of Christ also means **turning away from darkness**. Throughout Scripture, darkness is associated with **sin**, **ignorance**, and **separation from God**. To live in the light of Christ, we must actively choose to **reject** the darkness and to **embrace** the light.

In **1 John 1:6-7**, the apostle John writes:

> "If we say we have fellowship with Him while we walk in darkness, we lie and do not practice the truth. But if we walk in the light, as He is in the light, we have fellowship with one another, and the blood of Jesus His Son cleanses us from all sin."

Walking in the light requires a commitment to **holiness** and a willingness to confess our sins and allow Christ's light to cleanse and transform us.

B. Reflecting Christ's Light in the World

As believers, we are not only called to **walk in the light** but also to **reflect** Christ's light in the world. Just as the **lampstand's light** shone continually in the Holy Place, illuminating the way for the priests, so too are we called to let our light shine before others, pointing them to Christ and revealing the truth of the Gospel.

In **Philippians 2:15-16**, Paul encourages believers to shine as lights in the world:

> "That you may be blameless and innocent, children of God without blemish in the midst of a crooked and twisted generation, among whom you shine as lights in the world, holding fast to the word of life."

As **lights in the world**, we are called to live lives that reflect the **character of Christ**, demonstrating His love, truth, and grace to those around us. Our lives should be a testimony to the **transforming power** of Christ's light, leading others to **repentance** and faith in Him.

Fun Fact: The Olive Oil Used for the Lampstand

One interesting detail about the **Golden Lampstand** is the type of oil that was used to fuel its lamps. In **Exodus 27:20**, God commanded the people of Israel to bring **pure oil from beaten olives** for the lamps:

> "You shall command the people of Israel that they bring to you pure beaten olive oil for the light, that a lamp may regularly be set up to burn."

This **olive oil** was carefully prepared and represented the **best** and **purest** offering the people could bring. The use of olive oil to fuel the lamps is significant because **oil** is often associated with the **Holy Spirit** in Scripture. Just as the oil fueled the lamps and kept them burning, so too does the **Holy Spirit** fuel our spiritual lives, enabling us to **shine** as lights in the world and empowering us to walk in **fellowship** with God.

Christ, the True Light of the World

From the Tabernacle to Solomon's Temple to the Second Temple, the progression of God's dwelling among His people points toward a final and eternal fulfillment in Christ. The tearing of the temple veil at Jesus' crucifixion signifies the end of separation between God and humanity, and the beginning of the Church as the living temple, indwelt by the Spirit.

Solomon's Temple was the physical dwelling place of God among His people, where the Ark of the Covenant resided. As magnificent as it was, it served as a shadow of a greater reality. The destruction of this temple symbolized the passing of the old covenant system, pointing forward to the time when God's presence would dwell fully in Christ, the true Temple. The physical structure of the temple was temporary, but it laid the foundation for the spiritual temple found in Christ.

The Second Temple, rebuilt after the exile, held great significance for the Jewish people. It was the site of Jesus' ministry, and although it lacked the glory of Solomon's Temple, it still foreshadowed a greater fulfillment in Christ. The destruction of the Second Temple, as prophesied by Jesus, marks the end of the old sacrificial system and the transition to a new covenant where God's presence is no longer confined to a building but resides in Christ and His Church. Jesus, the ultimate Temple, fulfills what the Second Temple could only symbolize.

>The **Golden Lampstand** in the Tabernacle was a powerful symbol of **God's presence** and the **light of His truth**. Its **continual light** illuminated the **Holy Place**, enabling the priests to serve God and reminding the people of God's ongoing presence with them. However, the lampstand was only a **shadow** of the **greater light** that was to come—the light of **Jesus Christ**, who declared Himself to be the **Light of the World**.

>Through His life, death, and resurrection, Christ brought **spiritual light** into a world darkened by sin and separation from God. He continues to shine His light in the hearts of those who follow Him, guiding them into the truth and enabling them to walk in **fellowship** with God. As believers, we are called to **walk in the light**, to **reflect** Christ's light in the world, and to live lives that bring glory to God.

>Just as the **Golden Lampstand** illuminated the Holy Place, so too does Christ's light illuminate our hearts, dispelling the darkness and leading us into the **fullness of life** in Him. Let us, therefore, walk in the **light of Christ**, holding fast to His Word and allowing His light to shine through us as we serve Him in a world that so desperately needs His **illumination**.

CHAPTER 32: JONAH IN THE BELLY OF THE FISH: A TYPE OF CHRIST'S RESURRECTION

The story of **Jonah** in the Old Testament is one of the most well-known accounts in Scripture, often remembered for its dramatic imagery of a man swallowed by a **great fish** and miraculously surviving for three days. While this story captivates with its supernatural elements, it carries far deeper **theological significance** than merely being a tale of survival. **Jonah's experience** in the belly of the fish is a powerful **type** that prefigures the **death, burial**, and **resurrection of Jesus Christ**. In fact, Christ Himself references Jonah's time in the fish as a **foreshadowing** of His own **three days in the tomb**, thereby affirming Jonah's experience as a **type** of His redemptive work.

In this chapter, we will explore the typological connection between **Jonah's time in the belly of the fish** and Christ's **death, burial**, and **resurrection**. By delving into the **theological depth** of Jonah's experience and comparing it with Christ's resurrection, we gain a fuller understanding of how the **Old Testament** consistently points forward to the **New Testament** fulfillment in Christ. Furthermore, we will consider the **practical implications** of this typology for believers today, examining how Jonah's story calls us to reflect on the **power of resurrection** in our own spiritual lives.

I. JONAH'S EXPERIENCE: AN OVERVIEW (JONAH 1:17)

The story of Jonah begins with God's call for him to go to **Nineveh**, a great city of the **Assyrian Empire**, to call its people to

repentance. However, instead of obeying God's command, Jonah chooses to **flee in the opposite direction**, boarding a ship bound for **Tarshish**. Jonah's decision to run from God sets in motion a series of events that ultimately lead to him being swallowed by a **great fish**, in whose belly he spends three days and three nights.

In **Jonah 1:17**, we read the pivotal verse that sets the stage for Jonah's time in the fish:

> "And the Lord appointed a great fish to swallow up Jonah. And Jonah was in the belly of the fish three days and three nights."

Jonah's experience inside the fish is the central event of his story, not only because of its miraculous nature but also because it serves as the **turning point** for Jonah's **repentance** and subsequent **obedience** to God's call. While Jonah's time in the belly of the fish could be viewed as an isolated supernatural event, Christ's later reference to Jonah in the **Gospels** reveals that Jonah's experience foreshadowed the even greater event of Christ's **death** and **resurrection**.

A. Jonah's Three Days and Nights: A Period of Death and Resurrection

Jonah's **three days and three nights** in the belly of the fish serve as a **symbolic death**. When Jonah was thrown into the sea, it was as though he had been **given over to death**—a fate he expected would be his end. However, God's miraculous provision of the fish **preserved Jonah's life**, even though he was in a place of **darkness** and **isolation** for three days. This period of time mirrors the **three days** that Christ spent in the **tomb** after His crucifixion, before rising from the dead.

Jonah's experience of being swallowed by the fish can be seen as a **type of burial**, where he was entombed in the belly of the fish, separated from the land of the living. But just as Jonah was **delivered** after three days, Christ, too, rose from the dead on the third day, emerging from the **tomb** in victory over death.

1. The Symbolism of the Number Three in Scripture

The number **three** holds significant **symbolic meaning** throughout Scripture. It is often associated with **completeness** or **divine fulfillment**. In the case of Jonah and Christ, the three-day period represents the **completion** of a process leading to **deliverance** and **new life**. Jonah's three days in the fish symbolize his **rebellion** and subsequent **repentance**, while Christ's three days in the tomb represent His victory over **sin** and **death**, culminating in the **resurrection**.

In **Hosea 6:1-2**, the prophet Hosea speaks of God's restoration after two days, followed by revival on the third day, which mirrors the idea of **resurrection**:

> "Come, let us return to the Lord; for He has torn us, that He may heal us; He has struck us down, and He will bind us up. After two days He will revive us; on the third day He will raise us up, that we may live before Him."

This passage speaks to the **redemptive process** that takes place over three days, with the third day marking the moment of **restoration** and **new life**. In both Jonah's story and Christ's resurrection, the **third day** signifies the moment when God brings forth **life** from the **depths of death**.

2. Jonah's Prayer of Desperation and Repentance (Jonah 2:1-9)

While in the belly of the fish, Jonah experiences a profound **spiritual awakening**. His prayer, recorded in **Jonah 2:1-9**, reflects his **desperation**, **repentance**, and recognition of God's power to **save** him, even from the depths of the sea. Jonah's prayer echoes the **language of the Psalms**, particularly those Psalms that speak of **deliverance** from **death** and **despair**.

In **Jonah 2:2**, Jonah describes his experience as being in **Sheol**, the place of the dead:

> "I called out to the Lord, out of my distress, and He answered me; out of the belly of Sheol I cried, and You heard my voice."

Jonah's description of being in **Sheol** further reinforces the idea that his time in the fish represents a symbolic **death**. He views his situation as one of being on the brink of **death**, cut off from the land of the living and in need of **divine intervention**. This parallels Christ's **burial** in the tomb, where He was placed in the realm of the dead before being **raised to life**.

At the end of Jonah's prayer, he acknowledges God as the only source of **salvation**:

> "Salvation belongs to the Lord!" (Jonah 2:9)

This declaration of God's power to **save** prefigures the **resurrection** of Christ, through which God brought **salvation** to all who believe. Just as Jonah was delivered from the depths of the sea, Christ was delivered from the grave, securing eternal **salvation** for all humanity.

B. Jonah's Deliverance: A Type of Resurrection

After spending three days and three nights in the belly of the fish, Jonah is miraculously delivered when the fish **vomits him out** onto dry land. This moment of deliverance can be seen as a **type of resurrection**, where Jonah emerges from what was essentially his **tomb** and is given a **second chance** to fulfill God's command.

In **Jonah 2:10**, we read of Jonah's deliverance:

> "And the Lord spoke to the fish, and it vomited Jonah out upon the dry land."

This act of deliverance foreshadows Christ's **resurrection**, where He, too, was delivered from the **grave** on the **third day**. Just as Jonah's deliverance marked the beginning of his **obedience** to God's mission, Christ's resurrection marked the **inauguration** of His victorious reign over **sin** and **death**, as well as the beginning of the Church's mission to proclaim the **Gospel** to all nations.

1. Christ's Reference to Jonah as a Sign of His Resurrection (Matthew 12:40)

The typological connection between **Jonah** and **Christ's resurrection** is explicitly confirmed by Jesus Himself in the **Gospels**.

In **Matthew 12:40**, Jesus references Jonah's experience in the belly of the fish as a **sign** that prefigures His own death, burial, and resurrection:

> "For just as Jonah was three days and three nights in the belly of the great fish, so will the Son of Man be three days and three nights in the heart of the earth."

By making this comparison, Jesus affirms that Jonah's time in the fish was not only a historical event but also a **prophetic sign** that pointed forward to the **redemptive work** that Christ would accomplish through His death and resurrection. Just as Jonah's deliverance came after three days, so too would Christ's resurrection occur on the **third day**, bringing about the ultimate **deliverance** from sin and death.

2. Jonah's Mission After Deliverance: A Parallel to the Church's Mission

After Jonah's deliverance, God once again calls him to go to **Nineveh** and proclaim a message of **repentance**. This time, Jonah obeys, and as a result, the people of Nineveh repent, and God spares the city from destruction. Jonah's mission to Nineveh can be seen as a **parallel** to the Church's mission after Christ's resurrection.

Just as Jonah was sent to proclaim repentance and deliverance to the people of Nineveh, so too are believers called to **proclaim the Gospel** to the nations, calling people to **repent** and receive the **salvation** that comes through Christ. In **Matthew 28:18-20**, the **Great Commission** is given by the resurrected Christ, commanding His disciples to go into all the world and make disciples:

> "Go therefore and make disciples of all nations, baptizing them in the name of the Father and of the Son and of the Holy Spirit, teaching them to observe all that I have commanded you. And behold, I am with you always, to the end of the age."

Just as Jonah's mission brought **life** to the people of Nineveh, the Church's mission brings **eternal life** to those who believe in the message of Christ's **resurrection**.

II. JONAH AS A TYPE OF CHRIST'S DEATH, BURIAL, AND RESURRECTION

Having examined the key elements of Jonah's experience in the belly of the fish, we can now explore more fully how Jonah serves as a **type of Christ's death, burial, and resurrection**. Typology is a method of biblical interpretation in which a person or event in the **Old Testament** serves as a **foreshadowing** of a greater reality fulfilled in the **New Testament**. In Jonah's case, his time in the belly of the fish prefigures Christ's time in the tomb, while his deliverance from the fish prefigures Christ's **resurrection**.

A. Jonah's Descent as a Type of Christ's Death

Jonah's experience of being thrown into the sea and swallowed by the fish can be seen as a **symbolic death**. In **Jonah 1:15**, the sailors throw Jonah into the sea, which immediately calms the storm that had been threatening to destroy the ship:

> "So they picked up Jonah and hurled him into the sea, and the sea ceased from its raging."

Jonah's descent into the sea represents his **surrender** to the consequences of his disobedience, and it mirrors Christ's **surrender** to death on the cross. Just as Jonah willingly gave himself over to the sea, Christ willingly gave Himself over to death in order to bring **peace** and **salvation** to humanity. In **John 10:18**, Jesus speaks of His willingness to lay down His life:

> "No one takes it from me, but I lay it down of my own accord. I have authority to lay it down, and I have authority to take it up again."

Jonah's descent into the depths of the sea can be seen as a **type of Christ's descent into death**, where He took upon Himself the **sins of the world** and bore the **wrath of God** in order to bring about **reconciliation** between God and humanity.

1. The Imagery of the Deep: A Symbol of Death

Throughout Scripture, the **sea** and the **depths** are often used as metaphors for **death** and **chaos**. In **Jonah's prayer**, he describes his experience of being in the depths of the sea in language that evokes the **grave** and **Sheol**:

> "For You cast me into the deep, into the heart of the seas, and the flood surrounded me; all Your waves and Your billows passed over me. Then I said, 'I am driven away from Your sight; yet I shall again look upon Your holy temple.'" (Jonah 2:3-4)

The imagery of being surrounded by waves and cast into the heart of the seas reflects the **despair** and **isolation** that come with death. Jonah's experience of being submerged in the depths serves as a **type of Christ's death**, where He was buried in the **grave** and descended into the **realm of the dead**.

In the **Apostles' Creed**, we confess that Christ **"descended to the dead"** before rising on the third day. Jonah's descent into the depths of the sea foreshadows this **descent into death**, where Christ fully experienced the **consequences of sin** on behalf of humanity.

2. Jonah's Willing Sacrifice: A Parallel to Christ's Willing Sacrifice

One key element of Jonah's story that parallels Christ's sacrifice is the fact that Jonah **willingly** offered himself as a **sacrifice** to calm the storm and save the sailors. When the sailors cast lots to determine who was responsible for the storm, the lot fell on Jonah, and he confessed that his disobedience was the cause of the storm. In response, Jonah tells the sailors to throw him into the sea, knowing that his sacrifice will calm the storm.

In **Jonah 1:12**, Jonah says:

> "Pick me up and hurl me into the sea; then the sea will quiet down for you, for I know it is because of me that this great tempest has come upon you."

Jonah's willingness to be thrown into the sea to save the sailors is a **type** of Christ's willing sacrifice on the cross to save humanity. Just as Jonah gave himself up to the sea to bring peace, Christ gave Himself up to **death** to bring **peace** and **reconciliation** between God and humanity. In **Isaiah 53:5**, we read of the **suffering servant** who bore the punishment for our sins:

> "But He was pierced for our transgressions; He was crushed for our iniquities; upon Him was the chastisement that brought us peace, and with His wounds we are healed."

Jonah's sacrifice points forward to the **greater sacrifice** of Christ, who bore the weight of **sin** and **death** to bring **salvation** to the world.

B. Jonah's Time in the Belly of the Fish as a Type of Christ's Burial

After Jonah was thrown into the sea, he was swallowed by a great fish, where he remained for **three days and three nights**. This period of time inside the fish can be seen as a **type of Christ's burial**, where He was placed in the tomb for **three days** before rising from the dead. The belly of the fish serves as a **symbolic tomb**, where Jonah experienced a **temporary separation** from the land of the living.

In **Jonah 2:5-6**, Jonah describes his experience inside the fish:

> "The waters closed in over me to take my life; the deep surrounded me; weeds were wrapped about my head at the roots of the mountains. I went down to the land whose bars closed upon me forever; yet You brought up my life from the pit, O Lord my God."

Jonah's description of being **surrounded by water** and **trapped** in a place where the bars closed upon him forever reflects the **finality** of death and burial. Yet, even in this place of **death**, Jonah expresses hope that God will **deliver** him and **bring him back to life**. This hope of deliverance mirrors the **hope of resurrection** that is fulfilled in Christ, who was buried in the tomb but was raised to life on the third day.

1. The Significance of Three Days and Three Nights

The **three-day period** that Jonah spent in the belly of the fish holds great significance in the typology of **death** and **resurrection**. In the ancient world, the third day was often seen as the point at which **death was final**, and any hope of recovery was lost. However, the

third day also became a symbol of **new life** and **restoration**, as we see in the **resurrection** of Christ.

In **Hosea 6:1-2**, the prophet speaks of God's power to revive and restore after three days:

> "Come, let us return to the Lord; for He has torn us, that He may heal us; He has struck us down, and He will bind us up. After two days He will revive us; on the third day He will raise us up, that we may live before Him."

Jonah's **three days** in the fish prefigure Christ's **three days** in the tomb, where the power of death was broken, and **new life** was brought forth on the **third day**. This typology underscores the **pattern** of death, burial, and resurrection that runs throughout Scripture, culminating in the work of Christ.

2. The Belly of the Fish as a Symbolic Tomb

Jonah's experience inside the belly of the fish can also be viewed as a **symbolic burial**, where he was entombed in darkness and **cut off** from the land of the living. This image of Jonah in the depths of the sea serves as a **type** of Christ's burial, where He was laid in a **tomb** after His crucifixion.

In **Matthew 12:40**, Jesus explicitly connects Jonah's time in the fish with His own burial:

> "For just as Jonah was three days and three nights in the belly of the great fish, so will the Son of Man be three days and three nights in the heart of the earth."

Just as Jonah was temporarily **entombed** in the belly of the fish, Christ was **buried** in the tomb, where He remained for three days before rising from the dead. Jonah's experience points forward to the **greater reality** of Christ's death and resurrection, through which the power of death was **defeated** once and for all.

C. Jonah's Deliverance as a Type of Christ's Resurrection

After three days and three nights in the belly of the fish, Jonah is miraculously **delivered** when the fish vomits him out onto dry land. This moment of deliverance serves as a **type of resurrection**, where

Jonah emerges from his symbolic **tomb** and is given a **second chance** to fulfill God's mission. Just as Jonah's deliverance marked the beginning of his renewed **obedience** to God, Christ's resurrection marked the beginning of His victorious reign over **sin** and **death**.

In **Jonah 2:10**, we read of Jonah's deliverance:

> "And the Lord spoke to the fish, and it vomited Jonah out upon the dry land."

This act of deliverance prefigures Christ's **resurrection**, where He was raised from the dead on the third day, emerging from the tomb in victory over death. Just as Jonah's deliverance brought **new life** and renewed his mission, Christ's resurrection brings **eternal life** to all who believe in Him and inaugurates the Church's mission to proclaim the **Gospel** to the world.

1. Christ's Resurrection: The Fulfillment of Jonah's Deliverance

While Jonah's deliverance from the belly of the fish was a miraculous event, it ultimately points to the greater reality of **Christ's resurrection**, which is the fulfillment of God's plan for **salvation**. Through His resurrection, Christ conquered **sin** and **death**, bringing **eternal life** to all who believe in Him.

In **1 Corinthians 15:20-22**, Paul speaks of Christ's resurrection as the **firstfruits** of those who will be raised from the dead:

> "But in fact Christ has been raised from the dead, the firstfruits of those who have fallen asleep. For as by a man came death, by a man has come also the resurrection of the dead. For as in Adam all die, so also in Christ shall all be made alive."

Just as Jonah's deliverance from the fish was a **second chance** for him to fulfill his mission, Christ's resurrection is the ultimate victory that secures **eternal life** and the **hope of resurrection** for all who follow Him.

2. The Significance of Jonah's Mission After Deliverance

After being delivered from the belly of the fish, Jonah is once again called to go to **Nineveh** and proclaim God's message of **repentance**. This second chance to fulfill God's mission serves as a **type** of the Church's mission after Christ's resurrection. Just as Jonah was called to bring **repentance** and deliverance to the people of Nineveh, so too are believers called to proclaim the message of Christ's resurrection and **salvation** to the world.

In **Matthew 28:18-20**, the resurrected Christ gives His disciples the **Great Commission**, commanding them to go into all the world and make disciples:

> "Go therefore and make disciples of all nations, baptizing them in the name of the Father and of the Son and of the Holy Spirit, teaching them to observe all that I have commanded you. And behold, I am with you always, to the end of the age."

Jonah's mission to Nineveh foreshadows the Church's mission to proclaim the **Gospel** to the nations, calling people to **repent** and receive the salvation that comes through Christ's **resurrection**.

III. THE PRACTICAL IMPLICATIONS OF JONAH AS A TYPE OF CHRIST'S RESURRECTION

Having explored the typological connection between **Jonah's experience** in the belly of the fish and **Christ's resurrection**, we can now consider the **practical implications** of this typology for believers today. Jonah's story not only foreshadows Christ's work but also serves as a **call to reflection** on the power of **resurrection** in our own spiritual lives.

A. The Call to Repentance and Obedience

One of the key themes of Jonah's story is the call to **repentance** and **obedience**. Jonah's initial disobedience led to his **descent** into the sea and his time in the belly of the fish, but his deliverance was marked by a renewed commitment to **obey** God's command. This theme of repentance and obedience is also central to the message of **Christ's resurrection**.

In **Acts 17:30-31**, Paul speaks of the call to repentance in light of Christ's resurrection:

> "The times of ignorance God overlooked, but now He commands all people everywhere to repent, because He has fixed a day on which He will judge the world in righteousness by a man whom He has appointed; and of this He has given assurance to all by raising Him from the dead."

Just as Jonah was given a **second chance** to fulfill his mission, Christ's resurrection gives us the opportunity to **repent** of our sins and walk in **obedience** to God's will.

B. The Power of Resurrection in the Christian Life

The story of Jonah also reminds us of the power of **resurrection** in the **Christian life**. Just as Jonah was delivered from the depths of the sea, we, too, have been delivered from the **depths of sin** and **death** through the power of Christ's resurrection. This deliverance is not just a future hope but a present reality that transforms our lives and empowers us to walk in **newness of life**.

In **Romans 6:4**, Paul speaks of the transformative power of resurrection:

> "We were buried therefore with Him by baptism into death, in order that, just as Christ was raised from the dead by the glory of the Father, we too might walk in newness of life."

Just as Jonah emerged from the belly of the fish with a renewed sense of purpose, we, too, are called to walk in the **newness of life** that comes through Christ's resurrection.

Fun Fact: Jonah's Story in Jewish and Christian Tradition

While Jonah's story holds deep significance for **Christians**, it is also an important narrative in **Jewish tradition**. In fact, the story of

Jonah is read during the Jewish holiday of **Yom Kippur**, the Day of Atonement, as a reminder of God's **mercy** and the power of **repentance**. The reading of Jonah during this solemn day highlights the themes of **forgiveness**, **deliverance**, and the opportunity for a **second chance**.

For Christians, Jonah's story is further enriched by its typological connection to **Christ's resurrection**, serving as a powerful reminder of God's **mercy** and the **hope** of new life through the **resurrection of Jesus**.

Jonah as a Type of Christ's Death, Burial, and Resurrection

From the Tabernacle to Solomon's Temple to the Second Temple, the progression of God's dwelling among His people points toward a final and eternal fulfillment in Christ. The tearing of the temple veil at Jesus' crucifixion signifies the end of separation between God and humanity, and the beginning of the Church as the living temple, indwelt by the Spirit.

Solomon's Temple was the physical dwelling place of God among His people, where the Ark of the Covenant resided. As magnificent as it was, it served as a shadow of a greater reality. The destruction of this temple symbolized the passing of the old covenant system, pointing forward to the time when God's presence would dwell fully in Christ, the true Temple. The physical structure of the temple was temporary, but it laid the foundation for the spiritual temple found in Christ.

The Second Temple, rebuilt after the exile, held great significance for the Jewish people. It was the site of Jesus' ministry, and although it lacked the glory of Solomon's Temple, it still foreshadowed a greater fulfillment in Christ. The destruction of the Second Temple, as prophesied by Jesus, marks the end of the old sacrificial system and the transition to a new covenant where God's presence is no longer confined to a building but resides in Christ and His Church. Jesus, the ultimate Temple, fulfills what the Second Temple could only symbolize.

The story of **Jonah** in the belly of the fish serves as a powerful **type** of **Christ's death, burial, and resurrection**. Through Jonah's experience of **descent** into the depths, his time in the belly of the fish, and his subsequent deliverance, we see a **foreshadowing** of the work that Christ would accomplish on behalf of humanity. Just as Jonah's three days in the fish prefigured Christ's three days in the tomb, so too does Jonah's deliverance prefigure Christ's victorious **resurrection**.

This typology calls us to reflect on the **power of resurrection** in our own lives, reminding us of the **opportunity for repentance**, **new life**, and the mission to **proclaim the Gospel** to the world. Just as Jonah was given a second chance to fulfill God's mission, we, too, are called to walk in the **newness of life** that comes through Christ's resurrection, sharing the message of **salvation** with all who will hear.

Through Jonah's story, we are reminded that **salvation belongs to the Lord**, and through Christ's resurrection, we are assured of **eternal life** and **victory** over sin and death.

CHAPTER 33: THE JUDGES: TYPES OF CHRIST AS DELIVERER

The **Book of Judges** in the Old Testament chronicles a tumultuous time in Israel's history, following the death of **Joshua** and preceding the establishment of the monarchy. This period is marked by a cycle of **disobedience, oppression, repentance,** and **deliverance**. Time and again, the Israelites would fall into **idolatry** and **sin**, which led to oppression by foreign enemies. In response to their cries for help, God would raise up **judges** to deliver them, offering a temporary respite from their enemies and a return to faithfulness.

While the judges were flawed human beings, they played a pivotal role in God's plan to **rescue** and **restore** Israel. Each judge served as a **deliverer** in a time of need, pointing forward to the ultimate **Deliverer, Jesus Christ**, who would rescue His people from the greatest enemies: **sin, death,** and **spiritual oppression**. Throughout the Book of Judges, we see **types** of Christ—foreshadowings of His work as the **ultimate Judge** and **Deliverer** who would save His people once and for all.

In this chapter, we will explore the role of the **judges** in the Old Testament as types of Christ, examining how figures like **Gideon, Deborah,** and **Samson** prefigure the **redemptive work of Christ**. Through their stories, we gain a deeper understanding of how God's **deliverance** in the Old Testament points to the greater deliverance that Christ would accomplish through His **death** and **resurrection**. We will also consider the **theological themes** that emerge from the stories of the judges and how they relate to the **Christian life**.

I. THE CYCLE OF JUDGES: A PATTERN OF DELIVERANCE AND SIN

The **Book of Judges** covers a period of roughly 300 years in Israel's history, during which time the nation was governed not by kings or a central authority but by **judges**—military leaders and deliverers who were appointed by God to rescue Israel from its enemies. The book is characterized by a repetitive cycle in which the Israelites would turn away from God, fall into oppression, cry out for deliverance, and be rescued by a judge whom God raised up for that purpose.

This cycle is summarized in **Judges 2:16-19**:

"Then the Lord raised up judges, who saved them out of the hand of those who plundered them. Yet they did not listen to their judges, for they whored after other gods and bowed down to them. They soon turned aside from the way in which their fathers had walked, who had obeyed the commandments of the Lord, and they did not do so. Whenever the Lord raised up judges for them, the Lord was with the judge, and He saved them from the hand of their enemies all the days of the judge. For the Lord was moved to pity by their groaning because of those who afflicted and oppressed them. But whenever the judge died, they turned back and were more corrupt than their fathers, going after other gods, serving them and bowing down to them. They did not drop any of their practices or their stubborn ways."

This cycle of **sin**, **oppression**, and **deliverance** reflects the larger story of humanity's fall into **sin** and **rebellion** against God. Just as the Israelites needed a **deliverer** to rescue them from their earthly enemies, so too does humanity need a **Savior** to rescue them from the **spiritual enemies** of sin and death. The judges in the Old Testament serve as **types of Christ**, foreshadowing His role as the ultimate **Deliverer** who would bring eternal salvation to His people.

II. KEY JUDGES AS TYPES OF CHRIST

Throughout the **Book of Judges**, we encounter various judges who delivered Israel in times of crisis. These judges, despite their flaws and limitations, served as **vessels of God's deliverance**, pointing forward to the ultimate deliverance that would come through Christ. Below, we will examine some of the most prominent judges—**Gideon**, **Deborah**, and **Samson**—and explore how their stories prefigure Christ's work as the **Deliverer** of His people.

A. Gideon: A Type of Christ's Victory over Spiritual Enemies

One of the most well-known judges is **Gideon**, who is called by God to deliver Israel from the **Midianites**, a powerful enemy that had oppressed the Israelites for seven years. Gideon's story is remarkable not only for the **military victory** he achieves but also for the way in which his weakness and **fear** are transformed by God into **strength** and **courage**. Gideon's victory over the Midianites prefigures Christ's **victory** over the **spiritual enemies** of sin, death, and the devil.

In **Judges 6:12-16**, we read about Gideon's call:

"And the angel of the Lord appeared to him and said to him, 'The Lord is with you, O mighty man of valor.' And Gideon said to him, 'Please, my lord, if the Lord is with us, why then has all this happened to us? And where are all His wonderful deeds that our fathers recounted to us, saying, 'Did not the Lord bring us up from Egypt?' But now the Lord has forsaken us and given us into the hand of Midian.' And the Lord turned to him and said, 'Go in this might of yours and save Israel from the hand of Midian; do not I send you?' And he said to him, 'Please, Lord, how can I save Israel? Behold, my clan is the weakest in Manasseh, and I am the least in my father's house.' And the Lord said to him, 'But I will be with you, and you shall strike the Midianites as one man.'"

Gideon's **reluctance** and **doubt** reflect the human condition, which often struggles with **fear** and **insecurity** when faced with overwhelming challenges. Yet, God chooses to use Gideon's **weakness** to demonstrate His own **power** and **glory**, reminding us that God's deliverance does not depend on human strength but on His **sovereign will**.

1. Gideon's Victory with a Small Army: A Foreshadowing of Christ's Victory

One of the most striking aspects of Gideon's story is the way in which God reduces the size of his army to ensure that the **victory** is attributed to God's power rather than human effort. In **Judges 7:2**, God tells Gideon to reduce his army from 32,000 men to just 300:

"The Lord said to Gideon, 'The people with you are too many for Me to give the Midianites into their hand, lest Israel boast over Me, saying, 'My own hand has saved me.'"

With only 300 men, Gideon defeats the vast army of the **Midianites** in a battle that clearly demonstrates God's **sovereign power**. This victory foreshadows Christ's victory over **sin** and **death**, which was accomplished not through **military might** but through the apparent weakness of His **sacrifice on the cross**. Just as Gideon's victory was unexpected and miraculous, so too was Christ's **resurrection** and triumph over the powers of darkness.

In **1 Corinthians 1:27**, Paul speaks of how God uses the weak things of the world to shame the strong:

> "But God chose what is foolish in the world to shame the wise; God chose what is weak in the world to shame the strong."

Just as Gideon's weakness became the means through which God's power was displayed, Christ's death on the cross—an apparent defeat—became the means through which **salvation** and **victory** were achieved.

2. The Breaking of the Jars and the Light: A Type of Christ's Shining Light

Another key element of Gideon's victory over the Midianites is the **symbolism of light**. In **Judges 7:16-20**, Gideon instructs his men to carry **jars** with **torches** inside. At the right moment, they break the jars, revealing the light, and shout, "A sword for the Lord and for Gideon!" The sudden appearance of light and the sound of the jars breaking causes confusion among the Midianites, leading to their defeat.

The imagery of the **light** hidden within the jars and revealed at the moment of victory serves as a **type of Christ**, who is the **Light of the World**. Just as the light inside the jars was revealed at the moment of victory, Christ's light was revealed in its fullness through His **resurrection**, bringing victory over **sin** and **death**. In **John 8:12**, Jesus declares:

> "I am the light of the world. Whoever follows me will not walk in darkness, but will have the light of life."

Gideon's victory, which involved the breaking of jars and the revealing of light, foreshadows the **victory of Christ**, whose light shines in the darkness and whose death and resurrection brought **eternal salvation** to the world.

B. Deborah: A Type of Christ's Wise Leadership and Deliverance

Another important figure in the **Book of Judges** is **Deborah**, the only female judge, who is known for her **wisdom**, **courage**, and **faithfulness** to God. Deborah's leadership in a time of national crisis prefigures Christ's role as the **wise and faithful leader** who brings deliverance to His people.

In **Judges 4:4-5**, we are introduced to Deborah:

> "Now Deborah, a prophetess, the wife of Lappidoth, was judging Israel at that time. She used to sit under the palm of Deborah between Ramah and Bethel in the hill country of Ephraim, and the people of Israel came up to her for judgment."

Deborah's role as a **prophetess** and **judge** highlights her **wisdom** and **spiritual insight**, qualities that point forward to Christ, who is the ultimate **Prophet**, **Priest**, and **King**. Just as the people of Israel came to Deborah for judgment and guidance, so too do believers come to Christ for **wisdom** and **direction**.

1. Deborah's Leadership in Battle: A Type of Christ's Victory over the Enemy

Deborah's role as a **deliverer** is most clearly seen in her leadership during the battle against **Sisera**, the commander of the Canaanite army. When **Barak**, the military leader of Israel, expresses fear and hesitation about going into battle, Deborah responds with confidence in God's promise of victory.

In **Judges 4:14**, Deborah encourages Barak:

> "And Deborah said to Barak, 'Up! For this is the day in which the Lord has given Sisera into your hand. Does not the Lord go out before you?' So Barak went down from Mount Tabor with 10,000 men following him."

Deborah's **faith** and **courage** inspire Barak to lead the army into battle, and through God's power, Israel achieves a decisive victory over Sisera and the Canaanites. This victory, which was secured through **faith** in God's promises, serves as a **type** of the victory that Christ would achieve over the **spiritual enemies** of sin and death. Just as Deborah's leadership brought deliverance to Israel, Christ's leadership as the **Good Shepherd** brings deliverance to His people.

In **John 10:11**, Jesus declares:

"I am the good shepherd. The good shepherd lays down His life for the sheep."

Deborah's willingness to **trust in God** and lead the people into battle prefigures Christ's role as the **Good Shepherd**, who leads His people to victory through His sacrificial death and resurrection.

2. Jael's Role in Sisera's Defeat: A Type of Christ Crushing the Enemy

An important aspect of Deborah's story is the role of **Jael**, a woman who plays a decisive role in the defeat of Sisera. After Sisera flees the battlefield, he seeks refuge in the tent of Jael, who offers him hospitality. However, while Sisera is asleep, Jael drives a **tent peg** through his temple, killing him and securing Israel's victory.

In **Judges 4:21**, we read of Jael's actions:

"But Jael the wife of Heber took a tent peg, and took a hammer in her hand. Then she went softly to him and drove the peg into his temple until it went down into the ground, while he was lying fast asleep from weariness. So he died."

Jael's defeat of Sisera can be seen as a **type** of Christ's defeat of the **enemy**, as it echoes the imagery of **crushing** the head of the serpent found in **Genesis 3:15**. Just as Jael crushed Sisera's head with the tent peg, Christ crushed the head of the **serpent**, Satan, through His **death** and **resurrection**. In **Romans 16:20**, Paul reminds believers of the ultimate victory that Christ will bring:

"The God of peace will soon crush Satan under your feet. The grace of our Lord Jesus Christ be with you."

Jael's role in the defeat of Sisera prefigures Christ's **triumph** over the forces of **evil**, securing the ultimate victory for His people.

C. Samson: A Type of Christ's Sacrificial Strength

The final judge we will examine is **Samson**, a figure whose **physical strength** and **tragic downfall** make him one of the most complex characters in the **Book of Judges**. Despite his flaws, Samson serves as a **type** of Christ, particularly in his role as a **deliverer** who sacrifices himself to bring victory to Israel.

Samson's story is marked by his supernatural **strength**, which was given to him by God as part of his **Nazirite vow**. However, Samson's strength is not just a physical attribute; it symbolizes the **spiritual power** that Christ would demonstrate through His sacrificial death.

1. Samson's Supernatural Strength: A Type of Christ's Divine Power

Throughout Samson's life, his **supernatural strength** enables him to defeat Israel's enemies, particularly the **Philistines**, who were oppressing Israel at the time. In one of the most famous episodes of Samson's life, he defeats a thousand Philistines using nothing but the **jawbone of a donkey**.

In **Judges 15:15-16**, we read of Samson's victory:

> "And he found a fresh jawbone of a donkey, and put out his hand and took it, and with it he struck 1,000 men. And Samson said, 'With the jawbone of a donkey, heaps upon heaps, with the jawbone of a donkey have I struck down a thousand men.'"

Samson's **strength** is a type of the **divine power** that Christ would demonstrate through His **miracles**, His **teaching**, and ultimately, through His **victory over death**. Just as Samson's strength was a gift from God, so too was Christ's power rooted in His **divine identity** as the Son of God.

In **Matthew 28:18**, after His resurrection, Christ declares:

> "All authority in heaven and on earth has been given to me."

Samson's strength serves as a **foreshadowing** of the **divine power** that Christ would exercise in His role as the **ultimate Deliverer**, who brings salvation to His people.

2. Samson's Death as a Sacrificial Act: A Type of Christ's Sacrifice

The most significant parallel between Samson and Christ occurs at the end of Samson's life, when he sacrifices himself to defeat the Philistines. After being betrayed by **Delilah** and captured by the Philistines, Samson is blinded and brought to their temple as a spectacle for their amusement. In a final act of **sacrificial strength**, Samson prays for God to restore his strength, and he pulls down the pillars of the temple, killing himself along with thousands of Philistines.

In **Judges 16:28-30**, we read of Samson's final act:

"Then Samson called to the Lord and said, 'O Lord God, please remember me and please strengthen me only this once, O God, that I may be avenged on the Philistines for my two eyes.' And Samson grasped the two middle pillars on which the house rested, and he leaned his weight against them, his right hand on the one and his left hand on the other. And Samson said, 'Let me die with the Philistines.' Then he bowed with all his strength, and the house fell upon the lords and upon all the people who were in it. So the dead whom he killed at his death were more than those whom he had killed during his life."

Samson's **self-sacrifice** to defeat Israel's enemies serves as a **type** of Christ's sacrificial death on the cross, through which He defeated the ultimate enemies of **sin, death,** and **Satan**. Just as Samson's death brought deliverance to Israel, Christ's death and resurrection bring **eternal deliverance** to all who believe in Him.

In **Hebrews 2:14-15**, we read of Christ's victory over death:

"Since therefore the children share in flesh and blood, He Himself likewise partook of the same things, that through death He might destroy the one who has the power of death, that is, the devil, and deliver all those who through fear of death were subject to lifelong slavery."

Samson's final act of **self-sacrifice** points forward to the **greater sacrifice** of Christ, whose death brought **salvation** and **deliverance** to all who would follow Him.

III. THE THEOLOGICAL THEMES OF THE JUDGES AND THEIR FULFILLMENT IN CHRIST

The stories of the judges in the Old Testament reveal several key theological themes that find their ultimate fulfillment in the person and work of **Jesus Christ**. Below, we will explore these themes and how they relate to the **Christian life**.

A. The Need for Deliverance from Sin

The central theme of the **Book of Judges** is the need for **deliverance**. Time and again, the Israelites fall into sin and idolatry, leading to oppression by their enemies. Their need for a **deliverer** reflects the larger need for **deliverance from sin**, which is the condition of all humanity.

In **Romans 3:23**, Paul writes:

"For all have sinned and fall short of the glory of God."

Just as the Israelites needed judges to deliver them from their earthly enemies, so too do we need **Christ** to deliver us from the **spiritual enemies** of sin and death. The judges in the Old Testament serve as **types of Christ**, pointing to the ultimate **Deliverer** who would save His people from their sins.

B. The Imperfection of Human Deliverers

One of the striking aspects of the judges is their **imperfection**. Despite being used by God to bring deliverance, the judges were often flawed individuals who struggled with **sin**, **fear**, and **doubt**. This imperfection serves as a reminder that **human deliverers** are limited and fallible, pointing forward to the need for a **perfect Deliverer**—**Jesus Christ**—who was without sin and whose deliverance is eternal.

In **Hebrews 4:15**, we are reminded of Christ's perfection:

> "For we do not have a high priest who is unable to sympathize with our weaknesses, but one who in every respect has been tempted as we are, yet without sin."

The **imperfection** of the judges highlights the **perfection** of Christ, who is the only deliverer capable of bringing **eternal salvation**.

C. The Victory of God's Power

Throughout the **Book of Judges**, we see the theme of **God's power** working through weak and flawed individuals to bring about victory. Whether it is Gideon's small army, Deborah's leadership, or Samson's sacrificial strength, the victories of the judges are ultimately attributed to **God's power** rather than human effort.

In **2 Corinthians 12:9**, Paul speaks of the power of God being made perfect in weakness:

> "But He said to me, 'My grace is sufficient for you, for My power is made perfect in weakness.' Therefore I will boast all the more gladly of my weaknesses, so that the power of Christ may rest upon me."

The victories of the judges serve as a reminder that **salvation** and **deliverance** come through **God's power**, not through human strength. This theme finds its ultimate fulfillment in the **death and resurrection of Christ**, through which God's power was displayed in the most profound way.

Fun Fact: The Meaning of the Name "Judge"

The word **judge** in Hebrew is **"shofet,"** which not only refers to someone who **judges** or **administers justice** but also someone who **rules** and **delivers**. This broader meaning of **"shofet"** reflects the dual role of the judges in Israel: they were both **leaders** who delivered Israel from its enemies and **administrators** of justice who helped restore the nation to faithfulness.

In the same way, Christ serves as both our **Deliverer** and our **Judge**. He delivers us from the power of sin and death and will one day **judge the world** in righteousness, bringing justice and peace.

Christ as the Ultimate Deliverer

From the Tabernacle to Solomon's Temple to the Second Temple, the progression of God's dwelling among His people points toward a final and eternal fulfillment in Christ. The tearing of the temple veil at Jesus' crucifixion signifies the end of separation between God and humanity, and the beginning of the Church as the living temple, indwelt by the Spirit.

Solomon's Temple was the physical dwelling place of God among His people, where the Ark of the Covenant resided. As magnificent as it was, it served as a shadow of a greater reality. The destruction of this temple symbolized the passing of the old covenant system, pointing forward to the time when God's presence would dwell fully in Christ, the true Temple. The physical structure of the temple was temporary, but it laid the foundation for the spiritual temple found in Christ.

The Second Temple, rebuilt after the exile, held great significance for the Jewish people. It was the site of Jesus' ministry, and although it lacked the glory of Solomon's Temple, it still foreshadowed a greater fulfillment in Christ. The destruction of the Second Temple, as prophesied by Jesus, marks the end of the old sacrificial system and the transition to a new covenant where God's presence is no longer confined to a building but resides in Christ and His Church. Jesus, the ultimate Temple, fulfills what the Second Temple could only symbolize.

The **judges** of the Old Testament, despite their flaws and limitations, serve as powerful **types** of Christ, prefiguring His work as the **ultimate Deliverer** who rescues His people from the greatest enemies: **sin**, **death**, and **spiritual oppression**. Through the stories of Gideon, Deborah, Samson, and others, we see glimpses of the **salvation** that would come through Christ, who is the **perfect Judge** and **Deliverer**.

While the judges brought **temporary** deliverance to Israel, Christ brings **eternal salvation** through His **death and resurrection**, securing victory over the powers of darkness once and for all. As believers, we are called to trust in Christ as our **Deliverer** and to walk in the **victory** that He has secured for us.

The stories of the judges remind us of our need for **deliverance**, the **imperfection** of human leaders, and the **power of God** to bring about victory through weakness. These themes find their ultimate fulfillment in the person and work of **Jesus Christ**, who is the **Judge** and **Deliverer** of His people for all eternity.

CHAPTER 34: THE ALPHA AND THE OMEGA: CHRIST AS THE FULFILLMENT OF ALL TYPOLOGY

As we have journeyed through the rich tapestry of biblical types and shadows, we have seen how the Old Testament is filled with symbols, events, and people that point forward to the ultimate fulfillment found in Jesus Christ. From Adam as a type of Christ, to the Passover Lamb, to the Levitical sacrifices, and the prophets, each story is part of a grand narrative that reveals God's redemptive plan for the world.

The types and shadows we have explored were not just random illustrations or disconnected stories; they form the foundation upon which the entire narrative of Scripture is built. Through these types, God was laying the blueprint for the salvation of humanity. In this final chapter, we look at Christ as the Alpha and the Omega—the beginning and the end, the source and completion of all things.

I. THE ULTIMATE FULFILLMENT: CHRIST AS THE ALPHA AND OMEGA

Throughout Revelation, Jesus refers to Himself as the Alpha and Omega, the beginning and the end of all things:

Revelation 1:8 – "I am the Alpha and the Omega," says the Lord God, "who is and who was and who is to come, the Almighty."

Revelation 22:13 – "I am the Alpha and the Omega, the first and the last, the beginning and the end."

These titles highlight Jesus' role as the fulfillment of every promise in Scripture. From Genesis to Revelation, the entire Bible points to Him. Every type, every shadow, every prophecy, and every sacrifice finds its completion in the person of Jesus Christ.

Just as He is the beginning, He is also the end—the ultimate culmination of God's plan for the ages. He is both the promised seed of Genesis 3:15, the Lamb of God in Exodus 12, and the King of Kings in Revelation 19. In Christ, all things hold together, and through Him, all of creation will be restored and renewed.

II. THE FINAL SACRIFICE AND ETERNAL HIGH PRIEST

One of the central themes of biblical typology is the system of sacrifices established in the Old Testament. The Levitical priesthood, the animal sacrifices, and the Day of Atonement all pointed forward to a greater reality—the once-for-all sacrifice of Christ.

> Hebrews 10:12 – "But when Christ had offered for all time a single sacrifice for sins, He sat down at the right hand of God."

The priests of the Old Covenant had to continually offer sacrifices, for the blood of bulls and goats could never take away sins. But Christ, as our eternal High Priest, offered Himself as the final, perfect sacrifice. The work is finished. The veil is torn. Access to God is now open to all who come through Christ.

Just as Melchizedek, the priest-king, foreshadowed the eternal priesthood of Christ, so the tabernacle, temple, and veil all pointed to the reality that God would one day dwell among His people through the presence of the Holy Spirit. Now, in Christ, we have direct access to God, and we await the day when He will dwell with us for all eternity.

III. THE SECOND ADAM AND THE NEW CREATION

The story of the first Adam is the story of humanity's fall into sin. Through his disobedience, sin entered the world, and death reigned over humanity. Yet, in Christ, the second Adam, we see the reversal of the curse and the dawn of a new creation:

1 Corinthians 15:22 – "For as in Adam all die, so in Christ all will be made alive."

Romans 5:19 – "For as by the one man's disobedience the many were made sinners, so by the one man's obedience the many will be made righteous."

Just as Adam was a type of Christ, Christ represents the new creation, the restoration of all things. In Him, we are no longer bound to the curse of sin and death. Through His death and resurrection, Christ has inaugurated the new creation, and one day, the entire cosmos will be renewed.

As the second Adam, Christ is the head of a new humanity—those who have been redeemed by His blood and brought into the family of God. Through Him, the promise of eternal life is no longer a distant hope but a present reality that we now experience through the power of the Holy Spirit.

IV. THE BRIDE OF CHRIST AND THE ETERNAL MARRIAGE SUPPER

From the very beginning of Scripture, the marriage between Adam and Eve served as a type of the ultimate union between Christ and His Church. The Church is described as the bride of Christ, waiting for the day when the Bridegroom will return to take His bride to Himself.

> Revelation 19:7-9 – "Let us rejoice and exult and give Him the glory, for the marriage of the Lamb has come, and His Bride has made herself ready… Blessed are those who are invited to the marriage supper of the Lamb."

The marriage supper is the final culmination of the union between Christ and the Church. All of the types and shadows of the Old Testament are leading toward this moment—the day when Christ will return for His bride and usher in the eternal kingdom where God will dwell with His people forever.

This marriage imagery is seen throughout Scripture, from Eve's creation from Adam's side to the Song of Solomon. The union between Christ and His Church is the fulfillment of God's ultimate purpose—to bring a people to Himself and dwell with them forever.

V. THE FUTURE FULFILLMENT: NEW HEAVEN, NEW EARTH

The ultimate hope of every believer is the restoration of all things. In the book of Revelation, we see the final culmination of God's redemptive plan—the creation of a new heaven and a new earth, where sin, death, and suffering are no more:

> Revelation 21:1-4 – "Then I saw a new heaven and a new earth… He will wipe away every tear from their eyes, and death shall be no more."

All the types and shadows of the Old Testament point to this moment. The Garden of Eden, the tabernacle, the promised land, and the temple all pointed forward to the time when God's dwelling would be with humanity, in a perfect and restored creation.

In this new creation, the curse of sin will be undone, and the people of God will experience eternal life in the presence of God. Christ, the Alpha and the Omega, will reign forever, and His kingdom will have no end.

VI. OUR RESPONSE: LIVING IN LIGHT OF FULFILLMENT

As believers, understanding the types and shadows of Scripture should lead us to a deeper appreciation of Christ's work and a greater anticipation of His return. Each type points to the grace and mercy of God, and every shadow finds its substance in Christ.

Knowing that Christ is the fulfillment of all things, we are called to live in light of this reality—to walk in faith, to share the Gospel, and to eagerly await the day when we will see our Savior face to face.

> 2 Peter 3:11-12 – "Since all these things are thus to be dissolved, what sort of people ought you to be in lives of holiness and godliness, waiting for and hastening the coming of the day of God."

We stand in the middle of God's story, knowing that the promise of redemption has been fulfilled in Christ, but also awaiting the final culmination when all things will be made new. We are part of the great narrative of Scripture, and we look forward to the day when we will experience the fullness of God's plan.

CHAPTER 35: CHRIST, THE FULFILLMENT OF ALL TYPOLOGY

From the Tabernacle to Solomon's Temple to the Second Temple, the progression of God's dwelling among His people points toward a final and eternal fulfillment in Christ. The tearing of the temple veil at Jesus' crucifixion signifies the end of separation between God and humanity, and the beginning of the Church as the living temple, indwelt by the Spirit.

Solomon's Temple was the physical dwelling place of God among His people, where the Ark of the Covenant resided. As magnificent as it was, it served as a shadow of a greater reality. The destruction of this temple symbolized the passing of the old covenant system, pointing forward to the time when God's presence would dwell fully in Christ, the true Temple. The physical structure of the temple was temporary, but it laid the foundation for the spiritual temple found in Christ.

The Second Temple, rebuilt after the exile, held great significance for the Jewish people. It was the site of Jesus' ministry, and although it lacked the glory of Solomon's Temple, it still foreshadowed a greater fulfillment in Christ. The destruction of the Second Temple, as prophesied by Jesus, marks the end of the old sacrificial system and the transition to a new covenant where God's presence is no longer confined to a building but resides in Christ and His Church. Jesus, the ultimate Temple, fulfills what the Second Temple could only symbolize.

In the end, every story, every type, every shadow, and every symbol points to **Christ**. He is the **center** of Scripture, the **Alpha and Omega**, the **Lamb of God**, the **Bridegroom**, the **High Priest**, the **King**

of Kings, and the **New Adam**. He is the fulfillment of all **prophecy** and **promise**, and in Him, we find our **hope**, our **salvation**, and our **eternal destiny**.

As we close this journey through the **types and shadows** of Scripture, we are reminded that the **story of redemption** is not just about the past, but it is also about our **future**. Christ has come, and Christ will come again. And when He does, we will experience the **eternal fulfillment** of all things in Him.

> Revelation 22:20 – "He who testifies to these things says, 'Surely I am coming soon.' Amen. Come, Lord Jesus!"

Let us live in light of this **hope** and continually seek to make **Christ known**, knowing that **He is the fulfillment of all things**.

BIBLE VERSE INDEX FOR ALL CHAPTERS

Chapter 1: The House of God as the Bride of Christ

Old Testament

- **Psalms 127:1** – Except the LORD build the house, they labor in vain that build it.
- **Isaiah 6:1** – The Lord's train fills the temple.
- **Genesis 1-3** – Adam names Eve late in the third chapter, showing their unity as one.

New Testament

- **Revelation 18:4** – Come out of her, my people, that you do not partake in her sins.
- **Acts 7:52** – The fathers persecuted the prophets and betrayed the Just One.
- **Revelation 21:2-3, 9** – The holy city, New Jerusalem, as a bride adorned for her husband.
- **Ephesians 1:10** – All things will be gathered together in Christ.
- **Revelation 3:12** – He who overcomes will be made a pillar in the temple of God.
- **1 Corinthians 6:19** – Your body is the temple of the Holy Ghost.
- **Galatians 2:9** – James, Cephas, and John were pillars of the Church.

Chapter 2: Adam and Eve: Type of Christ and the Church

Old Testament

- **Genesis 2-3** – Eve is taken from Adam's side, signifying the Church coming from Christ.

New Testament

- **Romans 5:14** – Adam is a type of Christ.
- **Ephesians 5:31-32** – Marriage as a symbol of Christ and the Church.

Chapter 3: The Passover Lamb: A Type of Christ's Sacrifice

Old Testament

- **Exodus 12** – The Passover lamb and its blood spared Israel from death.

New Testament

- **John 1:29** – Jesus is the Lamb of God.
- **1 Corinthians 5:7** – Christ, our Passover, has been sacrificed.

Chapter 4: The Exodus and Red Sea Crossing: A Type of Baptism and Deliverance

Old Testament

- **Exodus 14** – The parting of the Red Sea, Israel's deliverance from Egypt.

New Testament

- **1 Corinthians 10:1-2** – Israel's crossing of the Red Sea as a type of baptism.

Chapter 5: Manna from Heaven: A Type of Christ as the Bread of Life

Old Testament

- **Exodus 16** – Manna provided daily sustenance to Israel in the wilderness.

New Testament

- **John 6:31-35** – Jesus is the true bread from heaven who gives life to the world.

Chapter 6: The Bronze Serpent: A Type of Christ's Crucifixion

Old Testament

- **Numbers 21:4-9** – The bronze serpent lifted up in the wilderness to heal the Israelites.

New Testament

- **John 3:14-15** – Jesus compares His crucifixion to the serpent lifted up in the wilderness.

Chapter 7: The Ark of Noah: A Type of Salvation in Christ

Old Testament

- **Genesis 6-9** – The ark saved Noah and his family from the flood.

New Testament

- **1 Peter 3:20-21** – The ark prefigures salvation through baptism in Christ.

Chapter 8: The Levitical Priesthood and Sacrifices: A Type of Christ's High Priesthood

Old Testament

- **Leviticus 8-10** – The consecration and role of the Levitical priests.
- **Leviticus 16** – The Day of Atonement sacrifices for the nation.

New Testament
- **Hebrews 7:23-27** – Jesus as the eternal High Priest.
- **Hebrews 9:11-12** – Jesus entered the holy places by His own blood.

Chapter 9: The Tabernacle: A Type of Christ's Ministry

As with the Tabernacle, Solomon's Temple represented God's dwelling among His people. However, even as the Second Temple was rebuilt, it lacked the Shekinah glory that filled the first. This absence symbolized the anticipation of the true fulfillment in Christ, in whom 'the fullness of deity dwells bodily' (Colossians 2:9). Jesus not only fulfills the typology of the Tabernacle but surpasses it, offering His own body as the ultimate temple.

Solomon's Temple was the physical dwelling place of God among His people, where the Ark of the Covenant resided. As magnificent as it was, it served as a shadow of a greater reality. The destruction of this temple symbolized the passing of the old covenant system, pointing forward to the time when God's presence would dwell fully in Christ, the true Temple. The physical structure of the temple was temporary, but it laid the foundation for the spiritual temple found in Christ.

The Second Temple, rebuilt after the exile, held great significance for the Jewish people. It was the site of Jesus' ministry, and although it lacked the glory of Solomon's Temple, it still foreshadowed a greater fulfillment in Christ. The destruction of the Second Temple, as prophesied by Jesus, marks the end of the old sacrificial system and the transition to a new covenant where God's presence is no longer confined to a building but resides in Christ and

His Church. Jesus, the ultimate Temple, fulfills what the Second Temple could only symbolize.

Old Testament

- **Exodus 25-31** – The tabernacle as God's dwelling among Israel.
- **Exodus 25:10-22** – The Ark of the Covenant in the Holy of Holies.

New Testament

- **Hebrews 8:5** – The tabernacle as a shadow of heavenly things.
- **Romans 3:25** – Jesus is the propitiation (mercy seat) for our sins.

Chapter 10: The Feasts of Israel: Types of Christ and Future Events

The Feast of Tabernacles not only recalled Israel's time in temporary shelters but also pointed to the future, where God would dwell permanently among His people. While Solomon's Temple stood as a physical representation of God's presence, it foreshadowed the true and eternal temple—Christ, whose body is the ultimate tabernacle.

Old Testament

- **Leviticus 23:5** – Passover, a type of Christ's death.
- **Leviticus 23:6** – Unleavened Bread, a type of Christ's sinless life.
- **Leviticus 23:10** – Firstfruits, a type of Christ's resurrection.
- **Leviticus 23:15-22** – Pentecost, a type of the Holy Spirit and the Church.

- **Leviticus 23:23-25** – Trumpets, pointing to the rapture of the Church.
- **Leviticus 23:27-32** – Day of Atonement, a type of Israel's future redemption.
- **Leviticus 23:33-43** – Tabernacles, pointing to the Millennial Kingdom.

New Testament

- **1 Corinthians 15:20** – Christ is the firstfruits of the dead.
- **Acts 2** – The Holy Spirit comes at Pentecost.
- **1 Thessalonians 4:16-17** – The trumpet will sound at the rapture.
- **Romans 11:26** – All Israel will be saved.
- **Zechariah 14:16-19** – Nations will celebrate Tabernacles in the Millennial Kingdom.
- **Revelation 21:3** – God will dwell with His people.

Chapter 11: Jonah: A Type of Christ's Death, Burial, and Resurrection

Old Testament

- **Jonah 1:17** – Jonah is swallowed by a great fish for three days.

New Testament

- **Matthew 12:40** – Jesus refers to Jonah as a type of His burial and resurrection.

Chapter 12: Joseph: A Type of Christ

Old Testament

- **Genesis 37-50** – Joseph's betrayal and exaltation as a type of Christ.

New Testament
- **Acts 7:9-10** – Joseph's suffering and rise to power prefigure Christ's redemptive work.

Chapter 13: The Sacrifice of Isaac: A Type of Christ's Sacrifice

Old Testament
- **Genesis 22** – Abraham's near-sacrifice of Isaac as a type of Christ's sacrifice.

New Testament
- **Hebrews 11:17-19** – Abraham's faith in God's promise prefigures resurrection.

Chapter 14: The Sabbath: A Type of the Eternal Rest in Christ

Just as the Sabbath prefigures the eternal rest believers will experience in Christ, Solomon's Temple—dedicated as a house of peace and rest—served as a shadow of the true rest found in Jesus. The temple, in its grandeur, was not an end but pointed toward the greater temple, Christ, in whom we find perfect rest.

Solomon's Temple was the physical dwelling place of God among His people, where the Ark of the Covenant resided. As magnificent as it was, it served as a shadow of a greater reality. The destruction of this temple symbolized the passing of the old covenant system, pointing forward to the time when God's presence would dwell fully in Christ, the true Temple. The physical structure of the temple was temporary, but it laid the foundation for the spiritual temple found in Christ.

Old Testament
- **Genesis 2:2-3** – God rested on the seventh day.

New Testament

- **Hebrews 4:9-10** – Believers enter into God's rest through Christ.

Chapter 15: Melchizedek: A Type of Christ's Eternal Priesthood

Old Testament

- **Genesis 14:18-20** – Melchizedek, both king and priest, blesses Abram.

New Testament

- **Hebrews 7:1-3** – Melchizedek prefigures Christ's eternal priesthood.

Chapter 16: The Exodus Plagues: A Type of Judgment and Deliverance

Old Testament

- **Exodus 7-12** – The plagues of Egypt as judgment on Pharaoh.

New Testament

- **Revelation 16** – The final judgments mirror the Exodus plagues.

Chapter 17: Boaz and Ruth: A Type of Christ as the Kinsman-Redeemer

Old Testament

- **Ruth 4:1-10** – Boaz redeems Ruth as her kinsman-redeemer.

New Testament

- **Ephesians 5:25-27** – Christ redeems and sanctifies the Church, His bride.

Chapter 18: The Tabernacle's Veil: A Type of Christ's Flesh

Old Testament

- **Exodus 26:31-35** – The veil separates the Holy of Holies from the rest of the tabernacle.

New Testament

- **Matthew 27:51** – The veil is torn at Christ's death, signifying access to God.
- **Hebrews 10:20** – Christ's flesh is the true veil that was torn for us.

Chapter 19: Joshua: A Type of Jesus Leading God's People into Rest

Old Testament

- **Joshua 1-6** – Joshua leads Israel into the Promised Land.

New Testament

- **Hebrews 4:8-9** – Joshua's rest points to the eternal rest in Christ.

Chapter 20: The Cities of Refuge: A Type of Christ as Our Refuge

Old Testament

- **Numbers 35:6-34** – Cities of refuge provided safety for those who accidentally killed someone.

New Testament

- **Hebrews 6:18** – Christ is our refuge and hope.

Chapter 21: The Rock in the Wilderness: A Type of Christ the Living Water

Old Testament

- **Exodus 17:6** – Moses strikes the rock, and water flows out to sustain Israel.

New Testament

- **1 Corinthians 10:4** – Christ is the spiritual Rock who provides living water.
- **John 7:37-39** – Jesus offers the living water of the Holy Spirit.

Chapter 22: The Scapegoat: A Type of Christ Bearing Our Sins

Old Testament

- **Leviticus 16:10** – The scapegoat bears the sins of Israel into the wilderness.

New Testament

- **Isaiah 53:6** – The Lord lays the iniquity of us all on Christ.
- **John 1:29** – Jesus is the Lamb of God who takes away the sin of the world.

Chapter 23: The Feasts of Israel: Types of Christ's Ministry and the Church

The Feast of Tabernacles not only recalled Israel's time in temporary shelters but also pointed to the future, where God would dwell permanently among His people. While Solomon's Temple stood as a physical representation of God's presence, it foreshadowed the true and eternal temple—Christ, whose body is the ultimate tabernacle.

Old Testament

- **Leviticus 23:6, 10, 15-21** – The Feasts of Israel point to key moments in Christ's ministry.

The Feast of Tabernacles not only recalled Israel's time in temporary shelters but also pointed to the future, where God would dwell permanently among His people. While Solomon's Temple stood as a physical representation of God's presence, it foreshadowed the true and eternal temple—Christ, whose body is the ultimate tabernacle.

New Testament

- **1 Corinthians 15:20-23** – Christ's resurrection as the firstfruits of the dead.
- **Acts 2** – The Holy Spirit comes at Pentecost.

Chapter 24: Samson: A Type of Christ's Sacrificial Strength

Old Testament

- **Judges 16:29-30** – Samson sacrifices himself to deliver Israel from the Philistines.

New Testament

- **Hebrews 2:14-15** – Christ's death destroys the power of death and delivers His people.

Chapter 25: The Manna and Quail: A Type of God's Provision in Christ

Old Testament

- **Exodus 16** – Manna and quail provided daily sustenance to Israel in the wilderness.

New Testament

- **John 6:32-35** – Jesus is the true Bread of Life who sustains believers.

Chapter 26: The Deliverance from Babylon: A Type of Spiritual Redemption

Old Testament

- **Ezra 1-2** – The Israelites return from Babylonian captivity.

New Testament

- **Revelation 18:4** – God calls His people to come out of Babylon (the world system).

Chapter 27: David as a Type of Christ the King

Old Testament

- **1 Samuel 16-2 Samuel 24** – David's reign as king of Israel foreshadows Christ's eternal reign.

New Testament

- **John 10:11** – Jesus is the Good Shepherd who lays down His life for His sheep.
- **Revelation 19:16** – Christ is the King of kings and Lord of lords.

Chapter 28: Moses as a Mediator: A Type of Christ the Mediator

Old Testament

- **Exodus 32:30-32** – Moses intercedes for Israel after their sin with the golden calf.

New Testament

- **1 Timothy 2:5** – Jesus is the one Mediator between God and man.

Chapter 29: Elijah as a Type of John the Baptist

Old Testament

- **1 Kings 17-2 Kings 2** – Elijah's prophetic ministry.

New Testament

- **Malachi 4:5-6** – Elijah will come before the day of the Lord.
- **Matthew 17:12** – Jesus identifies John the Baptist as the fulfillment of Elijah's ministry.

Chapter 30: The High Priest's Garments: A Type of Christ's Role as High Priest

Old Testament

- **Exodus 28** – The high priest's garments represent holiness, intercession, and mediation.

New Testament

- **Hebrews 4:14-16** – Jesus is the perfect High Priest who mediates for His people.

Chapter 31: The Golden Lampstand: A Type of Christ as the Light of the World

Old Testament

- **Exodus 25:31-40** – The golden lampstand in the tabernacle provided light.

New Testament

- **John 8:12** – Jesus is the Light of the World.

Chapter 32: Jonah in the Belly of the Fish: A Type of Christ's Resurrection

Old Testament

- **Jonah 1:17** – Jonah's three days in the belly of the fish.

New Testament

- **Matthew 12:40** – Jesus compares Jonah's experience to His own death, burial, and resurrection.

Chapter 33: The Judges: Types of Christ as Deliverer

Old Testament

- **Book of Judges** – The judges deliver Israel from its enemies.

New Testament

- **Romans 11:26** – Christ, the ultimate Deliverer, will save His people.

GLOSSARY OF THEOLOGICAL TERMS

This section provides definitions of key theological terms and concepts used throughout the book to aid in understanding the deeper symbolic and prophetic significance of the Old and New Testament narratives.

Antitype:
A greater reality that fulfills a type from the Old Testament. In Christian theology, Jesus Christ is often seen as the antitype of various figures, objects, or events from the Old Testament.

Ark of the Covenant:
A sacred chest that held the tablets of the Law, Aaron's rod, and a jar of manna. It represented God's presence among His people. Its loss during the Babylonian exile symbolized the departure of God's glory from Israel.

Atonement:
The act of covering or forgiving sin. In the Old Testament, this was achieved through animal sacrifices. In the New Testament, Jesus' death on the cross is the ultimate atonement, reconciling humanity to God.

Bride of Christ:
The Church, viewed symbolically as the bride prepared for union with Jesus, the Bridegroom. This metaphor reflects the intimacy, sanctity, and covenantal relationship between believers and Christ.

Cherubim:
Angelic beings associated with God's presence, often depicted guarding sacred spaces such as the Garden of Eden and the Ark of the Covenant.

Covenant:
A binding agreement between God and humanity. Two major covenants discussed are the Covenant of Works, made with Adam, and

the Covenant of Grace, fulfilled in Christ through His death and resurrection.

Covenant Theology:
A way of understanding the Bible that sees God's relationship with humanity as unfolding through a series of promises or agreements (covenants), which reveal God's redemptive plan.

Eschatological Hope:
The Christian belief in the future fulfillment of God's promises at the end of time, including Christ's return, the resurrection of the dead, final judgment, and the establishment of God's eternal kingdom.

Faith:
Trusting in God and believing in His promises, especially the promise of salvation through Jesus Christ. Faith is the means by which believers receive God's grace and are justified before Him.

Grace:
God's unmerited favor toward humanity, given freely through faith in Jesus Christ. It is through grace that believers are saved, not by their own works.

Holy of Holies:
The innermost and most sacred area of the temple where God's presence was believed to dwell, particularly in Solomon's Temple. Only the high priest could enter once a year on the Day of Atonement.

Ichabod:
A biblical term meaning "the glory has departed," signifying the loss of God's presence, particularly following the destruction of Solomon's Temple.

Imago Dei:
A Latin term meaning "Image of God." It refers to the belief that

humans are created in the image and likeness of God, giving every person inherent dignity and value.

Incarnation:

The Christian belief that God became human in the person of Jesus Christ. Jesus was fully divine and fully human, living among people to bring salvation.

Justification:

The act by which God declares a sinner to be righteous because of their faith in Jesus Christ. Through Christ's sacrifice, believers are forgiven of their sins and considered righteous before God.

Millennial Reign:

A thousand-year period described in Revelation 20, during which Christ will rule on earth with His Church. It is seen as a time of justice, peace, and righteousness before the final eternal state.

New Covenant:

The promise God made through Jesus Christ to establish a new relationship with humanity. Unlike the Old Covenant, which was based on the law, the New Covenant is based on grace, with the Holy Spirit dwelling in believers' hearts.

Passover Lamb:

A key symbol of Christ's sacrifice. In the Old Testament, the blood of the lamb spared Israelites from death during the final plague in Egypt. Jesus is referred to as the ultimate Passover Lamb, whose sacrifice delivers humanity from sin and death.

Protoevangelium:

The first mention of the Gospel in Genesis 3:15, where God promises that the offspring of the woman will crush the serpent's head. It is considered the first prophecy about Christ's victory over sin and Satan.

Redemptive Plan:
God's overarching plan to save humanity from sin and bring them back into a relationship with Him. This plan is fulfilled through the life, death, and resurrection of Jesus Christ.

Resurrection:
The Christian belief that all people will one day be raised from the dead. Believers will be resurrected to eternal life with God, while those who reject Christ will face eternal separation from God.

Sacrificial System:
The Old Testament system of offering animal sacrifices to atone for sin. These sacrifices pointed forward to the ultimate sacrifice of Jesus, who through His death paid the final price for humanity's sins.

Shekinah Glory:
The visible manifestation of God's presence, often associated with the cloud and fire that filled Solomon's Temple. Its absence in the Second Temple emphasized a spiritual loss for the people.

Sovereignty of God:
The belief that God is in complete control of all things, ruling over creation with absolute authority and power, working everything according to His will.

Tabernacle:
The portable sanctuary used by the Israelites before the construction of Solomon's Temple, where God's presence dwelled among His people.

Temple:
A structure representing God's dwelling place on earth. The first temple, Solomon's, was a physical symbol of God's presence, while the Second Temple played a significant role in Jewish worship and was

the site of Jesus' ministry. Jesus is seen as the ultimate fulfillment of the temple, and the Church is referred to as the spiritual temple.

Tearing of the Temple Veil:

At the moment of Christ's death, the veil in the temple separating the Holy of Holies from the rest of the temple was torn from top to bottom. This symbolizes the end of the division between God and humanity through Jesus' sacrifice.

Theodicy:

The study of why a good and powerful God allows the existence of evil and suffering in the world. It seeks to reconcile God's justice with the presence of evil.

Trinity:

The Christian belief that God exists as three persons—Father, Son (Jesus Christ), and Holy Spirit—yet is one God. Each person of the Trinity is fully God, sharing the same essence but distinct in role.

Type:

A person, event, or institution in the Old Testament that prefigures or symbolizes a greater reality fulfilled in Christ. Examples include Adam, Moses, and the Passover Lamb.

Typology:

A method of biblical interpretation where elements in the Old Testament (types) are seen as prefiguring or foreshadowing Christ and the events of the New Testament (antitypes).

AUTHOR'S NOTE

Thank you for taking the time to read *3 Temples: Types and Shadows*. This book is the product of my journey through Scripture, exploring the profound meanings behind the temples, covenants, and redemptive work of Christ. I hope that it has deepened your understanding of these biblical themes and how they connect to our faith today.

As I continue to write and grow in my work, I greatly value the feedback and thoughts of my readers. Your insights help me refine my approach and explore new ideas for future projects. I would love to hear what aspects of this book resonated with you and what further topics or themes you might want to see explored in future books.

Whether it's a deeper dive into the types and shadows of the Old Testament, a focus on other significant biblical figures, or reflections on the New Testament church, your suggestions are invaluable. What do you think could be expanded upon or clarified in the next book? Is there a particular area of theology, history, or doctrine you would like to explore further? Let me know your thoughts—every comment is a chance to make the next book better.

Please feel free to send your feedback, suggestions, or thoughts via admin@ETERNALROOTS.NET or through the EternalRoots.net website. I am always grateful for your support and encouragement as I continue this journey of writing and study.

Thank you again for being part of this journey, and I look forward to sharing more with you in the future.

With gratitude,
Eric Alger

Made in the USA
Columbia, SC
22 December 2024

56fee47a-8d13-4890-b40e-8360e5c9b467R01